THE GREAT
ENCYCLICAL
LETTERS OF
POPE LEO XIII

"Our epoch is rushing wildly along the straight road to destruction."
—Pope Leo XIII
Evils Affecting Modern Society
Page 12

D1547646

Pope Leo XIII—1878-1903
Prophesied by St. Malachy as "A Light in the Heavens."

THE GREAT
ENCYCLICAL LETTERS OF POPE LEO XIII

PLUS OTHER DOCUMENTS

Reigned 1878-1903.
Prophesied by St. Malachy as *Lumen in Coelo*—
"A Light in the Heavens."

Translations from Approved Sources

> "*And if society is to be healed now, in no other way can it be healed save by a return to Christian life and Christian institutions. When a society is perishing, the wholesome advice to give to those who would restore it is to recall it to the principles from which it sprang.*"
> —Pope Leo XIII
> *Condition of the Working Classes*
> Page 225 — Lazarus Nation

TAN BOOKS AND PUBLISHERS, INC.
Rockford, Illinois 61105

Nihil Obstat: Remigius Lafort, S.T.L.
                  Censor Librorum

Imprimatur: ✠ John M. Farley
                  Archbishop of New York
                  New York
                  August 4, 1903

ISBN: 0-89555-529-8

Library of Congress Catalog Card No.: 95-60850

Cover picture of Pope Leo XIII photographed by TAN Books and Publishers, Inc. courtesy of St. Joseph's Seminary, Dunwoodie, Yonkers, New York.

Printed and bound in the United States of America.

TAN BOOKS AND PUBLISHERS, INC.
P. O. Box 424
Rockford, Illinois 61105
1995

"When God, in His most wise providence, placed over human society both temporal and spiritual authority, He intended them to remain distinct indeed, but by no means disconnected and at war with each other. On the contrary, both the will of God and the common weal of human society imperatively require that the civil power should be in accord with the ecclesiastical in its rule and administration."

—Pope Leo XIII
The Reunion of Christendom
Page 313

"It would be very erroneous to draw the conclusion that in America is to be sought the type of the most desirable status of the Church, or that it would be universally lawful or expedient for State and Church to be, as in America, dissevered and divorced."

—Pope Leo XIII
Catholicity in the United States
Page 323

"Legislation is the work of men invested with power, and who, in fact, govern the nation; therefore it follows that, practically, the quality of the laws depends more upon the quality of these men than upon the form of power. The laws will be good or bad accordingly as the minds of the legislators are imbued with good or bad principles, and as they allow themselves to be guided by political prudence or by passion."

—Pope Leo XIII
Allegiance to the Republic
Page 259

PUBLISHER'S PREFACE

About the year 1140, St. Malachy, Bishop of Armagh and Primate of Ireland, on a visit to Rome, prophesied about all the Popes from his own time till the End of Time. And the prophecy describing Pope Leo XIII (1878-1903) was "A light in the heavens" (*Lumen in coelo*). And truly a "light" he was—and still is—to a world fast descending into the darkness of neo-paganism.

Why, indeed, should one read the encyclical letters of a Pope who wrote a hundred years ago? The answer is simple: The problems he addressed are the very problems that still beleaguer individuals and society today and which threaten to destroy the last vestiges of good in both.

For these great encyclicals read more like the chapters of a mighty book, a book as from a great and holy doctor of the Church, a pious physician of souls and of society, than they do as merely separate epistles on disparate subjects. In *The Condition of the Working Classes* (*Rerum Novarum*—1891), Leo's most famous letter, one discovers, for example, the Pope speaking on all sorts of related topics, giving the Church's common-sense, completely logical position on them. So it is with all his encyclicals; they are not about just the subject at hand, but taken together, they cover in their discussion the entire panoply of human exigencies, showing withal the transforming effect of Christ's one, true, holy, Catholic, apostolic Church upon every element of man's life.

The array of topics covered by Pope Leo XIII in these his major encyclicals is truly amazing: Not only does he boldly expose the chief evils of his day (which continue to menace our own)—namely, Liberalism, Secularism, Free-masonry, Socialism, Communism and Nihilism—he also makes the definitive statements on Anglican orders, the prohibition and censorship of books, Americanism, the condition of the working classes, the role and nature and types of government, private property, the duties of Christians as citizens, Christian Marriage, and so forth. But, as if these subjects were not enough, he treats also of the Holy Eucharist, the Holy Spirit, the study of Scripture, Scholastic philosophy, the epic contribution of Columbus, the unity of Faith, the reunion of Christendom and so on.

As already stated, these great encyclicals of Leo XIII read as the various chapters of a single, mighty book, all from a great and mighty mind. They show no evidence of being contrived and pieced together by assistant theologians, but reflect the synthesized and integrated thinking of a single brilliant intellect, one whose clear perspective of the past, present and future could only have been derived from the fabulously rich tradition of the Holy Catholic Church. Not only does he display a command of Scripture, theology, philosophy and government, but also of the history of our immediate and distant past, plus the direction in which our current history is taking us.

To our own age, bemused by a thousand errors—all heightened by the constant bombardment of T.V., cinema and the popular press, trumpeting their often foolish and contradictory ideas—the calm, learned, elevated, holy discussions of Pope Leo XIII (a great "Lion" of God) serve as a fresh breeze blowing away the stygian putrefaction arising from modern sin and error and present to us, truly, a "Light in the heavens" to guide our era to the safe haven of anchorage in Christ and in His holy Roman Catholic Church.

Where else will man today find that truth for which the human heart so longingly yearns than in the Church of Christ, the barque of Peter, the vessel from which He taught 2,000 years ago and from which today He still teaches, as

He has in all ages past. Let the present reader, Catholic or otherwise, consider Pope Leo XIII's holy, integrated, common-sense solutions to man's problems today, and then compare them, if he will, to the meager, tawdry answers parroted and paraded in our mass media for a day or a week and then replaced with others even cheaper. Mankind today needs a ROCK to anchor to, and I propose, Dear Reader, you will find that rock within this book! It is none other than the Rock of Peter on which Christ founded His Church and to which Church He prophesied, "Behold, I am with you all days, even to the consummation of the world." (*Matt.* 28:20). And if Leo is a "light" to us all today, it is because he was the Vicar of Him who said, "I am come a light into the world, that whosoever believeth in me, may not remain in darkness." (*John* 12:46).

Thomas A. Nelson
Publisher
July 8, 1995
St. Elizabeth, Queen of Portugal

*"Furthermore, that kind of civilization which con-
flicts with the doctrines and laws of holy Church is
nothing but a worthless imitation and a meaningless
name. Of this those peoples on whom the Gospel light
has never shown afford ample proof, since in their
mode of life a shadowy semblance only of civilization
is discoverable, while its true and solid blessings have
never been possessed. Undoubtedly that cannot by
any means be accounted the perfection of civilized
life which sets all legitimate authority boldly at defiance; nor can that be regarded as liberty which, shamefully and by the vilest means, spreading false principles,
and freely indulging the sensual gratification of lustful desires, claims impunity for all crime and misdemeanor, and thwarts the goodly influence of the
worthiest citizens of whatsoever class. Delusive, perverse, and misleading as are these principles, they cannot possibly have any inherent power to perfect the
human race and fill it with blessing, for 'sin maketh
nations miserable.' (Prov. 14:34). Such principles, as a
matter of course, must hurry nations, corrupted in mind
and heart, into every kind of infamy, weaken all right
order, and thus, sooner or later, bring the standing and
peace of the State to the very brink of ruin."*

—Pope Leo XIII
Evils Affecting Modern Society
Pages 12 & 13

THE GREAT

ENCYCLICAL LETTERS OF POPE LEO XIII

"Just as Christianity cannot penetrate in the soul without making it better, so it cannot enter into public life without establishing order. . . If it has transformed pagan society—and that transformation was a veritable resurrection—for barbarism disappeared in proportion as Christianity extended its sway, so, after the terrible shocks which unbelief has given to the world in our days, it will be able to put that world again on the true road, and bring back to order the states and peoples of modern times. But the return of Christianity will not be efficacious and complete if it does not restore the world to a sincere love of the One, Holy, Catholic and Apostolic Church."

—Pope Leo XIII
Review of His Pontificate
Pages 566-567

"For, to reject the supreme authority of God, and to cast off all obedience to Him in public matters, or even in private and domestic affairs, is the greatest perversion of liberty and the worst kind of Liberalism."

—Pope Leo XIII
Human Liberty
Page 159

"Take away the supremacy of God, who judges right and wrong, and law necessarily loses its paramount authority, while at the same time justice is undermined, these two being the strongest and most essential bonds of social union. In the same way, when the hope and expectation of immortality are gone, it is only human to seek greedily after perishable things, and every one will try, in proportion to his power, to clutch a larger share of them. Hence spring, jealousies, envies, hatreds; the most iniquitous plots to overthrow all power, and mad schemes of universal ruin are formed. There is no peace abroad, nor security at home, and social life is made hideous by crime."

—Pope Leo XIII
Christ Our Redeemer
Page 475

PREFACE.

THE popular demand for the Encyclicals and Apostolical Letters of a Roman Pontiff is something so novel as to constitute of itself a proof of the esteem in which he is held. It would seem that whatever is written of Leo XIII. in books or newspapers, instead of satisfying the universal desire for a knowledge of him, only inspires the wish to know more, and the conviction that the writings of a man of such powers and world-wide sympathies must contain messages of interest and benefit to all humanity.

It is precisely the merit of the Letters of the late Pope that no matter when they were written, or to whom they were addressed, they are of actual and universal interest, as intelligible to the layman and illiterate as to the theologian and scholar, as urgent in their appeals to those who are not within the fold of which he was chief pastor as to the children of the household. His arguments could not but command attention, drawn as they were from history, experience, and reason, as well as from Scripture and tradition; and his sincere interest in the civil and social improvements of every nation, whether Catholic or not, made all hearken to his plea for religion as the chief factor of true progress.

The Letters which we have selected are all characteristic of Leo. Taken together they express his sentiments on the chief questions of a time which, owing to his great influence in civil as well as in ecclesiastical matters, is really an epoch in the history of men. His influence on

3

scientific studies alone is sufficient proof of this. Never was science so arrogant as when Leo XIII. began to recommend to Catholics the study of sound philosophy. Twenty-five years ago, scientists everywhere were proclaiming oracularly, like Tyndall and Huxley among the English-speaking nations, the victory of science over religion, when Leo declared that there could be no question of victory where there was no conflict, and that only men who were ignorant of the true nature of religion and science could consider them mutually antagonistic. If to-day a Brunetière without fear of contradiction can proclaim science bankrupt, it is in a great measure because Leo's Encyclical on the Study of St. Thomas and Scholastic Philosophy inspired Catholic scientists, and through their influence non-Catholic scientists as well, to study both theology and science more ardently, systematically, and conservatively, and with such success in reconciling their apparent disagreements that the best scientists of our day recognize how each is but a study from a different aspect of the same great First Cause and its effects, and that each must necessarily, therefore, be in accord with the other. Lord Kelvin's words, "Science positively affirms Creative Power . . . we are absolutely forced by science to believe with perfect confidence in a Directive Power," and his further assertion, "If you think strong enough you will be forced by science to the belief in God, which is the foundation of all religion; you will find science not antagonistic but helpful to religion," are but a re-echo of Leo's utterances a quarter of a century ago. A perusal of the Letters contained in this volume will satisfy the reader that in other spheres as well as in that of science, in education, sociology, and statesmanship, the late Pontiff, by adapting himself to his age and studying carefully its needs and possibilities, has so far influenced its thought and tendencies, and so plainly altered its current of events, as to have opened a new era in its history.

It would perhaps be an exaggeration to say that never before had a Supreme Pontificate been exercised with more distinction than by Leo XIII., but surely in no Pontiff has the world at large appreciated so well as in him the nature, duties, and prerogatives of the papal office; and this appreciation is due chiefly, if not entirely, to his Pontifical acts as a teacher, ruler, and high priest, whose teachings, authority and spiritual ministration have exercised an influence on all humanity, as well as on his own subjects.

As teacher, Leo XIII. was not content with recommending true doctrine, or urging reforms and improvements in Catholic universities and seminaries; but, setting an example, he issued, in season and out of season, his own instructions based on the soundest principles of reason and revelation about the family, liberty, socialism, the relations of the working man with his employers, the right use of political powers, the menace of secret societies to the governments that harbor them, the duties of Christian citizens and the constitution of Christian States. As ruler, he exercised a singular power over his cardinals and bishops, many of whom he was magnanimous enough to appoint when their views and policy did not coincide entirely with his own. By counsel, direction, and command, he was ever aiding them to govern their dioceses, and to impart to the faithful proper guidance in every matter affecting faith and morals. As priest and Pontiff, he was solicitous for the unity, integrity, and splendor of Christian worship, instituting many reforms in the observance of the liturgy and in ecclesiastical music, but he was more solicitous still for the interior holiness of the faithful, as appears by his Letters on Human Liberty, The Right Ordering of Christian Life, Marriage, The Holy Spirit, Christ the Redeemer, and by his zeal in raising to the altars the approved models of Christian perfection in every walk of life.

An ardent love of truth, an unwavering determination

to preserve peace and concord not only among Catholics but between them and their fellow-citizens, whether believers in Christianity or not, and an unfailing spirit of hope, are the chief characteristics of Leo in these Encyclicals. The great Pontiff was no pessimist. If he never lost sight of the evils afflicting humanity, neither did he ever fail to provide a remedy, nor on occasion to take comfort in what was good, and to praise most generously all who had labored to accomplish it; in this he was really the Vicar of Christ, from his tribulations learning patience, from patience trial, and from trial hope—the hope that confoundeth not, because it shared in the supreme confidence of Christ in humanity, who, as Leo loved to remind men, was willing "when we were yet weak, according to the time, to die even for the ungodly."

For translations of Encyclicals not specially made for this book we are indebted to *The Tablet, The American Catholic Quarterly Review, The Catholic World, The Messenger, The Catholic Mind,* "The Pope and the People," and various pamphlets published by Benziger Brothers.

CONTENTS.

7

8 CONTENTS.

ENCYCLICAL LETTERS OF LEO XIII.

ON THE EVILS AFFECTING MODERN SOCIETY.

THEIR CAUSES AND REMEDIES.

Encyclical Letter Inscrutabili, April 21, 1878.

WHEN by God's unsearchable design, We, though all unworthy, were raised to the height of apostolic dignity, at once We felt Ourselves moved by an urgent desire and, as it were, necessity, to address you by letter, not merely to express to you Our very deep feeling of love, but further, in accordance with the task entrusted to Us from heaven, to strengthen you who are called to share Our solicitude, that you may help Us to carry on the battle now being waged on behalf of the Church of God and the salvation of souls.

For, from the very beginning of Our Pontificate, the sad sight has presented itself to Us of the evils by which the human race is oppressed on every side: the widespread subversion of the primary truths on which, as on its foundations, human society is based; the obstinacy of mind that will not brook any authority however lawful; the endless sources of disagreement, whence arrive civil strife, and ruthless war and bloodshed; the contempt of law which moulds characters and is the shield of righteousness; the insatiable craving for things perishable, with

9

complete forgetfulness of things eternal, leading up to the desperate madness whereby so many wretched beings, in all directions, scruple not to lay violent hands upon themselves; the reckless mismanagement, waste, and misappropriation of the public funds; the shamelessness of those who, full of treachery, make semblance of being champions of country, of freedom, and every kind of right; in fine, the deadly kind of plague which infects society in its inmost recesses, allowing it no respite and foreboding ever fresh disturbances and final disaster.

Now, the source of these evils lies chiefly, We are convinced, in this, that the holy and venerable authority of the Church, which in God's name rules mankind, upholding and defending all lawful authority, has been despised and set aside. The enemies of public order, being fully aware of this, have thought nothing better suited to destroy the foundations of society than to make an unflagging attack upon the Church of God, to bring her into discredit and odium by spreading infamous calumnies, and accusing her of being opposed to genuine progress. They labor to weaken her influence and power by wounds daily inflicted, and to overthrow the authority of the Bishop of Rome, in whom the abiding and unchangeable principles of right and good find their earthly guardian and champion. From these causes have originated laws that shake the structure of the Catholic Church, the enacting whereof we have to deplore in so many lands; hence too have flowed forth contempt of episcopal authority; the obstacles thrown in the way of the discharge of ecclesiastical duties; the dissolution of religious bodies; and the confiscation of property that was once the support of the Church's ministers and of the poor. Thereby public institutions, vowed to charity and benevolence, have been withdrawn from the wholesome control of the Church; thence also has arisen that unchecked freedom to teach and spread abroad all mischievous principles, while the Church's claim to train and educate youth is in every way outraged and baffled. Such too is the purpose of the seizing of the temporal power, conferred many centuries ago by Divine Providence on the Bishop of Rome, that he might without let or hindrance use the authority conferred by Christ for the eternal welfare of the nations.

We have recalled to your minds, Venerable Brothers, this deathly mass of ills, not to increase the sorrow naturally caused you by this most sad state of things, but because we believe that from its consideration you will most plainly see how serious are the matters claiming our attention as well as devotedness, and with what energy We should work and, more than ever, under the present adverse conditions, protect, so far as in Us lies, the Church of Christ and the honor of the Apostolic See—the objects of so many slanders—and assert their claims.

It is perfectly clear and evident, Venerable Brothers, that the very notion of civilization is a fiction of the brain if it rest not on the abiding principles of truth and the unchanging laws of virtue and justice, and if unfeigned love knit not together the wills of men, and gently control the interchange and the character of their mutual service. Now, who would make bold to deny that the Church, by spreading the Gospel throughout the nations, has brought the light of truth amongst people utterly savage and steeped in foul superstition, and has quickened them alike to recognize the Divine Author of nature and duly to respect themselves? Further, who will deny that the Church has done away with the curse of slavery and restored men to the original dignity of their noble nature; and—by uplifting the standard of Redemption in all quarters of the globe, by introducing, or shielding under her protection, the sciences and arts, by founding and taking into her keeping excellent charitable institutions which provide relief for ills of every kind—has throughout the world, in private or in public life, civilized the human race, freed it from degradation, and with all care trained it to a way of living such as befits the dignity and the hopes of man? And if any one of sound mind compare the age in which We live, so hostile to religion and to the Church of Christ, with those happy times when the Church was revered as a mother by the nations, beyond all question he will see that Our epoch is rushing wildly along the straight road to destruction; while in those times which most abounded in excellent institutions, peaceful life, wealth, and prosperity the people showed themselves most obedient to the Church's rule and laws. Therefore, if the many blessings We have mentioned, due to the agency and saving help of the Church, are the true and worthy outcome of civilization, the Church of Christ, far from being alien to or neglectful of progress, has a just claim to all men's praise as its nurse, its mistress, and its mother.

Furthermore, that kind of civilization which conflicts with the doctrines and laws of holy Church is nothing but a worthless imitation and a meaningless name. Of this those peoples on whom the gospel light has never shown afford ample proof, since in their mode of life a shadowy semblance only of civilization is discoverable, while its true and solid blessings have never been possessed. Undoubtedly that cannot by any means be accounted the perfection of civilized life which sets all legitimate authority boldly at defiance; nor can that be regarded as liberty which, shamefully and by the vilest means, spreading false principles, and freely indulging the sensual gratification of lustful desires, claims impunity for all crime and misdemeanor, and thwarts the goodly influence of the worthiest citizens of whatsoever class. Delusive, perverse, and misleading as are these principles, they cannot possibly have any inherent power to perfect the human race and fill it with blessing, for *sin maketh nations miserable*.[1] Such principles, as a matter of course, must hurry nations, corrupted in mind and heart, into every kind of infamy, weaken all right order, and thus, sooner or

[1] Prov. xiv. 34.

later, bring the standing and peace of the State to the very brink of ruin.

Again, if We consider the achievements of the See of Rome, what can be more wicked than to deny how much and how well the Roman Bishops have served civilized society at large? For Our predecessors, to provide for the peoples' good, encountered struggles of every kind, endured to the utmost burdensome toils, and never hesitated to expose themselves to most dangerous trials. With eyes fixed on heaven, they neither bowed down their head before the threats of the wicked, nor allowed themselves to be led by flattery or bribes into unworthy compliance. This Apostolic Chair it was that gathered and held together the crumbling remains of the old order of things; this was the kindly light by whose help the culture of Christian times shone far and wide; this was an anchor of safety in the fierce storms by which the human race has been convulsed; this was the sacred bond of union that linked together nations distant in region and differing in character; in short, this was a common centre from which was sought instruction in faith and religion, no less than guidance and advice for the maintenance of peace and the functions of practical life. In very truth it is the glory of the supreme Pontiffs that they steadfastly set themselves up as a wall and a bulwark to save human society from falling back into its former superstition and barbarism.

Would that this healing authority had never been slighted or set aside! Assuredly neither would the civil power have lost that venerable and sacred glory, the lustrous gift of religion, which alone renders the state of subjection noble and worthy of man; nor would so many revolutions and wars have been fomented to ravage the world with desolation and bloodshed; nor would kingdoms, once so flourishing, but now fallen from the height of prosperity, lie crushed beneath the weight of every kind of calamity. Of this the peoples of the East also furnish an example, who, by breaking the most sweet yoke that bound them to this Apostolic See, forfeited the splendor of their former greatness, their renown in science and art, and the dignity of their sway.

Of these remarkable benefits, however, which illustrious monuments of all ages prove to have flowed upon every quarter of the world from the Apostolic See, this land of Italy has had the most abounding experience. For it has derived advantages from the See of Rome proportionate to the greater nearness of its natural situation. Unquestionably to the Roman Pontiffs it is that Italy must own herself indebted for the substantial glory and majesty by which she has been pre-eminent amongst nations. The influence and fatherly care of the Popes have upon many occasions shielded her from hostile attack and brought her relief and aid, the effect of which is that the Catholic faith has been ever maintained inviolate in the hearts of Italians.

These services of Our predecessors, to omit mention of many others, have been witnessed to in a special manner by the records of the times of St. Leo the Great, Alexander III., Innocent III., St. Pius V., Leo X., and other Pontiffs, by whose exertions or protection Italy has escaped unscathed from the utter destruction threatened by barbarians; has kept unimpaired her old faith, and, amid the darkness and defilement of a ruder age, has cultivated and preserved in vigor the lustre of science and the splendor of art. To this furthermore bears witness Our Own fostering city, the home of the Popes, which, under their rule, reaped this special benefit, that it not only was the strong citadel of the faith, but also became the refuge of the liberal arts and the very abode of culture, winning for itself the admiration and respect of the whole world. As these facts in all their amplitude have been handed down in historical records for the perpetual remembrance of posterity, it is easy to understand that it is only with hostile design and shameless calumny—meant to mislead men—that any one can venture in speech and in writing to accuse the Apostolic See of being an obstacle to the civil progress of nations and to the prosperity of Italy.

Seeing, therefore, that all the hopes of Italy and of the whole world lie in the **power,** so beneficent to the common good and profit, wherewith the authority of the Apostolic See is endowed, and in the close union which binds all the faithful of Christ to the Roman Pontiff, We recognize that nothing should be nearer Our heart than how to preserve safe and sound the dignity of the Roman See, and to strengthen ever more and more the union ·of members with the Head, of the children with their Father.

Wherefore, that We may above all things, and in every possible way, maintain the rights and freedom of this Holy See, We shall never cease to strive that Our authority may meet with due deference; that obstacles may be removed which hamper the free exercise of Our ministry and that we may be restored to that condition of things in which the design of God's wisdom had long ago placed the Roman Pontiffs. We are moved to demand this restoration, Venerable Brethren, not by any feeling of ambition or desire of supremacy, but by the nature of Our office and by Our sacred promise confirmed on oath; and further, not only because this sovereignty is essential to protect and preserve the full liberty of the spiritual power but also because it is an ascertained fact that, when the temporal sovereignty of the Apostolic See is in question, the cause of the public good and the well-being of all human society in general are also at stake. Hence We cannot omit, in the discharge of Our duty, which obliges Us to guard the rights of Holy Church, to renew and confirm in every particular by this Our Letter those declarations and protests which Pius IX., of sacred memory, Our predecessor, on many and repeated occasions published against the seizing of the civil sovereignty and the infringement of rights belonging to the Roman Church. At the same time We address ourselves to princes and chief rulers of the nations, and earnestly beseech them in the august name of the most high God, not to refuse the Church's aid, proffered them in a season of such need, but with united and friendly aims to join themselves to her as the source of authority and salvation, and to attach themselves to her more and more in the bonds of hearty love and devotedness. God grant that—seeing the truth of Our words and considering within themselves that the teaching of Christ is, as Augustine used to say, "a great blessing to the State, if obeyed," [1] and that their own peace and safety, as well as that of their people, is bound up with the safety of the Church and the reverence due to her—they may give their whole thought and care to mitigating the evils by which the Church and its visible Head are harassed, and so it may at last come to pass that the peoples whom they govern may enter on the way of justice and peace, and rejoice in a happy era of prosperity and glory.

In the next place, in order that the union of hearts between their chief Pastor and the whole Catholic flock may daily be strengthened, We here call upon you, Venerable Brothers, with particular earnestness, and strongly urge you to kindle, with priestly zeal and pastoral care, the fire of the love of religion among the faithful entrusted to you, that their attachment to this chair of truth and justice may become closer and firmer, that they may welcome all its teachings with thorough assent of mind and will, wholly rejecting such opinions, even when most widely received, as they know to be contrary to the Church's doctrine. In this matter, the Roman Pontiffs, Our predecessors, and last of all, Pius IX. of sacred memory, especially in the General Council of the Vatican, have not neglected, so often as there was need, to condemn wide-spreading errors and to smite them with the Apostolic condemnation. This they did, keeping before their eyes the words of St. Paul: *Beware lest any man cheat you by*

---

[1] Epistola 138 (vel 5), ad Marcell, n. 15.

philosophy and vain deceit, according to the tradition of men, according to the elements of the world and not according to Christ.[1] All such censures, We, following in the steps of Our predecessors, do confirm and renew from this Apostolic Seat of truth, whilst We earnestly ask of the Father of Lights that all the faithful, brought to thorough agreement in the like feeling and the same belief, may think and speak even as Ourselves. It is your duty, Venerable Brothers, sedulously to strive that the seed of heavenly doctrine be sown broadcast in the field of God, and that the teachings of the Catholic faith may be implanted early in the souls of the faithful, may strike deep root in them, and be kept free from the ruinous blight of error. The more the enemies of religion exert themselves to offer the uninformed, especially the young, such instruction as darkens the mind and corrupts morals, the more actively should we endeavor that not only a suitable and solid method of education may flourish, but above all that this education be wholly in harmony with the Catholic faith in its literature and system of training, and chiefly in philosophy, upon which the foundation of other sciences in great measure depends. Philosophy seeks not the overthrow of divine revelation, but delights rather to prepare its way, and defend it against assailants, both by example and in written works, as the great Augustine and the Angelic Doctor, with all other teachers of Christian wisdom, have proved to Us.

Now, the training of youth most conducive to the defence of true faith and religion and to the preservation of morality must find its beginning from an early stage within the circle of home life; and this family Christian training, sadly undermined in these our times, cannot possibly be restored to its due dignity, save by those laws under which it was established in the Church by her Divine Founder Himself. Our Lord Jesus Christ, by raising to the dignity

---

[1] Coloss. ii. 8.

of a sacrament the contract of matrimony, in which He would have His Own union with the Church typified, not only made the marriage-tie more holy, but in addition provided efficacious sources of aid for parents and children alike, so that, by the discharge of their duties one to another, they might with greater ease attain to happiness both in time and in eternity. But when impious laws, setting at naught the sanctity of this great sacrament, put it on the same footing with mere civil contracts, the lamentable result followed, that, outraging the dignity of Christian matrimony, citizens made use of legalized concubinage in place of marriage; husband and wife neglected their bounden duty to each other; children refused obedience and reverence to their parents; the bonds of domestic love were loosened; and, alas! the worst scandal and of all the most ruinous to public morality, very frequently an unholy passion opened the door to disastrous and fatal separations. These most unhappy and painful consequences, Venerable Brothers, cannot fail to arouse your zeal and move you constantly and earnestly to warn the faithful committed to your charge, to listen with docility to your teaching regarding the holiness of Christian marriage, and to obey the laws by which the Church controls the duties of married people and of their offspring.

Then, indeed, will that most desirable result come about, that the character and conduct of individuals also will be reformed; for just as from a rotten stock are produced healthless branches or worthless fruits, so do the ravages of a pestilence which ruins the household spread wide their cruel infection to the hurt and injury of individual citizens. On the other hand, when domestic society is fashioned in the mould of Christian life, each member will gradually grow accustomed to the love of religion and piety, to the abhorrence of false and harmful teaching, to the pursuit of virtue, to obedience to elders, and to the restraint of that insatiable seeking after self-interest alone, which so spoils and weakens the character of men. To this end it will certainly help not a little to encourage and promote those pious associations which have been established, in our own times especially, with so great profit to the cause of the Catholic religion.

Great indeed and beyond the strength of man are these objects of our hopes and prayers, Venerable Brothers; but since God has *made the nations of the earth for health,*[1] when He founded the Church for the welfare of the peoples, and promised that He will abide with her by His assistance to the end of the world, We firmly trust that, through your endeavors, the human race, taking warning from so many evils and visitations, will submit themselves at length to the Church, and turn for health and prosperity to the infallible guidance of this Apostolic See.

Meanwhile, Venerable Brothers, before bringing this Letter to a close. We must express Our congratulations on the striking harmony and concord which unites your minds among yourselves and with this Apostolic See. This perfect union We regard as not merely an impregnable bulwark against hostile attacks, but also as an auspicious and happy omen, presaging better times for the Church; and, while it yields great relief to Our weakness, it seasonably encourages Us to endure with readiness all labors and all struggles on behalf of God's Church in the arduous task which We have undertaken.

Moreover, from the causes of hope and rejoicing which We have made known to you, We cannot separate those tokens of love and obedience which you, Venerable Brethren, in these first days of Our Pontificate, have shown Our lowliness, and with you so many of the clergy and the faithful, who, by letters sent, by offerings given, by pilgrimages undertaken, and by other works of love, have made it clear that the devotion and charity which they manifested to Our most worthy predecessor, still lasts, so strong and steadfast and unchanged, as not to slacken

---

[1] Wisdom i. 14.

towards the person of a successor so much inferior. For these splendid tokens of Catholic piety We humbly confess to the Lord that He is good and gracious, while to you, Venerable Brothers, and to all Our beloved children from whom We have received them, We publicly, from the bottom of Our heart, avow the grateful feelings of Our soul, cherishing the fullest confidence that, in the present critical state of things and in the difficulties of the times, this your devotion and love and the devotion and love of the faithful will never fail Us. Nor have We any doubt that these conspicuous examples of filial piety and Christian virtue will be of such avail as to make Our most merciful God, moved by these dutiful deeds, look with favor on His flock and grant the Church peace and victory. But as We are sure that this peace and victory will more quickly and more readily be given Us, if the faithful are unremitting in their prayers and supplications to obtain it, We earnestly exhort you, Venerable Brothers, to stir up for this end the zeal and ardor of the faithful, taking the Immaculate Queen of heaven as their intercessor with God, and having recourse as their advocates to St. Joseph, the heavenly Patron of the Church, and to SS. Peter and Paul, the Princes of the Apostles. To the powerful patronage of all these We humbly commit Our lowliness, all ranks of the ecclesiastical hierarchy, and all the flock of Christ our Lord.

For the rest, We trust that these days, on which We renew the memory of Jesus Christ, risen from the dead, may be to you, Venerable Brothers, and to all the fold of God, a source of blessing and salvation and fulness of holy joy, praying our most gracious God that by the blood of the Lamb without spot, which blotted out the handwriting that was against Us, the sins We have committed may be washed away, and the judgment We are suffering for them may mercifully be mitigated.

The grace of Our Lord Jesus Christ, and the charity of God, and the communication of the Holy Ghost be with you all,[1] Venerable Brothers; to each and all of whom, as well as to Our beloved children, the clergy and faithful of your churches, as a pledge of Our special good-will and as an earnest of the protection of heaven, We lovingly impart the Apostolic Benediction.

[1] 2 Cor. xiii. 13.

SOCIALISM, COMMUNISM, NIHILISM.

Encyclical Letter Quod Apostolici Muneris, December 28, 1878.

As the nature of Our Apostolic office required of Us, We have not omitted, from the very outset of Our Pontificate, addressing you, Venerable Brothers, in Encyclical Letters, in order to advert to the deadly plague which is tainting society to its very core and bringing it to a state of extreme peril. At the same time We call attention to certain most effectual remedies, by which society may be renewed unto salvation and enabled to escape the crisis now threatening.

But the evils which We then deplored have taken in a brief space of time such widespread growth that We are compelled to address you anew, with the words of the prophet resounding as it were in Our ears: *Cry, cease not, lift up thy voice like a trumpet.*[1]

You understand as a matter of course, Venerable Brothers, that We are alluding to that sect of men who, under the motley and all but barbarous terms and titles of Socialists, Communists, and Nihilists, are spread abroad throughout the world and, bound intimately together in baneful alliance, no longer look for strong support in secret meetings held in darksome places, but standing forth openly and boldly in the light of day, strive to carry out the purpose long resolved upon, of uprooting the foundations of civilized society at large.

These are they in very truth who, as the sacred text

[1] Isai. lviii. 1.

bears witness, *defile the flesh, and despise dominion, and blaspheme majesty.*[1] They leave nothing scathless or uninjured of that which human and divine laws alike have wisely ordained to ensure the preservation and honor of life. From the heads of States to whom, as the Apostle admonishes, all owe submission, and on whom the rights of authority are bestowed by God Himself, these sectaries withhold obedience and preach up the perfect equality of all men in regard to rights alike and duties. The natural union of man and woman, which is held sacred even among barbarous nations, they hold in scorn; and its bond, whereby family life is chiefly maintained, they slacken, or else yield up to the sway of lust. In short, spurred on by greedy hankering after things present, which is *the root of all evils, which some coveting have erred from the faith,*[2] they attack the right of property, sanctioned by the law of nature, and with signal depravity, while pretending to feel solicitous about the needs, and anxious to satisfy the requirements of all, they strain every effort to seize upon and hold in common all that has been individually acquired by title of lawful inheritance, through intellectual or manual labor, or economy in living. These monstrous views they proclaim in public meetings, uphold in booklets, and spread broadcast everywhere through the daily press. Hence the hallowed dignity and authority of rulers has incurred such odium on the part of rebellious subjects that evil-minded traitors, spurning all control, have many a time within a recent period boldly raised impious hands against even the very heads of States.

Such daring conduct on the part of disloyal individuals, which threatens the civilized community from day to day with even graver perils, and troubles the mind of all with anxious fears, draws its cause and origin from those venomous teachings which, like pernicious seed scattered far and wide among the nations, have produced in course

---

[1] Jude 8.   [2] 1 Tim. vi. 10.

of time death-bearing fruit. In fact, Venerable Brothers, you know full well that the atrocious war which, starting from the sixteenth century, was declared against the Catholic faith by the Reformers, and which has been growing amain from day to day in vehemence, aimed at giving free course to the rejection of all revelation, the subversion of the supernatural order, and the enthronement of unaided reason, with its vagaries or rather ravings. Deriving pretentiously its name from Reason, this false doctrine, by flattering and stimulating the eagerness to outstrip others which is interwoven with man's nature, and giving the rein to every kind of unlawful desire, has taken willing possession of the minds of great numbers, and has even pervaded the whole of civilized society. Hence by a fresh act of impiety, unknown even to very pagans, governments have been organized without God and the order established by Him being taken at all into account. It has even been contended that public authority, with its dignity and its power of ruling, originates not from God but from the mass of the people, which, considering itself unfettered by all divine sanction, refuses to submit to any laws that it has not itself passed of its own free will. Next, after having attacked and cast away the supernatural truths of faith as being contrary to reason, the very Author and Redeemer of mankind has been forced slowly and gradually to withdraw from the scheme of studies at universities, colleges, and high-schools, as well as from all the practical working of public life. In fine, after having consigned to oblivion the rewards and punishments of a future and never-ending existence, the keen longing after happiness has been narrowed down to the range of the present life.   With such doctrines spread far and wide, and such license in thought and action, it is no wonder that men of the most lowly condition, heart-sick of a humble home or poor workshop, should fix eager eyes on the abodes and fortunes of the wealthy; no wonder that tranquillity no longer prevails in public or private life, or that the human race has been hurried onward to well-nigh the verge of ruin.

But the supreme pastors of the Church, on whom devolves the charge of guarding the Lord's flock from the snares of the enemy, have in good time devoted their energies to avert the danger impending, and to provide for the safety of the faithful. In fact, as soon as secret societies began to take extension, in the midst whereof the germs of those evil principles already adverted to were nursed, the Roman Pontiffs Clement XV. and Benedict XIV. failed not to unmask the impious designs of the sectaries, and to warn the faithful throughout the world concerning the mischiefs they were thus hatching in secret. But when by those who gloried in the title of "philosophers" a certain unbridled liberty was assigned to man, and the "new law," as they term it, began in opposition to the divine and natural law to be set forth and gather sanction, Pius VI. of happy memory forthwith laid bare by public documents the pernicious character and falsity of those principles, and at the same time, with apostolic foresight, predicted the utter ruin to which the deluded multitudes were being hurried. But since, notwithstanding the measures resorted to, none proved of avail to prevent their wicked doctrines from day by day gaining ground with the people, and obtaining ascendency even in public decisions of government, Popes Pius VII. and Leo XII. excommunicated secret societies, and once more gave warning to society of the perils that threatened it. In fine, the world at large is fully aware in what earnest terms, and with what resoluteness of soul and unflinching constancy, Our glorious predecessor, Pius IX. of happy memory, by Allocutions alike and Encyclical Letters addressed to the Bishops of the whole world, levied war against the iniquitous endeavors of these sects, and furthermore even denounced by name the plague of Socialism thence bursting forth.

It is to be deplored, however, that they to whom has

been entrusted the care of the common welfare, allowing
themselves to be circumvented by the fraudulent devices
of infamous men and terror-stricken at their threats,
have ever displayed towards the Church feelings of suspicion or even of hostility, not understanding that the
endeavors of these sects would have been of no effect
had the doctrine of the Catholic Church and the authority
of the Roman Pontiffs, among rulers and peoples alike,
always remained in due honor.   For the *Church of the
living God, which is the pillar and ground of truth,*[1] proclaims those doctrines and precepts whereby the security
and calm of society is provided for, and the accursed brood
of Socialism is utterly destroyed.

For although the Socialists, turning to evil use the
Gospel itself so as to deceive more readily the unwary,
have been wont to twist it to their meaning, still so striking
is the disagreement between their criminal teachings and
the pure doctrine of Christ, that no greater can exist: *For
what participation hath justice with injustice, or what fellowship hath light with darkness?*[2] They in good sooth cease
not from asserting—as we have already mentioned—that
all men are by nature equal, and hence they contend that
neither honor nor respect is owed to public authority, nor
any obedience to the laws, saving perhaps to those which
have been sanctioned according to their good pleasure.
Contrariwise, from the Gospel records, equality among
men consists in this, that one and all, possessing the same
nature, are called to the sublime dignity of being sons of
God; and, moreover, that one and the same end being set
before all, each and every one has to be judged according
to the same laws and to have punishments or rewards
meted out according to individual deserts.   There is, however, an inequality of right and authority which emanates
from the Author of nature Himself, *of whom all paternity
in heaven and earth is named.*[3] As regards rulers and

---

[1] 1 Tim. iii. 15.   [2] 2 Cor. vi. 14.   [3] Eph. iii. 15.

subjects, all without exception, according to Catholic teaching and precept, are mutually bound by duties and rights, in such manner that, on the one hand, moderation is enjoined on the appetite for power, and, on the other, obedience is shown to be easy, stable, and wholly honorable. Therefore does the Church constantly urge upon each and all who are subject to her the apostolic precept: *There is no power but from God; and those that are, are ordained of God. Therefore, he that resisteth the powers resisteth the ordinance of God. And they that resist, purchase to themselves damnation.* And again: *Be subject of necessity, not only for wrath, but also for conscience' sake; and render to all men their dues. Tribute to whom tribute is due; custom to whom custom; fear to whom fear; honor to whom honor.*[1] For He who has created and governs all things, has in His provident wisdom so disposed them that the lowest attain to their end by the middlemost, and the middlemost by the highest. Just then as the Almighty willed that, in the heavenly kingdom itself, the choirs of angels should be of differing ranks, subordinated the one to the other; again just as in the Church God has established different grades of orders with diversity of functions, so that all should not be *apostles, all not doctors, all not prophets;*[2] so also has He established in civil society many orders of varying dignity, right, and power. And this, to the end that the State, like the Church, should form one body comprising many members, some excelling others in rank and importance, but all alike necessary to one another and solicitous for the common welfare.

But to the end that the rulers of the people shall employ the power bestowed for the advancement, and not detriment, of those under rule, the Church of Christ very fittingly warns the rulers themselves that the Sovereign Judge will call them to a strict and speedy account, and evoking the words of divine wisdom, she addresses them

---

[1] Rom. xiii. 1–7.   [2] 1 Cor. xii. 29.

one and all in God's name. *Give ear, you that rule the people, and that please yourselves in multitudes of nations; for power is given you by the Lord, and strength by the Most High, who will examine your works, and search out your thoughts; . . . for a most severe judgment shall be for them that bear rule. . . . For God will not accept any man's person, neither will He stand in awe of any one's greatness: for He hath made the little and the great, and He hath equally care of all. But a greater punishment is ready for the more mighty.*[1] Should it, however, happen, at any time, that in the public exercise of authority rulers act rashly and arbitrarily, the teaching of the Catholic Church does not allow subjects to rise against them, without further warranty, lest peace and order become more and more disturbed, and society run the risk of greater detriment. And when things have come to such a pass as to hold out no further hope, she teaches that a remedy is to be sought in the virtue of Christian patience and in urgent prayer to God. But should it please legislators and rulers to enjoin or sanction anything repugnant to the divine and natural law, the dignity and duty of the name of Christian and the Apostolic injunction proclaim that one *ought to obey God rather than men.*[2]

Moreover, the salutary influence of the Church, which redounds to the upholding of well-regulated order in civil society and promotes its conservation, the family circle itself (which is the starting-point of every city and every State) necessarily feels and experiences. For you are fully aware, Venerable Brothers, that the governing principle of family life has, in accordance with the requirements of natural law, its basis in the indissoluble union of husband and wife, and its superstructure in the duties and rights of parents and children, and of masters and servants towards each other. You are further aware that the theories of socialism would quickly destroy this

[1] Wisd. vi. 3 seqq.   [2] Acts v. 29.

family life, since the stability afforded by marriage under
religious sanction once lost, paternal authority over
children and the duties of children to parents are necessarily and most harmfully slackened. Contrariwise, *marriage, honorable to all*,[1] which from the beginning of the
world God Himself instituted for the propagation and
preservation of the human race, and decreed to be indissoluble, the Church holds to have become more stable and
holy through Christ, who conferred on it the dignity of a
sacrament, and willed to make it an image of His own
union with the Church. Wherefore, as the Apostle admonishes: *As Christ is the head of the Church,* so is *the
husband the head of the wife;*[2] and just as the Church is
subject to Christ, who cherishes it with most chaste and
lasting love, so is it becoming that women also should be
subject to their husbands, and by them in turn be loved
with faithful and constant affection.

In like manner the Church regulates the authority of
the father and the master in such mode as to keep
children and servants within their duty, without, however,
allowing authority to be overstepped. For, according
to Catholic teaching, the authority of the heavenly Father
and Lord flows forth upon parents and masters, and on
that account receives not only its origin and power from
God, but also its very nature and character. Hence does
the Apostle exhort children to *obey their parents in the
Lord, and to honor their father and their mother, which is the
first commandment with a promise.*[3] *And you, fathers,
provoke not your children to anger, but bring them up in
the discipline and correction of the Lord.*[4] And again by
the same divine apostolic injunction it is urged on servants and masters that the former *should obey their masters
according to the flesh . . . as to Christ . . . with a good
will serving as to the Lord, . . .*[5] but the latter should

---

[1] Heb. xiii. 4.   [2] Eph. v. 23.   [3] Ibid. vi. 1, 2.
[4] Ibid. vi. 4.   [5] Ibid. vi. 5-7.

forbear threatenings, knowing that the Lord of all is in heaven, and there is no respect of persons with Him.[1] Were all these things observed by every one whom they concern, according to the intent of the divine Will, each family would truly present a likeness of the heavenly home, and the wondrous benefits thence resulting would not be limited simply to the family circle, but would spread abroad abundantly over the State at large.

As regards the maintenance of public and private tranquillity, Catholic wisdom, sustained by both divine and natural law, prudently provides through what it holds and teaches touching the right of ownership and the apportioning of personal property which has been accumulated for the wants and requirements of life. For the Socialists wrongly assume the right of property to be of mere human invention, repugnant to the natural equality between men, and, preaching up the community of goods, declare that no one should endure poverty meekly, and that all may with impunity seize upon the possessions and usurp the rights of the wealthy. More wisely and profitably the Church recognizes the existence of inequality amongst men, who are by nature unlike in mental endowment and strength of body, and even in amount of fortune; and she enjoins that the right of property and of its disposal, derived from nature, should in the case of every individual remain intact and inviolate. She knows full well indeed that robbery and rapine have been so forbidden by God, the Author and Protector of every right, that it is unlawful even to covet the goods of others, and that thieves and robbers no less than adulterers and idolaters are excluded from the kingdom of heaven. Nor does she, on this account, loving mother as she is, omit solicitude for the poor or fail to provide for their needs; nay, taking them to her arms with maternal affection, and knowing that they in a manner represent the person

---

[1] Eph. vi. 9.

of Christ Himself, who accounts as done unto Him any benefit conferred upon the lowliest among the poor, she holds them in great account, brings them aid to the utmost of her power, takes thought to have erected in every land in their behoof homes and refuges where they can be received, nurtured, and tended; and takes these charitable foundations under her protecting care. Moreover, she lays the rich under strict command to give of their superfluity to the poor, impressing them with fear of the divine judgment which will exact the penalty of eternal punishment unle   they succor the wants of the needy. In fine, she cheers and comforts exceedingly the hearts of the poor, either by setting before them the example of Christ, who, *being rich became poor for our sakes,*[1] or by reminding them of the words by which Jesus pronounced the poor to be *blessed,* and enjoined them to hope for the reward of eternal bliss. Who then does not perceive that herein lies the best means of appeasing the undying conflict between the rich and poor? For, as the evidence of things and facts clearly demonstrates, if such conclusion be disallowed or made light of, it must come about either that the vast majority of mankind will fall back into that most abject condition of bondage which through a long lapse of time obtained amongst pagan nations, or else that human society will be agitated by constant outbreaks and ravaged by plunder and rapine, such as even of late years we have had occasion to deplore.

Since things have come to this pass, Venerable Brothers, We, on whom is laid the charge of governing the Universal Church, pointed out even at the very outset of Our Pontificate to the nations and their rulers, tossed about by so dire a tempest, the port to which they could betake themselves in all safety. And now, moved greatly by the extreme peril which actually threatens, We lift up anew Our Apostolic voice, and conjure them again and again,

---

[1] 2 Cor. viii. 9.

for the sake of their own safety and that of the State, to welcome and obey the teaching of that Church which has deserved so well in promoting the public prosperity of nations, and to recognize once for all that the relations of the State and of Religion are so bound together as that whatever is withdrawn from religion impairs by so much the dutiful submission of the subject and the dignity of authority. And when they shall have recognized that the Church of Christ is possessed of a power to stave off the pest of Socialism, too mighty to be found in human enactments or in the strong hand of the civil power or in military force, let them re-establish that Church in the condition and liberty needed in order to be able to exercise her most salutary influence for the good of society in general. Do you, however, Venerable Brothers, who have keen insight as to the nature and origin of the ills thickening ever in the world, apply yourselves with all zeal and energy of spirit to inculcate Catholic doctrine, that it may reach and strike deep root in the souls of all. Provide as far as may be that from early years all may grow accustomed to cherish a filial love towards God, and to revere His sovereign sway; to show due submission to rulers and the laws; to bridle their passions and zealously uphold the authority which God has established alike in the State and in the family circle. Moreover, it behooves you to strive earnestly that the children of the Catholic Church venture not to lend their name, nor in any way to give countenance to this hateful sect, but on the contrary that by worthy deeds and honorable line of action in all particulars, they show how well and happily human society would prosper were the individual members distinguishable for the regularity of their conduct and for their virtuous life. Finally, as the confederates of Socialism are sought mainly among those who occupy themselves in business pursuits, or give themselves to manual labor, and who, wearied out by sheer hard work, are more easily entrapped by the hope of wealth and promise of prosperity, it seems expedient to encourage associations for handicraftsmen and laboring men, which, placed under the sheltering care of religion, may render the members content with their lot and resigned to toil, inducing them to lead a peaceful and tranquil life.

On Our undertakings, Venerable Brothers, and on yours, may He confer favoring aid to whom we are bound to refer the beginning and the end of all good. We have ample ground to hope for speedy help during these auspicious days when the festival of Our Lord's Nativity is being celebrated. That new deliverance which Christ, born into a world sinking with years and well-nigh crushed with the weight of ills, charges us to hope for; that peace which then He announced to men through the ministry of angels, He has promised to bestow likewise on us. For *the hand of the Lord is not shortened, that He cannot save, neither is His ear heavy, that it cannot hear.*[1] During these days, then, of most happy augury, Venerable Brothers, wishing to you and to all the faithful of your churches all joy and prosperity, We earnestly pray the Giver of all good gifts that anew to men may appear *the goodness and kindness of God our Saviour,*[2] who, after having snatched us from the power of a ruthless enemy, has raised us up to the most exalted dignity of being sons of God. And in order that our vows may be the more speedily and abundantly satisfied, join with Us, Venerable Brothers, in addressing to God fervent prayers, invoking also the patronage of the Blessed Virgin Mary, ever immaculate, and of her spouse, Joseph, as also of the blessed Apostles, Peter and Paul, in whose intercession we greatly confide. And in the meantime, with inmost affection of heart to you, Venerable Brothers, to your clergy and to all the faithful throughout the world, as a harbinger of the divine gifts, We impart Our Apostolic blessing.

[1] Is. lix. 1.   [2] Tit. iii. 4.

THE STUDY OF SCHOLASTIC PHILOSOPHY.

Encyclical Letter Æterni Patris, August 4, 1879.

THE only-begotten Son of the Eternal Father, who came on earth to bring salvation and the light of divine wisdom to men, conferred a great and wonderful blessing on the world when, about to ascend again into heaven, He commanded the apostles to go and teach all nations,[1] and left the Church which He had founded to be the common and supreme teacher of the peoples. For men, whom the truth had set free, were to be preserved by the truth; nor would the fruits of heavenly doctrines, by which salvation comes to men, have long remained had not the Lord Christ appointed an unfailing authority for the instruction of the faithful. And the Church built upon the promises of its own divine Author, whose charity it imitated, so faithfully followed out His commands that its constant aim and chief wish was this: to teach true religion and contend forever against errors. To this end assuredly have tended the incessant labors of individual bishops; to this end also the published laws and decrees of Councils, and especially the constant watchfulness of the Roman Pontiffs, to whom, as successors, of the blessed Peter in the primacy of the apostles, belongs the right and office of teaching and confirming their brethren in the faith. Since, then, according to the warning of the apostle, the minds of Christ's faithful are apt to be deceived and the integrity of the faith to be corrupted among men by philosophy and vain deceit,[2] the supreme pastors of the Church have always thought

---

[1] Matt. xxviii. 19.   [2] Coloss. ii. 8.

34

it their duty to advance, by every means in their power, science truly so called, and at the same time to provide with special care that all studies should accord with the Catholic faith, especially philosophy, on which a right apprehension of the other sciences in great part depends. Indeed, Venerable Brethren, on this very subject among others, We briefly admonished you in Our first Encyclical Letter; but now, both by reason of the gravity of the subject and the condition of the time, we are again compelled to speak to you on the mode of taking up the study of philosophy which shall respond most fitly to the true faith, and at the same time be most consonant with the dignity of human knowledge.

Whoso turns his attention to the bitter strifes of these days and seeks a reason for the troubles that vex public and private life, must come to the conclusion that a fruitful cause of the evils which now afflict, as well as of those which threaten us, lies in this: that false conclusions concerning divine and human things, which originated in the schools of philosophy, have crept into all the orders of the State, and have been accepted by the common consent of the masses. For since it is in the very nature of man to follow the guide of reason in his actions, if his intellect sins at all his will soon follows; and thus it happens that looseness of intellectual opinion influences human actions and perverts them. Whereas, on the other hand, if men be of sound mind and take their stand on true and solid principles, there will result a vast amount of benefits for the public and private good. We do not, indeed, attribute such force and authority to philosophy as to esteem it equal to the task of combating and rooting out all errors; for, when the Christian religion was first constituted, it came upon earth to restore it to its primeval dignity by the admirable light of faith, diffused not by persuasive words of human wisdom, but in the manifestation of spirit and of power;[1] so also

[1] 1 Cor. ii. 4.

at the present time we look above all things to the powerful help of Almighty God to bring back to a right understanding the minds of men and dispel the darkness of
error. But the natural helps with which the grace of
the divine wisdom, strongly and sweetly disposing all
things, has supplied the human race are neither to be
despised nor neglected, chief among which is evidently
the right use of philosophy. For not in vain did God
set the light of reason in the human mind; and so far
is the superadded light of faith from extinguishing or
lessening the power of the intelligence that it completes
it rather, and by adding to its strength renders it capable
of greater things.

Therefore divine Providence itself requires that in
calling back the peoples to the paths of faith and salvation advantage should be taken of human science also—
an approved and wise practice which history testifies was
observed by the most illustrious Fathers of the Church.
They, indeed, were wont neither to belittle nor under-
value the part that reason had to play, as is summed up
by the great Augustine when he attributes to this science
"that by which the most wholesome faith is begotten, . . .
is nourished, defended, and made strong." [1]

In the first place, philosophy, if rightly made use of by
the wise, in a certain way tends to smooth and fortify
the road to true faith, and to prepare the souls of its
disciples for the fit reception of revelation; for which
reason it is well called by ancient writers sometimes a
stepping-stone to the Christian faith, [2] sometimes the prelude and help of Christianity, [3] sometimes the Gospel
teacher. [4] And assuredly the God of all goodness, in all
that pertains to divine things, has not only manifested
by the light of faith those truths which human intelligence

[1] De Trim., lib. xiv. c. 1.
[2] Clem. Alex., Strom., lib. i. c. 16; l. vii. c. 3.
[3] Orig. ad Greg. Thaum.
[4] Clem. Alex., Strom., i. c. 5.

could not attain of itself, but others also not altogether unattainable by reason, that by the help of divine authority they may be made known to all at once and without any admixture of error. Hence it is that certain truths which were either divinely proposed for belief, or were bound by the closest chains to a doctrine of faith, were discovered by pagan sages with nothing but their natural reason to guide them, were demonstrated and proved by becoming arguments. For, as the apostle says, the invisible things of Him, from the creation of the world, are clearly seen, being understood by the things that are made: His eternal power also and divinity;[1] and the Gentiles who have not the law show, nevertheless, the work of the law written in their hearts.[2] But it is most fitting to turn these truths, which have been discovered by the pagan sages even, to the use and purposes of revealed doctrine, in order to show that both human wisdom and the very testimony of our adversaries serve to support the Christian faith—a method which is not of recent introduction, but of established use, and has often been adopted by the holy Fathers of the Church. For instance, those venerable men, the witnesses and guardians of religious traditions, recognize a certain form and figure of this in the action of the Hebrews, who, when about to depart out of Egypt, were commanded to take with them the gold and silver vessels and precious robes of the Egyptians, that by a change of use the things might be dedicated to the service of the true God which had formerly been the instruments of ignoble and superstitious rites. Gregory of Neocæsarea [3] praises Origen expressly because, with singular dexterity, as one snatches weapons from the enemy, he turned to the defence of Christian wisdom and to the destruction of superstition many arguments drawn from the writings of the pagans. And both Gregory of Nazianzen [4] and

---

[1] Rom. i. 20.
[2] Ibid. ii. 14, 15.
[3] Orat. paneg. ad Origen.
[4] Vit. Moys.

Gregory of Nyssa [1] praise and commend a like mode of disputation in Basil the Great; while Jerome especially commends it in Quadratus, a disciple of the apostles, in Aristides, Justin, Irenæus, and very many others. [2] Augustine says: " Do we not see Cyprian, that mildest of doctors and most blessed of martyrs, going out of Egypt laden with gold and silver and vestments? And Lactantius also and Victorinus, Optatus and Hilary? And, not to speak of the living, how many Greeks have done likewise?" [3] But if natural reason first sowed this rich field of doctrine before it was rendered fruitful by the power of Christ, it must assuredly become more prolific after the grace of the Saviour has renewed and added to the native faculties of the human mind. And who does not see that a plain and easy road is opened up to faith by such a method of philosophic study?

But the advantage to be derived from such a school of philosophy is not to be confined within these limits. The foolishness of those men is gravely reproved in the words of divine wisdom who by these good things that are seen could not understand Him that is, neither by attending to the works could have acknowledged who was the workman. [4] In the first place, then, this great and noble fruit is gathered from human reason, that it demonstrates that God *is;* for by the greatness of the beauty and of the creature the Creator of them may be seen so as to be known thereby. [5] Again, it shows God to excel in the height of all perfections, in infinite wisdom before which nothing lies hidden, and in absolute justice which no depraved affection could possibly shake; and that God, therefore, is not only true but truth itself, which can neither deceive nor be deceived. Whence it clearly follows that human reason finds the fullest faith and authority united in the word of God. In like manner

[1] Carm. i. Iamb. 3.   [4] Wisdom xiii. 1.
[2] Epist. ad Magn.   [5] Ibid. xiii. 5
[3] De Doctr. christ., l. ii. c. 40.

reason declares that the doctrine of the Gospel has even from its very beginning been made manifest by certain wonderful signs, the established proofs, as it were, of unshaken truth; and that all, therefore, who set faith in the Gospel do not believe rashly as though following cunningly devised fables,[1] but, by a most reasonable consent, subject their intelligence and judgment to an authority which is divine. And of no less importance is it that reason most clearly sets forth that the Church instituted by Christ (as laid down in the Vatican Synod), on account of its wonderful spread, its marvellous sanctity, and its inexhaustible fecundity in all places, as well as of its Catholic unity and unshaken stability, is in itself a great and perpetual motive of belief and an irrefragable testimony of its own divine mission.[2]

Its solid foundations having been thus laid, a perpetual and varied service is further required of philosophy, in order that sacred theology may receive and assume the nature, form, and genius of a true science. For in this, the most noble of studies, it is of the greatest necessity to bind together, as it were, in one body the many and various parts of the heavenly doctrines, that, each being allotted to its own proper place and derived from its own proper principles, the whole may join together in a complete union; in order, in fine, that all and each part may be strengthened by its own and the others' invincible arguments. Nor is that more accurate or fuller knowledge of the things that are believed, and somewhat more lucid understanding, as far as it can go, of the very mysteries of faith which Augustine and the other Fathers commended and strove to reach, and which the Vatican Synod itself [3] declared to be most fruitful, to be passed over in silence or belittled. Those will certainly more fully and more easily attain that knowledge and understanding who to integrity of life and love of faith join a mind rounded

[1] 2 Petr. i. 16.   [2] Const. dogm. de Fid. Cath., cap. 3,
[3] Const. cit. cap. 4.

and finished by philosophic studies, as the same Vatican Synod teaches that the knowledge of such sacred dogmas ought to be sought as well from analogy of the things that are naturally known as from the connection of those mysteries one with another and with the final end of man.[1]

Lastly, the duty of religiously defending the truths divinely delivered, and of resisting those who dare oppose them, pertains to philosophic pursuits. Wherefore it is the glory of philosophy to be esteemed as the bulwark of faith and the strong defence of religion. As Clement of Alexandria testifies, the doctrine of the Saviour is indeed perfect in itself and wanteth naught, since it is the power and wisdom of God. And the assistance of the Greek philosophy maketh not the truth more powerful; but inasmuch as it weakens the contrary arguments of the sophists and repels the veiled attacks against the truth, it has been fitly called the hedge and fence of the vine.[2] For as the enemies of the Catholic name, when about to attack religion, are in the habit of borrowing their weapons from the arguments of philosophers, so the defenders of sacred science draw many arguments from the store of philosophy which may serve to uphold revealed dogmas. Nor is the triumph of the Christian faith a small one in using human reason to repel powerfully and speedily the attacks of its adversaries by the hostile arms which human reason itself supplied. Which species of religious strife St. Jerome, writing to Magnus, notices as having been adopted by the apostle of the Gentiles himself : Paul, the leader of the Christian army and the invincible orator, battling for the cause of Christ, skilfully turns even a chance inscription into an argument for the faith; for he had learned from the true David to wrest the sword from the hands of the enemy and to cut off the head of the boastful Goliath with his

---

[1] Const. cit. cap. 4.   [2] Strom., lib. i. c. 20.

own weapon.[1] Moreover, the Church herself not only urges, but even commands, Christian teachers to seek help from philosophy. For the fifth Council of Lateran, after it had decided that "every assertion contrary to the truth of revealed faith is altogether false, for the reason that it contradicts, however slightly, the truth,"[2] advises teachers of philosophy to pay close attention to the exposition of fallacious arguments; since, as Augustine testifies, "if reason is turned against the authority of sacred Scripture, no matter how specious it may seem, it errs in the likeness of truth; for true it cannot be."[3]

But in order that philosophy may be found equal to the gathering of those precious fruits which we have indicated, it behooves it above all things never to turn aside from that path which the Fathers have entered upon from a venerable antiquity, and which the Vatican Council solemnly and authoritatively approved. As it is evident that very many truths of the supernatural order which are far beyond the reach of the keenest intellect must be accepted, human reason, conscious of its own infirmity, dare not affect to itself too great powers, nor deny those truths, nor measure them by its own standard, nor interpret them at will; but receive them rather with a full and humble faith, and esteem it the highest honor to be allowed to wait upon heavenly doctrines like a handmaid and attendant, and by God's goodness attain to them in any way whatsoever. But in the case of such doctrines as the human intelligence may perceive, it is equally just that philosophy should make use of its own method, principles, and arguments—not indeed in such fashion as to seem rashly to withdraw from the divine authority. But since it is established that those things which become known by revelation have the force of certain truth, and that those things which war against faith war equally against right reason,

---

[1] Epist. ad Magn.　　[2] Bulla Apostolici regiminis.
[3] Epist. 143 (al. 7), ad. Marcellin., n. 7.

the Catholic philosopher will know that he violates at once faith and the laws of reason if he accepts any conclusion which he understands to be opposed to revealed doctrine.

We know that there are some who, in their overestimate of the human faculties, maintain that as soon as man's intellect becomes subject to divine authority it falls from its native dignity, and, hampered by the yoke of this species of slavery, is much retarded and hindered in its progress towards the supreme truth and excellence. Such an idea is most false and deceptive, and its sole tendency is to induce foolish and ungrateful men wilfully to repudiate the most sublime truths, and reject the divine gift of faith, from which the fountains of all good things flow out upon civil society. For the human mind, being confined within certain limits, and those narrow enough, is exposed to many errors and is ignorant of many things; whereas the Christain faith, reposing on the authority of God, is the unfailing mistress of truth, whom whoso followeth he will be neither immeshed in the snares of error nor tossed hither and thither on the waves of fluctuating opinion. Those, therefore, who to the study of philosophy unite obedience to the Christian faith are philosophers indeed; for the splendor of the divine truths, received into the mind, helps the understanding, and not only detracts in nowise from its dignity, but adds greatly to its nobility, keenness, and stability. For surely that is a worthy and most useful exercise of reason when men give their minds to disproving those things which are repugnant to faith and proving the things which conform to faith. In the first case they cut the ground from under the feet of error and expose the viciousness of the arguments on which error rests; while in the second case they make themselves masters of weighty reasons for the sound demonstration of truth and the satisfactory instruction of any reasonable person. Whoever denies that such study and practice tend to add to the resources and expand the faculties of the mind must necessarily and absurdly hold that the mind gains nothing from discriminating between the true and the false. Justly, therefore, does the Vatican Council commemorate in these words the great benefits which faith has conferred upon reason: *Faith frees and saves reason from error, and endows it with manifold knowledge.*[1] A wise man, therefore, would not accuse faith and look upon it as opposed to reason and natural truths, but would rather offer heartfelt thanks to God, and sincerely rejoice that, in the density of ignorance and in the flood-tide of error, holy faith, like a friendly star, shines down upon his path and points out to him the fair gate of truth beyond all danger of wandering.

If, Venerable Brethren, you open the history of philosophy, you will find all We have just said proved by experience. The philosophers of old who lacked the gift of faith, yet were esteemed so wise, fell into many appalling errors. You know how often among some truths they taught false and incongruous things; what vague and doubtful opinions they held concerning the nature of the Divinity, the first origin of things, the government of the world, the divine knowledge of the future, the cause and principle of evil, the ultimate end of man, the eternal beatitude, concerning virtue and vice, and other matters, a true and certain knowledge of which is most necessary to the human race; while, on the other hand, the early Fathers and Doctors of the Church, who well understood that, according to the divine plan, the restorer of human science is Christ, who is the power and the wisdom of God,[2] and in whom are hid all the treasures of wisdom and knowledge,[3] took up and investigated the books of the ancient philosophers, and compared their teachings with the doctrines of revelation, and, carefully sifting them, they cherished what was true and wise in them and

---

[1] Const. dogm. de Fid. Cath., cap. 4.   [2] 1 Cor. i. 24.
[3] Coloss. ii. 3.

amended or rejected all else. For as the all-seeing God against the cruelty of tyrants raised up mighty martyrs to the defence of the Church, men prodigal of their great lives, in like manner to false philosophers and heretics he opposed men of great wisdom, to defend, even by the aid of human reason, the treasure of revealed truths. Thus from the very first ages of the Church the Catholic doctrine has encountered a multitude of most bitter adversaries, who, deriding the Christian dogmas and institutions, maintained that there were many gods, that the material world never had a beginning or cause, and that the course of events was one of blind and fatal necessity, not regulated by the will of divine Providence.

But the learned men whom We call apologists speedily encountered these teachers of foolish doctrine, and, under the guidance of faith, found arguments in human wisdom also to prove that one God, who stands pre-eminent in every kind of perfection, is to be worshipped; that all things were created from nothing by His omnipotent power; that by His wisdom they flourish and serve each their own special purposes. Among these St. Justin Martyr claims the chief place. After having tried the most celebrated academies of the Greeks, he saw clearly, as he himself confesses, that he could only draw truths in their fulness from the doctrines of revelation. These he embraced with all the ardor of his soul, purged of calumny, courageously and fully defended before the Roman emperors, and reconciled with them not a few of the sayings of the Greek philosophers.

Quadratus also and Aristides, Hermias and Athenagoras, stood nobly forth in that time. Nor did Irenæus, the invincible martyr and bishop of Lyons, win less glory in the same cause when, forcibly refuting the perverse opinions of the Orientals, the work of the Gnostics, scattered broadcast over the territories of the Roman Empire, he explained (according to Jerome) the origin of each

heresy and in what philosophic source it took its rise.[1]
But who knows not the disputations of Clement of Alexandria, which the same Jerome thus honorably com-
memorates: "What is there in them that is not learned,
and what that is not of the very heart of philosophy?"[2]
He himself, indeed, with marvellous versatility treated
of many things of the greatest utility for preparing a
history of philosophy, for the exercise of the dialectic
art, and for showing the agreement between reason and
faith. After him came Origen, who graced the chair of
the school of Alexandria, and was most learned in the
teachings of the Greeks and Orientals. He published
many volumes, involving great labor, which were wonderfully adapted to explain the divine writings and illustrate
the sacred dogmas; which, though, as they now stand,
not altogether free from error, contain nevertheless a
wealth of knowledge tending to the growth and advance
of natural truths. Tertullian opposes heretics with the
authority of the sacred writings; with the philosophers
he changes his fence and disputes philosophically; but
so learnedly and accurately did he confute them that he
made bold to say, "Neither in science nor in schooling
are we equals, as you imagine." [3] Arnobius also, in his
works against the pagans, and Lactantius in the divine
Institutions especially, with equal eloquence and strength
strenuously strive to move men to accept the dogmas and
precepts of Catholic wisdom, not by philosophic juggling,
after the fashion of the academicians,[4] but vanquishing
them partly by their own arms, and partly by arguments
drawn from the mutual contentions of the philosophers.[5]
But the writings on the human soul, the divine attributes,
and other questions of mighty moment which the great
Athanasius and Chrysostom, the prince of orators, have
left behind them are, by common consent, so supremely
excellent that it seems scarcely anything could be added

[1] Epist. ad Magn.   [3] Apologet., § 46.   [5] De opif. Dei, cap. 21.
[2] Loc. cit.   [4] Inst. vii. cap. 7.

to their subtlety and fulness. And, not to cover too wide
a range, we add to the number of the great men of whom
mention has been made the names of Basil the Great and
of the two Gregories, who, on going forth from Athens,
that home of all learning, thoroughly equipped with all
the harness of philosophy, turned the wealth of knowledge
which each had gathered up in a course of zealous study
to the work of refuting heretics and preparing Christians.

But Augustine would seem to have wrested the palm
from all. Of a most powerful genius and thoroughly
saturated with sacred and profane learning, with the
loftiest faith and with equal knowledge, he combated
most vigorously all the errors of his age. What height
of philosophy did he not reach? What region of it did
he not diligently explore, either in expounding the loftiest
mysteries of the faith to the faithful, or defending them
against the fell onslaught of adversaries, or again when,
in demolishing the fables of the academicians or the
Manichæans, he laid the safe foundations and sure structure of human science, or followed up the reason, origin,
and causes of the evils that afflict man? How subtly he
reasoned on the angels, the soul, the human mind, the
will and free choice, on religion and the life of the blessed,
on time and eternity, and even on the very nature of
changeable bodies. Afterwards, in the East John Dama-
scene treading in the footsteps of Basil and of Gregory
Nazianzen, and in the West Boëtius and Anselm following
the doctrines of Augustine, added largely to the patrimony
of philosophy.

Later on the doctors of the middle ages, who are called
scholastics, addressed themselves to a great work—that
of diligently collecting, and sifting, and storing up, as it
were, in one place, for the use and convenience of posterity
the rich and fertile harvests of Christian learning scattered
abroad in the voluminous works of the holy Fathers.
And with regard, Venerable Brethren, to the origin, drift,
and excellence of this scholastic learning, it may be well

here to speak more fully in the words of one of the wisest of Our predecessors, Sixtus V.: "By the divine favor of Him who alone gives the spirit of science, and wisdom, and understanding, and who through all ages, as there may be need, enriches His Church with new blessings and strengthens it with new safeguards, there was founded by Our fathers, men of eminent wisdom, the scholastic theology, which two glorious doctors in particular, the angelic St. Thomas and the seraphic St. Bonaventure, illustrious teachers of this faculty, . . . with surpassing genius, by unwearied diligence, and at the cost of long labors and vigils, set in order and beautified, and, when skilfully arranged and clearly explained in a variety of ways, handed down to posterity.

"And, indeed, the knowledge and use of so salutary a science, which flows from the fertilizing founts of the sacred writings, the Sovereign Pontiffs, the holy Fathers and the councils, must always be of the greatest assistance to the Church, whether with the view of really and soundly understanding and interpreting the Scriptures, or more safely and to better purpose reading and explaining the Fathers, or for exposing and refuting the various errors and heresies; and in these late days, when those dangerous times described by the apostle are already upon us, when the blasphemers, the proud, and the seducers go from bad to worse, erring themselves and causing others to err, there is surely a very great need of confirming the dogmas of Catholic faith and confuting heresies." [1]

Although these words seem to bear reference solely to scholastic theology, nevertheless they may plainly be accepted as equally true of philosophy and its praises. For the noble endowments which make the scholastic theology so formidable to the enemies of truth—to wit, as the same pontiff adds, "that ready and close coherence of cause and effect, that order and array as of a disciplined

---

[1] Bulla Triumphantis, an. 1588.

army in battle, those clear definitions and distinctions, that strength of argument and those keen discussions, by which light is distinguished from darkness, the true from the false, expose and strip naked, as it were, the falsehoods of heretics wrapped around by a cloud of subterfuges and fallacies"[1]—those noble and admirable endowments, We say, are only to be found in a right use of that philosophy which the scholastic teachers have been accustomed carefully and prudently to make use of even in theological disputations. Moreover, since it is the proper and special office of the scholastic theologians to bind together by the fastest chain human and divine science, surely the theology in which they excelled would not have gained such honor and commendation among men if they had made use of a lame and imperfect or vain philosophy.

Among the scholastic doctors, the chief and master of all, towers Thomas Aquinas, who, as Cajetan observes, because "he most venerated the ancient doctors of the Church, in a certain way seems to have inherited the intellect of all."[2] The doctrines of those illustrious men, like the scattered members of a body, Thomas collected together and cemented, distributed in wonderful order, and so increased with important additions that he is rightly and deservedly esteemed the special bulwark and glory of the Catholic faith. With his spirit at once humble and swift, his memory ready and tenacious, his life spotless throughout, a lover of truth for its own sake, richly endowed with human and divine science, like the sun he heated the world with the ardor of his virtues and filled it with the splendor of his teaching. Philosophy has no part which he did not touch finely at once and thoroughly; on the laws of reasoning, on God and incorporeal substances, on man and other sensible things, on human actions and their principles, he reasoned in

---

[1] Bull. cit. [2] In 2m. 2æ. q. 148, a. 4, in fin.

such a manner that in him there is wanting neither a full array of questions, nor an apt disposal of the various parts, nor the best method of proceeding, nor soundness of principles or strength of argument, nor clearness and elegance of style, nor a facility for explaining what is abstruse.

Moreover, the Angelic Doctor pushed his philosophic conclusions into the reasons and principles of the things which are most comprehensive and contain in their bosom, so to say, the seeds of almost infinite truths, to be unfolded in good time by later masters and with a goodly yield. And as he also used this philosophic method in the refutation of error, he won this title to distinction for himself: that single-handed he victoriously combated the errors of former times, and supplied invincible arms to put those to rout which might in after-times spring up. Again, clearly distinguishing, as is fitting, reason from faith, while happily associating the one with the other, he both preserved the rights and had regard for the dignity of each; so much so, indeed, that reason, borne on the wings of Thomas to its human height, can scarcely rise higher, while faith could scarcely expect more or stronger aids from reason than those which she has already obtained through Thomas.

For these reasons learned men, in former ages especially, of the highest repute in theology and philosophy, after mastering with infinite pains the immortal works of Thomas, gave themselves up not so much to be instructed in his angelic wisdom as to be nourished upon it. It is known that nearly all the founders and framers of laws of the religious orders commanded their associates to study and religiously adhere to the teachings of St. Thomas, fearful lest any of them should swerve even in the slightest degree from the footsteps of so great a man. To say nothing of the family of St. Dominic, which rightly claims this great teacher for its own glory, the statutes of the Benedictines, the Carmelites, the Augustinians, the

Society of Jesus, and many others, all testify that they are bound by this law.

And here how pleasantly one's thoughts fly back to those celebrated schools and academies which flourished of old in Europe—to Paris, Salamanca, Alcala, to Douay, Toulouse, and Louvain, to Padua and Bologna, to Naples and Coimbra, and to many another! All know how the fame of these seats of learning grew with their years, and that their judgment, often asked in matters of grave moment, held great weight everywhere. And we know how in those great homes of human wisdom, as in his own kingdom, Thomas reigned supreme; and that the minds of all, of teachers as well as of taught, rested in wonderful harmony under the shield and authority of the Angelic Doctor.

But, furthermore, Our predecessors in the Roman pontificate have celebrated the wisdom of Thomas Aquinas by exceptional tributes of praise and the most ample testimonials. Clement VI.,[1] Nicholas V.,[2] Benedict XIII.,[3] and others bear witness that the universal Church borrows lustre from his admirable teaching; while St. Pius V.[4] confesses that heresies, confounded and convicted by the same teaching, were dissipated, and the whole world daily freed from fatal errors; others affirm with Clement XII.[5] that most fruitful blessings have spread abroad from his writings over the whole Church, and that he is worthy of the honor which is bestowed on the greatest doctors of the Church, on Gregory and Ambrose, Augustine and Jerome; while others have not hesitated to propose St. Thomas for the exemplar and master of the academies and great lyceums, whom they may follow with unfaltering feet. On which point the words of Blessed Urban V. to the Academy of Toulouse are worthy of recall: "It is our will, which we hereby enjoin upon you, that ye follow the teaching of Blessed

---

[1] Bulla In Ordine.   [2] Breve ad FF. Ord. Prædic., 1451.
[3] Bulla Pretiosus.   [4] Bulla Mirabilis.   [5] Bulla Verbo Dei.

Thomas as the true and Catholic doctrine, and that ye labor with all your force to profit by the same." [1] Innocent XII. [2] followed the example of Urban in the case of the University of Louvain, and Benedict XIV. [3] with the Dionysian College of Granada; while to these judgments of great Pontiffs on Thomas Aquinas comes the crowning testimony of Innocent VI.: "His teaching above that of others, the canons alone excepted, enjoys such an elegance of phraseology, a method of statement, a truth of proposition, that those who hold to it are never found swerving from the path of truth, and he who dare assail it will always be suspected of error." [4]

The œcumenical councils also, where blossoms the flower of all earthly wisdom, have always been careful to hold Thomas Aquinas in singular honor. In the councils of Lyons, Vienna, Florence, and the Vatican one might almost say that Thomas took part and presided over the deliberations and decrees of the Fathers, contending against the errors of the Greeks, of heretics and rationalists, with invincible force and with the happiest results. But the chief and special glory of Thomas, one which he has shared with none of the Catholic doctors, is that the Fathers of Trent made it part of the order of the conclave to lay upon the altar, together with the code of sacred Scripture and the decrees of the Supreme Pontiffs, the *Summa* of Thomas Aquinas, whence to seek counsel, reason, and inspiration.

A last triumph was reserved for this incomparable man—namely, to compel the homage, praise, and admiration of even the very enemies of the Catholic name. For it has come to light that there were not lacking among the leaders of heretical sects some who openly declared that, if the teaching of Thomas Aquinas were only taken

---

[1] Const. 5a. dat. die 3 Aug. 1368 ad Cancell. Univ. Tolos.
[2] Litt. in form Brev., die 6 Feb. 1694.
[3] Ibid., die 21 Aug. 1752.
[4] Serm. de St. Thom.

away they could easily battle with all Catholic teachers, gain the victory, and abolish the Church.[1] A vain hope indeed, but no vain testimony.

Therefore, Venerable Brethern, as often as We contemplate the good, the force, and the singular advantages to be derived from this system of philosophy which Our Fathers so dearly loved, We think it hazardous that its special honor should not always and everywhere remain, especially when it is established that daily experience, and the judgment of the greatest men, and, to crown all, the voice of the Church, have favored the scholastic philosophy. Moreover, to the old teaching a novel system of philosophy has succeeded here and there, in which We fail to perceive those desirable and wholesome fruits which the Church and civil society itself would prefer. For it pleased the struggling innovators of the sixteenth century to philosophize without any respect for faith, the power of inventing in accordance with his own pleasure and bent being asked and given in turn by each one. Hence it was natural that systems of philosophy multiplied beyond measure, and conclusions differing and clashing one with another arose about those matters even which are the most important in human knowledge. From a mass of conclusions men often come to wavering and doubt; and who knows not how easily the mind slips from doubt to error? But as men are apt to follow the lead given them, this new pursuit seems to have caught the souls of certain Catholic philosophers, who, throwing aside the patrimony of ancient wisdom, chose rather to build up a new edifice than to strengthen and complete the old by aid of the new—ill-advisedly, in sooth, and not without detriment to the sciences. For a multiform system of this kind, which depends on the authority and choice of any professor, has a foundation open to change, and consequently gives us a philosophy not firm, and

[1] Beza—Bucerus.

stable, and robust like that of old, but tottering and feeble. And if perchance it sometimes finds itself scarcely equal to sustain the shock of its foes, it should recognize that the cause and the blame lie in itself. In saying this We have no intention of discountenancing the learned and able men who bring their industry and erudition, and, what is more, the wealth of new discoveries, to the service of philosophy; for, of course, We understand that this tends to the development of learning. But one should be very careful lest all or his chief labor be exhausted in these pursuits and in mere erudition. And the same thing is true of sacred theology, which, indeed, may be assisted and illustrated by all kinds of erudition, though it is absolutely necessary to approach it in the grave manner of the scholastics, in order that, the forces of revelation and reason being united in it, it may continue to be "the invincible bulwark of the faith."[1]

With wise forethought, therefoer, not a few of the advocates of philosophic studies, when turning their minds recently to the practical reform of philosophy, aimed and aim at restoring the renowned teaching of Thomas Aquinas and winning it back to its ancient beauty.

We have learned with great joy that many members of your order, Venerable Brethren, have taken this plan to heart; and while We earnestly commend their efforts, We exhort them to hold fast to their purpose, and remind each and all of you that Our first and most cherished idea is that you should all furnish a generous and copious supply to studious youth of those crystal rills of wisdom flowing in a never-ending and fertilizing stream from the fountain-head of the Angelic Doctor.

Many are the reasons why We are so desirous of this. In the first place, then, since in the tempest that is on us the Christian faith is being constantly assailed by the machinations and craft of a certain false wisdom, all

---

[1] Sixtus V., Bull. cit.

youths, but especially those who are the growing hope
of the Church, should be nourished on the strong and
robust food of doctrine, that so, mighty in strength and
armed at all points, they may become habituated to
advance the cause of religion with force and judgment,
"being ready always, according to the apostolic counsel,
to satisfy every one that asketh you a reason of that hope
which is in you," [1] and that they may be able to exhort
in sound doctrine and to convince the gainsayers.[2]   Many
of those who, with minds alienated from the faith, hate
Catholic institutions, claim reason as their sole mistress and
guide.   Now, We think that, apart from the supernatural
help of God, nothing is better calculated to heal those
minds and to bring them into favor with the Catholic
faith than the solid doctrine of the Fathers and the scholastics, who so clearly and forcibly demonstrate the firm
foundations of the faith, its divine origin, its certain truth,
the arguments that sustain it, the benefits it has conferred
on the human race, and its perfect accord with reason, in
a manner to satisfy completely minds open to persuasion,
however unwilling and repugnant.

Domestic and civil society even, which, as all see,
is exposed to great danger from this plague of perverse
opinions, would certainly enjoy a far more peaceful and
secure existence if a more wholesome doctrine were taught
in the academies and schools—one more in conformity
with the teaching of the Church, such as is contained in
the works of Thomas Aquinas.

For the teachings of Thomas on the true meaning of
liberty, which at this time is running into license, on the
divine origin of all authority, on laws and their force,
on the paternal and just rule of princes, on obedience
to the higher powers, on mutual charity one towards
another—on all of these and kindred subjects have very
great and invincible force to overturn those principles of

[1] 1 Peter iii. 15.   [2] Tit. i. 9.

the new order which are well known to be dangerous to the peaceful order of things and to public safety. In short, all studies ought to find hope of advancement and promise of assistance in this restoration of philosophic discipline which We have proposed. The arts were wont to draw from philosophy, as from a wise mistress, sound judgment and right method, and from it also their spirit as from the common fount of life. When philosophy stood stainless in honor and wise in judgment, then, as facts and constant experience showed, the liberal arts flourished as never before or since; but, neglected and almost blotted out, they lay prone since philosophy began to lean to error and join hands with folly. Nor will the physical sciences, which are now in such great repute, and by the renown of so many inventions draw such universal admiration to themselves, suffer detriment but find very great assistance in the re-establishment of the ancient philosophy. For the investigation of facts and the contemplation of nature is not alone sufficient for their profitable exercise and advance; but when facts have been established it is necessary to rise and apply ourselves to the study of the nature of corporeal things, to inquire into the laws which govern them and the principles whence their order and varied unity and mutual attraction in diversity arise. To such investigations it is wonderful what force and light and aid the scholastic philosophy, if judiciously taught, would bring.

And here it is well to note that Our philosophy can only by the grossest injustice be accused of being opposed to the advance and development of natural science. For when the scholastics, following the opinion of the holy Fathers, always held in anthropology that the human intelligence is only led to the knowledge of things without body and matter by things sensible, they well understood that nothing was of greater use to the philosopher than diligently to search into the mysteries of nature and to be earnest and constant in the study of physical things.

And this they confirmed by their own example; for St. Thomas, Blessed Albertus Magnus, and other leaders of the scholastics were never so wholly rapt in the study of philosophy as not to give large attention to the knowledge of natural things; and, indeed, the number of their sayings and writings on these subjects, which recent professors approve of and admit to harmonize with truth, is by no means small. Moreover, in this very age many illustrious professors of the physical sciences openly testify that between certain and accepted conclusions of modern physics and the philosophic principles of the schools there is no conflict worthy of the name.

While, therefore, We hold that every word of wisdom, every useful thing by whomsoever discovered or planned, ought to be received with a willing and grateful mind, We exhort you, Venerable Brethren, in all earnestness to restore the golden wisdom of St. Thomas, and to spread it far and wide for the defence and beauty of the Catholic faith, for the good of society, and for the advantage of all the sciences. The wisdom of St. Thomas, We say; for if anything is taken up with too great subtlety by the scholastic doctors, or too carelessly stated—if there be anything that ill agrees with the discoveries of a later age, or, in a word, improbable in whatever way, it does not enter Our mind to propose that for imitation to Our age. Let carefully selected teachers endeavor to implant the doctrine of Thomas Aquinas in the minds of students, and set forth clearly his solidity and excellence over others. Let the academies already founded or to be founded by you illustrate and defend this doctrine, and use it for the refutation of prevailing errors. But, lest the false for the true or the corrupt for the pure be drunk in, be ye watchful that the doctrine of Thomas be drawn from his own fountains, or at least from those rivulets which derived from the very fount, have thus far flowed, according to the established agreement of learned men, pure and clear; be careful to guard the minds of youth from those which are said to flow thence, but in reality are gathered from strange and unwholesome streams.

But well do We know that vain will be Our efforts unless, Venerable Brethren, He helps Our common cause who, in the words of divine Scripture, is called the God of all knowledge;[1] by which we are also admonished that "every best gift and every perfect gift is from above, coming down from the Father of lights";[2] and again: "If any of you want wisdom, let him ask of God, who giveth to all men abundantly, and upbraideth not: and it shall be given him."[3]

Therefore in this also let us follow the example of the Angelic Doctor, who never gave himself to reading or writing without first begging the blessing of God, who modestly confessed that whatever he knew he had acquired not so much by his own study and labor as by the divine gift; and therefore let us all, in humble and united prayer, beseech God to send forth the spirit of knowledge and of understanding to the children of the Church, and open their senses for the understanding of wisdom. And that we may receive fuller fruits of the divine goodness, offer up to God the most efficacious patronage of the Blessed Virgin Mary, who is called the seat of wisdom; having at the same time as advocates St. Joseph, the most chaste spouse of the Virgin, and Peter and Paul, the chiefs of the apostles, whose truth renewed the earth, which had fallen under the impure blight of error, filling it with the light of heavenly wisdom.

In fine, relying on the divine assistance and confiding in your pastoral zeal, We bestow on all of you, Venerable Brethren, on all the clergy and the flocks committed to your charge, the apostolic benediction as a pledge of heavenly gifts and a token of Our special esteem.

---

[1] 1 Kings ii. 3.   [2] James i. 17.   [3] Ibid. i. 5.

CHRISTIAN MARRIAGE.

Encyclical Letter Arcanum Divinæ, February 10, 1880.

THE hidden design of the divine wisdom, which Jesus Christ the Saviour of men came to carry out on earth, had this end in view, that, by Himself and in Himself, He should divinely renew the world, which was sinking as it were, with length of years, into decline. The Apostle Paul summed this up in words of dignity and majesty when he wrote to the Ephesians, thus: *That He might make known unto us the mystery of His will . . . to re-establish all things in Christ that are in heaven and on earth.*[1]

In truth, Christ our Lord, setting Himself to fulfil the commandment which His Father had given Him, straightway imparted a new form and fresh beauty to all things, taking away the effects of their time-worn age. For He healed the wounds which the sin of our first father had inflicted on the human race; He brought all men, by nature children of wrath, into favor with God; He led to the light of truth men wearied out by long-standing errors; He renewed to every virtue those who were weakened by lawlessness of every kind; and, giving them again an inheritance of never-ending bliss, He added a sure hope that their mortal and perishable bodies should one day be partakers of immortality and of the glory of heaven. In order that these unparalleled benefits might last as long as men should be found on earth, He trusted to His Church the continuance of His work; and, looking to future times,

[1] Ephes. i. 9, 10.

He commanded her to set in order whatever might have become deranged in human society, and to restore whatever might have fallen into ruin.

Although the divine renewal we have spoken of chiefly and directly affected men as constituted in the supernatural order of grace, nevertheless some of its precious and salutary fruits were also bestowed abundantly in the order of nature. Hence not only individual men, but also the whole mass of the human race, have in every respect received no small degree of worthiness. For, so soon as Christian order was once established in the world, it became happily possible for all men, one by one, to learn what God's fatherly providence is, and to dwell in it habitually, thereby fostering that hope of heavenly help which never confoundeth. From all this outflowed fortitude, self-control, constancy, and the evenness of a peaceful mind, together with many high virtues and noble deeds.

Wondrous, indeed, was the extent of dignity, steadfastness, and goodness which thus accrued to the State as well as to the family. The authority of rulers became more just and revered; the obedience of the people more ready and unforced; the union of citizens closer; the rights of dominion more secure. In very truth, the Christian religion thought of and provided for all things which are held to be advantageous in a State; so much so indeed that, according to St. Augustine, one cannot see how it could have offered greater help in the matter of living well and happily, had it been instituted for the single object of procuring or increasing those things which contribute to the conveniences or advantages of this mortal life.

Still the purpose We have set before Us is not to recount, in detail, benefits of this kind; Our wish is rather to speak about that family union of which *marriage* is the beginning and the foundation.

The true origin of marriage, Venerable Brothers, is

well known to all. Though the revilers of the Christian faith refuse to acknowledge the never-interrupted doctrine of the Church on this subject, and have long striven to destroy the testimony of all nations and of all times, they have nevertheless failed not only to quench the powerful light of truth, but even to lessen it. We record what is to all known, and cannot be doubted by any, that God, on the sixth day of creation, having made man from the slime of the earth, and having breathed into his face the breath of life, gave him a companion, whom He miraculously took from the side of Adam when he was locked in sleep. God thus, in His most far-reaching foresight, decreed that this husband and wife should be the natural beginning of the human race, from whom it might be propagated and preserved by an unfailing fruitfulness throughout all futurity of time. And this union of man and woman, that it might answer more fittingly to the infinitely wise counsels of God, even from that beginning manifested chiefly two most excellent properties—deeply sealed, at it were, and signed upon it—namely, unity and perpetuity. From the Gospel we see clearly that this doctrine was declared and openly confirmed by the divine authority of Jesus Christ. He bore witness to the Jews and to His apostles that marriage, from its institution, should exist between two only, that is, between one man and one woman; that of two they are made, so to say, one flesh; and that the marriage bond is by the will of God so closely and strongly made fast that no man may dissolve it or render it asunder. *For this cause shall a man leave father and mother, and shall cleave to his wife, and they two shall be in one flesh. Therefore now they are not two, but one flesh. What, therefore, God hath joined together, let no man put asunder.*[1]

This form of marriage, however, so excellent and so pre-eminent, began to be corrupted by degrees, and to

---

[1] Matt. xix. 5, 6.

disappear among the heathen; and became even among the Jewish race clouded in a measure and obscured. For in their midst a common custom was gradually introduced, by which it was accounted as lawful for a man to have more than one wife; and eventually when *by reason of the hardness of their heart,*[1] Moses indulgently permitted them to put away their wives, the way was open to divorce.

But the corruption and change which fell on marriage among the Gentiles seem almost incredible, inasmuch as it was exposed in every land to floods of error and of the most shameful lusts. All nations seem, more or less, to have forgotten the true notion and origin of marriage; and thus everywhere laws were enacted with reference to marriage, prompted to all appearance by State reasons, but not such as nature required. Solemn rites, invented at will of the lawgivers, brought about that women should, as might be, bear either the honorable name of wife or the disgraceful name of concubine; and things came to such a pitch that permission to marry, or the refusal of the permission, depended on the will of the heads of the State, whose laws were greatly against equity or even to the highest degree unjust. Moreover, plurality of wives and husbands, the abounding source of divorces, caused the nuptial bond to be relaxed exceedingly. Hence, too, sprang up the greatest confusion as to the mutual rights and duties of husbands and wives, inasmuch as a man assumed right of dominion over his wife, ordering her to go about her business, often without any just cause; while he was himself at liberty (as St. Jerome says) "to run headlong with impunity into lust, unbridled and unrestrained, in houses of ill-fame and amongst his female slaves, as if the dignity of the persons sinned with, and not the will of the sinner, made the guilt."[2] When the licentiousness of a husband thus showed itself,

---

[1] Matt. xix. 8.   [2] Op. tom. i. col. 455.

nothing could be more piteous than the wife, sunk so low as to be all but reckoned as a means for the gratification of passion, or for the production of offspring. Without any feeling of shame marriageable girls were bought and sold, just like so much merchandise;[1] and power was sometimes given to the father and to the husband to inflict capital punishment on the wife. Of necessity the offspring of such marriages as these were either reckoned among the stock in trade of the commonwealth or held to be the property of the father of the family;[2] and the law permitted him to make and unmake the marriages of his children at his mere will, and even to exercise against them the monstrous power of life and death.

So manifold being the vices and so great the ignominies with which marriage was defiled, an alleviation and a remedy were at length bestowed from on high. Jesus Christ, who restored our human dignity and who perfected the Mosaic law, applied early in His ministry no little solicitude to the question of marriage. He ennobled the marriage in Cana of Galilee by His presence, and made it memorable by the first of the miracles which He wrought;[3] and for this reason, even from that day forth, it seemed as if the beginnings of new holiness had been conferred on human marriages. Later on He brought back matrimony to the nobility of its primeval origin, by condemning the customs of the Jews in their abuse of the plurality of wives and of the power of giving bills of divorce; and still more by commanding most strictly that no one should dare to dissolve that union which God Himself had sanctioned by a bond perpetual. Hence, having set aside the difficulties which were adduced from the law of Moses, He, in character of supreme Lawgiver, decreed as follows concerning husbands and wives: *I say to you, that whosoever shall put away his wife, except it be for fornication, and shall marry another, committeth*

---

[1] Arnob. adv. Gent. 4.   [2] Dionys. Halicar. lib. ii. cc. 26, 27.
[3] John ii.

adultery; and he that shall marry her that is put away committeth adultery.[1]

But what was decreed and constituted in respect to marriage by the authority of God, has been more fully and more clearly handed down to us, by tradition and the written Word, through the apostles, those heralds of the laws of God. To the apostles, indeed, as our masters, are to be referred the doctrines which *our holy Fathers, the Councils, and the Tradition of the Universal Church have always taught,*[2] namely, that Christ our Lord raised marriage to the dignity of a sacrament; that to husband and wife, guarded and strengthened by the heavenly grace which His merits gained for them, He gave power to attain holiness in the married state; and that, in a wondrous way, making marriage an example of the mystical union between Himself and His Church, He not only perfected that love which is according to nature,[3] but also made the natural union of one man with one woman far more perfect through the bond of heavenly love. Paul says to the Ephesians: *Husbands, love your wives, as Christ also loved the Church, and delivered Himself up for it, that He might sanctify it. . . . So also ought men to love their wives as their own bodies. . . . For no man ever hated his own flesh, but nourisheth and cherisheth it, as also Christ doth the Church; because we are members of His body, of His flesh, and of His bones. For this cause shall a man leave His father and mother, and shall cleave to his wife, and they shall be two in one flesh. This is a great sacrament; but I speak in Christ and in the Church.*[4] In like manner from the teaching of the apostles we learn that the unity of marriage and its perpetual indissolubility, the indispensable conditions of its very origin, must, according to the command of Christ, be holy and inviolable without exception. Paul says again: *To them that are married, not I, but the Lord commandeth that the wife depart not*

---

[1] Matt. xix. 9. [3] Trid. sess. xxiv. cap. i. de reform. matr.
[2] Trid. sess. xxiv. in pr. [4] Eph. v. 25–32.

from her husband; and if she depart, that she remain un-married or be reconciled to her husband.[1] And again: *A woman is bound by the law as long as her husband liveth; but if her husband die, she is at liberty.*[2] It is for these reasons that marriage *is a great sacrament;*[3] *honorable in all;*[4] holy, pure, and to be reverenced as a type and symbol of most high mysteries.

Furthermore, the Christian perfection and complete-ness of marriage are not comprised in those points only which have been mentioned.

For, first, there has been vouchsafed to the marriage union a higher and nobler purpose than was ever previously given to it. By the command of Christ, it not only looks to the propagation of the human race, but to the bringing forth of children for the Church, *fellow-citizens with the saints, and the domestics of God;*[5] so that *a people might be born and brought up for the worship and religion of the true God and our Saviour Jesus Christ.*[6]

Secondly, the mutual duties of husband and wife have been defined, and their several rights accurately estab-lished. They are bound, namely, to have such feelings for one another as to cherish always very great mutual love, to be ever faithful to their marriage vow, and to give one another an unfailing and unselfish help. The husband is the chief of the family and the head of the wife. The woman, because she is flesh of his flesh, and bone of his bone, must be subject to her husband and obey him; not, indeed, as a servant, but as a com-panion, so that her obedience shall be wanting in neither honor nor dignity. Since the husband represents Christ, and since the wife represents the Church, let there always be, both in him who commands and in her who obeys, a heaven-born love guiding both in their respec-tive duties. For *the husband is the head of the wife; as Christ is the head of the Church. . . . Therefore, as the*

---

[1] 1 Zor. vii. 10, 11.   [3] Eph. v. 32.   [5] Eph. ii. 19.
[2] 1 Cor. vii. 39.   [4] Heb. xiii. 4.   [6] Catech. Rom. c. viii.

Church is subject to Christ, so also let wives be to their husbands in all things.[1]

As regards children, they ought to submit to the parents and obey them, and give them honor for conscience' sake; while, on the other hand, parents are bound to give all care and watchful thought to the education of their offspring and their virtuous bringing up: *Fathers, . . . bring them up* (that is, your children) *in the discipline and correction of the Lord.*[2] From this we see clearly that the duties of husbands and wives are neither few nor light; although to married people who are good these burdens become not only bearable but agreeable, owing to the strength which they gain through the sacrament.

Christ, therefore,.having renewed marriage to such and so great excellence, commended and entrusted all the discipline bearing upon these matters to his Church. The Church, always and everywhere, has so used her power with reference to the marriages of Christians, that men have seen clearly how it belongs to her as of native right; not being made hers by any human grant, but given divinely to her by the will of her Founder. Her constant and watchful care in guarding Marriage, by the preservation of its sanctity, is so well understood as to not need proof. That the judgment of the Council of Jerusalem reprobated licentious and free love,[3] we all know; as also that the incestuous Corinthian was condemned by the authority of blessed Paul.[4] Again, in the very beginning of the Christian Church were repulsed and defeated, with the like unremitting determination, the efforts of many who aimed at the destruction of Christian marriage, such as the Gnostics, Manicheans, and Montanists; and in our own time Mormons, St. Simonians, Phalansterians, and Communists.

In like manner, moreover, a law of marriage just to all, and the same for all, was enacted by the abolition of the

[1] Eph. v. 23, 24.
[2] Ibid. vi. 4.
[3] Acts xv. 29.
[4] 1 Cor. v. 5.

old distinction between slaves and free-born men and
women; and thus the rights of husbands and wives were
made equal: for, as St. Jerome says, "with us that which
is unlawful for women is unlawful for men also, and the
same restraint is imposed on equal conditions."[1] The
self-same rights also were firmly established for reciprocal
affection and for the interchange of duties; the dignity of
the woman was asserted and assured; and it was forbidden
to the man to inflict capital punishment for adultery, or
lustfully and shamelessly to violate his plighted faith.

It is also a great blessing that the Church has limited,
so far as is needful, the power of fathers of families,
so that sons and daughters, wishing to marry, are not in
any way deprived of their rightful freedom; that, for the
purpose of spreading more widely the supernatural love of
husbands and wives, she has decreed marriages within
certain degrees of consanguinity or affinity to be null and
void; that she has taken the greatest pains to safeguard
marriage, as much as is possible, from error and violence
and deceit; that she has always wished to preserve the
holy chasteness of the marriage bed, personal rights, the
honor of husband and wife, and the security of religion.

Lastly, with such power and with such foresight of
legislation has the Church guarded its divine institution,
that no one who thinks rightfully of these matters can fail
to see how, with regard to marriage, she is the best guardian and defender of the human race; and how withal her
wisdom has come forth victorious from the lapse of years,
from the assaults of men, and from the countless changes
of public events.

Yet, owing to the efforts of the arch-enemy of mankind,
there are persons who, thanklessly casting away so many
other blessings of redemption, despise also or utterly ignore
the restoration of marriage to its original perfection. It
is the reproach of some of the ancients that they showed

---

[1] Oper. tom. 1 col. 455.

themselves the enemies of marriage in many ways; but in our own age, much more pernicious is the sin of those who would fain pervert utterly the nature of marriage, perfect though it is, and complete in all its details and parts. The chief reason why they act in this way is because very many, imbued with the maxims of a false philosophy and corrupted in morals, judge nothing so unbearable as submission and obedience; and strive with all their might to bring about that not only individual men, but families also, nay indeed, human society itself, may in haughty pride despise the sovereignty of God.

Now since the family and human society at large spring from marriage, these men will on no account allow matrimony to be the subject of the jurisdiction of the Church. Nay, they endeavor to deprive it of all holiness, and so bring it within the contracted sphere of those rights which, having been instituted by man, are ruled and administered by the civil jurisprudence of the community. Wherefore it necessarily follows that they attribute all power over marriage to civil rulers, and allow none whatever to the Church; and when the Church exercises any such power, they think that she acts either by favor of the civil authority or to its injury. Now is the time, they say, for the heads of the State to vindicate their rights unflinchingly, and to do their best to settle all that relates to marriage according as to them seems good.

Hence are owing *civil marriages,* commonly so called; hence laws are framed which impose impediments to marriage; hence arise judicial sentences affecting the marriage contract, as to whether or not it have been rightly made. Lastly, all power of prescribing and passing judgment in this class of cases is, as we see, of set purpose denied to the Catholic Church, so that no regard is paid either to her divine power or to her prudent laws. Yet under these, for so many centuries, have the nations lived on whom the light of civilization shone bright with the wisdom of Christ Jesus.

Nevertheless, all those who reject what is supernatural, as well as all who profess that they worship above all things the divinity of the State, and strive to disturb whole communities with such wicked doctrines, cannot escape the charge of delusion. Marriage has God for its Author, and was from the very beginning a kind of foreshadowing of the Incarnation of His Son; and therefore there abides in it a something holy and religious; not extraneous, but innate; not derived from men, but implanted by nature. Innocent III., therefore, and Honorius III., our predecessors, affirmed not falsely nor rashly that a certain sacredness of marriage rites existed ever amongst the faithful and unbelievers.[1] We call to witness the monuments of antiquity, as also the manners and customs of those people who, being the most civilized, had the greatest knowledge of law and equity. In the minds of all of them it was a fixed and foregone conclusion that, when marriage was thought of, it was thought of as conjoined with religion and holiness. Hence among those, marriages were commonly celebrated with religious ceremonies, under the authority of pontiffs, and with the ministry of priests. So mighty, even in the souls ignorant of heavenly doctrine, was the force of nature, of the remembrance of their origin, and of the conscience of the human race. As, then, marriage is holy by its own power, in its own nature, and of itself, it ought not to be regulated and administered by the will of civil rulers, but by the divine authority of the Church, which alone in sacred matters professes the office of teaching.

Next, the dignity of the sacrament must be considered; for through addition of the sacrament the marriages of Christians have become far the noblest of all matrimonial unions. But to decree and ordain concerning the sacrament is, by the will of Christ Himself, so much a part of

[1] Apud fideles et infideles existere sacramentum conjugii.

the power and duty of the Church, that it is plainly absurd to maintain that even the very smallest fraction of such power has been transferred to the civil ruler.

Lastly should be borne in mind the great weight and crucial test of history, by which it is plainly proved that the legislative and judicial authority of which We are speaking has been freely and constantly used by the Church, even in times when some foolishly suppose the head of the State either to have consented to it or connived at it. It would, for instance, be incredible and altogether absurd to assume that Christ our Lord condemned the long-standing practice of polygamy and divorce by authority delegated to Him by the procurator of the province, or the principal ruler of the Jews. And it would be equally extravagant to think that, when the Apostle Paul taught that divorces and incestuous marriages were not lawful, it was because Tiberius, Caligula, and Nero agreed with him or secretly commanded him so to teach. No man in his senses could ever be persuaded that the Church made so many laws about the holiness and indissolubility of marriage, and the marriages of slaves with the free-born, by power received from Roman emperors most hostile to the Christian name, whose strongest desire was to destroy by violence and murder the rising Church of Christ. Still less could any one believe this to be the case, when the law of the Church was sometimes so divergent from the civil law that Ignatius the Martyr, Justin, Athenagoras, and Tertullian publicly denounced as unjust and adulterous certain marriages which had been sanctioned by Imperial law.

Furthermore, after all power had devolved upon the Christian emperors, the supreme Pontiffs and Bishops assembled in Council persisted, with the same independence and consciousness of their right, in commanding or forbidding in regard to marriage whatever they judged to be profitable or expedient for the time being, however much it might seem to be at variance with the laws of the

State. It is well known that, with respect to the impediments arising from the marriage bond, through vow, disparity of worship, blood relationship, certain forms of crime, and from previously plighted troth, many decrees were issued by the rulers of the Church in the Councils of Granada, Arles, Chalcedon, the second of Milevum, and others, which were often widely different from the decrees sanctioned by the laws of the empire. Furthermore, so far were Christian princes from arrogating any power in the matter of Christian marriage, that they on the contrary acknowledged and declared that it belonged exclusively in all its fulness to the Church. In fact, Honorius, the younger Theodosius, and Justinian also, hesitated not to confess that the only power belonging to them in relation to marriage was that of acting as guardians and defenders of the Holy Canons. If at any time they enacted anything by their edicts concerning impediments of marriage, they voluntarily explained the reason, affirming that they took it upon themselves so to act, by leave and authority of the Church, whose judgment they were wont to appeal to and reverently to accept, in all questions that concerned legitimacy and divorce; as also in all those points which in any way have a necessary connection with the marriage-bond. The Council of Trent, therefore, had the clearest right to define that it is in the Church's power "to establish diriment impediments of matrimony," and that "matrimonial causes pertain to ecclesiastical judges." [1]

Let no one then be deceived by the distinction which some court legists have so strongly insisted upon—the distinction, namely, by virtue of which they sever the matrimonial contract from the sacrament, with intent to hand over the contract to the power and will of the rulers of the State, while reserving questions concerning the sacrament to the Church. A distinction, or rather severance,

---

[1] Trid. sess. xxiv. can. 4, 12.

of this kind cannot be approved; for certain it is that in Christian marriage the contract is inseparable from the sacrament; and that, for this reason, the contract cannot be true and legitimate without being a sacrament as well. For Christ our Lord added to marriage the dignity of a sacrament; but marriage is the contract itself, whenever that contract is lawfully concluded.

Marriage, moreover, is a sacrament, because it is a holy sign which gives grace, showing forth an image of the mystical nuptials of Christ with the Church. But the form and image of these nuptials is shown precisely by the very bond of that most close union in which man and woman are bound together in one; which bond is nothing else but the marriage itself. Hence it is clear that among Christians every true marriage is, in itself and by itself, a sacrament; and that nothing can be further from the truth than to say that the sacrament is a certain added ornament, or outward endowment, which can be separated and torn away from the contract at the caprice of man. Neither therefore by reasoning can it be shown, nor by any testimony of history be proved, that power over the marriages of Christians has ever lawfully been handed over to the rulers of the State. If, in this matter, the right of any one else has ever been violated, no one can truly say that it has been violated by the Church.

Would that the teaching of those who reject what is supernatural, besides being full of falsehood and injustice, were not also the fertile source of much detriment and calamity! But it is easy to see at a glance the greatness of the evil which unhallowed marriages have brought, and ever will bring, on the whole of human society.

From the beginning of the world, indeed, it was divinely ordained that things instituted by God and by Nature should be proved by us to be the more profitable and salutary the more they remain unchanged in their full integrity. For God, the Maker of all things, well knowing what was good for the institution and preservation of each of His creatures, so ordered them by His will and mind that each might adequately attain the end for which it was made. If the rashness or the wickedness of human agency venture to change or disturb that order of things which has been constituted with fullest foresight, then the designs of infinite wisdom and usefulness begin either to be hurtful or cease to be profitable, partly because through the change undergone they have lost their power of benefiting, and partly because God chooses to inflict punishment on the pride and audacity of man. Now those who deny that marriage is holy, and who relegate it, stripped of all holiness, among the class of common things, uproot thereby the foundations of nature, not only resisting the designs of Providence, but, so far as they can, destroying the order that God has ordained. No one, therefore, should wonder if from such insane and impious attempts there spring up a crop of evils pernicious in the highest degree both to the salvation of souls and to the safety of the commonwealth.

. If, then, we consider the end of the divine institution of marriage, we shall see very clearly that God intended it to be a most fruitful source of individual benefit and of public welfare. Not only, in strict truth, was marriage instituted for the propagation of the human race, but also that the lives of husbands and wives might be made better and happier. This comes about in many ways: by their lightening each other's burdens through mutual help; by constant and faithful love; by having all their possessions in common; and by the heavenly grace which flows from the sacrament. Marriage also can do much for the good of families, for, so long as it is conformable to nature and in accordance with the counsels of God, it has power to strengthen union of heart in the parents; to secure the holy education of children; to attemper the authority of the father by the example of the divine authority; to render children obedient to their parents and servants obedient to their masters. From such marriages as these the State may rightly expect a race of citizens animated by a good spirit and filled with reverence and love for God, recognizing it their duty to obey those who rule justly and lawfully, to love all, and to injure no one.

These many and glorious fruits were ever the product of marriage, so long as it retained those gifts of holiness, unity, and indissolubility from which proceeded all its fertile and saving power; nor can any one doubt but that it would always have brought forth such fruits, at all times and in all places, had it been under the power and guardianship of the Church, the trustworthy preserver and protector of these gifts. But now there is a spreading wish to supplant natural and divine law by human law; and hence has begun a gradual extinction of that most excellent ideal of marriage which Nature herself had impressed on the soul of man, and sealed, as it were, with her own seal; nay, more, even in Christian marriages this power, productive of so great good, has been weakened by the sinfulness of man. Of what advantage is it if a State can institute nuptials estranged from the Christian religion, which is the mother of all good, cherishing all sublime virtues, quickening and urging us to everything that is the glory of a lofty and generous soul? When the Christian religion is rejected and repudiated, marriage sinks of necessity into the slavery of man's vicious nature and vile passions, and finds but little protection in the help of natural goodness. A very torrent of evil has flowed from this source, not only into private families, but also into States. For the salutary fear of God being removed, and there being no longer that refreshment in toil which is nowhere more abounding than in the Christian religion, it very often happens, as from facts is evident, that the mutual services and duties of marriage seem almost unbearable; and thus very many yearn for the loosening of the tie which they believe to be woven by human law and of their own will, whenever incompatibility of temper, or quarrels, or the violation of the marriage vow, or mutual consent, or other reasons induce them to think that it would be well to be set free. Then, if they are hindered by law from carrying out this shameless desire, they contend that the laws are iniquitous, inhuman, and at variance with the rights of free citizens; adding that every effort should be made to repeal such enactments, and to introduce a more humane code sanctioning divorce.

Now, however much the legislators of these our days may wish to guard themselves against the impiety of men such as we have been speaking of, they are unable to do so, seeing that they profess to hold and defend the very same principles of jurisprudence; and hence they have to go with the times, and render divorce easily obtainable. History itself shows this; for, to pass over other instances, we find that, at the close of the last century, divorces were sanctioned by law in that upheaval, or rather, as it might be called, conflagration in France, when society was wholly degraded by the abandoning of God. Many at the present time would fain have those laws re-enacted, because they wish God and His Church to be altogether exiled and excluded from the midst of human society, madly thinking that in such laws a final remedy must be sought for that moral corruption which is advancing with rapid strides.

Truly, it is hardly possible to describe how great are the evils that flow from divorce. Matrimonial contracts are by it made variable; mutual kindness is weakened; deplorable inducements to unfaithfulness are supplied; harm is done to the education and training of children; occasion is afforded for the breaking up of homes; the seeds of dissension are sown among families; the dignity of womanhood is lessened and brought low, and women run the risk of being deserted after having ministered to the pleasures of men. Since, then, nothing has such power to lay waste families and destroy the mainstay of kingdoms as the corruption of morals, it is easily seen that divorces are in the highest degree hostile to the prosperity of families and States, springing as they do from the depraved morals of the people, and, as experience shows us, opening out a way to every kind of evil-doing in public alike and in private life.

Further still, if the matter be duly pondered, we shall clearly see these evils to be the more especially dangerous, because, divorce once being tolerated, there will be no restraint powerful enough to keep it within the bounds marked out or presurmised. Great indeed is the force of example, and even greater still the might of passion. With such incitements it must needs follow that the eagerness for divorce, daily spreading by devious ways, will seize upon the minds of many like a virulent contagious disease, or like a flood of water bursting through every barrier. These are truths that doubtlessly are all clear in themselves; but they will become clearer yet if we call to mind the teachings of experience. So soon as the road to divorce began to be made smooth by law, at once quarrels, jealousies, and judicial separations largely increased; and such shamelessness of life followed, that men who had been in favor of these divorces repented of what they had done, and feared that, if they did not carefully seek a remedy by repealing the law, the State itself might come to ruin.

The Romans of old are said to have shrunk with horror from the first examples of divorce, but ere long all sense of decency was blunted in their soul; the meagre restraint of passion died out, and the marriage vow was so often broken that what some writers have affirmed would seem to be true—namely, women used to reckon years not by the change of consuls, but of their husbands.

In like manner, at the beginning, Protestants allowed legalized divorces in certain although but few cases, and yet from the affinity of circumstances of like kind, the number of divorces increased to such extent in Germany, America, and elsewhere, that all wise thinkers deplored the boundless corruption of morals, and judged the reck-lessness of the laws to be simply intolerable.

Even in Catholic States the like evil existed. For whenever at any time divorce was introduced, the abundance of misery that followed far exceeded all that the framers of the law could have foreseen. In fact, many lent their minds to contrive all kinds of fraud and device, and by accusations of cruelty, violence, and adultery to feign grounds for the dissolution of the matriomnial bond of which they had grown weary; and all this with so great havoc to morals that an amendment of the laws was deemed to be urgently needed.

Can any one, therefore, doubt that laws in favor of divorce would have a result equally baneful and calamitous were they to be passed in these our days? There exists not, indeed, in the projects and enactments of men any power to change the character and tendency which things have received from nature. Those men therefore show but little wisdom in the idea they have formed of the well-being of the commonwealth who think that the inherent character of marriage can be perverted with impunity; and who, disregarding the sanctity of religion and of the sacrament, seem to wish to degrade and dishonor marriage more basely than was done even by heathen laws. Indeed, if they do not change their views, not only private families, but all public society, will have unceasing cause to fear lest they should be miserably driven into that general confusion and overthrow of order which is even now the wicked aim of Socialists and Communists.

Thus we see most clearly how foolish and senseless it is to expect any public good from divorce, when, on the contrary, it tends to the certain destruction of society.

It must consequently be acknowledged that the Church has deserved exceedingly well of all nations by her ever-watchful care in guarding the sanctity and the indis-solubility of marriage. Again, no small amount of gratitude is owing to her for having, during the last hundred years, openly denounced the wicked laws which have grievously offended on this particular subject; as well as for her having branded with anathema the baneful heresy obtaining among Protestants touching divorce and separation; also for having in many ways condemned the habitual dissolution of marriage among the Greeks; for having declared invalid all marriages contracted upon the understanding that they may be at some future time dissolved; and lastly, for having, from the earliest times, repudiated the imperial laws which disastrously favored divorce.

As often, indeed, as the supreme Pontiffs have resisted the most powerful among rulers, in their threatening demands that divorces carried out by them should be confirmed by the Church, so often must we account them to have been contending for the safety, not only of religion, but also of the human race. For this reason all generations of men will admire the proofs of unbending courage which are to be found in the decrees of Nicholas I. against Lothair; of Urban II. and Paschal II. against Philip I. of France; of Celestine III. and Innocent III. against Alphonsus of Leon and Philip II. of France; of Clement VII. and Paul III. against Henry VIII.; and lastly, of Pius VII., that holy and courageous Pontiff, against Napoleon I., when at the height of his prosperity and in the fulness of his power.

This being so, all rulers and administrators of the State who are desirous of following the dictates of reason and wisdom, and anxious for the good of their people, ought to make up their minds to keep the holy laws of marriage intact, and to make use of the proffered aid of the Church for securing the safety of morals and the happiness of families, rather than suspect her of hostile intention, and falsely and wickedly accuse her of violating the civil law.

They should do this the more readily because the Catholic Church, though powerless in any way to abandon the duties of her office or the defence of her authority,

still very greatly inclines to kindness and indulgence
whenever they are consistent with the safety of her rights
and the sanctity of her duties. Wherefore she makes
no decrees in relation to marriage without having regard
to the state of the body politic and the condition of the
general public; and has besides more than once mitigated,
as far as possible, the enactments of her own laws when
there were just and weighty reasons. Moreover, she is
not unaware, and never calls in doubt, that the Sacrament
of Marriage, being instituted for the preservation and
increase of the human race, has a necessary relation to
circumstances of life which, though connected with
marriage, belong to the civil order, and about which the
State rightly makes strict inquiry and justly promulgates
decrees.

Yet no one doubts that Jesus Christ, the Founder of
the Church, willed her sacred power to be distinct from
the civil power, and each power to be free and unshackled
in its own sphere: with this condition, however—a condition good for both, and of advantage to all men—that
union and concord should be maintained between them;
and that on those questions which are, though in different
ways, of common right and authority, the power to which
secular matters have been intrusted should happily and
becomingly depend on the other power which has in its
charge the interests of heaven. In such arrangement
and harmony is found not only the best line of action
for each power, but also the most opportune and efficacious method of helping men in all that pertains to their
life here, and to their hope of salvation hereafter. For,
as We have shown in former Encyclical Letters, the intellect of man is greatly ennobled by the Christian faith,
and made better able to shun and banish all error, while
faith borrows in turn no little help from the intellect; and
in like manner. when the civil power is on friendly terms
with the sacred authority of the Church, there accrues
to both a great increase of usefulness. The dignity of

the one is exalted, and so long as religion is its guide it will never rule unjustly; while the other receives help of protection and defence for the public good of the faithful.

Being moved, therefore, by these considerations, as We have exhorted rulers at other times, so still more earnestly We exhort them now, to concord and friendly feeling; and We are the first to stretch out Our hand to them with fatherly benevolence, and to offer to them the help of Our supreme authority, a help which is the more necessary at this time when, in public opinion, the authority of rulers is wounded and enfeebled. Now that the minds of so many are inflamed with a reckless spirit of liberty, and men are wickedly endeavoring to get rid of every restraint of authority, however legitimate it may be, the public safety demands that both powers should unite their strength to avert the evils which are hanging, not only over the Church, but also over civil society.

But, while earnestly exhorting all to a friendly union of will, and beseeching God, the Prince of peace, to infuse a love of concord into all hearts, We cannot, Venerable Brothers, refrain from urging you more and more to fresh earnestness, and zeal, and watchfulness, though we know that these are already very great. With every effort and with all authority, strive, as much as you are able, to preserve whole and undefiled among the people committed to your charge the doctrine which Christ our Lord taught us; which the apostles, the interpreters of the will of God, have handed down; and which the Catholic Church has herself scrupulously guarded, and commanded to be believed in all ages by the faithful of Christ.

Let special care be taken that the people be well instructed in the precepts of Christian wisdom, so that they may always remember that marriage was not instituted by the will of man, but, from the very beginning, by the authority and command of God; that it does not admit of plurality of wives or husbands; that Christ, the author of the New Covenant, raised it from a rite of nature to be a sacrament, and gave to His Church legislative and judicial power with regard to the bond of union. On this point the very greatest care must be taken to instruct them, lest their minds should be led into error by the unsound conclusions of adversaries who desire that the Church should be deprived of that power.

In like manner, all ought to understand clearly that, if there be any union of a man and a woman among the faithful of Christ which is not a sacrament, such union has not the force and nature of a proper marriage; that although contracted in accordance with the laws of the State, it cannot be more than a rite or custom introduced by the civil law. Further, the civil law can deal with and decide those matters alone which in the civil order spring from marriage, and which cannot possibly exist, as is evident, unless there be a true and lawful cause for them, that is to say, the nuptial bond. It is of the greatest consequence to husband and wife that all these things should be known and well understood by them, in order that they may conform to the laws of the State, if there be no objection on the part of the Church; for the Church wishes the effects of marriage to be guarded in all possible ways, and that no harm may come to the children.

In the great confusion of opinions, however, which day by day is spreading more and more widely, it should further be known that no power can dissolve the bond of Christian marriage whenever this has been ratified and consummated; and that, of a consequence, those husbands and wives are guilty of a manifest crime who plan, for whatever reason, to be united in a second marriage before the first one has been ended by death. When, indeed, matters have come to such a pitch that it seems impossible for them to live together any longer, then the Church allows them to live apart, and strives at the same time to soften the evils of this separation by such remedies and helps as are suited to their condition; yet she never ceases to endeavor to bring about a reconciliation, and never despairs of doing so. But these are extreme cases; and they would seldom exist if men and women entered into the married state with proper dispositions, not influenced by passion, but entertaining right ideas of the duties of marriage and of its noble purpose; neither would they anticipate their marriage by a series of sins drawing down upon them the wrath of God.

To sum up all in a few words, there would be a calm and quiet constancy in marriage if married people would gather strength and life from the virtue of religion alone, which imparts to us resolution and fortitude; for religion would enable them to bear tranquilly and even gladly the trials of their state, such as, for instance, the faults that they discover in one another, the difference of temper and character, the weight of a mother's cares, the wearing anxiety about the education of children, reverses of fortune, and the sorrows of life.

Care also must be taken that they do not easily enter into marriage with those who are not Catholics; for when minds do not agree as to the observances of religion, it is scarcely possible to hope for agreement in other things. Other reasons also proving that persons should turn with dread from such marriages are chiefly these: that they give occasion to forbidden association and communion in religious matters; endanger the faith of the Catholic partner; are a hindrance to the proper education of the children; and often lead to a mixing up of truth and falsehood, and to the belief that all religions are equally good.

Lastly, since We well know that none should be excluded from Our charity, We commend, Venerable Brothers, to your fidelity and piety those unhappy persons who, carried away by the heat of passion, and being utterly indifferent to their salvation, live wickedly together without the bond of lawful marriage. Let your utmost care be exercised in bringing such persons back to their duty; and, both by your own efforts and by those of good men who will consent to help you, strive by every means that they may see how wrongly they have acted; that they may do penance; and that they may be induced to enter into a lawful marriage according to the Catholic rite.

You will at once see, Venerable Brothers, that the doctrine and precepts in relation to Christian marriage, which We have thought good to communicate to you in this letter, tend no less to the preservation of civil society than to the everlasting salvation of souls. May God grant that, by reason of their gravity and importance, minds may everywhere be found docile and ready to obey them! For this end let us all suppliantly, with humble prayer, implore the help of the Blessed and Immaculate Virgin Mary, that, our hearts being quickened to the obedience of faith, she may show herself our mother and our helper. With equal earnestness let us ask the princes of the apostles, Peter and Paul, the destroyers of heresies, the sowers of the seed of truth, to save the human race by their powerful patronage from the deluge of errors that is surging afresh.

In the meantime, as an earnest of heavenly gifts, and a testimony of Our special benevolence, We grant you all, Venerable Brothers, and to the people confided to your charge, from the depths of Our heart, the Apostolic Benediction.

FREEMASONRY.

Encyclical Letter Humanum Genus, April 20, 1884.

THE race of man, after its miserable fall from God, the Creator and the Giver of heavenly gifts, "through the envy of the devil," separated into two diverse and opposite parts, of which the one steadfastly contends for truth and virtue, the other for those things which are contrary to virtue and to truth. The one is the kingdom of God on earth, namely, the true Church of Jesus Christ; and those who desire from their heart to be united with it, so as to gain salvation, must of necessity serve God and His only-begotten Son with their whole mind and with an entire will. The other is the kingdom of Satan, in whose possession and control are all whosoever follow the fatal example of their leader and of our first parents, those who refuse to obey the divine and eternal law, and who have many aims of their own in contempt of God, and many aims also against God.

This twofold kingdom St. Augustine keenly discerned and described after the manner of two cities, contrary in their laws because striving for contrary objects; and with a subtle brevity he expressed the efficient cause of each in these words: "Two loves formed two cities: the love of self, reaching even to contempt of God, an earthly city; and the love of God, reaching to contempt of self, a heavenly one." At every period of time each has been in conflict with the other, with a variety and multiplicity of weapons, and of warfare, although not always with equal ardor and assault. At this period, however, the

83

partisans of evil seem to be combining together, and to
be struggling with united vehemence, led on or assisted
by that strongly organized and widespread association
called the Freemasons. No longer making any secret
of their purposes, they are now boldly rising up against
God Himself. They are planning the destruction of holy
Church publicly and openly, and this with the set purpose of utterly despoiling the nations of Christendom,
if it were possible, of the blessings obtained for us through
Jesus Christ our Saviour. Lamenting these evils, We are
constrained by the charity which urges Our heart to cry
out often to God: "For lo, Thy enemies have made a noise;
and they that hate Thee have lifted up the head. They
have taken a malicious counsel against Thy people, and
they have consulted against Thy saints. They have said,
'Come, and let us destroy them, so that they be not a
nation.'"

At so urgent a crisis, when so fierce and so pressing an
onslaught is made upon the Christian name, it is Our
office to point out the danger, to mark who are the adversaries, and to the best of Our power to make head against
their plans and devices, that those may not perish whose
salvation is committed to Us, and that the kingdom of
Jesus Christ intrusted to Our charge may not only stand
and remain whole, but may be enlarged by an ever-
increasing growth throughout the world.

The Roman Pontiffs Our predecessors, in their incessant
watchfulness over the safety of the Christian people,
were prompt in detecting the presence and the purpose
of this capital enemy immediately it sprang into the
light instead of hiding as a dark conspiracy; and moreover they took occasion with true foresight to give, as
it were, the alarm, and to admonish both princes and
nations to stand on their guard, and not allow themselves
to be caught by the devices and snares laid out to deceive
them.

The first warning of the danger was given by Clement

XII. in the year 1738, and his Constitution was confirmed and renewed by Benedict XIV. Pius VII. followed the same path; and Leo XII., by his Apostolic Constitution, "*Quo graviora*," put together the acts and decrees of former Pontiffs on this subject, and ratified and confirmed them forever. In the same sense spoke Pius VIII., Gregory XVI., and many times over Pius IX.

For as soon as the constitution and the spirit of the Masonic sect were clearly discovered by manifest signs of its action, by cases investigated, by the publication of its laws, and of its rites and commentaries, with the addition often of the personal testimony of those who were in the secret, this Apostolic See denounced the sect ·of the Freemasons, and publicly declared its constitution, as contrary to law and right, to be pernicious no less to Christendom than to the State; and it forbade any one to enter the society, under the penalties which the Church is wont to inflict upon exceptionally guilty persons. The sectaries, indignant at this, thinking to elude or to weaken the force of these decrees, partly by contempt of them, and partly by calumny, accused the Sovereign Pontiffs who had passed them either of exceeding the bounds of moderation in their decrees or of decreeing what was not just. This was the manner in which they endeavored to elude the authority and the weight of the Apostolic Constitutions of Clement XII. and Benedict XIV., as well as of Pius VII. and Pius IX. Yet in the very society itself there were to be found men who unwillingly acknowledged that the Roman Pontiffs had acted within their right, according to the Catholic doctrine and discipline. The Pontiffs received the same assent, and in strong terms, from many princes and heads of governments, who made it their business either to delate the Masonic society to the Apostolic See, or of their own accord by special enactments to brand it as pernicious, as, for example, in Holland, Austria, Switzerland, Spain, Bavaria, Savoy, and other parts of Italy.

But, what is of highest importance, the course of events has demonstrated the prudence of Our predecessors. For their provident and paternal solicitude had not always and everywhere the result desired; and this, either because of the simulation and cunning of some who were active agents in the mischief, or else of the thoughtless levity of the rest who ought, in their own interest, to have given to the matter their diligent attention. In consequence the sect of Freemasons grew with a rapidity beyond conception in the course of a century and a half, until it came to be able, by means of fraud or of audacity, to gain such entrance into every rank of the State as to seem to be almost its ruling power. This swift and formidable advance has brought upon the Church, upon the power of princes, upon the public well-being, precisely that grievous harm which Our predecessors had long before foreseen. Such a condition has been reached that henceforth there will be grave reason to fear, not indeed for the Church—for her foundation is much too firm to be overturned by the effort of men—but for those States in which prevails the power, either of the sect of which we are speaking or of other sects not dissimilar which lend themselves to it as disciples and subordinates.

For these reasons We no sooner came to the helm of the Church than We clearly saw and felt it to be Our duty to use Our authority to the very utmost against so vast an evil. We have several times already, as occasion served, attacked certain chief points of teaching which showed in a special manner the perverse influence of Masonic opinions. Thus, in Our Encyclical Letter, *"Quod Apostolici muneris,"* We endeavored to refute the monstrous doctrines of the Socialists and Communists; afterwards, in another beginning *"Arcanum,"* We took pains to defend and explain the true and genuine idea of domestic life, of which marriage is the spring and origin; and again, in that which begins *"Diuturnum,"* We described the ideal of political government conformed to the principles of Christian wisdom, which is marvellously in harmony, on the one hand, with the natural order of things, and, on the other, with the well-being of both sovereign princes and of nations. It is now Our intention, following the example of Our predecessors, directly to treat of the Masonic society itself, of its whole teaching, of its aims, and of its manner of thinking and acting, in order to bring more and more into the light its power for evil, and to do what We can to arrest the contagion of this fatal plague.

There are several organized bodies which, though differing in name, in ceremonial, in form and origin, are nevertheless so bound together by community of purpose and by the similarity of their main opinions, as to make in fact one thing with the sect of the Freemasons, which is a kind of centre whence they all go forth, and whither they all return. Now, these no longer show a desire to remain concealed; for they hold their meetings in the daylight and before the public eye, and publish their own newspaper organs; and yet, when thoroughly understood, they are found still to retain the nature and the habits of secret societies. There are many things like mysteries which it is the fixed rule to hide with extreme care, not only from strangers, but from very many members also; such as their secret and final designs, the names of the chief leaders, and certain secret and inner meetings, as well as their decisions, and the ways and means of carrying them out. This is, no doubt, the object of the manifold difference among the members as to right, office, and privilege—of the received distinction of orders and grades, and of that severe discipline which is maintained. Candidates are generally commanded to promise —nay, with a special oath, to swear—that they will never, to any person, at any time or in any way, make known the members, the passes, or the subjects discussed. Thus, with a fraudulent external appearance, and with a style of simulation which is always the same, the Freemasons, like the Manichees of old, strive, as far as possible, to conceal themselves, and to admit no witnesses but their own members. As a convenient manner of concealment, they assume the character of literary men and scholars associated for purposes of learning. They speak of their zeal for a more cultured refinement, and of their love for the poor; and they declare their one wish to be the amelioration of the condition of the masses, and to share with the largest possible number all the benefits of civil life. Were these purposes aimed at in real truth, they are by no means the whole of their object. Moreover, to be enrolled, it is necessary that the candidates promise and undertake to be thenceforward strictly obedient to their leaders and masters with the utmost submission and fidelity, and to be in readiness to do their bidding upon the slightest expression of their will; or, if disobedient, to submit to the direst penalties and death itself. As a fact, if any are judged to have betrayed the doings of the sect or to have resisted commands given, punishment is inflicted on them not infrequently, and with so much audacity and dexterity that the assassin very often escapes the detection and penalty of his crime.

But to simulate and wish to lie hid; to bind men like slaves in the very tightest bonds, and without giving any sufficient reason; to make use of men enslaved to the will of another for any arbitrary act; to arm men's right hands for bloodshed after securing impunity for the crime—all this is an enormity from which nature recoils. Wherefore reason and truth itself make it plain that the society of which we are speaking is in antagonism with justice and natural uprightness. And this becomes still plainer, inasmuch as other arguments also, and those very manifest, prove that it is essentially opposed to natural virtue. For, no matter how great may be men's cleverness in concealing and their experience in lying, it is impossible to prevent the effects of any cause from showing, in some way, the intrinsic nature of the cause whence they come. "A good tree cannot produce bad fruit, nor a bad tree produce good fruit." Now, the Masonic sect produces fruits that are pernicious and of the bitterest savor. For, from what We have above most clearly shown, that which is their ultimate purpose forces itself into view—namely, the utter overthrow of that whole religious and political order of the world which the Christian teaching has produced, and the substitution of a new state of things in accordance with their ideas, of which the foundations and laws shall be drawn from mere "Naturalism."

What We have said, and are about to say, must be understood of the sect of the Freemasons taken generically, and in so far as it comprises the associations kindred to it and confederated with it, but not of the individual members of them. There may be persons amongst these, and not a few, who, although not free from the guilt of having entangled themselves in such associations, yet are neither themselves partners in their criminal acts, nor aware of the ultimate object which they are endeavoring to attain. In the same way, some of the affiliated societies, perhaps, by no means approve of the extreme conclusions which they would, if consistent, embrace as necessarily following from their common principles, did not their very foulness strike them with horror. Some of these, again, are led by circumstances of times and places either to aim at smaller things than the others usually attempt, or than they themselves would wish to attempt. They are not, however, for this reason, to be reckoned as alien to the Masonic federation; for the Masonic federation is to be judged not so much by the things which it has done, or brought to completion, as by the sum of its pronounced opinions.

Now, the fundamental doctrine of the Naturalists, which they sufficiently make known by their very name, is that human nature and human reason ought in all things to be mistress and guide. Laying this down, they care little for duties to God, or pervert them by erroneous and vague opinions. For they deny that anything has been taught by God; they allow no dogma of religion or truth which cannot be understood by the human intelligence, nor any teacher who ought to be believed by reason of his authority. And since it is the special and exclusive duty of the Catholic Church fully to set forth in words truths divinely received, to teach, besides other divine helps to salvation, the authority of its office, and to defend the same with perfect purity, it is against the Church that the rage and attack of the enemies are principally directed.

In those matters which regard religion let it be seen how the sect of the Freemasons acts, especially where it is more free to act without restraint, and then let any one judge whether in fact it does not wish to carry out the policy of the Naturalists. By a long and persevering labor, they endeavor to bring about this result—namely, that the office and authority of the Church may become of no account in the civil State; and for this same reason they declare to the people and contend that Church and State ought to be altogether disunited. By this means they reject from the laws and from the commonwealth the wholesome influence of the Catholic religion; and they consequently imagine that States ought to be constituted without any regard for the laws and precepts of the Church.

Nor do they think it enough to disregard the Church —the best of guides—unless they also injure it by their hostility. Indeed, with them it is lawful to attack with impunity the very foundations of the Catholic religion, in speech, in writing, and in teaching; and even the rights of the Church are not spared, and the offices with which it is divinely invested are not safe. The least possible liberty to manage affairs is left to the Church; and this is done by laws not apparently very hostile, but in reality framed and fitted to hinder freedom of action. Moreover, We see exceptional and onerous laws imposed upon the clergy, to the end that they may be continually diminished in number and in necessary means. We see also the remnants of the possessions of the Church fettered by the strictest conditions, and subjected to the power and arbitrary will of the administrators of the State, and the religious orders rooted up and scattered.

But against the Apostolic See and the Roman Pontiff the contention of these enemies has been for a long time directed. The Pontiff was first, for specious reasons, thrust out from the bulwark of his liberty and of his right, the civil princedom; soon he was unjustly driven into a condition which was unbearable because of the difficulties raised on all sides; and now the time has come when the partisans of the sects openly declare, what in secret among themselves they have for a long time plotted, that the sacred power of the Pontiffs must be abolished, and that the Pontificate itself, founded by divine right, must be utterly destroyed. If other proofs were wanting, this fact would be sufficiently disclosed by the testimony of men well informed, of whom some at other times, and others again recently, have declared it to be true of the Freemasons that they especially desire to assail the Church with irreconcilable hostility, and that they will never rest until they have destroyed whatever the supreme Pontiffs have established for the sake of religion.

If those who are admitted as members are not commanded to abjure by any form of words the Catholic doctrines, this omission, so far from being adverse to the designs of the Freemasons, is more useful for their purposes. First, in this way they easily deceive the simpleminded and the heedless, and can induce a far greater number to become members. Again, as all who offer themselves are received whatever may be their form of religion, they thereby teach the great error of this age

—that a regard for religion should be held as an indifferent matter, and that all religions are alike. This manner of reasoning is calculated to bring about the ruin of all forms of religion, and especially of the Catholic religion, which, as it is the only one that is true, cannot, without great injustice, be regarded as merely equal to other religions.

But the Naturalists go much further; for having, in the highest things, entered upon a wholly erroneous course, they are carried headlong to extremes, either by reason of the weakness of human nature, or because God inflicts upon them the just punishment of their pride. Hence it happens that they no longer consider as certain and permanent those things which are fully understood by the natural light of reason, such as certainly are—the existence of God, the immaterial nature of the human soul, and its immortality. The sect of the Freemasons, by a similar course of error, is exposed to these same dangers; for although in a general way they may profess the existence of God, they themselves are witnesses that they do not all maintain this truth with the full assent of the mind or with a firm conviction. Neither do they conceal that this question about God is the greatest source and cause of discords among them; in fact, it is certain that a considerable contention about this same subject has existed among them very lately. But indeed the sect allows great liberty to its votaries, so that to each side is given the right to defend its own opinion, either that there is a God, or that there is none; and those who obstinately contend that there is no God are as easily initiated as those who contend that God exists, though, like the Pantheists, they have false notions concerning Him: all which is nothing else than taking away the reality, while retaining some absurd representation of the divine nature.

When this greatest fundamental truth has been overturned or weakened, it follows that those truths also which are known by the teaching of nature must begin to fall—namely, that all things were made by the free will of God the Creator; that the world is governed by Providence; that souls do not die; that to this life of men upon the earth there will succeed another and an everlasting life.

When these truths are done away with, which are as the principles of nature and important for knowledge and for practical use, it is easy to see what will become of both public and private morality. We say nothing of those more heavenly virtues, which no one can exercise or even acquire without a special gift and grace of God; of which necessarily no trace can be found in those who reject as unknown the redemption of mankind, the grace of God, the sacraments, and the happiness to be obtained in heaven. We speak now of the duties which have their origin in natural probity. That God is the Creator of the world and its provident Ruler; that the eternal law commands the natural order to be maintained, and forbids that it be disturbed; that the last end of men is a destiny far above human things and beyond this sojourning upon the earth: these are the sources and these the principles of all justice and morality. If these be taken away, as the Naturalists and Freemasons desire, there will immediately be no knowledge as to what constitutes justice and injustice, or upon what principle morality is founded. And, in truth, the teaching of morality which alone finds favor with the sect of Freemasons, and in which they contend that youth should be instructed, is that which they call "civil," and "independent," and "free," namely, that which does not contain any religious belief. But how insufficient such teaching is, how wanting in soundness, and how easily moved by every impulse of passion, is sufficiently proved by its sad fruits, which have already begun to appear. For wherever, by removing Christian education, the sect has begun more completely to rule, there goodness and integrity of morals have begun quickly to perish, monstrous and shameful opinions have grown up, and the audacity of evil deeds has risen to a high degree. All this is commonly complained of and deplored; and not a few of those who by no means wish to do so are compelled by abundant evidence to give not infrequently the same testimony.

Moreover, since human nature was stained by original sin, and is therefore more disposed to vice than to virtue, for a virtuous life it is absolutely necessary to restrain the disorderly movements of the soul, and to make the passions obedient to reason. In this conflict human things must very often be despised, and the greatest labors and hardships must be undergone, in order that reason may always hold its sway. But the Naturalists and Freemasons, having no faith in those things which we have learned by the revelation of God, deny that our first parents sinned, and consequently think that free will is not at all weakened and inclined to evil. On the contrary, exaggerating rather our natural virtue and excellence and placing therein alone the principle and rule of justice, they cannot even imagine that there is any need at all of a constant struggle and a perfect steadfastness to overcome the violence and rule the passions of our nature. Wherefore we see that men are publicly tempted by the many allurements of pleasure; that there are journals and pamphlets with neither moderation nor shame; that stage-plays are remarkable for license; that designs for works of art are shamelessly sought in the laws of a so-called *realism;* that the contrivances for a soft and delicate life are most carefully devised; and that all the blandishments of pleasure are diligently sought out by which virtue may be lulled to sleep. Wickedly also, but at the same time quite consistently, do those act who do away with the expectation of the joys of heaven, and bring down all happiness to the level of mortality, and, as it were, sink it in the earth. Of what We have said the following fact, astonishing not so much in itself as in its open expression, may serve as a confirmation. For since generally no one is accustomed to obey crafty and clever men so submissively as those whose soul is weakened and broken down by the domination of the passions, there have been in the sect of the Freemasons some who have plainly determined and proposed that, artfully and of set purpose, the multitude should be satiated with a boundless license of vice, as, when this had been done, it would easily come under their power and authority for any acts of daring.

What refers to domestic life in the teaching of the Naturalists is almost all contained in the following declarations. That marriage belongs to the genus of commercial contracts, which can rightly be revoked by the will of those who made them, and that the civil rulers of the State have power over the matrimonial bond; that in the education of youth nothing is to be taught in the matter of religion as of certain and fixed opinion; and each one must be left at liberty to follow, when he comes of age, whatever he may prefer. To these things the Freemasons fully assent; and not only assent, but have long endeavored to make them into a law and institution. For in many countries, and those nominally Catholic, it is enacted that no marriages shall be considered lawful except those contracted by the civil rite; in other places the law permits divorce; and in others every effort is used to make it lawful as soon as may be. Thus the time is quickly coming when marriages will be turned into another kind of contract—that is, into changeable and uncertain unions which fancy may join together, and which the same when changed may disunite. With the greatest unanimity the sect of the Freemasons also endeavors to take to itself the education of youth. They think that they can easily mould to their opinions that soft and pliant age, and bend it whither they will; and that nothing can be more fitted than this to enable them to bring up the youth of the State after their own plan. Therefore in the education and instruction of children they allow no share, either of teaching or of discipline, to the ministers of the Church; and in many places they have procured that the education of youth shall be exclusively in the hands of laymen, and that nothing which treats of the most important and most holy duties of men to God shall be introduced into the instructions on morals.

Then come their doctrines of politics, in which the Naturalists lay down that all men have the same right, and are in every respect of equal and like condition; that each one is naturally free; that no one has the right to command another; that it is an act of violence to require men to obey any authority other than that which is obtained from themselves. According to this, therefore, all things belong to the free people; power is held by the command or permission of the people, so that, when the popular will changes, rulers may lawfully be deposed; and the source of all rights and civil duties is either in the multitude or in the governing authority when this is constituted according to the latest doctrines. It is held also that the State should be without God; that in the various forms of religion there is no reason why one should have precedence of another; and that they are all to occupy the same place.

That these doctrines are equally acceptable to the Freemasons, and that they would wish to constitute States according to this example and model, is too well known to require proof. For some time past they have openly endeavored to bring this about with all their strength and resources; and in this they prepare the way for not a few bolder men who are hurrying on even to worse things, in their endeavor to obtain equality and community of all goods by the destruction of every distinction of rank and property.

What therefore the sect of the Freemasons is, and what course it pursues, appears sufficiently from the summary We have briefly given. Their chief dogmas are so greatly and manifestly at variance with reason, that nothing can be more perverse. To wish to destroy the religion and the Church which God Himself has established, and whose perpetuity He insures by His protection, and to bring back after a lapse of eighteen centuries the manners and customs of the pagans, is signal folly and audacious impiety. Neither is it less horrible nor more tolerable that they should repudiate the benefits which Jesus Christ has mercifully obtained, not only for individuals, but also for the family and for civil society, benefits which, even according to the judgment and testimony of enemies of Christianity, are very great. In this insane and wicked endeavor we may almost see the implacable hatred and spirit of revenge with which Satan himself is inflamed against Jesus Christ.—So also the studious endeavor of the Freemasons to destroy the chief foundations of justice and honesty, and to co-operate with those who would wish, as if they were mere animals, to do what they please, tends only to the ignominious and disgraceful ruin of the human race. The evil, too, is increased by the dangers which threaten both domestic and civil society. As We have elsewhere shown, in marriage, according to the belief of almost every nation, there is something sacred and religious; and the law of God has determined that marriages shall not be dissolved. If they are deprived of their sacred character, and made dissoluble, trouble and confusion in the family will be the result, the wife being deprived of her dignity and the children left without protection as to their interests and well-being.—To have in public matters no care for religion, and in the arrangement and administration of civil affairs to have no more regard for God than if He did not exist, is a rashness unknown to the very pagans; for in their heart and soul the notion of a divinity and the need of public religion were so firmly fixed that they would have thought it easier to have a city without foundation than a city without God. Human society, indeed, for which by nature we are formed, has been constituted by God the Author of nature; and from Him, as from their principle and source, flow in all their strength and permanence the countless benefits with which society abounds. As we are each of us admonished by the very voice of nature to worship God in piety and holiness, as the Giver unto us of life and of all that is good therein, so also and for the same reason, nations and States are bound to worship Him; and therefore it is clear that those who would absolve society from all religious duty act not only unjustly but also with ignorance and folly.

As men are by the will of God born for civil union and society, and as the power to rule is so necessary a bond of society that, if it be taken away, society must at once be broken up, it follows that from Him who is the Author of society has come also the authority to rule; so that whosoever rules, he is the minister of God. Wherefore, as the end and nature of human society so requires, it is right to obey the just commands of lawful authority, as it is right to obey God who ruleth all things; and it is most untrue that the people have it in their power to cast aside their obedience whensoever they please.

In like manner, no one doubts that all men are equal one to another, so far as regards their common origin and nature, or the last end which each one has to attain, or the rights and duties which are thence derived. But as the abilities of all are not equal, as one differs from another in the powers of mind or body, and as there are very many dissimilarities of manner, disposition, and character, it is most repugnant to reason to endeavor to confine all within the same measure, and to extend complete equality to the institutions of civil life. Just as a perfect condition of the body results from the conjunction and composition of its various members, which, though differing in form and purpose, make, by their union and the distribution of each one to its proper place, a combination beautiful to behold, firm in strength, and necessary for use; so, in the commonwealth, there is an almost infinite dissimilarity of men, as parts of the whole. If they are to be all equal, and each is to follow his own will, the State will appear most deformed; but if, with a distinction of degrees of dignity, of pursuits and employments, all aptly conspire for the common good, they will present a natural image of a well-constituted State.

Now, from the disturbing errors which We have described the greatest dangers to States are to be feared. For, the fear of God and reverence for divine laws being taken away, the authority of rulers despised, sedition permitted and approved, and the popular passions urged on to lawlessness, with no restraint save that of punishment, a change and overthrow of all things will necessarily follow. Yea, this change and overthrow is deliberately planned and put forward by many associations of *Communists* and *Socialists;* and to their undertakings the sect of Freemasons is not hostile, but greatly favors their designs, and holds in common with them their chief opinions. And if these men do not at once and everywhere endeavor to carry out their extreme views, it is not to be attributed to their teaching and their will, but to the virtue of that divine religion which cannot be destroyed; and also because the sounder part of men, refusing to be enslaved to secret societies, vigorously resist their insane attempts.

Would that all men would judge of the tree by its fruits, and would acknowledge the seed and origin of the evils which press upon us, and of the dangers that are impending! We have to deal with a deceitful and crafty enemy, who, gratifying the ears of people and of princes, has ensnared them by smooth speeches and by adulation. Ingratiating themselves with rulers under a pretence of friendship, the Freemasons have endeavored to make them their allies and powerful helpers for the destruction of the Christian name; and that they might more strongly urge them on, they have, with determined calumny, accused the Church of invidiously contending with rulers in matters that affect their authority and sovereign power. Having, by these artifices, insured their own safety and audacity, they have begun to exercise great weight in the government of States; but nevertheless they are prepared to shake the foundations of empires, to harass the rulers of the State, to accuse, and to cast them out, as often as they appear to govern otherwise than they themselves could have wished. In like manner they have by flattery deluded the people. Proclaiming with a loud voice liberty and public prosperity, and saying that it was owing to the Church and to sovereigns that the multitude were not drawn out of their unjust servitude and poverty, they have imposed upon the people; and, exciting them by a thirst for novelty, they have urged them to assail both the Church and the civil power. Nevertheless, the expectation of the benefits which were hoped for was greater than the reality; indeed, the common people, more oppressed than they were before, are deprived in their misery of that solace which, if things had been arranged in a Christian manner, they would have had with ease and in abundance. But whoever strive against the order which divine Providence has constituted pay usually the penalty of their pride, and meet with affliction and misery where they rashly hoped to find all things prosperous and in conformity with their desires.

The Church, if she directs men to render obedience chiefly and above all to God the sovereign Lord, is wrongly and falsely believed either to be envious of the civil power or to arrogate to herself something of the rights of sovereigns. On the contrary, she teaches that what is rightly due to the civil power must be rendered to it with a conviction and consciousness of duty. In teaching that from God Himself comes the right of ruling, she adds a great dignity to civil authority, and no small help towards obtaining the obedience and good-will of the citizens. The friend of peace and sustainer of concord, she embraces all with maternal love; and, intent only upon giving help to mortal man, she teaches that to justice must be joined clemency, equity to authority, and moderation to law-giving; that no one's right must be violated; that order and public tranquillity are to be maintained; and that the poverty of those who are in need is, as far as possible, to be relieved by public and private charity. "But for this reason," to use the words of St. Augustine, "men think, or would have it believed, that Christian teaching is not suited to the good of the State; for they wish the State to be founded not on solid virtue, but on the impunity of vice." Knowing these things, both princes and people would act with political wisdom, and according to the needs of general safety, if, instead of joining with Freemasons to destroy the Church, they joined with the Church in repelling their attacks.

Whatever the future may be, in this grave and widespread evil it is Our duty, Venerable Brethren, to endeavor to find a remedy. And because We know that Our best and firmest hope of a remedy is in the power of that divine religion which the Freemasons hate in proportion to their fear of it, We think it to be of chief importance to call that most saving power to Our aid against the common enemy. Therefore, whatsoever the Roman Pontiffs Our predecessors have decreed for the purpose of opposing the undertakings and endeavors of the Masonic sect, and whatsoever they have enacted to deter or withdraw men from societies of this kind, We ratify and confirm it all by Our Apostolic authority: and trusting greatly to the good-will of Christians, We pray and beseech each one, for the sake of his eternal salvation, to be most conscientiously careful not in the least to depart from what the Apostolic See has commanded in this matter.

We pray and beseech you, Venerable Brethren, to join your efforts with Ours, and earnestly to strive for the extirpation of this foul plague, which is creeping through the veins of the State. You have to defend the glory of God and the salvation of your neighbor; and with this object of your strife before you, neither courage nor

strength will be wanting. It will be for your prudence
to judge by what means you can best overcome the
difficulties and obstacles you meet with. But as it befits
the authority of Our office that We Ourselves should
point out some suitable way of proceeding, We wish it
to be your rule first of all to tear away the mask from
Freemasonry, and to let it be seen as it really is; and by sermons and Pastoral Letters to instruct the people as to
the artifices used by societies of this kind in seducing men
and enticing them into their ranks, and as to the depravity of their opinions and the wickedness of their acts.
As Our predecessors have many times repeated, let no
man think that he may for any reason whatsoever join
the Masonic sect, if he values his Catholic name and his
eternal salvation as he ought to value them. Let no one
be deceived by a pretence of honesty. It may seem to
some that Freemasons demand nothing that is openly
contrary to religion and morality; but, as the whole principle and object of the sect lies in what is vicious and
criminal, to join with these men or in any way to help
them cannot be lawful.

Further, by assiduous teaching and exhortation, the
multitude must be drawn to learn diligently the precepts
of religion; for which purpose We earnestly advise that
by opportune writings and sermons they be taught the
elements of those sacred truths in which Christian philosophy is contained. The result of this will be that the
minds of men will be made sound by instruction, and
will be protected against many forms of error and inducements to wickedness, especially in the present unbounded freedom of writing and insatiable eagerness for
learning.

Great, indeed, is the work; but in it the clergy will
share your labors if, through your care, they are fitted for
it by learning and a well-trained life. This good and
great work requires to be helped also by the industry of
those amongst the laity in whom a love of religion and

of country is joined to learning and goodness of life. By uniting the efforts of both clergy and laity, strive, Venerable Brethren, to make men thoroughly know and love the Church; for the greater their knowledge and love of the Church, the more will they be turned away from clandestine societies.

Wherefore, not without cause do We use this occasion to state again what We have stated elsewhere, namely, that the Third Order of St. Francis, whose discipline We a little while ago prudently mitigated, should be studiously promoted and sustained: for the whole object of this Order, as constituted by its founder, is to invite men to an imitation of Jesus Christ, to a love of the Church, and to the observance of all Christian virtues; and therefore it ought to be of great influence in suppressing the contagion of wicked societies. Let, therefore, this holy sodality be strengthened by a daily increase. Amongst the many benefits to be expected from it will be the great benefit of drawing the minds of men to liberty, fraternity, and equality of right; not such as the Freemasons absurdly imagine, but such as Jesus Christ obtained for the human race and St. Francis aspired to: the liberty, We mean, of *sons of God,* through which we may be free from slavery to Satan or to our passions, both of them most wicked masters; the fraternity whose origin is in God, the common Creator and Father of all; the equality which, founded on justice and charity, does not take away all distinctions among men, but, out of the varieties of life, of duties, and of pursuits, forms that union and that harmony which naturally tend to the benefit and dignity of the State.

In the third place, there is a matter wisely instituted by our forefathers, but in course of time laid aside, which may now be used as a pattern and form of something similar. We mean the associations or guilds of workmen, for the protection, under the guidance of religion, both of their temporal interests and of their morality.

If our ancestors, by long use and experience, felt the benefit of these guilds, our age perhaps will feel it the more by reason of the opportunity which they will give of crushing the power of the sects. Those who support themselves by the labor of their hands, besides being, by their very condition, most worthy above all others of charity and consolation, are also especially exposed to the allurements of men whose ways lie in fraud and deceit. Therefore they ought to be helped with the greatest possible kindness, and to be invited to join associations that are good, lest they be drawn away to others that are evil. For this reason, We greatly wish, for the salvation of the people, that, under the auspices and patronage of the Bishops, and at convenient times, these guilds may be generally restored. To Our great delight, sodalities of this kind and also associations of masters, have in many places already been established, having, each class of them, for their object to help the honest workman, to protect and guard his children and family, and to promote in them piety, Christian knowledge, and a moral life. And in this matter We cannot omit mentioning that exemplary society, named after its founder, St. Vincent, which has deserved so well of the people of the lower order. Its acts and its aims are well known. Its whole object is to give relief to the poor and miserable. This it does with singular prudence and modesty; and the less it wishes to be seen, the better is it fitted for the exercise of Christian charity, and for the relief of suffering.

In the fourth place, in order more easily to attain what We wish, to your fidelity and watchfulness We commend in a special manner the young, as being the hope of human society. Devote the greatest part of your care to their instruction; and do not think that any precaution can be great enough in keeping them from masters and schools whence the pestilent breath of the sects is to be feared Under your guidance, let parents, religious instructors, and priests having the cure of souls, use every opportunity, in their Christian teaching, of warning their children and pupils of the infamous nature of these societies so that they may learn in good time to beware of the various and fraudulent artifices by which their promoters are accustomed to ensnare people. And those who instruct the young in religious knowledge will act wisely, if they induce all of them to resolve and to undertake never to bind themselves to any society without the knowledge of their parents, or the advice of their parish priest or director.

We well know, however, that our united labors will by no means suffice to pluck up these pernicious seeds from the Lord's field, unless the Heavenly Master of the vineyard shall mercifully help us in our endeavors. We must, therefore, with great and anxious care, implore of Him the help which the greatness of the danger and of the need requires. The sect of the Freemasons shows itself insolent and proud of its success, and seems as if it would put no bounds to its pertinacity. Its followers, joined together by a wicked compact and by secret counsels, give help one to another, and excite one another to an audacity for evil things. So vehement an attack demands an equal defence—namely, that all good men should form the widest possible association of action and of prayer. We beseech them, therefore, with united hearts, to stand together and unmoved against the advancing force of the sects; and in mourning and supplication to stretch out their hands to God, praying that the Christian name may flourish and prosper, that the Church may enjoy its needed liberty, that those who have gone astray may return to a right mind, that error at length may give place to truth, and vice to virtue. Let us take as our helper and intercessor the Virgin Mary, Mother of God, so that she, who from the moment of her conception overcame Satan, may show her power over these evil sects, in which is revived the contumacious spirit of the demon, together with his unsubdued perfidy and deceit. Let us beseech Michael, the prince of the heavenly angels, who drove out the infernal foe; and Joseph, the spouse of the Most Holy Virgin, and heavenly Patron of the Catholic Church; and the great apostles, Peter and Paul, the fathers and victorious champions of the Christian faith. By their patronage, and by perseverance in united prayer, We hope that God will mercifully and opportunely succor the human race, which is encompassed by so many dangers.

As a pledge of heavenly gifts and of Our benevolence We lovingly grant in the Lord, to you, Venerable Brethren, and to the clergy and all the people committed to your watchful care, Our Apostolic Benediction.

THE CHRISTIAN CONSTITUTION OF STATES.

Encyclical Letter Immortale Dei, November 1, 1885.

THE Catholic Church, that imperishable handiwork of our all-merciful God, has for her immediate and natural purpose the saving of souls and securing our happiness in heaven. Yet in regard to things temporal she is the source of benefits as manifold and great as if the chief end of her existence were to ensure the prospering of our earthly life. And in truth, wherever the Church has set her foot, she has straightway changed the face of things, and has attempered the moral tone of the people with a new civilization, and with virtues before unknown. All nations which have yielded to her sway have become eminent for their culture, their sense of justice, and the glory of their high deeds.

And yet a hackneyed reproach of old date is levelled against her, that the Church is opposed to the rightful aims of the civil government, and is wholly unable to afford help in spreading that welfare and progress which justly and naturally are sought after by every well-regulated State. From the very beginning Christians were harassed by slanderous accusations of this nature, and on that account were held up to hatred and execration, for being (so they were called) enemies of the empire. The Christian religion was moreover commonly charged with being the cause of the calamities that so frequently befell the State, whereas, in very truth, just punishment was being awarded to guilty nations by an avenging God. This odious calumny, with most valid reason, nerved the genius and

107

sharpened the pen of St. Augustine, who, notably in his treatise *On the City of God*, set forth in so bright a light the worth of Christian wisdom in its relation to the public weal, that he seems not merely to have pleaded the cause of the Christians of his day, but to have refuted for all future times impeachments so grossly contrary to truth. The wicked proneness, however, to levy the like charges and accusations has not been lulled to rest. Many, indeed, are they who have tried to work out a plan of civil society based on doctrines other than those approved by the Catholic Church. Nay, in these latter days a novel scheme of law has begun here and there to gain increase and influence, the outcome, as it is maintained, of an age arrived at full stature, and the result of liberty in evolution. But though endeavors of various kinds have been ventured on, it is clear that no better mode has been devised for the building up and ruling the State than that which is the necessary growth of the teachings of the Gospel. We deem it, therefore, of the highest moment, and a strict duty of Our Apostolic office, to contrast with the lessons taught by Christ the novel theories now advanced touching the State. By this means We cherish hope that the bright shining of the truth may scatter the mists of error and doubt, so that one and all may see clearly the imperious law of life which they are bound to follow and obey.

It is not difficult to determine what would be the form and character of the State were it governed according to the principles of Christian philosophy. Man's natural instinct moves him to live in civil society, for he cannot, if dwelling apart, provide himself with the necessary requirements of life, nor procure the means of developing his mental and moral faculties. Hence it is divinely ordained that he should lead his life—be it family, social, or civil—with his fellow-men, amongst whom alone his several wants can be adequately supplied. But as no society can hold together unless some one be over all, directing all to strive earnestly for the common good; every civilized community must have a ruling authority, and this authority, no less than society itself, has its source in nature, and has, consequently, God for its author. Hence it follows that all public power must proceed from God. For God alone is the true and supreme Lord of the world. Everything, without exception, must be subject to Him, and must serve Him, so that whosoever holds the right to govern, holds it from one sole and single source, namely, God, the Sovereign Ruler of all. *There is no power but from God.*[1]

The right to rule is not necessarily, however, bound up with any special mode of government. It may take this or that form, provided only that it be of a nature to insure the general welfare. But whatever be the nature of the government, rulers must ever bear in mind that God is the paramount ruler of the world, and must set Him before themselves as their exemplar and law in the administration of the State. For, in things visible, God has fashioned secondary causes, in which His divine action can in some wise be discerned, leading up to the end to which the course of the world is ever tending. In like manner in civil society, God has always willed that there should be a ruling authority, and that they who are invested with it should reflect the divine power and providence in some measure over the human race.

They, therefore, who rule should rule with even-handed justice, not as masters, but rather as fathers, for the rule of God over man is most just, and is tempered always with a father's kindness. Government should, moreover, be administered for the well-being of the citizens because they who govern others possess authority solely for the welfare of the State. Furthermore, the civil power must not be subservient to the advantage of any one individual or of some few persons, inasmuch as it was established

[1] Rom. xiii. 1.

for the common good of all. But if those who are in authority rule unjustly, if they govern overbearingly or arrogantly, and if their measures prove hurtful to the people, they must remember that the Almighty will one day bring them to account, the more strictly in proportion to the sacredness of their office and pre-eminence of their dignity. *The mighty shall be mightily tormented.*[1] Then truly will the majesty of the law meet with the dutiful and willing homage of the people, when they are convinced that their rulers hold authority from God, and feel that it is a matter of justice and duty to obey them, and to show them reverence and fealty, united to a love not unlike that which children show their parents. *Let every soul be subject to higher powers.*[2] To despise legitimate authority, in whomsoever vested, is unlawful, as a rebellion against the divine will, and whoever resists that, rushes wilfully to destruction. *He that resisteth the power resisteth the ordinance of God, and they that resist, purchase to themselves damnation.*[3] To cast aside obedience, and by popular violence to incite to revolt, is therefore treason, not against man only, but against God.

As a consequence, the State, constituted as it is, is clearly bound to act up to the manifold and weighty duties linking it to God, by the public profession of religion. Nature and reason, which command every individual devoutly to worship God in holiness, because we belong to Him and must return to Him since from Him we came, bind also the civil community by a like law. For men living together in society are under the power of God no less than individuals are, and society, not less than individuals, owes gratitude to God, who gave it being and maintains it, and whose ever-bounteous goodness enriches it with countless blessings. Since, then, no one is allowed to be remiss in the service due to God, and since the chief duty of all men is to cling to religion in both its teaching

---

[1] Wisd. vi. 7.   [2] Rom. xiii. 1.   [3] Ibid. xiii. 2.

and practice—not such religion as they may have a preference for, but the religion which God enjoins, and which
certain and most clear marks show to be the only one true
religion—it is a public crime to act as though there were
no God. So, too, is it a sin in the State not to have care
for religion, as a something beyond its scope, or as of no
practical benefit; or out of many forms of religion to adopt
that one which chimes in with the fancy; for we are
bound absolutely to worship God in that way which He
has shown to be His will. All who rule, therefore, should
hold in honor the holy name of God, and one of their
chief duties must be to favor religion, to protect it, to
shield it under the credit and sanction of the laws, and
neither to organize nor enact any measure that may
compromise its safety. This is the bounden duty of rulers
to the people over whom they rule. For one and all are
we destined by our birth and adoption to enjoy, when
this frail and fleeting life is ended, a supreme and final
good in heaven, and to the attainment of this every
endeavor should be directed. Since, then, upon this
depends the full and perfect happiness of mankind, the
securing of this end should be of all imaginable interests
the most urgent. Hence civil society, established for
the common welfare, should not only safeguard the well-
being of the community, but have also at heart the interests of its individual members, in such mode as not in any
way to hinder, but in every manner to render as easy as
may be, the possession of that highest and unchangeable
good for which all should seek. Wherefore, for this purpose, care must especially be taken to preserve unharmed
and unimpeded the religion whereof the practice is the
link connecting man with God.

Now, it cannot be difficult to find out which is the true
religion, if only it be sought with an earnest and unbiassed
mind; for proofs are abundant and striking. We have,
for example, the fulfilment of prophecies; miracles in
great number; the rapid spread of the faith in the midst

of enemies and in face of overwhelming obstacles; the witness of the martyrs, and the like. From all these it is evident that the only true religion is the one established by Jesus Christ Himself, and which He committed to His Church to protect and to propagate.

For the only-begotten Son of God established on earth a society which is called the Church, and to it He handed over the exalted and divine office which He had received from His Father, to be continued through the ages to come. *As the Father hath sent Me, I also send you.*[1] *Behold I am with you all days, even to the consummation of the world.*[2] Consequently, as Jesus Christ came into the world that men *might have life and have it more abundantly,*[3] so also has the Church for its aim and end the eternal salvation of souls, and hence it is so constituted as to open wide its arms to all mankind, unhampered by any limit of either time or place. *Preach ye the Gospel to every creature.*[4]

Over this mighty multitude God has Himself set rulers with power to govern; and He has willed that one should be the head of all, and the chief and unerring teacher of truth, to whom He has given *the keys of the kingdom of heaven.*[5] *Feed My lambs, feed My sheep.*[6] *I have prayed for thee that thy faith fail not.*[7]

This society is made up of men, just as civil society is, and yet is supernatural and spiritual, on account of the end for which it was founded, and of the means by which it aims at attaining that end. Hence it is distinguished and differs from civil society, and what is of highest moment, it is a society chartered as of right divine, perfect in its nature and in its title, to possess in itself and by itself, through the will and loving kindness of its Founder, all needful provision for its maintenance and action. And just as the end at which the Church aims is by far the

[1] John xx. 21.
[2] Matt. xxviii. 20.
[3] John x. 10.
[4] Mark xvi. 15.
[5] Matt. xvi. 19.
[6] John xxi. 16, 17.
[7] Luke xxii. 32.

noblest of ends, so is its authority the most exalted of all authority, nor can it be looked upon as inferior to the civil power, or in any manner dependent upon it.

In very truth Jesus Christ gave to His apostles unrestrained authority in regard to things sacred, together with the genuine and most true power of making laws, as also with the twofold right of judging and of punishing, which flow from that power. *All power is given to Me in heaven and on earth : going therefore teach all nations . . . teaching them to observe all things whatsoever I have commanded you.*[1] And in another place, *If he will not hear them, tell the Church.*[2] And again, *In readiness to revenge all disobedience.*[3] And once more, *That . . . I may not deal more severely according to the power which the Lord hath given me, unto edification and not unto destruction.*[4] Hence it is the Church, and not the State, that is to be man's guide to heaven. It is to the Church that God has assigned the charge of seeing to, and legislating for, all that concerns religion; of teaching all nations; of spreading the Christian faith as widely as possible; in short, of administering freely and without hindrance, in accordance with her own judgment, all matters that fall within its competence.

Now this authority, perfect in itself, and plainly meant to be unfettered, so long assailed by a philosophy that truckles to the State, the Church has never ceased to claim for herself and openly to exercise. The apostles themselves were the first to uphold it, when, being forbidden by the rulers of the Synagogue to preach the Gospel, they courageously answered, *We must obey God rather than men.*[5] This same authority the holy Fathers of the Church were always careful to maintain by weighty arguments, according as occasion arose, and the Roman Pontiffs have never shrunk from defending it with unbending constancy.

[1] Matt. xxviii. 18–20.
[2] Matt. xviii. 17.
[3] 2 Cor. x. 6.
[4] 2 Cor. xiii. 10.
[5] Acts v. 29.

Nay more, princes and all invested with power to rule have themselves approved it, in theory alike and in practice. It cannot be called in question that in the making of treaties, in the transaction of business matters, in the sending and receiving ambassadors, and in the interchange of other kinds of official dealings, they have been wont to treat with the Church as with a supreme and legitimate power. And assuredly all ought to hold that it was not without a singular disposition of God's providence that this power of the Church was provided with a civil sovereignty as the surest safeguard of her independence.

The Almighty, therefore, has appointed the charge of the human race between two powers, the ecclesiastical and the civil, the one being set over divine, and the other over human, things. Each in its kind is supreme, each has fixed limits within which it is contained, limits which are defined by the nature and special object of the province of each, so that there is, we may say, an orbit traced out within which the action of each is brought into play by its own native right. But inasmuch as each of these two powers has authority over the same subjects, and as it might come to pass that one and the same thing—related differently, but still remaining one and the same thing—might belong to the jurisdiction and determination of both, therefore God, who foresees all things, and who is the author of these two powers, has marked out the course of each in right correlation to the other. *For the powers that are, are ordained of God.*[1] Were this not so, deplorable contentions and conflicts would often arise, and not infrequently men, like travellers at the meeting of two roads, would hesitate in anxiety and doubt, not knowing what course to follow. Two powers would be commanding contrary things, and it would be a dereliction of duty to disobey either of the two.

---

[1] Rom. xiii. 1.

But it would be most repugnant to deem thus of the wisdom and goodness of God. Even in physical things, albeit of a lower order, the Almighty has so combined the forces and springs of nature with tempered action and wondrous harmony that no one of them clashes with any other, and all of them most fitly and aptly work together for the great purpose of the universe. There must, accordingly, exist, between these two powers, a certain orderly connection, which may be compared to the union of the soul and body in man. The nature and scope of that connection can be determined only, as We have laid down, by having regard to the nature of each power, and by taking account of the relative excellence and nobleness of their purpose. One of the two has for its proximate and chief object the well-being of this mortal life; the other the everlasting joys of heaven. Whatever, therefore, in things human is of a sacred character, whatever belongs either of its own nature or by reason of the end to which it is referred, to the salvation of souls, or to the worship of God, is subject to the power and judgment of the Church. Whatever is to be ranged under the civil and political order is rightly subject to the civil authority. Jesus Christ has Himself given command that what is Cæsar's is to be rendered to Cæsar, and that what belongs to God is to be rendered to God.

There are, nevertheless, occasions when another method of concord is available for the sake of peace and liberty: We mean when rulers of the State and the Roman Pontiff come to an understanding touching some special matter. At such times the Church gives signal proof of her motherly love by showing the greatest possible kindliness and indulgence.

Such then, as We have briefly pointed out, is the Christian organization of civil society; not rashly or fancifully shaped out, but educed from the highest and truest principles, confirmed by natural reason itself.

In such an organization of the State, there is nothing

that can be thought to infringe upon the dignity of rulers, and nothing unbecoming them; nay, so far from degrading the sovereign power in its due rights, it adds to it permanence and lustre. Indeed, when more fully pondered, this mutual co-ordination has a perfection in which all other forms of government are lacking, and from which excellent results would flow, were the several component parts to keep their place and duly discharge the office and work appointed respectively for each. And, doubtless, in the constitution of the State such as we have described, divine and human things are equitably shared; the rights of citizens assured to them, and fenced round by divine, by natural, and by human law; the duties incumbent on each one being wisely marked out, and their fulfilment fittingly insured. In their uncertain and toilsome journey towards *the city made without hands*, all see that they have safe guides and helpers on their way, and are conscious that others have charge to protect their persons alike and their possessions, and to obtain or preserve for them everything essential for their present life. Furthermore, domestic society acquires that firmness and solidity so needful to it, from the holiness of marriage, one and indissoluble, wherein the rights and duties of husband and wife are controlled with wise justice and equity; due honor is assured to the woman; the authority of the husband is conformed to the pattern afforded by the authority of God; the power of the father is tempered by a due regard for the dignity of the mother and her offspring; and the best possible provision is made for the guardianship, welfare, and education of the children.

In political affairs, and all matters civil, the laws aim at securing the common good, and are not framed according to the delusive caprices and opinions of the mass of the people, but by truth and by justice; the ruling powers are invested with a sacredness more than human, and are withheld from deviating from the path of duty, and from overstepping the bounds of rightful authority; and the obedience of citizens is rendered with a feeling of honor and dignity, since obedience is not the servitude of man to man, but submission to the will of God, exercising His sovereignty through the medium of men. Now, this being recognized as undeniable, it is felt that the high office of rulers should be held in respect; that public authority should be constantly and faithfully obeyed; that no act of sedition should be committed; and that the civic order of the commonwealth should be maintained as sacred.

So, also, as to the duties of each one towards his fellow-men, mutual forbearance, kindliness, generosity, are placed in the ascendant; the man who is at once a citizen and a Christian is not drawn aside by conflicting obligations; and, lastly, the abundant benefits with which the Christian religion, of its very nature, endows even the mortal life of man, are acquired for the community and civil society. And this to such an extent that it may be said in sober truth: "The condition of the commonwealth depends on the religion with which God is worshipped: and between one and the other there exists an intimate and abiding connection." [1]

Admirably, according to his wont, does St. Augustine, in many passages, enlarge upon the potency of these advantages; but nowhere more markedly and to the point than when he addresses the Catholic Church in the following words: "Thou dost teach and train children with much tenderness, young men with much vigor, old men with much gentleness; as the age not of the body alone, but of the mind of each requires. Women thou dost subject to their husbands in chaste and faithful obedience, not for the gratifying of their lust, but for bringing forth children, and for having a share in the family concerns. Thou dost set husbands over their wives, not that they may play false to the weaker sex, but according to the

[1] Sacr. Imp. ad Cyrillum Alexand. et Episcopos Metrop. Cfr. Labbe, Collect. Conc., T. iii.

requirements of sincere affection. Thou dost subject children to their parents in a kind of free service, and dost establish parents over their children with a benign rule. . . . Thou joinest together, not in society only, but in a sort of brotherhood, citizen with citizen, nation with nation, and the whole race of men, by reminding them of their common parentage. Thou teachest kings to look to the interests of their people, and dost admonish the people to be submissive to their kings. With all care dost thou teach all to whom honor is due, and affection, and reverence, and fear, consolation, and admonition and exhortation, and discipline, and reproach, and punishment. Thou showest that all these are not equally incumbent on all, but that charity is owing to all, and wrong-doing to none."[1]   And in another place, blaming the false wisdom of certain time-saving philosophers, he observes: "Let those who say that the teaching of Christ is hurtful to the State, produce such armies as the maxims of Jesus have enjoined soldiers to bring into being; such governors of provinces; such husbands and wives; such parents and children; such masters and servants; such kings; such judges, and such payers and collectors of tribute, as the Christian teaching instructs them to become, and then let them dare to say that such teaching is hurtful to the State. Nay, rather will they hesitate to own that this discipline, if duly acted up to, is the very main-stay of the commonwealth?"[2]

There was once a time when States were governed by the principles of Gospel teaching. Then it was that the power and divine virtue of Christian wisdom had diffused itself throughout the laws, institutions, and morals of the people; permeating all ranks and relations of civil society. Then, too, the religion instituted by Jesus Christ, established firmly in befitting dignity, flourished everywhere, by the favor of princes and the legitimate protection of

---

[1] De moribus Eccl. Cathol., xxx. 63.
[2] Epist. 138, al. 5, ad Marcellinum, ii. 15.

magistrates; and Church and State were happily united in concord and friendly interchange of good offices. The State, constituted in this wise, bore fruits important beyond all expectation, whose remembrance is still, and always will be, in renown, witnessed to as they are by countless proofs which can never be blotted out or even obscured by any craft of any enemies. Christian Europe has subdued barbarous nations, and changed them from a savage to a civilized condition, from superstition to true worship. It victoriously rolled back the tide of Mohammedan conquest; retained the headship of civilization; stood forth in the front rank as the leader and teacher of all, in every branch of national culture; bestowed on the world the gift of true and many-sided liberty; and most wisely founded very numerous institutions for the solace of human suffering. And if we inquire how it was able to bring about so altered a condition of things, the answer is—Beyond all question, in large measure, through religion; under whose auspices so many great undertakings were set on foot, through whose aid they were brought to completion.

A similar state of things would certainly have continued had the agreement of the two powers been lasting. More important results even might have been justly looked for, had obedience waited upon the authority, teaching, and counsels of the Church, and had this submission been specially marked by greater and more unswerving loyalty. For that should be regarded in the light of an ever-changeless law which Ivo of Chartres wrote to Pope Paschal II.: "When kingdom and priesthood are at one, in complete accord, the world is well ruled, and the Church flourishes, and brings forth abundant fruit. But when they are at variance, not only smaller interests prosper not, but even things of greatest moment fall into deplorable decay." [1]

---

[1] Epist. 238.

Sad it is to call to mind how the harmful and lamentable rage for innovation which rose to a climax in the sixteenth century, threw first of all into confusion the Christian religion, and next, by natural sequence, invaded the precincts of philosophy, whence it spread amongst all classes of society. From this source, as from a fountain-head, burst forth all those later tenets of unbridled license which, in the midst of the terrible upheavals of the last century, were wildly conceived and boldly proclaimed as the principles and foundation of that *new jurisprudence* which was not merely previously unknown, but was at variance on many points with not only the Christian, but even with the natural law.

Amongst these principles the main one lays down that as all men are alike by race and nature, so in like manner all are equal in the control of their life; that each one is so far his own master as to be in no sense under the rule of any other individual; that each is free to think on every subject just as he may choose, and to do whatever he may like to do; that no man has any right to rule over other men. In a society grounded upon such maxims, all government is nothing more nor less than the will of the people, and the people, being under the power of itself alone, is alone its own ruler. It does choose nevertheless some to whose charge it may commit itself, but in such wise that it makes over to them not the right so much as the business of governing, to be exercised, however, in its name.

The authority of God is passed over in silence, just as if there were no God; or as if He cared nothing for human society; or as if men, whether in their individual capacity or bound together in social relations, owed nothing to God; or as if there could be a government of which the whole origin and power and authority did not reside in God Himself. Thus, as is evident, a State becomes nothing but a multitude, which is its own master and ruler. And since the populace is declared to contain within itself the spring-head of all rights and of all power, it follows that the State does not consider itself bound by any kind of duty towards God. Moreover, it believes that it is not obliged to make public profession of any religion; or to inquire which of the very many religions is the only one true; or to prefer one religion to all the rest; or to show to any form of religion special favor; but, on the contrary, is bound to grant equal rights to every creed, so that public order may not be disturbed by any particular form of religious belief.

And it is a part of this theory that all questions that concern religion are to be referred to private judgment; that every one is to be free to follow whatever religion he prefers, or none at all if he disapprove of all. From this the following consequences logically flow: that the judgment of each one's conscience is independent of all law; that the most unrestrained opinions may be openly expressed as to the practice or omission of divine worship; and that every one has unbounded license to think whatever he chooses and to publish abroad whatever he thinks.

Now when the State rests on foundations like those just named—and for the time being they are greatly in favor —it readily appears into what and how unrightful a position the Church is driven. For when the management of public business is in harmony with doctrines of such a kind, the Catholic religion is allowed a standing in civil society equal only, or inferior, to societies alien from it; no regard is paid to the laws of the Church, and she who, by the order and commission of Jesus Christ, has the duty of teaching all nations, finds herself forbidden to take any part in the instruction of the people. With reference to matters that are of twofold jurisdiction, they who administer the civil power lay down the law at their own will, and in matters that appertain to religion defiantly put aside the most sacred decrees of the Church. They claim jurisdiction over the marriages of Catholics, even over the bond as well as the unity and the indissolubility of matrimony. They lay hands on the goods of the clergy, contending that the Church cannot possess property. Lastly, they treat the Church with such arrogance that, rejecting entirely her title to the nature and rights of a perfect society, they hold that she differs in no respect from other societies in the State, and for this reason possesses no right nor any legal power of action, save that which she holds by the concession and favor of the government. If in any State the Church retains her own right—and this with the approval of the civil law, owing to an agreement publicly entered into by the two powers—men forthwith begin to cry out that matters affecting the Church must be separated from those of the State.

Their object in uttering this cry is to be able to violate unpunished their plighted faith, and in all things to have unchecked control. And as the Church, unable to abandon her chiefest and most sacred duties, cannot patiently put up with this, and asks that the pledge given to her be fully and scrupulously acted up to, contentions frequently arise between the ecclesiastical and the civil power, of which the issue commonly is, that the weaker power yields to the one which is stronger in human resources.

Accordingly, it has become the practice and determination under this condition of public polity (now so much admired by many) either to forbid the action of the Church altogether, or to keep her in check and bondage to the State. Public enactments are in great measure framed with this design. The drawing up of laws, the administration of State affairs, the godless education of youth, the spoliation and suppression of religious orders, the overthrow of the temporal power of the Roman Pontiff, all alike aim at this one end—to paralyze the action of Christian institutions, to cramp to the utmost the freedom of the Catholic Church, and to curtail her every single prerogative.

Now, natural reason itself proves convincingly that such concepts of the government of a State are wholly at variance with the truth. Nature itself bears witness that all power, of every kind, has its origin from God, who is its chief and most august source.

The sovereignty of the people, however, and this without any reference to God, is held to reside in the multitude; which is doubtless a doctrine exceedingly well calculated to flatter and to inflame many passions, but which lacks all reasonable proof, and all power of insuring public safety and preserving order. Indeed from the prevalence of this teaching, things have come to such a pass that many hold as an axiom of civil jurisprudence that seditions may be rightfully fostered. For the opinion prevails that princes are nothing more than delegates chosen to carry out the will of the people; whence it necessarily follows that all things are as changeable as the will of the people, so that risk of public disturbance is ever hanging over our heads.

To hold therefore that there is no difference in matters of religion between forms that are unlike each other, and even contrary to each other, most clearly leads in the end to the rejection of all religion in both theory and practice. And this is the same thing as atheism, however it may differ from it in name. Men who really believe in the existence of God must, in order to be consistent with themselves and to avoid absurd conclusions, understand that differing modes of divine worship involving dissimilarity and conflict even on most important points, cannot all be equally probable, equally good, and equally acceptable to God.

So, too, the liberty of thinking, and of publishing, whatsoever each one likes, without any hindrance, is not in itself an advantage over which society can wisely rejoice. On the contrary, it is the fountain-head and origin of many evils. Liberty is a power perfecting man, and hence should have truth and goodness for its object.

But the character of goodness and truth cannot be changed at option. These remain ever one and the same, and are no less unchangeable than Nature herself. If the mind assents to false opinions, and the will chooses and follows after what is wrong, neither can attain its native fulness, but both must fall from their native dignity into an abyss of corruption. Whatever, therefore, is opposed to virtue and truth, may not rightly be brought temptingly before the eye of man, much less sanctioned by the favor and protection of the law. A well-spent life is the only passport to heaven, whither all are bound, and on this account the State is acting against the laws and dictates of nature whenever it permits the license of opinion and of action to lead minds astray from truth and souls away from the practice of virtue. To exclude the Church, founded by God Himself, from the business of life, from the power of making laws, from the training of youth, from domestic society, is a grave and fatal error. A State from which religion is banished can never be well regulated; and already perhaps more than is desirable is known of the nature and tendency of the so-called *civil* philosophy of life and morals. The Church of Christ is the true and sole teacher of virtue and guardian of morals. She it is who preserves in their purity the principles from which duties flow, and by setting forth most urgent reasons for virtuous life, bids us not only to turn away from wicked deeds, but even to curb all movements of the mind that are opposed to reason, even though they be not carried out in action.

To wish the Church to be subject to the civil power in the exercise of her duty is a great folly and a sheer injustice. Whenever this is the case, order is disturbed, for things natural are put above things supernatural; the many benefits which the Church, if free to act, would confer on society are either prevented or at least lessened in number; and a way is prepared for enmities and contentions between the two powers, with how evil result to both the issue of events has taught us only too frequently.

Doctrines such as these, which cannot be approved by human reason, and most seriously affect the whole civil order, Our predecessors the Roman Pontiffs (well aware of what their apostolic office required of them) have never allowed to pass uncondemned. Thus Gregory XVI. in his Encyclical Letter *Mirari vos,* of date August 15, 1832, inveighed with weighty words against the sophisms, which even at his time were being publicly inculcated—namely, that no preference should be shown for any particular form of worship; that it is right for individuals to form their own personal judgments about religion; that each man's conscience is his sole and all-sufficing guide; and that it is lawful for every man to publish his own views, whatever they may be, and even to conspire against the State. On the question of the separation of Church and State the same Pontiff writes as follows: "Nor can We hope for happier results either for religion or for the civil government from the wishes of those who desire that the Church be separated from the State, and the concord between the secular and ecclesiastical authority be dissolved. It is clear that these men, who yearn for a shameless liberty, live in dread of an agreement which has always been fraught with good, and advantageous alike to sacred and civil interests." To the like effect, also, as occasion presented itself, did Pius IX. brand publicly many false opinions which were gaining ground, and afterwards ordered them to be condensed in summary form in order that in this sea of error Catholics might have a light which they might safely follow.[1]

[1] It will suffice to indicate a few of them:
Prop. xix. The Church is not a true, perfect, and wholly independent society, possessing its own unchanging rights conferred upon it by its Divine Founder; but it is for the civil power to determine what are the rights of the Church, and the limits within which it may use them.

From these pronouncements of the Popes it is evident that the origin of public power is to be sought for in God Himself, and not in the multitude, and that it is repugnant to reason to allow free scope for sedition. Again, that it is not lawful for the State, any more than for the individual, either to disregard all religious duties or to hold in equal favor different kinds of religion; that the unrestrained freedom of thinking and of openly making known one's thoughts is not inherent in the rights of citizens, and is by no means to be reckoned worthy of favor and support. In like manner it is to be understood that the Church no less than the State itself is a society perfect in its own nature and its own right, and that those who exercise sovereignty ought not so to act as to compel the Church to become subservient or subject to them, or to hamper her liberty in the management of her own affairs, or to despoil her in any way of the other privileges conferred upon her by Jesus Christ. In matters, however, of mixed jurisdiction, it is in the highest degree consonant to nature, as also to the designs of God, that so far from one of the powers separating itself from the other, or still less coming into conflict with it, complete harmony, such as is suited to the end for which each power exists, should be preserved between them.

This then is the teaching of the Catholic Church concerning the constitution and government of the State. By the words and decrees just cited, if judged dispassionately, no one of the several forms of government is in itself condemned, inasmuch as none of them contain

Prop. xxxix. The State, as the origin and source of all rights enjoys a right that is unlimited.

Prop. lv. The Church must be separated from the State, and the State from the Church.

Prop. lxxix. . . . It is untrue that the civil liberty of every form of worship, and the full power given to all of openly and publicly manifesting whatsoever opinions and thoughts, lead to the more ready corruption of the minds and morals of the people, and to the spread of the plague of religious indifference.

anything contrary to Catholic doctrine, and all of them are capable, if wisely and justly managed, to insure the welfare of the State. Neither is it blameworthy in itself, in any manner, for the people to have a share, greater or less, in the government: for at certain times, and under certain laws, such participation may not only be of benefit to the citizens, but may even be of obligation. Nor is there any reason why any one should accuse the Church of being wanting in gentleness of action or largeness of view, or of being opposed to real and lawful liberty. The Church, indeed, deems it unlawful to place the various forms of divine worship on the same footing as the true religion, but does not, on that account, condemn those rulers who, for the sake of securing some great good or of hindering some great evil, allow patiently custom or usage to be a kind of sanction for each kind of religion having its place in the State. And in fact the Church is wont to take earnest heed that no one shall be forced to embrace the Catholic faith against his will, for, as St. Augustine wisely reminds us, "Man cannot believe otherwise than of his own free will."

In the same way the Church cannot approve of that liberty which begets a contempt of the most sacred laws of God, and casts off the obedience due to lawful authority, for this is not liberty so much as license, and is most correctly styled by St. Augustine the "liberty of self-ruin," and by the apostle St. Peter the *cloak of malice*.[1] Indeed, since it is opposed to reason, it is a true slavery, *for whosoever committeth sin is the slave of sin*.[2] On the other hand, that liberty is truly genuine, and to be sought after, which in regard to the individual does not allow men to be the slaves of error and of passion, the worst of all masters; which, too, in public administration guides the citizens in wisdom and provides for them increased means of well-being; and which, further, protects the State from foreign interference.

[1] 1 Peter ii. 16.   [2] John viii. 34.

This honorable liberty, alone worthy of human beings, the Church approves most highly and has never slackened her endeavor to preserve, strong and unchanged, among nations. And in truth whatever in the State is of chief avail for the common welfare; whatever has been usefully established to curb the license of rulers who are opposed to the true interests of the people, or to keep in check the leading authorities from unwarrantably interfering in municipal or family affairs;—whatever tends to uphold the honor, manhood, and equal rights of individual citizens;—of all these things, as the monuments of past ages bear witness, the Catholic Church has always been the originator, the promotor, or the guardian. Ever therefore consistent with herself, while on the one hand she rejects that exorbitant liberty which in individuals and in nations ends in license or in thraldom, on the other hand, she willingly and most gladly welcomes whatever improvements the age brings forth, if these really secure the prosperity of life here below, which is as it were a stage in the journey to the life that will know no ending.

Therefore, when it is said that the Church is jealous of modern political systems, and that she repudiates the discoveries of modern research, the charge is a ridiculous and groundless calumny. Wild opinions she does repudiate, wicked and seditious projects she does condemn, together with that habit of mind which points to the beginning of a wilful departure from God. But as all truth must necessarily proceed from God, the Church recognizes in all truth that is reached by research, a trace of the divine intelligence. And as all truth in the natural order is powerless to destroy belief in the teachings of revelation, but can do much to confirm it, and as every newly discovered truth may serve to further the knowledge or the praise of God, it follows that whatsoever spreads the range of knowledge will always be willingly and even joyfully welcomed by the Church. She will always encourage and promote, as she does in other branches of knowledge, all study occupied with the investigation of nature. In these pursuits, should the human intellect discover anything not known before, the Church makes no opposition. She never objects to search being made for things that minister to the refinements and comforts of life So far indeed from opposing these she is now, as she ever has been, hostile alone to indolence and sloth, and earnestly wishes that the talents of men may bear more and more abundant fruit by cultivation and exercise. Moreover she gives encouragement to every kind of art and handicraft, and through her influence, directing all strivings after progress towards virtue and salvation, she labors to prevent man's intellect and industry from turning him away from God and from heavenly things.

All this, though so reasonable and full of counsel, finds little favor nowadays when States not only refuse to conform to the rules of Christian wisdom, but seem even anxious to recede from them further and further on each successive day. Nevertheless, since truth when brought to light is wont, of its own nature, to spread itself far and wide, and gradually take possession of the minds of men, We, moved by the great and holy duty of Our apostolic mission to all nations, speak, as We are bound to do, with freedom. Our eyes are not closed to the spirit of the times. We repudiate not the assured and useful improvements of our age, but devoutly wish affairs of State to take a safer course than they are now taking, and to rest on a more firm foundation without injury to the true freedom of the people; for the best parent and guardian of liberty amongst men is truth. *The truth shall make you free.*[1]

If in the difficult times in which our lot is cast, Catholics will give ear to Us, as it behooves them to do, they will readily see what are the duties of each one in matters of opinion as well as action. As regards opinion, whatever

---

[1] John viii. 32.

the Roman Pontiffs have hitherto taught, or shall hereafter teach, must be held with a firm grasp of mind, and, so often as occasion requires, must be openly professed.

Especially with reference to the so-called "Liberties" which are so greatly coveted in these days, all must stand by the judgment of the Apostolic See, and have the same mind. Let no man be deceived by the outward appearance of these *liberties*, but let each one reflect whence these have had their origin, and by what efforts they are everywhere upheld and promoted. Experience has made us well acquainted with their results to the State, since everywhere they have borne fruits which the good and wise bitterly deplore. If there really exist anywhere, or if we in imagination conceive, a State, waging wanton and tyrannical war against Christianity, and if we compare with it the modern form of government just described, this latter may seem the more endurable of the two. Yet, undoubtedly, the principles on which such a government is grounded are, as We have said, of a nature which no one can approve.

Secondly, action may relate to private and domestic matters, or to matters public. As to private affairs, the first duty is to conform life and conduct to the gospel precepts, and to refuse to shrink from this duty when Christian virtue demands some sacrifice difficult to make. All, moreover, are bound to love the Church as their common mother, to obey her laws, promote her honor, defend her rights, and to endeavor to make her respected and loved by those over whom they have authority. It is also of great moment to the public welfare to take a prudent part in the business of municipal administration, and to endeavor above all to introduce effectual measures, so that, as becomes a Christian people, public provision may be made for the instruction of youth in religion and true morality. Upon these things the well-being of every State greatly depends.

Furthermore, it is in general fitting and salutary that

Catholics should extend their efforts beyond this restricted sphere, and give their attenton to national politics. We say *in general,* because these Our precepts are addressed to all nations. However, it may in some places be true that, for most urgent and just reasons, it is by no means expedient for Catholics to engage in public affairs or to take an active part in politics. Nevertheless, as We have laid down, to take no share in public matters would be equally as wrong (We speak in general) as not to have concern for, or not to bestow labor upon, the common good. And this all the more because Catholics are admonished, by the very doctrines which they profess, to be upright and faithful in the discharge of duty, while if they hold aloof, men whose principles offer but small guarantee for the welfare of the State will the more readily seize the reins of government. This would tend also to the injury of the Christian religion, forasmuch as those would come into power who are badly disposed towards the Church, and those who are willing to befriend her would be deprived of all influence.

It follows therefore clearly that Catholics have just reasons for taking part in the conduct of public affairs.

For in so doing they assume not the responsibility of approving what is blameworthy in the actual methods of government, but seek to turn these very methods, so far as is possible, to the genuine and true public good, and to use their best endeavors at the same time to infuse, as it were, into all the veins of the State the healthy sap and blood of Christian wisdom and virtue. The morals and ambitions of the heathens differed widely from those of the Gospel, yet Christians were to be seen living undefiled everywhere in the midst of pagan superstition, and, while always true to themselves, coming to the front boldly wherever an opening was presented. Models of loyalty to their rulers, submissive, so far as was permitted, to the sovereign power, they shed around them on every side a halo of sanctity; they strove to be helpful to their brethren, and to attract others to the wisdom of Jesus Christ, yet were bravely ready to withdraw from public life, nay, even to lay down their life, if they could not without loss of virtue retain honors, dignities, and offices. For this reason Christian ways and manners speedily found their way not only into private houses but into the camp, the senate, and even into the imperial palaces. "We are but of yesterday," wrote Tertullian, "yet we swarm in all your institutions, we crowd your cities, islands, villages, towns, assemblies, the army itself, your wards and corporations, the palace, the senate, and the law courts." So that the Christian faith, when once it became lawful to make public profession of the Gospel, appeared in most of the cities of Europe, not like an infant crying in its cradle, but already grown up and full of vigor.

In these our days it is well to revive these examples of our forefathers. First and foremost it is the duty of all Catholics worthy of the name and wishful to be known as most loving children of the Church, to reject without swerving whatever is inconsistent with so fair a title; to make use of popular institutions, so far as can honestly be done, for the advancement of truth and righteousness; to strive that liberty of action shall not transgress the bounds marked out by nature and the law of God; to endeavor to bring back all civil society to the pattern and form of Christianity which We have described. It is barely possible to lay down any fixed method by which such purposes are to be attained, because the means adopted must suit places and times widely differing from one another. Nevertheless, above all things, unity of aim must be preserved, and similarity must be sought after in all plans of action. Both these objects will be carried into effect without fail if all will follow the guidance of the Apostolic See as their rule of life and obey the bishops whom the Holy Ghost has placed to rule the

Church of God.[1] The defence of Catholicism, indeed, necessarily demands that in the profession of doctrines taught by the Church all shall be of one mind and all steadfast in believing; and care must be taken never to connive, in any way, at false opinions, never to withstand them less strenuously than truth allows. In mere matters of opinion it is permissible to discuss things with moderation, with a desire of searching into the truth, without unjust suspicion or angry recriminations.

Hence, lest concord be broken by rash charges, let this be understood by all, that the integrity of Catholic faith cannot be reconciled with opinions verging on Naturalism or Rationalism, the essence of which is utterly to sterilize Christianity, and to instal in society the supremacy of man to the exclusion of God. Further, it is unlawful to follow one line of conduct in private and another in public, respecting privately the authority of the Church, but publicly rejecting it; for this would amount to joining together good and evil, and to putting man in conflict with himself; whereas he ought always to be consistent, and never in the least point nor in any condition of life to swerve from Christian virtue.

But in matters merely political, as for instance the best form of government, and this or that system of administration, a difference of opinion is lawful. Those, therefore, whose piety is in other respects known, and whose minds are ready to accept in all obedience the decrees of the Apostolic See, cannot in justice be accounted as bad men because they disagree as to subjects We have mentioned; and still graver wrong will be done them, if—as We have more than once perceived with regret—they are accused of violating, or of wavering in, the Catholic faith.

Let this be well borne in mind by all who are in the habit of publishing their opinions, and above all by journalists. In the endeavor to secure interests of the highest

[1] Acts xx. 28.

order there is no room for intestine strife or party rivalries; since all should aim with one mind and purpose to make safe that which is the common object of all—the maintenance of Religion and of the State. If, therefore, there have hitherto been dissensions, let them henceforth be gladly buried in oblivion. If rash or injurious acts have been committed, whoever may have been at fault, let mutual charity make amends, and let the past be redeemed by a special submission of all to the Apostolic See.

In this way Catholics will attain two most excellent results: they will become helpers to the Church in preserving and propagating Christian wisdom; and they will confer the greatest benefit on civil society, the safety of which is exceedingly imperilled by evil teachings and bad passions.

This, Venerable Brethren, is what We have thought it Our duty to expound to all nations of the Catholic world touching the Christian constitution of States and the duties of individual citizens.

It behooves Us now with earnest prayer to implore the protection of heaven, beseeching God, who alone can enlighten the minds of men and move their will, to bring about those happy ends for which We yearn and strive, for His greater glory and the general salvation of mankind. As a happy augury of the divine benefits, and in token of Our paternal benevolence, to you, Venerable Brothers, and to the clergy and to the whole people committed to your charge and vigilance, We grant lovingly in the Lord the Apostolic Benediction.

HUMAN LIBERTY.

Encyclical Letter Libertas Præstantissimum, June 20, 1888.

LIBERTY, the highest of natural endowment, being the portion only of intellectual or rational natures, confers on man this dignity—that he is *in the hand of his counsel* and has power over his actions. But the manner in which such dignity is exercised is of the greatest moment, inasmuch as on the use that is made of liberty the highest good and the greatest evil alike depend. Man, indeed, is free to obey his reason, to seek moral good, and to strive unswervingly after his last end. Yet he is free also to turn aside to all other things; and, in pursuing the empty semblance of good, to disturb rightful order and to fall headlong into the destruction which he has voluntarily chosen. The Redeemer of mankind, Jesus Christ, having restored and exalted the original dignity of nature, vouchsafed special assistance to the will of man; and by the gifts of His grace here, and the promise of heavenly bliss hereafter, He raised it to a nobler state. In like manner this great gift of nature has ever been, and always will be, deservingly cherished by the Catholic Church; for to her alone has been committed the charge of handing down to all ages the benefits purchased for us by Jesus Christ. Yet there are many who imagine that the Church is hostile to human liberty. Having a false and absurd notion as to what liberty is, either they pervert the very idea of freedom, or they extend it at their pleasure to many things in respect of which man cannot rightly be regarded as free.

We have on other occasions, and especially in Our Encyclical Letter *Immortale Dei,* in treating of the so-called *modern liberties,* distinguished between their good and evil elements; and We have shown that whatsoever is good in those liberties is as ancient as truth itself, and that the Church has always most willingly approved and practised that good: but whatsoever has been added as new is, to tell the plain truth, of a vitiated kind, the fruit of the disorders of the age, and of an insatiate longing after novelties. Seeing, however, that many cling so obstinately to their own opinion in this matter as to imagine these modern liberties, cankered as they are, to be the greatest glory of our age, and the very basis of civil life, without which no perfect government can be conceived, We feel it a pressing duty, for the sake of the common good, to treat separately of this subject.

It is with *moral* liberty, whether in individuals or in communities, that We proceed at once to deal. But, first of all, it will be well to speak briefly of *natural* liberty; for, though it is distinct and separate from moral liberty, natural freedom is the fountain-head from which liberty of whatsoever kind flows, *sua vi suaque sponte.* The unanimous consent and judgment of men, which is the trusty voice of nature, recognizes this natural liberty in those only who are endowed with intelligence or reason; and it is by his use of this that man is rightly regarded as responsible for his actions. For, while other animate creatures follow their senses, seeking good and avoiding evil only by instinct, man has reason to guide him in each and every act of his life. Reason sees that whatever things that are held to be good upon earth, may exist or may not, and discerning that none of them are of necessity for us, it leaves the will free to choose what it pleases. But man can judge of this *contingency,* as We say, only because he has a soul that is simple, spiritual, and intellectual—a soul, therefore, which is not produced by matter, and does not depend on matter for its existence;

but which is created immediately by God, and, far surpassing the condition of things material, has a life and action of its own—so that, knowing the unchangeable and necessary reasons of what is true and good, it sees that no particular kind of good is necessary to us. When, therefore, it is established that man's soul is immortal and endowed with reason and not bound up with things material, the foundation of natural liberty is at once most firmly laid.

As the Catholic Church declares in the strongest terms the simplicity, spirituality, and immortality of the soul, so with unequalled constancy and publicity she ever also asserts its freedom. These truths she has always taught, and has sustained them as a dogma of faith; and whensoever heretics or innovators have attacked the liberty of man, the Church has defended it and protected this noble possession from destruction. History bears witness to the energy with which she met the fury of the Manicheans and others like them; and the earnestness with which in later years she defended human liberty in the Council of Trent, and against the followers of Jansenius, is known to all. At no time, and in no place, has she held truce with *fatalism*.

Liberty, then, as We have said, belongs only to those who have the gift of reason or intelligence. Considered as to its nature, it is the faculty of choosing means fitted for the end proposed; for he is master of his actions who can choose one thing out of many. Now, since everything chosen as a means is viewed as good or useful, and since good, as such, is the proper object of our desire, it follows that freedom of choice is a property of the will, or rather is identical with the will in so far as it has in its action the faculty of choice. But the will cannot proceed to act until it is enlightened by the knowledge possessed by the intellect. In other words, the good wished by the will is necessarily good in so far as it is known by the intellect; and this the more, because in all voluntary acts choice is subsequent to a judgment upon the truth of the good presented, declaring to which good preference should be given. No sensible man can doubt that judgment is an act of reason, not of the will. The end, or object, both of the rational will and of its liberty is that good only which is in conformity with reason.

Since, however, both these faculties are imperfect, it is possible, as is often seen, that the reason should propose something which is not really good, but which has the appearance of good, and that the will should choose accordingly. For, as the possibility of error, and actual error, are defects of the mind and attest its imperfection, so the pursuit of what has a false appearance of good, though a proof of our freedom, just as a disease is a proof of our vitality, implies defect in human liberty. The will also, simply because of its dependence on the reason, no sooner desires anything contrary thereto, than it abuses its freedom of choice and corrupts its very essence. Thus it is that the infinitely perfect God, although supremely free, because of the supremacy of His intellect and of His essential goodness, nevertheless cannot choose evil; neither can the angels and saints, who enjoy the beatific vision. St. Augustine and others urged most admirably against the Pelagians, that, if the possibility of deflection from good belonged to the essence or perfection of liberty, then God, Jesus Christ, and the angels and saints, who have not this power, would have no liberty at all, or would have less liberty than man has in his state of pilgrimage and imperfection. This subject is often discussed by the Angelic Doctor in his demonstration that the possibility of sinning is not freedom, but slavery. It will suffice to quote his subtle commentary on the words of our Lord: *Whosoever committeth sin is the slave of sin.*[1] "Everything," he says, "is that

---

[1] John viii. 34.

which belongs to it naturally. When, therefore, it acts through a power outside itself, it does not act of itself, but through another, that is, as a slave. But man is by nature rational. When, therefore, he acts according to reason, he acts of himself and according to his free will; and this is liberty. Whereas, when he sins, he acts in opposition to reason, is moved by another, and is the victim of foreign misapprehensions. Therefore, *Whosoever committeth sin is the slave of sin.*" Even the heathen philosophers clearly recognized this truth, especially they who held that the wise man alone is free; and by the term "wise man" was meant, as is well known, the man trained to live in accordance with his nature, that is, in justice and virtue.

Such then being the condition of human liberty, it necessarily stands in need of light and strength to direct its actions to good and to restrain them from evil. Without this the freedom of our will would be our ruin. First of all there must be *law;* that is, a fixed rule of teaching what is to be done and what is to be left undone. This rule cannot affect the lower animals in any true sense, since they act of necessity, following their natural instinct, and cannot of themselves act in any other way. On the other hand, as was said above, he who is free can either act or not act, can do this or do that, as he pleases, because his judgment precedes his choice. And his judgment not only decides what is right or wrong of its own nature, but also what is practically good and therefore to be chosen, and what is practically evil and therefore to be avoided. In other words the reason prescribes to the will what it should seek after or shun, in order to the eventual attainment of man's last end, for the sake of which all his actions ought to be performed. This ordination of *reason* is called law. In man's free will, therefore, or in the moral necessity of our voluntary acts being in accordance with reason, lies the very root of the necessity of law. Nothing more foolish can be uttered or

conceived than the notion that because man is free by
nature, he is therefore exempt from law. Were this
the case, it would follow that to become free we must
be deprived of reason; whereas the truth is that we are
bound to submit to law precisely because we are free
by our very nature. For law is the guide of man's actions;
it turns him towards good by its rewards, and deters
him from evil by its punishments.

Foremost in this office comes the *natural law,* which is
written and engraved in the mind of every man; and
this is nothing but our reason, commanding us to do
right and forbidding sin. Nevertheless all prescriptions
of human reason can have force of law only inasmuch
as they are the voice and the interpreters of some higher
power on which our reason and liberty necessarily depend. For, since the force of law consists in the imposing
of obligations and the granting of rights, authority is the
one and only foundation of all law—the power, that is, of
fixing duties and defining rights, as also of assigning the
necessary sanctions of reward and chastisement to each
and all of its commands. But all this, clearly, cannot
be found in man, if, as his own supreme legislator, he
is to be the rule of his own actions. It follows therefore that the law of nature is the same thing as the *eternal
law,* implanted in rational creatures, and inclining them
to their right action and end; and can be nothing else but
the eternal reason of God, the Creator and Ruler of all
the world. To this rule of action and restraint of evil
God has vouchsafed to give special and most suitable
aids for strengthening and ordering the human will.
The first and most excellent of these is the power of His
divine *grace,* whereby the mind can be enlightened and the
will wholesomely invigorated and moved to the constant
pursuit of moral good, so that the use of our inborn liberty
becomes at once less difficult and less dangerous. Not
that the divine assistance hinders in any way the free
movement of our will; just the contrary, for grace works

inwardly in man and in harmony with his natural inclinations, since it flows from the very Creator of his mind and will, by whom all things are moved in conformity with their nature. As the Angelic Doctor points out, it is because divine grace comes from the Author of nature, that it is so admirably adapted to be the safeguard of all natures, and to maintain the character, efficiency, and operations of each.

What has been said of the liberty of individuals is no less applicable to them when considered as bound together in civil society. For, what reason and the natural law do for individuals, that *human law*, promulgated for their good, does for the citizens of States. Of the laws enacted by men, some are concerned with what is good or bad by its very nature; and they command men to follow after what is right and to shun what is wrong, adding at the same time a suitable sanction. But such laws by no means derive their origin from civil society; because just as civil society did not create human nature, so neither can it be said to be the author of the good which befits human nature, or of the evil which is contrary to it. Laws come before men live together in society, and have their origin in the natural, and consequently in the eternal, law. The precepts, therefore, of the natural law, contained bodily in the laws of men, have not merely the force of human law, but they possess that higher and more august sanction which belongs to the law of nature and the eternal law. And within the sphere of this kind of laws, the duty of the civil legislator is, mainly, to keep the community in obedience by the adoption of a common discipline and by putting restraint upon refractory and viciously inclined men, so that, deterred from evil, they may turn to what is good, or at any rate may avoid causing trouble and disturbance to the State. Now there are other enactments of the civil authority, which do not follow directly, but somewhat remotely, from the natural law, and decide many points which the law of nature treats only in a general and indefinite way. For instance, though nature commands all to contribute to the public peace and prosperity, still whatever belongs to the manner and circumstances, and conditions under which such service is to be rendered must be determined by the wisdom of men and not by Nature herself. It is in the constitution of these particular rules of life, suggested by reason and prudence, and put forth by competent authority, that human law, properly so called, consists, binding all citizens to work together for the attainment of the common end proposed to the community, and forbidding them to depart from this end; and in so far as human law is in conformity with the dictates of nature, leading to what is good, and deterring from evil.

From this it is manifest that the eternal law of God is the sole standard and rule of human liberty, not only in each individual man, but also in the community and civil society which men constitute when united. Therefore, the true liberty of human society does not consist in every man doing what he pleases, for this would simply end in turmoil and confusion, and bring on the overthrow of the State; but rather in this, that through the injunctions of the civil law all may more easily conform to the prescriptions of the eternal law. Likewise, the liberty of those who are in authority does not consist in the power to lay unreasonable and capricious commands upon their subjects, which would equally be criminal and would lead to the ruin of the commonwealth; but the binding force of human laws is in this, that they are to be regarded as applications of the eternal law, and incapable of sanctioning anything which is not contained in the eternal law, as in the principle of all law. Thus St. Augustine most wisely says: " I think that you can see, at the same time, that there is nothing just and lawful in that temporal law, unless what men have gathered from this eternal law." [1] If, then, by any one in author-

_____
[1] De Libero Arbitrio, lib. i. cap. 6, n. 15.

ity, something be sanctioned out of conformity with the principles of right reason, and consequently hurtful to the commonwealth, such an enactment can have no binding force of law, as being no rule of justice, but certain to lead men away from that good which is the very end of civil society.

Therefore, the nature of human liberty, however it be considered, whether in individuals or in society, whether in those who command or in those who obey, supposes the necessity of obedience to some supreme and eternal law, which is no other than the authority of God, commanding good and forbidding evil. And so far from this most just authority of God over men diminishing, or even destroying their liberty, it protects and perfects it, for the real perfection of all creatures is found in the prosecution and attainment of their respective ends; but the supreme end to which human liberty must aspire is God.

These precepts of the truest and highest teaching, made known to us by the light of reason itself, the Church, instructed by the example and doctrine of her divine Author, has ever propagated and asserted; for she has ever made them the measure of her office and of her teaching to the Christian nations. As to morals, the laws of the Gospel not only immeasurably surpass the wisdom of the heathen, but are an invitation and an introduction to a state of holiness unknown to the ancients; and, bringing man nearer to God, they make him at once the possessor of a more perfect liberty. Thus the powerful influence of the Church has ever been manifested in the custody and protection of the civil and political liberty of the people. The enumeration of its merits in this respect does not belong to our present purpose. It is sufficient to recall the fact that slavery, that old reproach of the heathen nations, was mainly abolished by the beneficent efforts of the Church. The impartiality of law and the true brotherhood of man were first asserted by Jesus Christ;

and His apostles re-echoed His voice when they declared that in future there was to be neither Jew, nor Gentile, nor Barbarian, nor Scythian, but all were brothers in Christ. So powerful, so conspicuous in this respect, is the influence of the Church, that experience abundantly testifies how savage customs are no longer possible in any land where she has once set her foot; but that gentleness speedily takes the place of cruelty, and the light of truth quickly dispels the darkness of barbarism. Nor has the Church been less lavish in the benefits she has conferred on civilized nations in every age, either by resisting the tyranny of the wicked, or by protecting the innocent and helpless from injury; or finally by using her influence in the support of any form of government which commended itself to the citizens at home, because of its justice, or was feared by their enemies without, because of its power.

Moreover, the highest duty is to respect authority, and obediently to submit to just law; and by this the members of a community are effectually protected from the wrongdoing of evil men. Lawful power is from God, *and whosoever resisteth authority resisteth the ordinance of God;* wherefore obedience is greatly ennobled when subjected to an authority which is the most just and supreme of all. But where the power to command is wanting, or where a law is enacted contrary to reason, or to the eternal law, or to some ordinance of God, obedience is unlawful, lest, while obeying man, we become disobedient to God. Thus, an effectual barrier being opposed to tyranny, the authority in the State will not have all its own way, but the interests and rights of all will be safeguarded—the rights of individuals, of domestic society, and of all the members of the commonwealth; all being free to live according to law and right reason; and in this, as We have shown, true liberty really consists.

If when men discuss the question of liberty they were careful to grasp its true and legitimate meaning, such as reason and reasoning have just explained, they would never venture to affix such a calumny on the Church as to assert that she is the foe to individual and public liberty. But many there are who follow in the footsteps of Lucifer, and adopt as their own his rebellious cry, "I will not serve"; and consequently substitute for true liberty what is sheer and most foolish license. Such, for instance, are the men belonging to that widely spread and powerful organization, who, usurping the name of liberty, style themselves *Liberals*.

What *Naturalists* or *Rationalists* aim at in philosophy, that the supporters of *Liberalism*, carrying out the principles laid down by Naturalism, are attempting in the domain of morality and politics. The fundamental doctrine of *Rationalism* is the supremacy of the human reason, which, refusing due submission to the divine and eternal reason, proclaims its own independence, and constitutes itself the supreme principle and source and judge of truth. Hence these followers of Liberalism deny the existence of any divine authority to which obedience is due, and proclaim that every man is the law to himself; from which arises that ethical system which they style *independent* morality, and which, under the guise of liberty, exonerates man from any obedience to the commands of God, and substitutes a boundless license. The end of all this it is not difficult to foresee, especially when society is in question. For, when once man is firmly persuaded that he is subject to no one, it follows that the efficient cause of the unity of civil society is not to be sought in any principle external to man, or superior to him, but simply in the free will of individuals; that the authority in the State comes from the people only; and that, just as every man's individual reason is his only rule of life, so the collective reason of the community should be the supreme guide in the management of all public affairs. Hence the doctrine of the supremacy of the greater number, and that all right and all duty reside in the majority. But, from what has been said, it is clear that all this is in contradiction to reason. To refuse any bond of union between man and civil society, on the one hand, and God the Creator and consequently the supreme Law-giver, on the other, is plainly repugnant to the nature, not only of man, but of all created things; for, of necessity, all effects must in some proper way be connected with their cause; and it belongs to the perfection of every nature to contain itself within that sphere and grade which the order of nature has assigned to it, namely, that the lower should be subject and obedient to the higher.

Moreover, besides this, a doctrine of such character is most hurtful both to individuals and to the State. For, once ascribe to human reason the only authority to decide what is true and what is good, and the real distinction between good and evil is destroyed; honor and dishonor differ not in their nature, but in the opinion and judgment of each one; pleasure is the measure of what is lawful; and, given a code of morality which can have little or no power to restrain or quiet the unruly propensities of man, a way is naturally opened to universal corruption. With reference also to public affairs: authority is severed from the true and natural principle whence it derives all its efficacy for the common good; and the law determining what it is right to do and avoid doing is at the mercy of a majority. Now this is simply a road leading straight to tyranny. The empire of God over man and civil society once repudiated, it follows that religion, as a public institution, can have no claim to exist, and that everything that belongs to religion will be treated with complete indifference. Furthermore, with ambitious designs on sovereignty, tumult and sedition will be common amongst the people; and when duty and conscience cease to appeal to them, there will be nothing to hold them back but force, which of itself alone is powerless to keep their covetousness in check. Of this we have almost daily evidence in the conflict with *Socialists* and members of other seditious societies, who labor unceasingly to bring about revolution. It is for those, then, who are capable of forming a just estimate of things to decide whether such doctrines promote that true liberty which alone is worthy of man, or rather pervert and destroy it.

There are, indeed, some adherents of Liberalism who do not subscribe to these opinions, which we have seen to be fearful in their enormity, openly opposed to the truth, and the cause of most terrible evils. Indeed, very many amongst them, compelled by the force of truth, do not hesitate to admit that such liberty is vicious, nay, is simple license, whenever intemperate in its claims, to the neglect of truth and justice; and therefore they would have liberty ruled and directed by right reason, and consequently subject to the natural law and to the divine eternal law. But here they think they may stop, holding that man as a free being is bound by no law of God, except such as He makes known to us through our natural reason. In this they are plainly inconsistent. For if—as they must admit, and no one can rightly deny —the will of the divine Law-giver is to be obeyed, because every man is under the power of God, and tends toward Him as his end, it follows that no one can assign limits to His legislative authority without failing in the obedience which is due. Indeed, if the human mind be so presumptuous as to define the nature and extent of God's rights and its own duties, reverence for the divine law will be apparent rather than real, and arbitrary judgment will prevail over the authority and providence of God. Man must, therefore, take his standard of a loyal and religious life from the eternal law; and from all and every one of those laws which God, in His infinite wisdom and power, has been pleased to enact, and to make known to us by such clear and unmistakable signs as to leave no room for doubt. And the more so because laws of this kind have the same origin, the same author, as the eternal law, are absolutely in accordance with right reason, and perfect the natural law. These laws it is that embody the government of God, who graciously guides and directs both the intellect and the will of man lest these fall into error. Let, then, that continue to remain in a holy and inviolable union, which neither can nor should be separated; and in all things—for this is the dictate of right reason itself—let God be dutifully and obediently served.

There are others, somewhat more moderate though not more consistent, who affirm that the morality of individuals is to be guided by the divine law, but not the morality of the State, so that in public affairs the commands of God may be passed over, and may be entirely disregarded in the framing of laws. Hence follows the fatal theory of the need of separation between Church and State. But the absurdity of such a position is manifest. Nature herself proclaims the necessity of the State providing means and opportunities whereby the community may be enabled to live properly, that is to say, according to the laws of God. For since God is the source of all goodness and justice, it is absolutely ridiculous that the State should pay no attention to these laws or render them abortive by contrary enactments. Besides, those who are in authority owe it to the commonwealth not only to provide for its external well-being and the conveniences of life, but still more to consult the welfare of men's souls in the wisdom of their legislation. But, for the increase of such benefits, nothing more suitable can be conceived than the laws which have God for their author; and, therefore, they who in their government of the State take no account of these laws, abuse political power by causing it to deviate from its proper end and from what nature itself prescribes. And, what is still more important, and what We have more than once pointed out, although the civil authority has not the same proximate end as the spiritual, nor proceeds on the same lines, nevertheless in the exercise of their separate powers they must occasionally meet. For their subjects are the same, and not infrequently they deal with the same objects, though in different ways. Whenever this occurs, since a state of conflict is absurd and manifestly repugnant to the most wise ordinance of God, there must necessarily exist some order or mode of procedure to remove the occasions of difference and contention, and to secure harmony in all things. This harmony has been not inaptly compared to that which exists between the body and the soul for the well-being of both one and the other, the separation of which brings irremediable harm to the body, since it extinguishes its very life.

To make this more evident, the growth of liberty ascribed to our age must be considered apart in its various details. And, first, let us examine that liberty in individuals which is so opposed to the virtue of religion, namely, the *liberty of worship*, as it is called. This is based on the principle that every man is free to profess as he may choose any religion or none.

But, assuredly, of all the duties which man has to fulfil, that, without doubt, is the chiefest and holiest which commands him to worship God with devotion and piety. This follows of necessity from the truth that we are ever in the power of God, are ever guided by His will and providence, and, having come forth from Him, must return to Him. Add to which no true virtue can exist without religion, for moral virtue is concerned with those things which lead to God as man's supreme and ultimate good; and therefore religion, which (as St. Thomas says) " performs those actions which are directly and immediately ordained for the divine honor," [1] rules and tempers all virtues. And if it be asked which of the many conflicting religions it is necessary to adopt, reason and the natural law unhesitatingly tell us to practise that one which God enjoins, and which men can easily recognize by certain exterior notes, whereby divine Providence has willed that it should be distinguished, because, in a matter of such

---

[1] Summa, 2a 2æ, q. lxxxi. a. 6.

moment, the most terrible loss would be the consequence of error. Wherefore, when a liberty such as We have described is offered to man, the power is given him to pervert or abandon with impunity the most sacred of duties, and to exchange the unchangeable good for evil; which, as We have said, is no liberty, but its degradation, and the abject submission of the soul to sin.

This kind of liberty, if considered in relation to the State, clearly implies that there is no reason why the State should offer any homage to God, or should desire any public recognition of Him; that no one form of worship is to be preferred to another, but that all stand on an equal footing, no account being taken of the religion of the people, even if they profess the Catholic faith. But, to justify this, it must needs be taken as true that the State has no duties towards God, or that such duties, if they exist, can be abandoned with impunity, both of which assertions are manifestly false. For it cannot be doubted but that, by the will of God, men are united in civil society; whether its component parts be considered; or its form, which implies authority; or the object of its existence; or the abundance of the vast services which it renders to man. God it is who has made man for society, and has placed him in the company of others like himself, so that what was wanting to his nature, and beyond his attainment if left to his own resources, he might obtain by association with others. Wherefore civil society must acknowledge God as its Founder and Parent, and must obey and reverence His power and authority. Justice therefore forbids, and reason itself forbids, the State to be godless; or to adopt a line of action which would end in godlessness—namely, to treat the various religions (as they call them) alike, and to bestow upon them promiscuously equal rights and privileges. Since, then, the profession of one religion is necessary in the State, that religion must be professed which alone is true, and which can be recognized without difficulty, especially in Catholic

States, because the marks of truth are, as it were, engraven upon it. This religion, therefore, the rulers of the State must preserve and protect, if they would provide —as they should do—with prudence and usefulness for the good of the community. For public authority exists for the welfare of those whom it governs; and although its proximate end is to lead men to the prosperity found in this life, yet, in so doing, it ought not to diminish, but rather to increase, man's capability of attaining to the supreme good in which his everlasting happiness consists: which never can be attained if religion be disregarded.

All this, however, We have explained more fully elsewhere. We now only wish to add the remark that liberty of so false a nature is greatly hurtful to the true liberty of both rulers and their subjects. Religion, of its essence, is wonderfully helpful to the State. For since it derives the prime origin of all power directly from God Himself, with grave authority it charges rulers to be mindful of their duty, to govern without injustice or severity, to rule their people kindly and with almost paternal charity; it admonishes subjects to be obedient to lawful authority, as to the ministers of God; and it binds them to their rulers, not merely by obedience, but by reverence and affection, forbidding all seditions and venturesome enterprises calculated to disturb public order and tranquillity, and cause greater restrictions to be put upon the liberty of the people. We need not mention how greatly religion conduces to pure morals, and pure morals to liberty. Reason shows, and history confirms the fact, that the higher the morality of States, the greater are the liberty and wealth and power which they enjoy.

We must now consider briefly *liberty of speech*, and liberty of the Press. It is hardly necessary to say that there can be no such right as this, if it be not used in moderation, and if it pass beyond the bounds and end of all true liberty. For right is a moral power which—as We have before said and must again and again repeat—it is absurd to suppose that nature has accorded indifferently to truth and falsehood, to justice and injustice. Men have a right freely and prudently to propagate throughout the State what things soever are true and honorable, so that as many as possible may possess them; but lying opinions, than which no mental plague is greater, and vices which corrupt the heart and moral life, should be diligently repressed by public authority, lest they insidiously work the ruin of the State. The excesses of an unbridled intellect, which unfailingly end in the oppression of the untutored multitude, are no less rightly controlled by the authority of the law than are the injuries inflicted by violence upon the weak. And this all the more surely, because by far the greater part of the community is either absolutely unable, or able only with great difficulty, to escape from illusions and deceitful subtleties, especially such as flatter the passions. If unbridled license of speech and of writing be granted to all, nothing will remain sacred and inviolate; even the highest and truest mandates of nature, justly held to be the common and noblest heritage of the human race, will not be spared. Thus, truth being gradually obscured by darkness, pernicious and manifold error, as too often happens, will easily prevail. Thus, too, license will gain what liberty loses; for liberty will ever be more free and secure, in proportion as license is kept in fuller restraint. In regard, however, to all matters of opinion which God leaves to man's free discussion, full liberty of thought and of speech is naturally within the right of every one; for such liberty never leads men to suppress the truth, but often to discover it and make it known.

A like judgment must be passed upon what is called *liberty of teaching.* There can be no doubt that truth alone should imbue the minds of men; for in it are found the well-being, the end, and the perfection of every intelligent nature; and therefore nothing but truth should be taught both to the ignorant and to the educated, so as to bring knowledge to those who have it not, and to preserve it in those who possess it. For this reason it is plainly the duty of all who teach to banish error from the mind, and by sure safeguards to close the entry to all false convictions. From this it follows, as is evident, that the liberty of which We have been speaking, is greatly opposed to reason, and tends absolutely to pervert men's minds, in as much as it claims for itself the right of teaching whatever it pleases—a liberty which the State cannot grant without failing in its duty. And the more so, because the authority of teachers has great weight with their hearers, who can rarely decide for themselves as to the truth or falsehood of the instruction given to them.

Wherefore, this liberty also, in order that it may deserve the name, must be kept within certain limits, lest the office of teaching be turned with impunity into an instrument of corruption. Now truth, which should be the only subject-matter of those who teach, is of two kinds, natural and supernatural. Of natural truths, such as the principles of nature and whatever is derived from them immediately by our reason, there is a kind of common patrimony in the human race. On this, as on a firm basis, morality, justice, religion, and the very bonds of human society rest: and to allow people to go unharmed who violate or destroy it, would be most impious, most foolish, and most inhuman. But with no less religious care must we preserve that great and sacred treasure of the truths which God Himself has taught us. By many and convincing arguments, often used by defenders of Christianity, certain leading truths have been laid down: namely, that some things have been revealed by God; that the only-begotten Son of God was made flesh, to bear witness to the truth; that a perfect society was founded by Him—the Church namely, of which He is the head, and with which He has promised to abide till the end of the world. To this society He entrusted all the truths which he had taught, in order that it might keep and guard them and with lawful authority explain them; and at the same time He commanded all nations to hear the voice of the Church, as if it were His own, threatening those who would not hear it with everlasting perdition. Thus it is manifest that man's best and surest teacher is God, the source and principle of all truth; and the only-begotten Son, who is in the bosom of the Father, the Way, the Truth, and the Life, the true Light which enlightens every man, and to whose teaching all must submit: *And they shall all be taught of God.*[1] In faith and in the teaching of morality, God Himself made the Church a partaker of His divine authority, and through His heavenly gift she cannot be deceived. She is therefore the greatest and most reliable teacher of mankind, and in her dwells an inviolable right to teach them. Sustained by the truth received from her divine Founder, the Church has ever sought to fulfil holily the mission entrusted to her by God; unconquered by the difficulties on all sides surrounding her, she has never ceased to assert her liberty of teaching, and in this way the wretched superstition of paganism being dispelled, the wide world was renewed unto Christian wisdom. Now, reason itself clearly teaches that the truths of divine revelation and those of nature cannot really be opposed to one another, and that whatever is at variance with them must necessarily be false. Therefore the divine teaching of the Church, so far from being an obstacle to the pursuit of learning and the progress of science, or in any way retarding the advance of civilization, in reality brings to them the sure guidance of shining light. And for the same reason it is of no small advantage for the perfecting of human liberty, since our Saviour Jesus Christ has said that by truth is man made free: *You shall know the truth, and the truth shall make you free.*[2] Therefore there is no reason why genuine liberty should grow indignant, or true science feel aggrieved, at having to

[1] John vi. 45.   [2] John viii. 32.

bear the just and necessary restraint of laws by which, in the judgment of the Church and of Reason itself, human teaching has to be controlled. The Church, indeed—as facts have everywhere proved—looks chiefly and above all to the defence of the Christian faith, while careful at the same time to foster and promote every kind of human learning. For learning is in itself good, and praiseworthy, and desirable; and further, all erudition which is the outgrowth of sound reason, and in conformity with the truth of things, serves not a little to confirm what we believe on the authority of God. The Church, truly, to our great benefit, has carefully preserved the monuments of ancient wisdom; has opened everywhere homes of science, and has urged on intellectual progress by fostering most diligently the arts by which the culture of our age is so much advanced. Lastly, We must not forget that a vast field lies freely open to man's industry and genius, containing all those things which have no necessary connection with Christian faith and morals, or as to which the Church, exercising no authority, leaves the judgment of the learned free and unconstrained. From all this may be understood the nature and character of that liberty which the followers of *Liberalism* so eagerly advocate and proclaim. On the one hand, they demand for themselves and for the State a license which opens the way to every perversity of opinion; and on the other, they hamper the Church in divers ways, restricting her liberty within narrowest limits, although from her teaching not only is there nothing to be feared, but in every respect very much to be gained.

Another liberty is widely advocated, namely, *liberty of conscience.* If by this is meant that every one may, as he chooses, worship God or not, it is sufficiently refuted by the arguments already adduced. But it may also be taken to mean that every man in the State may follow the will of God and, from a consciousness of duty and free from every obstacle, obey His commands. This, indeed, is true liberty, a liberty worthy of the sons of God, which nobly maintains the dignity of man, and is stronger than all violence or wrong—a liberty which the Church has always desired and held most dear. This is the kind of liberty the apostles claimed for themselves with intrepid constancy, which the apologists of Christianity confirmed by their writings, and which the martyrs in vast numbers consecrated by their blood. And deservedly so; for this Christian liberty bears witness to the absolute and most just dominion of God over man, and to the chief and supreme duty of man towards God. It has nothing in common with a seditious and rebellious mind; and in no tittle derogates from obedience to public authority; for the right to command and to require obedience exists only so far as it is in accordance with the authority of God, and is within the measure that He has laid down. But when anything is commanded which is plainly at variance with the will of God, there is a wide departure from this divinely constituted order, and at the same time a direct conflict with divine authority; therefore it is right not to obey.

By the patrons of *Liberalism*, however, who make the State absolute and omnipotent, and proclaim that man should live altogether independently of God, the liberty of which We speak, which goes hand in hand with virtue and religion, is not admitted; and whatever is done for its preservation is accounted an injury and an offence against the State. Indeed, if what they say were really true, there would be no tyranny, no matter how monstrous, which we should not be bound to endure and submit to.

The Church most earnestly desires that the Christian teaching, of which We have given an outline, should penetrate every rank of society in reality and in practice; for it would be of the greatest efficacy in healing the evils of our day, which are neither few nor slight, and are the offspring in great part of the false liberty which is so much extolled, and in which the germs of safety and glory were supposed to be contained. The hope has been disappointed by the result. The fruit, instead of being sweet and wholesome, has proved cankered and bitter. If then a remedy is desired, let it be sought for in a restoration of sound doctrine, from which alone the preservation of order and, as a consequence, the defence of true liberty can be confidently expected. Yet, with the discernment of a true mother, the Church weighs the great burden of human weakness, and well knows the course down which the minds and actions of men are in this our age being borne. For this reason, while not conceding any right to anything save what is true and honest, she does not forbid public authority to tolerate what is at variance with truth and justice, for the sake of avoiding some greater evil, or of obtaining or preserving some greater good. God Himself, in His providence, though infinitely good and powerful permits evil to exist in the world, partly that greater good may not be impeded, and partly that greater evil may not ensue. In the government of States it is not forbidden to imitate the Ruler of the world; and, as the authority of man is powerless to prevent every evil, it has (as St. Augustine says) *to overlook and leave unpunished many things which are punished, and rightly, by divine Providence.*[1] But if, in such circumstances, for the sake of the common good (and this is the only legitimate reason), human law may or even should tolerate evil, it may not and should not approve or desire evil for its own sake; for evil of itself, being a privation of good, is opposed to the common welfare which every legislator is bound to desire and defend to the best of his ability. In this, human law must endeavor to imitate God, who, as St. Thomas teaches, in allowing evil to exist in the world, *" neither wills evil to be done, nor wills it not to be done, but wills only to permit it to be done; and this is good."*[2] This

---

[1] St. August., de lib. arb., lib. 1. cap. 6, num. 14.
[2] St. Thomas, 1 q. xix. a 9 ad. 3.

saying of the Angelic Doctor contains briefly the whole doctrine of the permission of evil. But, to judge aright, we must acknowledge that the more a State is driven to tolerate evil the further is it from perfection; and that the tolerance of evil which is dictated by political prudence should be strictly confined to the limits which its justifying cause, the public welfare, requires. Wherefore, if such tolerance would be injurious to the public welfare, and entail greater evils on the State, it would not be lawful; for in such case the motive of good is wanting. And although in the extraordinary condition of these times the Church usually acquiesces in certain modern liberties, not because she prefers them in themselves, but because she judges it expedient to permit them, she would in happier times exercise her own liberty; and, by persuasion, exhortation, and entreaty, would endeavor, as she is bound, to fulfil the duty assigned to her by God of providing for the eternal salvation of mankind. One thing, however, remains always true— that the liberty which is claimed for all to do all things is not, as We have often said, of itself desirable, inasmuch as it is contrary to reason that error and truth should have equal rights. And as to *tolerance*, it is surprising how far removed from the equity and prudence of the Church are those who profess what is called *Liberalism*. For, in allowing that boundless license of which We have spoken, they exceed all limits, and end at last by making no apparent distinction between truth and error, honesty and dishonesty. And because the Church, the pillar and ground of truth, and the unerring teacher of morals, is forced utterly to reprobate and condemn *tolerance* of such an abandoned and criminal character, they calumniate her as being wanting in patience and gentleness, and thus fail to see that, in so doing, they impute to her as a fault what is in reality a matter for commendation. But, in spite of all this show of *tolerance*, it very often happens that, while they profess themselves ready to lavish liberty on all in the greatest profusion, they are utterly intolerant towards the Catholic Church, by refusing to allow her the liberty of being herself free.

And now to reduce for clearness' sake to its principal heads all that has been set forth with its immediate conclusions, the summing up is this briefly: that man, by a necessity of his nature, is wholly subject to the most faithful and ever-enduring power of God; and that as a consequence any liberty, except that which consists in submission to God and in subjection to His will, is unintelligible. To deny the existence of this authority in God, or to refuse to submit to it, means to act, not as a free man, but as one who treasonably abuses his liberty; and in such a disposition of mind the chief and deadly vice of *Liberalism* essentially consists. The form, however, of the sin is manifold; for in more ways and degrees than one can the will depart from the obedience which is due to God or to those who share the divine power.

For, to reject the supreme authority of God, and to cast off all obedience to Him in public matters, or even in private and domestic affairs, is the greatest perversion of liberty and the worst kind of *Liberalism:* and what We have said must be understood to apply to this alone in its fullest sense.

Next comes the system of those who admit indeed the duty of submitting to God, the Creator and Ruler of the world, inasmuch as all nature is dependent on His will, but who boldly reject all laws of faith and morals which are above natural reason, but are revealed by the authority of God; or who at least impudently assert that there is no reason why regard should be paid to these laws, at any rate publicly, by the State. How mistaken these men also are, and how inconsistent, we have seen above. From this teaching, as from its source and principle, flows that fatal principle of the separation of Church and State; whereas it is, on the contrary, clear that the two powers, though dissimilar in functions and unequal in degree, ought nevertheless to live in concord, by harmony in their action and the faithful discharge of their respective duties.

But this teaching is understood in two ways. Many wish the State to be separated from the Church wholly and entirely, so that regard to every right of human society, in institutions, customs, and laws, the offices of State, and the education of youth, they would pay no more regard to the Church than if she did not exist; and, at most, would allow the citizens individually to attend to their religion in private if so minded. Against such as these, all the arguments by which We disprove the principle of separation of Church and State are conclusive; with this superadded, that it is absurd the citizen should respect the Church, while the State may hold her in contempt.

Others oppose not the existence of the Church, nor indeed could they; yet they despoil her of the nature and rights of a perfect society, and maintain that it does not belong to her to legislate, to judge, or to punish, but only to exhort, to advise, and to rule her subjects in accordance with their own consent and will. By such opinion they pervert the nature of this divine society, and attenuate and narrow its authority, its office of teacher, and its whole efficiency; and at the same time they aggrandize the power of the civil government to such extent as to subject the Church of God to the empire and sway of the State, like any voluntary association of citizens. To refute completely such teaching, the arguments often used by the defenders of Christianity, and set forth by Us, especially in the Encyclical Letter *Immortale Dei*, are of great avail; for by those arguments it is proved that, by a divine provision, all the rights which essentially belong to a society that is legitimate, supreme, and perfect in all its parts exist in the Church.

Lastly, there remain those who, while they do not

approve the separation of Church and State, think nevertheless that the Church ought to adapt herself to the times and conform to what is required by the modern system of government. Such an opinion is sound, if it is to be understood of some equitable adjustment consistent with truth and justice; in so far, namely, that the Church, in the hope of some great good, may show herself indulgent, and may conform to the times in so far as her sacred office permits. But it is not so in regard to practices and doctrines which a perversion of morals and a warped judgment have unlawfully introduced. Religion, truth, and justice, must ever be maintained; and, as God has intrusted these great and sacred matters to the care of the Church, she can never be so unfaithful to her office as to dissemble in regard to what is false or unjust, or to connive at what is hurtful to religion.

From what has been said, it follows that it is quite unlawful to demand, to defend, or to grant unconditional freedom of thought, of speech, of writing, or of worship, as if these were so many rights given by nature to man. For if nature had really granted them, it would be lawful to refuse obedience to God, and there would be no restraint on human liberty. It likewise follows that freedom in these things may be tolerated wherever there is just cause; but only with such moderation as will prevent its degenerating into license and excess. And where such liberties are in use, men should employ them in doing good, and should estimate them as the Church does; for liberty is to be regarded as legitimate in so far only as it affords greater facility for doing good, but no farther.

Whenever there exists, or there is reason to fear, an unjust oppression of the people on the one hand, or a deprivation of the liberty of the Church on the other, it is lawful to seek for such a change of government as will bring about due liberty of action. In such case an excessive and vicious liberty is not sought for, but only some relief, for the common welfare, in order that, while license for evil is allowed by the State, the power of doing good may not be hindered.

Again, it is not of itself wrong to prefer a democratic form of government, if only the Catholic doctrine be maintained as to the origin and exercise of power. Of the various forms of government, the Church does not reject any that are fitted to procure the welfare of the subject; she wishes only—and this nature itself requires —that they should be constituted without involving wrong to any one, and especially without violating the rights of the Church.

Unless it be otherwise determined, by reason of some exceptional condition of things, it is expedient to take part in the administration of public affairs. And the Church approves of every one devoting his services to the common good, and doing all that he can for the defence, preservation, and prosperity of his country.

Neither does the Church condemn those who, if it can be done without violation of justice, wish to make their country independent of any foreign or despotic power. Nor does she blame those who wish to assign to the State the power of self-government, and to its citizens the greatest possible measure of prosperity. The Church has always most faithfully fostered civil liberty, and this was seen especially in Italy, in the municipal prosperity, and wealth, and glory, which were obtained at a time when the salutary power of the Church had spread, without opposition, to all parts of the State.

These things, Venerable Brothers, which, under the guidance of faith and reason, in the discharge of Our Apostolic office, We have now delivered to you, We hope, especially by your co-operation with Us, will be useful unto very many. In lowliness of heart We raise Our eyes in supplication to God, and earnestly beseech Him to shed mercifully the light of His wisdom and of His counsel upon men, so that, strengthened by these heavenly gifts, they may in matters of such moment discern what is true, and may afterwards, in public and in private, at all times and with unshaken constancy, live in accordance with the truth. As a pledge of these heavenly gifts, and in witness of Our good will to you, Venerable Brothers, and to the clergy and people committed to each of you, We most lovingly grant in the Lord the Apostolic Benediction.

THE RIGHT ORDERING OF CHRISTIAN LIFE.

Encyclical Letter Exeunte Jam Anno, December 25, 1888.

AT the close of the year in which, by the singular blessing and benefit of God, We have in sound health celebrated the fiftieth anniversary of Our priesthood, We naturally look back upon the past months, and with great pleasure recall to memory each and all of them. And not without reason; for while the event, so far as it regarded Us personally, was of itself neither great nor wonderful, it has moved the hearts of men in an unusual manner, and has been celebrated with so many manifestations of joy and congratulation that nothing was left to be desired. This general joy was indeed most pleasing to Us, and most gratifying; but what We valued most in connection with it was the significance of these heartfelt demonstrations, and the constancy of faith which they so unmistakably displayed. For the congratulations which came to Us from all sides expressed clearly this fact, that in all places the minds and hearts of men are turned to the Vicar of Jesus Christ; that, in the many evils which press upon us from every quarter, men look with confidence to the Apostolic See as to an ever-flowing and ever-pure source of salvation; and that, in every land where the Catholic religion flourishes, the Roman Church, mother and mistress of all churches, is reverenced and honored, as is right and fitting, with one mind and with ardent love.

For these reasons We have often during the past months lifted up Our eyes to the ever holy and eternal God, in thanksgiving for the most gracious gift of life bestowed upon Us, and for the many consolations vouchsafed to Us in Our sorrows; and during all this time We have used every occasion of showing Our gratitude to those to whom it was due. Now, however, the closing days of the year and of the Jubilee bid Us renew the recollection of benefits received; and, to Our very great satisfaction, the whole Church is joining with us in fresh thanksgiving. At the same time We anxiously wish by this letter to declare publicly that as so many testimonies of devotion and kindness and love have done much to lighten Our burden, so too a grateful remembrance of them will live always in Our mind.

But a holier and higher duty yet remains. For, in this affectionate and extraordinary eagerness to show honor to the Roman Pontiff, We seem called upon to acknowledge the power and the design of God, who often draws, and alone can draw, the beginnings of great good from events of the smallest moment. For God, in His most loving providence, seems to have wished to arouse faith in the midst of widespread disbelief, and to recall the Christian people to the pursuit of a higher life. Wherefore we must strive diligently that, laying the foundation of good, a favorable change may be inaugurated, and that the intentions of God may be both understood and put in practice. The obedience shown to the Apostolic See will indeed be full and perfect, if, joined with the admiration for Christian virtue, it lead to the salvation of souls—the only end worth seeking, and one which will abide forever.

In the exercise of the high Apostolic office bestowed upon Us by the goodness of God, We have many times, as in duty bound, undertaken the defence of truth, and have striven to expound particularly that teaching which seemed the most opportune for the public welfare, so that, in seeking the truth, all might watchfully and carefully avoid the dangers of error. But now, as a loving parent of his children, We wish to address all Christians, and in simple homely words to exhort all and each to lead a holy life. For, beyond the mere profession of faith, Christian virtues and practices are necessary for the Christian; and upon these depend, not only the eternal salvation of souls, but also the stable peace and true prosperity of the human family and of society.

If we inquire into the kind of life men everywhere lead, it is impossible for any one to avoid the conclusion that public and private morals differ vastly from the precepts of the Gospel. Too sadly, alas! do the words of the apostle St. John apply to our age: *All that is in the world is the concupiscence of the flesh, and the concupiscence of the eyes, and the pride of life.*[1] For in truth most men, with little heed as to whence they have come or whither they are going, place all their thoughts and all their care upon the vain and fleeting goods of this life; and, contrary to nature and right order, they voluntarily give themselves up to serve things of which their reason tells them they should be the masters. It is a short step from the desire of comfort and luxury to the striving after the means to obtain them. Hence arises the unbridled eagerness to become rich which binds those whom it possesses, and while they are seeking the gratification of their passion, hurries them along, often without reference to justice or injustice, and not infrequently even with insolent contempt for the penury of others. Thus very many who live in luxury call themselves the brethren of the multitudes whom in the depths of their hearts they despise. With minds puffed up with pride, they strive to be subject to no law and to have respect for no authority. They call self-love liberty, and think themselves *born free like a wild ass's colt.*[2] Snares and temptations to sin abound; impious and immoral dramas are exhibited on the stage; books and the daily press jeer at virtue and ennoble crime; and the fine arts themselves, which were intended for virtuous use and for rightful recreation, are

[1] 1 John ii. 16.   [2] Job xi. 12.

made to minister to depraved passions. Nor can we look to the future without fear; for new seeds of evil are continually being sown broadcast in the hearts of the rising generation. As for the public schools, it is well known to you that there is no ecclesiastical authority left in them; and during the years when tender minds should be trained carefully and conscientiously in Christian virtue, the precepts of religion are for the most part even left untaught. Youths somewhat advanced in age encounter a still graver peril, namely, from evil teaching; which is of such a kind as to deceive them by misleading words, instead of filling them with a knowledge of what is true. For many nowadays seek to learn truth by the aid of reason alone, putting divine faith entirely aside; and, through the exclusion of this strength and of this light, they fall into many errors and fail to discover the truth. They teach, for instance, that matter alone exists in the world; that men and beasts have the same origin and a like nature; and some even there are who go so far as to doubt the existence of God, the Ruler and Maker of the world, or to err most grievously, like unto the heathen, as to His divine nature. Hence the very essence and form of virtue, of justice, and of duty are of necessity distorted. Thus it is that, while they hold up to admiration the high authority of reason, and unduly extol the subtlety of the human intellect, they fall into the just punishment of pride through ignorance of what is of the greatest importance. When the mind has thus been poisoned, the moral character becomes at the same time deeply and substantially corrupt; and so diseased a state can be cured only with the utmost difficulty in this class of men, because on the one side their opinions vitiate the judgment of what is right, and on the other they have not the light of Christian faith, which is the principle and foundation of all righteousness.

Daily we see, with our own eyes, as it were, the numerous evils that afflict all classes of men from these causes.

Poisonous doctrines have corrupted both public and private life; rationalism, materialism, and atheism have begotten socialism, communism, and nihilism—fatal and pestilential evils, which naturally, and almost necessarily, flow forth from such principles. In good sooth, if the Catholic religion may be rejected with impunity, whose divine origin is made clear by such unmistakable signs, why should not all other forms of religion be rejected, when it is clear that they have not the same evidence of truth? If the soul is by nature one with the body, and if therefore no hope of a happy eternity remains when the body dies, what reason is there why man should endure toil and suffering here in the endeavor to subject the appetites to right reason? The highest good of man will consist in enjoying the comforts and pleasures of life, and since there is absolutely no one who does not by an instinct and impulse of nature strive after happiness, every man will naturally lay hands on all he can in the hope of living happily on the spoils of others. Nor will there be any power mighty enough to bridle passions when fully set astir; for if the supreme and eternal law, which commands what is right and forbids what is wrong, be rejected, it follows that the power of law is thwarted, and that all authority is loosened. Hence the bonds of civil society will be utterly shattered, when every man is driven by insatiable greed to a perpetual struggle, some striving to keep what they possess, others to obtain what they covet. Such is more or less the spirit and tone of our age.

There is, nevertheless, some consolation for us, even while looking at existing evils, and we may lift up our heart in good hope. For God *created all things that they might be: and He made the nations of the earth for health.*[1] But as all this world cannot be upheld save by the will and providence of Him who called it out of nothing, so also can men be healed only by the power of Him by whose good-

[1] Wisd. i. 14.

ness they were recalled from death to life. For Jesus Christ redeemed the human race once by the abundant shedding of His blood; and the efficacy of this great work and gift is for all ages: *Neither is there salvation in any other.*[1] Hence they who strive by the enforcement of law to extinguish the ever-growing flame of popular passions, strive indeed for what is right and just; but they will labor with little or no result so long as they obstinately reject the power of the Gospel and refuse the assistance of the Church. These evils can be cured only by a change of principles, and by returning in public and private conduct to Jesus Christ and to a Christian rule of life.

Now the whole essence of a Christian life is not to take part in the corruption of the world, but to oppose constantly any indulgence in that corruption. This is taught by all the words and actions, by all the laws and institutions, by the very life and death of Jesus Christ, *the author and finisher of faith.*[2] Hence, however strongly we are drawn back by our evil nature and the profligacy that is around us, it is our duty to run to the *fight proposed to us,*[3] armed and prepared with the same courage and the same weapons as He who, *having joy set before Him, endured the cross.*[4] Wherefore men are bound to consider and understand this above all, that it is contrary to the profession and duty of a Christian to follow, as they are wont to do, every kind of pleasure, to shrink from the hardship attending a virtuous life, and to allow oneself all that gratifies and delights the senses. *They that are Christ's have crucified their flesh with the vices and concupiscences.*[5] Hence it follows that they who are not accustomed to suffer, and to disregard ease and pleasure, belong not to Christ. By the infinite goodness of God, man was restored to the hope of an immortal life from which he had been cut off; but he cannot attain to it if he strives not to walk in the very

[1] Acts iv 12.
[2] Heb. xii. 2.
[3] Heb. xii. 1.
[4] Heb. xii. 2.
[5] Gal. v. 24.

footsteps of Christ, and to conform his mind and life to that of Christ by meditating on His example. Therefore this is not a counsel, but a duty; and the duty, not only of those who desire a more perfect life, but of all—*always bearing about in our body the mortification of Jesus.*[1] How else shall the natural law, which commands man to live virtuously, be kept? For by holy baptism the sin which we contracted at birth is taken away; but the evil and perverse roots which sin has planted in our hearts are by no means removed. That part of man which is without reason, although harmless to those who fight manfully by the grace of Christ, nevertheless struggles with reason for supremacy, disturbs the whole soul, and tyrannically bends the will away from virtue with such power that we cannot escape vice or do our duty except by a daily struggle. The Council of Trent says: "This holy synod teaches that in the baptized there remains concupiscence or an inclination to evil, which, being left to be fought against, cannot hurt those who, instead of yielding to it, manfully fight against it by the grace of Jesus Christ; *for he who hath lawfully striven shall be crowned.*"[2] There is in this struggle a degree of valor to which only a very perfect virtue attains, such as belongs to those who, by putting to flight impulses opposed to right reason, have made such advances in virtue as to seem almost to live a heavenly life on earth. Granted that few attain excellence so great, yet even the philosophy of the ancients taught that every man should conquer his evil desires; and still more and with greater care should those do so who, from daily contact with the world, are more sorely tempted—unless it be foolishly thought that where the danger is greater watchfulness is less needed, or that they whose maladies are most grievous need medicine more seldom.

But the toil which has to be borne in this conflict is compensated by great blessings over and above its eternal reward in heaven; and particularly because by the quell-

---

[1] 2 Cor. iv. 10.   [2] Sess. v. can. 5.

ing of the passions, nature is in a measure restored to its original dignity. For man has been born under a law that the soul should rule the body, and that the appetites should be restrained by mind and reason; and hence it follows that to restrain evil passions striving for the mastery over us is our noblest and greatest freedom. Moreover, it is difficult to see what can be expected of a man, even as a member of society, who is not thus disposed. Will any one be inclined to do right who has been accustomed to make self-love the sole rule of what he should do or avoid doing? No man can be high-souled, or kind, or merciful, or restrained who has not learned to conquer self, and to despise all worldly things when opposed to virtue.

Nor must We refrain from affirming that it seems to have been determined in the designs of God that there should be no salvation for men without struggle and pain. Indeed, when God gave to man pardon for sin, He gave it under the condition that His only-begotten Son should pay its just and due penalty; and though Jesus Christ might have satisfied divine justice in other ways, nevertheless He preferred to satisfy it by the utmost suffering and the sacrifice of His life. Therefore He has imposed it upon His followers as a law signed with His blood that their life should be an endless strife with the vices of their age. What made the apostles unconquerable in their mission of teaching truth to the world? What strengthened our countless martyrs in bearing witness by their blood to the Christian faith? Their more than readiness to obey fearlessly this law. All who have taken heed to live a Christian life and to seek after virtue have trodden the same path. We, too, must walk along this road if we desire to assure either our own salvation or that of others. Therefore, in the unbounded license that prevails, it is necessary for every one to guard manfully against the allurements of luxury; and since on every side there is so much pretentious display of enjoyment in wealth, the soul must be strengthened against the dangerous snare of wealth, lest, in striving after what are called the good things of life, which cannot satisfy and soon fade away, the soul should lose *the treasure in heaven which faileth not.* Finally, it is a further matter of deep grief that free thought and evil example have had such an influence in enfeebling the minds of men as to make many ashamed of the name of Christian—a shame which is the sign either of hopeless wickedness or of extreme cowardice. Each of these is detestable, and each injurious in the extreme. For what salvation remains for men, or on what hope can they rely, if they cease to glory in the name of Jesus Christ, if they openly and constantly refuse to live by the precepts of the Gospel? It is a common complaint that the age is barren of courageous men. Bring back into vogue a Christian rule of life and the minds of men will forthwith regain their strength and constancy.

But man's power of itself is not equal to the responsibility of so many and such various duties. As we must ask of God our daily bread for the sustenance of the body, so must we pray to Him for strength of soul that we may be sustained in virtue. Hence that universal condition and law of our life, which We have said is a perpetual warfare, brings with it the necessity of prayer to God. For, as is well and gracefully said by St. Augustine, devout prayer passes beyond the world's space and calls down the mercy of God from heaven. In order to conquer the assaults of our passions and the snares of the devil, lest we be led into evil, we are commanded to seek the divine help in the words, *Pray that ye enter not into temptation.*[1] How much more is this necessary if we wish to labor profitably for the salvation of others also! Christ our Lord, the only-begotten Son of God, the source of all grace and virtue, first showed by example what He taught in word: *He passed the whole night in the prayer of*

[1] Matt. xxvi. 41.

God;[1] and when nigh to the sacrifice of His life, *He prayed the longer.*[2] The frailty of nature would be much less perilous, and the moral character less weak and languid, if that divine precept of prayer were not so much disregarded and treated almost with dislike. God is easily appeased. He desires to do good to men, having clearly promised to give His grace in abundance to those who ask for it. Nay, He even invites men to ask, and almost insists upon their asking, with most loving words: *I say unto you, ask, and it shall be given to you: seek and you shall find: knock and it shall be opened unto you.*[3] And that we may have no fear in doing this with all confidence and familiarity, He makes use of tender phrases, comparing Himself to a most loving father who desires nothing so much as the love of his children: *If you then, being evil, know how to give good gifts to your children: how much more will your Father, who is in heaven, give good things to them that ask Him?*[4]

Whoever considers these things will not wonder at the efficacy of human prayer seeming so great to St. John Chrysostom that he thought it might be compared with the divine power. For, as God created all things by His word, so man by prayer obtains whatever he wills. Nothing has so great a power to obtain grace for us as prayer when rightly made; for it contains the motives by which God easily allows Himself to be appeased and to incline to mercy. In prayer we separate ourselves from things of earth; filled with the thought of God alone, we become conscious of our human weakness; and therefore, resting in the goodness and embrace of our Heavenly Father, we seek refuge in the power of Him who created us. We approach the Author of all good as if pressing Him to look upon our weak souls, unsteadfast strength, and great poverty; and, full of hope, we implore His aid and guardianship, who alone can heal our infirmities,

---

[1] Luke vi. 12.
[2] Luke xxii. 43.
[3] Luke xi. 9.
[4] Matt. vii. 11.

and give help to us in our weakness and misery. By such a condition of mind, in which, as is fitting, we think humbly of ourselves, God is greatly moved to mercy, for *God resisteth the proud, but to the humble He giveth grace.*[1]

Let, then, the habit of prayer be sacred to all; let the mind and heart and voice pray together; and let our life be in conformity with our prayer, so that by keeping the divine laws, the course of our days may seem a continual ascent towards God.

The virtue of prayer of which we are speaking is, like other virtues, produced and nourished by divine faith. For God is the author of all true and alone desirable blessings; and to Him also we owe our knowledge of His infinite goodness, and of the merits of Jesus our Redeemer. But, on the other hand, nothing is more fitted for the nourishment and increase of faith than the pious habit of prayer. And the need of the virtue of faith is seen plainly at this our time through its weakness in most men, and its absence in so many. For faith is especially the source whereby not only each one's life may be amended, but also right judgment may be obtained as to those matters which by their conflict hinder States from living in peace and security. If the multitude thirsts and raves for excessive liberty; if the indignation of the lower orders is with difficulty constrained; if the greed of the wealthier classes is insatiable, and if to these be added other evils of the same kind which We have elsewhere fully set forth, it will be found that nothing can remedy them more fully or more surely than Christian faith.

And here it is fitting that We should turn Our thoughts and words to you whom God has made His helpers, by giving you His divine power to dispense His mysteries. If the sources of public and private moral welfare are examined, it will, without doubt, be found that the lives of the clergy may be of immense influence. Let them

---

[1] 1 Peter v. 5.

therefore remember that they have been called by Jesus
Christ *the light of the world;* and that "the soul of the
priest should shine like a light illuminating the whole
world." [1] The light of learning, and this in no small
degree, is needed in the priest, because it is his duty to
fill others with wisdom, to overcome error, and to be a
guide to the many in the steep and slippery paths of life.
Learning, however, must above all be accompanied by
innocence of life, because in the reformation of man example avails far more than precept. *Let your light shine
before men, that they may see your good works.* [2] The
meaning of this divine precept is, that the perfection of
virtue in priests should be such that they should be like
a mirror to the rest of men. "Nothing leads others more
surely to the love and worship of God than the life and
example of those dedicated to the divine ministry; for,
since they are separated from the world and placed in a
higher sphere, others look on them as on a mirror, to
seek from them an example which they may follow." [3]
Therefore, if all men must watchfully take heed against
the allurements of sin, and against a too eager seeking
after fleeting pleasures, it is clear that priests ought to
do the same much more faithfully and steadfastly. But it
is not enough for them merely to restrain their passions:
their sacred dignity requires of them in addition the habit
of stringent self-denial, and that they should devote all
the powers of their soul, particularly the intellect and
will, which hold the highest powers in man, to the service
of Christ. "If thou hast a mind to leave all," says St.
Bernard, "remember to reckon thyself among the things
that thou wishest to abandon—nay, deny thyself first
and before everything." [4] Not until their soul is unshackled and free from every unhallowed desire will

---

[1] St. John Chrysost. De Sac. l. 3, c. 1.
[2] Matt. v. 16.
[3] Con. Trid. Sess. xxii. 1, de Ref.
[4] Declam., c. 1.

priests have a ready and generous zeal for the salvation of others, and without this they cannot properly secure their own. "One thing only shall they seek and rejoice at in those subject to them, in one thing only shall they glory—to make of them, if possible, a perfect people. For this they will strive in every way, with great labor of mind and body, in toil and suffering, in hunger and thirst, in cold and nakedness." [1] Frequent meditation upon the things of heaven wonderfully nourishes and strengthens virtue of this kind, and makes it always ready and fearless of the greatest difficulties for the good of others. The more pains they take in such meditation, the more clearly will priests understand the greatness, the excellence, the holiness of their office. They will see how sad it is that so many men, redeemed by Jesus Christ, should run headlong to eternal ruin; and by meditation upon the divine nature they will themselves be more strongly moved, and will more effectually excite others to the love of God.

Such, then, is the surest way to secure the general welfare. But let us not be frightened by the greatness of our difficulties, or despair of cure by reason of the long continuance of evil. The impartial and unchangeable justice of God reserves due reward for good deeds and fitting punishment for sin. But since the life of peoples and nations does not outlast this world, these necessarily receive their retribution upon this earth. Indeed, it is not a new thing for prosperity to have place in a sinful nation; and this by the just designs of God, who from time to time rewards good deeds with prosperity, for no people is altogether without worth. This St. Augustine considered to have been the case with the Roman people. The law, nevertheless, remains clear: that nations may prosper, it is to the interest of all that virtue—and especially justice, the mother of all virtues—should be publicly practised. *Justice exalteth a nation; but sin maketh*

---

[1] St. Bern., De Consid., iv. 2.

nations miserable.[1] It is not our purpose here to consider how far evil deeds may succeed, or whether some kingdoms, while flourishing according to their desires, may nevertheless bear within them the seeds of ruin and misery. This one thing, of which history has innumerable examples, We wish to be understood, that injustice is always punished, and with greater severity the longer it has been continued. We, however, are greatly consoled by the words of the Apostle St. Paul: *For all things are yours; and you are Christ's, and Christ is God's.*[2] That is, by the hidden dispensation of divine Providence the course of earthly things is so guided and governed that all things that happen to man turn to the glory of God, and lead to the salvation of the true disciples of Jesus Christ. Of these the mother and sustainer, the leader and guardian, is the Church; which, united to Christ her spouse in intimate and unchangeable charity, is also joined to Him in common contest and in common conquest. Hence We are not, and cannot be, anxious for the sake of the Church; but We greatly fear for the salvation of very many who in their pride despise the Church, and by many kinds of error are borne along to their own destruction. We are anxious for those States which We cannot but see have turned from God, and are sleeping in the midst of danger with dull security and insensibility. "Nothing is equal in power to the Church. . . . How many have opposed the Church and have themselves perished! The Church reaches to the heavens. Such is the Church's greatness: she conquers when attacked; when beset by snares she triumphs; . . . she struggles, and is not overthrown; she fights, and is not overcome."[3]

Not only is she not conquered, but she preserves entire that reforming power and efficient principle of salvation which she derives unceasingly from God, and which

---

[1] Prov. xiv. 34.   [2] 1 Cor. iii. 22, 23.
[3] St. John Chrysost.

remains unchanged by time. And, if by this power she freed the world grown old in vice and lost in superstition, why should she not by the same bring it back again to the right way? Let suspicion and enmity cease at length; let all obstacles be removed, and let the Church, whose duty it is to guard and spread abroad the benefits obtained by Jesus Christ, be restored everywhere to her rights. Then shall we know by experience how far the light of the Gospel can reach, and what the power of Christ our Redeemer can effect. This year, now coming to a close, has given, as We have said, many signs of a reviving faith. Would that this little spark may increase till it becomes a mighty flame, which, burning up the roots of vice, may quickly prepare the way for the restoration of morals and for salutary works. We, indeed, who command the mystical barque of the Church in so formidable a storm, fix Our mind and heart upon the divine Pilot who sits unseen at the helm. Thou seest, O Lord, how the winds have burst forth from every side; how the sea rages, and the waves are lashed to fury. Command, we beseech Thee, who alone canst do so, the winds and the sea. Give back to mankind that tranquillity of order, that true peace which the world cannot give. By Thy grace and impulse let men be restored to proper order, with piety towards God, with justice and love towards their neighbor, with temperance in regard to themselves, and with reason controlling all their passions. Let Thy kingdom come; let the duty of submitting to Thee and serving Thee be learnt by those who, far from Thee, seek truth and salvation with a purpose that is all vain. In Thy laws justice and a father's gentleness are found: and Thou grantest to us of Thy own good-will the power to keep Thy commands. The life of man on earth is a warfare, but Thou lookest down upon the struggle and helpest man to conquer; Thou raisest him that falls, and crownest him that triumphs." [1]

[1] Cf. St. Aug. on Ps. 32.

Our mind is upheld by these thoughts to a joyful and firm hope; and as a pledge of heavenly favors, and of our good-will, we most lovingly in the Lord grant to you, Venerable Brothers, and to the clergy and people of the whole Catholic world, the Apostolic Blessing.

ON THE CHIEF DUTIES OF CHRISTIANS AS CITIZENS.

Encyclical Letter Sapientiæ Christianæ, January 10, 1890.

FROM day to day it becomes more and more evident how needful it is that the principles of Christian wisdom should be ever borne in mind, and that the life, the morals, and the institutions of nations should be wholly conformed to them. From the fact of these principles having been disregarded, mischiefs so vast have accrued that no right-minded man can face the trials of the time being without grave solicitude, nor contemplate the future without serious alarm. Progress, not inconsiderable indeed, has been made towards securing the well-being of the body and of material things; but all natural advantages that administer to the senses of man, while bringing in their train the possession of wealth, power, and limitless resources may indeed greatly avail to procure the comforts and increase the enjoyments of life, but are incapable of satisfying the soul created for higher and more glorious benefits. To fix the gaze on God, and to aim earnestly at becoming like Him, is the supreme law of the life of man. For we were created in the divine image and likeness, and are vehemently urged, by our very nature, to return to Him from whom we have origin. But not by bodily motion or effort do we make advance towards God, but through acts of the soul, that is, through knowledge and love. God is, in very deed, the primal and supreme truth, and truth the food on which alone the soul is nourished; and God is holiness in perfection and the sovereign good,

180

to which solely the will may aspire and which it may attain, when virtue is its guide.

But what applies to individual men applies equally to society—domestic alike and civil. Nature did not fashion society with intent that man should seek in it his last end, but that in it and through it he should find suitable aids whereby to attain to his own perfection. If, then, a civil government strives after external advantages merely, and the attainment of such objects as adorn life; if in administering public affairs it is wont to put God aside, and show no solicitude for the upholding of moral law; it deflects wofully from its right course and from the injunctions of nature: nor should such a gathering together and association of men be accounted as a commonwealth, but only as a deceitful imitation and make-believe of civil organization.

As to what We have termed the well-being of the soul, which consists chiefly in the practice of the true religion and unswerving observance of the Christian precepts, We perceive that it is daily losing esteem among men, either by reason of forgetfulness or disregard, in such wise that the greater the advance made in the well-being of the body, the greater is the falling away in that of the soul. A striking proof of the lessening and enfeebling of Christian faith is seen in the insults that are, alas! so frequently, in open day, and before Our very eyes, offered to the Catholic Church—insults, indeed, to which an age cherishing religion would on no account have submitted. For these reasons how great a multitude of men is involved in danger as to their eternal salvation surpasses belief; but, more than this, nations and even vast empires themselves cannot long remain unharmed, since upon the lapsing of Christian institutions and morality, the main foundation of human society must necessarily be uprooted. Force alone will remain to preserve public tranquillity and order; force, however, is very feeble when the bulwark of religion has been removed; and being more apt to beget slavery than obedience, it bears within itself the germs of ever-increasing troubles. The present century has encountered notable disasters, nor is it clear that some equally terrible are not impending. The very times in which we live are warning us to seek remedies there where alone they are to be found—namely, by re-establishing in the family circle and throughout the whole range of society the doctrines and practices of the Christian religion. In this lies the sole means of freeing us from the ills now weighing us down, of forestalling the dangers now threatening the world. For the accomplishment of this end, Venerable Brothers, We must bring to bear all the activity and diligence that lie within Our power. Although We have already, under other circumstances, and whenever occasion required, treated of these matters in other Letters, We deem it expedient in this message to you, to define more in detail the duties of Catholics, inasmuch as these would, if strictly observed, avail with wondrous power to save society in all its length and breadth. We are engaged, as regards matters of highest moment, in a violent and well-nigh daily struggle, wherein it is hard at times for the minds of many not to be deluded, not to go astray, not to yield. It behooves Us, Venerable Brothers, to warn, instruct, and exhort each of the faithful with an earnestness befitting the occasion: *that none may abandon the way of truth.*

It cannot be doubted that duties more numerous and of greater moment devolve on Catholics than upon such as are either not sufficiently enlightened in relation to the Catholic faith, or who are entirely unacquainted with its doctrines. Considering that forthwith upon salvation being brought out for mankind, Jesus Christ laid upon His apostles the injunction to *preach the Gospel to every creature*, He imposed, it is evident, upon all men the duty of learning thoroughly and believing what they were taught. This duty is intimately bound up with the gaining of eternal salvation: *He that believeth and is bap-*

*tized shall be saved; but he that believeth not, shall be con-
demned.*[1] But the man who has embraced the Christian
faith, as in duty bound, is by that very fact a subject of
the Church as one of the children born of her, and becomes
a member of that greatest and holiest body, which it is
the special charge of the Roman Pontiff to rule with
supreme power, under its invisible head, Jesus Christ.
Now, if the natural law enjoins us to love devotedly and
to defend the country in which we had birth, and in which
we were brought up, so that every good citizen hesitates
not to face death for his native land, very much more is
it the urgent duty of Christians to be ever quickened by
like feelings towards the Church. For the Church is the
holy city of the living God, born of God Himself, and by
Him built up and established. Upon this earth indeed
she accomplishes her pilgrimage, but by instructing and
guiding men, she summons them to eternal happiness.
We are bound, then, to love dearly the country whence
we have received the means of enjoyment this mortal
life affords, but we have a much more urgent obligation
to love, with ardent love, the Church to which we owe
the life of the soul, a life that will endure for ever. For
fitting it is to prefer the good of the soul to the well-being
of the body, inasmuch as duties toward God are of a far
more hallowed character than those toward men.

Moreover, if we would judge aright, the supernatural
love for the Church and the natural love of our own
country proceed from the same eternal principle, since
God himself is their Author and originating Cause. Consequently it follows that between the duties they respectively enjoin, neither can come into collision with the other.
We can, certainly, and should love ourselves, bear ourselves kindly towards our fellow-men, nourish affection
for the State and the governing powers; but at the same
time we can and must cherish towards the Church a feeling

---

[1] Mark xvi. 16.

of filial piety, and love God with the deepest love of which we are capable. The order of precedence of these duties is, however, at times, either under stress of public calamities, or through the perverse will of men, inverted. For instances occur where the State seems to require from men as subjects one thing, and religion, from men as Christians, quite another; and this in reality without any other ground, than that the rulers of the State either hold the sacred power of the Church of no account, or endeavor to subject it to their own will. Hence arises a conflict, and an occasion, through such conflict, of virtue being put to the proof. The two powers are confronted and urge their behests in a contrary sense; to obey both is wholly impossible. *No man can serve two masters*,[1] for to please the one amounts to contemning the other. As to which should be preferred no one ought to balance for an instant. It is a high crime indeed to withdraw allegiance from God in order to please men; an act of consummate wickedness to break the laws of Jesus Christ, in order to yield obedience to earthly rulers, or, under pretext of keeping the civil law, to ignore the rights of the Church; *we ought to obey God rather than men*.[2] This answer, which of old Peter and the other apostles were used to give the civil authorities who enjoined unrighteous things, we must, in like circumstances, give always and without hesitation. No better citizen is there, whether in time of peace or war, than the Christian who is mindful of his duty; but such a one should be ready to suffer all things, even death itself, rather than abandon the cause of God or of the Church.

Hence they who blame, and call by the name of sedition, this steadfastness of attitude in the choice of duty, have not rightly apprehended the force and nature of true law. We are speaking of matters widely known, and which We have before now more than once fully explained.

---

[1] Matt. vi. 24.   [2] Acts v 29.

Law is of its very essence a mandate of right reason, proclaimed by a properly constituted authority, for the common good. But true and legitimate authority is void of
sanction, unless it proceed from God the supreme Ruler
and Lord of all. The Almighty alone can commit power
to a man over his fellow-men; nor may that be accounted
as right reason which is in disaccord with truth and with
divine reason; nor that held to be true good which is repugnant to the supreme and unchangeable good, or that
wrests aside and draws away the wills of men from the
charity of God.

Hallowed therefore in the minds of Christians is the
very idea of public authority, in which they recognize
some likeness and symbol as it were of the divine Majesty, even when it is exercised by one unworthy. A just
and due reverence to the laws abides in them, not from
force and threats, but from a consciousness of duty; *for
God hath not given us the spirit of fear.*[1]

But if the laws of the State are manifestly at variance
with the divine law, containing enactments hurtful to
the Church, or conveying injunctions adverse to the duties
imposed by religion, or if they violate in the person of
the supreme Pontiff the authority of Jesus Christ, then
truly, to resist becomes a positive duty, to obey, a crime;
a crime, moreover, combined with misdemeanor against
the State itself, inasmuch as every offence levelled against
religion is also a sin against the State. Here anew it
becomes evident how unjust is the reproach of sedition:
for the obedience due to rulers and legislators is not
refused; but there is a deviation from their will in those
precepts only which they have no power to enjoin. Commands that are issued adversely to the honor due to God,
and hence are beyond the scope of justice, must be looked
upon as anything rather than laws. You are fully aware,
Venerable Brothers, that this is the very contention of

[1] 2 Timothy i. 7.

the Apostle St. Paul, who, in writing to Titus, after reminding Christians that they are *to be subject to princes and powers, and to obey at a word,* at once adds, *And to be ready to every good work.*[1] Thereby he openly declares that if laws of men contain injunctions contrary to the eternal law of God, it is right not to obey them. In like manner the prince of the apostles gave this courageous and sublime answer to those who would have deprived him of the liberty of preaching the Gospel: *If it be just in the sight of God to hear you rather than God, judge ye, for we cannot but speak the things which we have seen and heard.*[2]

Wherefore, to love both countries, that of earth below and that of heaven above, yet in such mode that the love of our heavenly surpass the love of our earthly home, and that human laws be never set above the divine law, is the essential duty of Christians, and the fountain-head, so to say, from which all other duties spring. The Redeemer of mankind of Himself has said: *For this was I born, and for this came I into the world, that I should give testimony to the truth.*[3] In like manner, *I am come to cast fire upon earth, and what will I but that it be kindled?*[4] In the knowledge of this truth, which constitutes the highest perfection of the mind; in divine charity which, in like manner, completes the will, all Christian life and liberty abide. This noble patrimony of truth and charity entrusted by Jesus Christ to the Church, she defends and maintains ever with untiring endeavor and watchfulness.

But with what bitterness and in how many guises war has been waged against the Church, it would be ill-timed now to urge. From the fact that it has been vouchsafed to human reason to snatch from nature, through the investigations of science, many of her treasured secrets and to apply them befittingly to the divers requirements of life, men have become possessed with so arrogant a sense of their own powers, as already to consider them-

[1] Tit. iii. i.
[2] Acts iv. 19, 20.
[3] John xviii. 37.
[4] Luke xii. 49.

selves able to banish from social life the authority and empire of God. Led away by this delusion, they make over
to human nature the dominion of which they think God
has been despoiled; from nature, they maintain, we must
seek the principle and rule of all truth; from nature, they
aver, alone spring, and to it should be referred, all the duties
that religious feeling prompts. Hence they deny all revelation from on high, and all fealty due to the Christian
teaching of morals as well as all obedience to the Church;
and they go so far as to deny her power of making laws
and exercising every other kind of right, even disallowing
the Church any place among the civil institutions of the
State. These men aspire unjustly, and with their might
strive, to gain control over public affairs and lay hands
on the rudder of the State, in order that the legislation
may the more easily be adapted to these principles, and
the morals of the people influenced in accordance with
them. Whence it comes to pass that in many countries
Catholicism is either openly assailed or else secretly inter-
fered with, full impunity being granted to the most pernicious doctrines, while the public profession of Christian
truth is shackled oftentimes with manifold constraints.

Under such evil circumstances therefore each one is
bound in conscience to watch over himself, taking all
means possible to preserve the faith inviolate in the depths
of his soul, avoiding all risks, and arming himself on all
occasions, especially against the various specious sophisms
rife among non-believers. In order to safeguard this
virtue of faith in its integrity, We declare it to be very
profitable and consistent with the requirements of the
time, that each one, according to the measure of his capacity and intelligence, should make a deep study of Christian doctrine, and imbue his mind with as perfect a knowledge as may be of those matters that are interwoven
with religion and lie within the range of reason. And as
it is necessary that faith should not only abide untarnished
in the soul, but should grow with ever painstaking increase,

the suppliant and humble entreaty of the apostles ought constantly to be addressed to God: *Increase our faith.*[1]

But in this same matter, touching Christian faith, there are other duties whose exact and religious observance, necessary at all times in the interests of eternal salvation, become more especially so in these our days. Amid such reckless and widespread folly of opinion, it is, as we have said, the office of the Church to undertake the defence of truth and uproot errors from the mind, and this charge has to be at all times sacredly observed by her, seeing that the honor of God and the salvation of men are confided to her keeping. But when necessity compels, not those only who are invested with power of rule are bound to safeguard the integrity of faith, but, as St. Thomas maintains, "Each one is under obligation to show forth his faith, either to instruct and encourage others of the faithful, or to repel the attacks of unbelievers."[2] To recoil before an enemy, or to keep silence when from all sides such clamors are raised against truth, is the part of a man either devoid of character or who entertains doubt as to the truth of what he professes to believe. In both cases such mode of behaving is base and is insulting to God, and both are incompatible with the salvation of mankind. This kind of conduct is profitable only to the enemies of the faith, for nothing emboldens the wicked so greatly as the lack of courage on the part of the good. Moreover, want of vigor on the part of Christians is so much the more blameworthy, as not seldom little would be needed on their part to bring to naught false charges and refute erroneous opinions; and by always exerting themselves more strenuously they might reckon upon being successful. After all, no one can be prevented from putting forth that strength of soul which is the characteristic of true Christians; and very frequently by such display of courage our enemies lose heart and their designs

---

[1] Luke xvii. 5.   [2] 2a 2æ Q. ii, a. 2 ad. 2.

are thwarted. Christians are, moreover, born for combat, whereof the greater the vehemence, the more assured, God aiding, the triumph: *Have confidence; I have overcome the world.*[1] Nor is there any ground for alleging that Jesus Christ, the Guardian and Champion of the Church, needs not in any manner the help of men. Power certainly is not wanting to Him, but in His loving kindness He would assign to us a share in obtaining and applying the fruits of salvation procured through His grace.

The chief elements of this duty consist in professing openly and unflinchingly the Catholic doctrine, and in propagating it to the utmost of our power. For, as is often said, with the greatest truth, there is nothing so hurtful to Christian wisdom as that it should not be known, since it possesses, when loyally received, inherent power to drive away error. So soon as Catholic truth is apprehended by a simple and unprejudiced soul, reason yields assent. Now faith, as a virtue, is a great boon of divine grace and goodness; nevertheless, the objects themselves to which faith is to be applied are scarcely known in any other way than through the hearing. *How shall they believe Him of whom they have not heard? and how shall they hear without a preacher? Faith then cometh by hearing, and hearing by the word of Christ.*[2] Since, then, faith is necessary for salvation, it follows that the word of Christ must be preached. The office indeed of preaching, that is, of teaching, lies by divine right in the province of the pastors, namely of the bishops whom *the Holy Ghost has placed to rule the Church of God.*[3] It belongs above all to the Roman Pontiff, vicar of Jesus Christ, established as head of the universal Church, teacher of all that pertains to morals and faith. No one, however, must entertain the notion that private individuals are prevented from taking some active part in this duty of teaching, especially those on whom God has bestowed gifts of mind with the

---

[1] John xvi. 33.   [2] Rom. x. 14, 17.   [3] Acts xx. 28.

strong wish of rendering themselves useful. These, so often as circumstances demand, may take upon themselves, not indeed the office of the pastor, but the task of communicating to others what they have themselves received, becoming, as it were, living echoes of their masters in the faith. Such co-operation on the part of the laity has seemed to the Fathers of the Vatican Council so opportune and fruitful of good that they thought well to invite it. " All faithful Christians, but those chiefly who are in a prominent position, or engaged in teaching, we entreat, by the compassion of Jesus Christ, and enjoin by the authority of the same God and Saviour, that they bring aid to ward off and eliminate these errors from Holy Church, and contribute their zealous help in spreading abroad the light of undefiled faith."[1] Let each one therefore bear in mind that he both can and should, so far as may be, preach the Catholic faith by the authority of his example, and by open and constant profession of the obligations it imposes. In respect consequently to the duties that bind us to God and the Church, it should be borne earnestly in mind that in propagating Christian truth and warding off errors, the zeal of the laity should, as far as possible, be brought actively into play.

The faithful would not, however, so completely and advantageously satisfy these duties as is fitting they should were they to enter the field as isolated champions of the faith. Jesus Christ, indeed, has clearly intimated that the hostility and hatred of men, which He first and foremost experienced, would be shown in like degree towards the work founded by Him, so that many would be barred from profiting by the salvation for which all are indebted to His loving kindness. Wherefore He willed not only to train disciples in His doctrine, but to unite them into one society, and closely conjoin them in one body, *which is the Church*,[2] whereof He would be the Head.

---

[1] Const. Dei Filius, sub fine.   [2] Coloss. i. 24.

The life of Jesus Christ pervades, therefore, the entire framework of this body, cherishes and nourishes its every member, uniting each with each, and making all work together to the same end, albeit the action of each be not the same.[1] Hence it follows that not only is the Church a perfect society far excelling every other, but it is enjoined by her Founder that for the salvation of mankind she is to contend *as an army drawn up in battle array.*[2] The organization and constitution of Christian society can in no wise be changed, neither can any one of its members live as he may choose, nor elect that mode of fighting which best pleases him. For in effect he scatters and gathers not, who gathers not with the Church and with Jesus Christ, and all who fight not jointly with him and with the Church are in very truth contending against God.[3]

To bring about such a union of minds and uniformity of action—not without reason so greatly feared by the enemies of Catholicism,—the main point is that a perfect harmony of opinion should prevail; in which intent we find Paul the Apostle exhorting the Corinthians with earnest zeal and solemn weight of words: *Now I beseech you, brethren, by the name of our Lord Jesus Christ, that you all speak the same thing, and that there be no schisms among you: but that you be perfectly in the same mind, and in the same judgment.*[4]

The wisdom of this precept is readily apprehended. In truth, thought is the principle of action, and hence there cannot exist agreement of will, nor similarity of action, if people all think differently one from the other.

In the case of those who profess to take reason as their

---

[1] As in one body we have many members, but all the members have not the same office.—Rom. xii. 4, 5.

[2] Canticles vi. 9.

[3] Who is not with Me, is against Me, and he who gathereth not with Me, scattereth.—Luke xi. 22.

[4] 1 Cor. i. 10.

sole guide, there would hardly be found, if, indeed, there ever could be found, unity of doctrine Indeed, the art of knowing things as they really are is exceedingly difficult; moreover, the mind of man is by nature feeble and drawn this way and that by a variety of opinions, and not seldom led astray by impressions coming from without; and furthermore, the influence of the passions oftentimes takes away, or certainly at least diminishes, the capacity for grasping the truth. On this account, in controlling State affairs means are often taken to keep those together by force who cannot agree in their way of thinking.

It happens far otherwise with Christians: they receive their rule of faith from the Church, by whose authority and under whose guidance they are conscious that they have beyond question attained to truth. Consequently as the Church is one, because Jesus Christ is one, so throughout the whole Christian world there is, and ought to be, but one doctrine: *One Lord, one faith;*[1] *but having the same spirit of faith,*[2] they possess the saving principle whence proceed spontaneously one and the same will in all, and one and the same tenor of action.

Now, as the Apostle Paul urges, this unanimity ought to be perfect. Christian faith reposes not on human but on divine authority, for what God has revealed "we believe not on account of the intrinsic evidence of the truth perceived by the natural light of our reason, but on account of the authority of God revealing, who cannot be deceived nor himself deceive."[3] It follows as a consequence, that whatever things are manifestly revealed by God we must receive with a similar and equal assent. To refuse to believe any one of them is equivalent to rejecting them all; for those at once destroy the very groundwork of faith who deny that God has spoken to men, or who bring into doubt His infinite truth and wisdom. To determine, however, which are the doctrines divinely

---

[1] Eph. iv. 5.   [2] 2 Cor. iv. 13.   [3] Conc. Vat. Const. Dei Filius.

revealed, belongs to the teaching Church, to whom God has entrusted the safe-keeping and interpretation of His utterances. But the supreme teacher in the Church is the Roman Pontiff. Union of minds, therefore, requires, together with a perfect accord in the one faith, complete submission and obedience of will to the Church and to the Roman Pontiff, as to God Himself. This obedience should, however, be perfect, because it is enjoined by faith itself, and has this in common with faith, that it cannot be given in shreds;—nay, were it not absolute and perfect in every particular, it might wear the name of obedience, but its essence would disappear. Christian usage attaches such value to this perfection of obedience that it has been, and will ever be, accounted the distinguishing mark by which we are able to recognize Catholics. Admirably does the following passage from St. Thomas of Aquin set before us the right view: "The formal object of faith is primary truth, as it is shown forth in the Holy Scriptures, and in the teaching of the Church, which proceeds from the fountain-head of truth. It follows, therefore, that he who does not adhere, as to an infallible divine rule, to the teaching of the Church, which proceeds from the primary truth manifested in the Holy Scriptures, possesses not the habit of faith; but matters of faith he holds otherwise than true faith. Now it is evident that he who clings to the doctrines of the Church as to an infallible rule yields his assent to everything the Church teaches; but otherwise, if with reference to what the Church teaches he holds what he likes, but does not hold what he does not like, he adheres not to the teaching of the Church as to an infallible rule, but to his own will." [1]

"The faith of the whole Church should be one, according to the precept (1 Corinthians i.10): *Let all speak the same thing, and let there be no schisms among you;* and this cannot be observed save on condition that questions which arise

---

[1] 2a 2æ, q. v. art. 3.

touching faith should be determined by him who presides over the whole Church, whose sentence must consequently be accepted without wavering. And hence to the sole authority of the supreme Pontiff does it pertain to publish a new revision of the Symbol,*as also to decree all other matters that concern the universal Church." [1]

In defining the limits of the obedience owed to the pastors of souls, but most of all to the authority of the Roman Pontiff, it must not be supposed that it is only to be yielded in relation to dogmas of which the obstinate denial cannot be disjoined from the crime of heresy. Nay, further, it is not enough sincerely and firmly to assent to doctrines which, though not defined by any solemn pronouncement of the Church, are by her proposed to belief, as divinely revealed, in her common and universal teaching, and which the Vatican Council declared are to be believed *with Catholic and divine faith.* But this likewise must be reckoned amongst the duties of Christians, that they allow themselves to be ruled and directed by the authority and leadership of bishops, and above all of the Apostolic See. And how fitting it is that this should be so any one can easily perceive. For the things contained in the divine oracles have reference to God in part, and in part to man, and to whatever is necessary for the attainment of his eternal salvation. Now, both these, that is to say, what we are bound to believe, and what we are obliged to do, are laid down, as we have stated, by the Church using her divine right, and in the Church by the supreme Pontiff. Wherefore it belongs to the Pope to judge authoritatively what things the sacred oracles contain, as well as what doctrines are in harmony, and what in disagreement, with them; and also for the same reason, to show forth what things are to be accepted as right, and what to be rejected as worthless; what it is necessary to do and what to avoid doing, in order to attain eternal salvation. For, otherwise, there would be no sure interpreter

*Symbol, i.e., the Creed.　　　[1]2a 2ae, q. i. art. 10

of the commands of God, nor would there be any safe guide showing man the way he should live.

In addition to what has been laid down, it is necessary to enter more fully into the nature of the Church. She is not an association of Christians brought together by chance, but is a divinely established and admirably constituted society, having for its direct and proximate purpose to lead the world to peace and holiness. And since the Church alone has, through the grace of God, received the means necessary to realize such end, she has her fixed laws, special spheres of action, and a certain method, fixed and conformable to her nature, of governing Christian peoples. But the exercise of such governing power is difficult, and leaves room for numberless conflicts, inasmuch as the Church rules peoples scattered through every portion of the earth, differing in race and customs, who, living under the sway of the laws of their respective countries, owe obedience alike to the civil and religious authorities. The duties enjoined are incumbent on the same persons, as already stated, and between them there exists neither contradiction nor confusion; for some of these duties have relation to the prosperity of the State, others refer to the general good of the Church, and both have as their object to train men to perfection.

The tracing out of these rights and duties being thus set forth, it is plainly evident that the governing powers are wholly free to carry out the business of the State; and this not only not against the wish of the Church, but manifestly with her co-operation, inasmuch as she strongly urges to the practice of piety, which implies right feeling towards God, and by that very fact inspires a right-mindedness towards the rulers in the State. The spiritual power, however, has a far loftier purpose, the Church directing her aim to govern the minds of men in the defending of the *kingdom of God, and His justice,*[1] a task she is wholly bent upon accomplishing.

[1] Matt. vi. 33.

No one can, however, without risk to faith, foster any doubt as to the Church alone having been invested with such power of governing souls as to exclude altogether the civil authority. In truth it was not to Cæsar but to Peter that Jesus Christ entrusted the keys of the kingdom of heaven. From this doctrine touching the relations of politics and religion originate important consequences which We cannot pass over in silence.

A notable difference exists between every kind of civil rule and that of the kingdom of Christ. If this latter bear a certain likeness and character to a civil kingdom, it is distinguished from it by its origin, principle, and essence. The Church, therefore, possesses the right to exist and to protect herself by institutions and laws in accordance with her nature. And since she not only is a perfect society in herself, but superior to every other society of human growth, she resolutely refuses, prompted alike by right and by duty, to link herself to any mere party and to subject herself to the fleeting exigencies of politics. On like grounds the Church, the guardian always of her own right and most observant of that of others, holds that it is not her province to decide which is the best amongst many diverse forms of government and the civil institutions of Christian States, and amid the various kinds of State rule she does not disapprove of any, provided the respect due to religion and the observance of good morals be upheld. By such standard of conduct should the thoughts and mode of acting of every Catholic be directed. There is no doubt but that in the sphere of politics ample matter may exist for legitimate difference of opinion, and that, the single reserve being made of the rights of justice and truth, all may strive to bring into actual working the ideas believed likely to be more conducive than others to the general welfare. But to attempt to involve the Church in party strife, and seek to bring her support to bear against those who take opposite views, is only worthy of partisans. Religion should, on the contrary, be accounted by every one as holy and inviolate; nay, in the public order itself of States—which cannot be severed from the laws influencing morals and from religious duties—it is always urgent, and indeed the main preoccupation, to take thought how best to consult the interests of Catholicism. Wherever these appear by reason of the efforts of adversaries to be in danger, all differences of opinion among Catholics should forthwith cease, so that, like thoughts and counsels prevailing, they may hasten to the aid of religion, the general and supreme good, to which all else should be referred. We think it well to treat this matter somewhat more in detail.

The Church alike and the State, doubtless, both possess individual sovereignty; hence, in the carrying out of public affairs, neither obeys the other within the limits to which each is restricted by its constitution. It does not hence follow, however, that Church and State are in any manner severed, and still less antagonistic. Nature, in fact, has given us not only physical existence, but moral life likewise. Hence, from the tranquillity of public order, whose immediate purpose is civil society, man expects that this may be able to secure all his needful well-being, and still more supply the sheltering care which perfects his moral life, which consists mainly in the knowledge and practice of virtue. He wishes moreover at the same time, as in duty bound, to find in the Church the aids necessary to his religious perfection, which consists in the knowledge and practice of the true religion; of that religion which is the queen of virtues, because in binding these to God it completes them all and perfects them. Therefore they who are engaged in framing constitutions and in enacting laws should bear in mind the moral and religious nature of man, and take care to help him, but in a right and orderly way, to gain perfection, neither enjoining nor forbidding anything save what is reasonably consistent with civil as well as with religious requirements. On this very account the Church cannot stand by, indifferent as to the import and significance of laws enacted by the State; not in so far indeed as they refer to the State, but in so far as, passing beyond their due limits, they trench upon the rights of the Church. From God has the duty been assigned to the Church not only to interpose resistance, if at any time the State rule should run counter to religion, but, further, to make a strong endeavor that the power of the Gospel may pervade the law and institutions of the nations. And inasmuch as the destiny of the State depends mainly on the disposition of those who are at the head of affairs, it follows that the Church cannot give countenance or favor to those whom she knows to be imbued with a spirit of hostility to her; who refuse openly to respect her rights; who make it their aim and purpose to tear asunder the alliance that should, by the very nature of things, connect the interests of religion with those of the State. On the contrary, she is (as she is bound to be) the upholder of those who are themselves imbued with the right way of thinking as to the relations between Church and State, and who strive to make them work in perfect accord for the common good. These precepts contain the abiding principle by which every Catholic should shape his conduct in regard to public life. In short, where the Church does not forbid taking part in public affairs, it is fit and proper to give support to men of acknowledged worth, and who pledge themselves to deserve well in the Catholic cause, and on no account may it be allowed to prefer to them any such individuals as are hostile to religion.

Whence it appears how urgent is the duty to maintain perfect union of minds, especially at these our times, when the Christian name is assailed with designs so concerted and subtle. All who have it at heart to attach themselves earnestly to the Church, which is *the pillar and ground of the truth*,[1] will easily steer clear of masters who

---

[1] 1 Tim. iii. 15.

are *lying and promising them liberty, when they themselves are slaves of corruption.*[1] Nay, more, having made themselves sharers in the divine virtue which resides in the Church, they will triumph over the craft of their adversaries by wisdom, and over their violence by courage. This is not now the time and place to inquire whether and how far the inertness and internal dissensions of Catholics have contributed to the present condition of things; but it is certain at least that the perverse-minded would exhibit less boldness, and would not have brought about such an accumulation of ills, if the faith *which worketh by charity*[2] had been generally more energetic and lively in the souls of men, and had there not been so universal a drifting away from the divinely established rule of morality throughout Christianity. May at least the lessons afforded by the memory of the past have the good result of leading to a wiser mode of acting in the future.

As to those who mean to take part in public affairs they should avoid with the very utmost care two criminal excesses: so-called prudence and false courage. Some there are, indeed, who maintain that it is not opportune boldly to attack evil-doing in its might and when in the ascendant, lest, as they say, opposition should exasperate minds already hostile. These make it a matter of guess-work as to whether they are for the Church or against her; since on the one hand they give themselves out as professing the Catholic faith, and yet wish that the Church should allow certain opinions, at variance with her teaching, to be spread abroad with impunity. They moan over the loss of faith and the perversion of morals, yet trouble themselves not to bring any remedy; nay, not seldom, even add to the intensity of the mischief through too much forbearance or harmful dissembling. These same individuals would not have any one entertain a doubt as to their good-will towards the Holy See; yet they have

[1] 2 Peter ii. 1, 19.   [2] Gal. v. 6.

always a something by way of reproach against the supreme Pontiff. The prudence of men of this cast is of that kind which is termed by the Apostle Paul *wisdom of the flesh* and *death* of the soul, *because it is not subject to the law of God, neither can it be.*[1] Nothing is less calculated to amend such ills than prudence of this kind. For the enemies of the Church have for their object—and they hesitate not to proclaim it, and many among them boast of it—to destroy outright, if possible, the Catholic religion, which is alone the true religion. With such a purpose in hand they shrink from nothing; for they are fully conscious that the more faint-hearted those who withstand them become, the more easy will it be to work out their wicked will. Therefore they who cherish the *prudence of the flesh* and who pretend to be unaware that every Christian ought to be a valiant soldier of Christ; they who would fain obtain the rewards owing to conquerors, while they are leading the lives of cowards, untouched in the fight, are so far from thwarting the onward march of the evil-disposed that, on the contrary, they even help it forward.

On the other hand, not a few, impelled by a false zeal, or—what is more blameworthy still—affecting sentiments which their conduct belies, take upon themselves to act a part which does not belong to them. They would fain see the Church's mode of action influenced by their ideas and their judgment to such an extent that everything done otherwise they take ill or accept with repugnance. Some, yet again, expend their energies in fruitless contention, being worthy of blame equally with the former. To act in such manner is not to follow lawful authority but to forestall it, and, unauthorized, assume the duties of the spiritual rulers, to the great detriment of the order which God established in His Church to be observed forever, and which He does not permit to be violated with impunity by any one, whoever he may be.

[1] The wisdom of the flesh is an enemy to God; for it is not subject to the law of God, neither can it be.—Rom. viii. 6, 7

Honor, then, to those who shrink not from entering the arena as often as need calls, believing and being convinced that the violence of injustice will be brought to an end and finally give way to the sanctity of right and religion! They truly seem invested with the dignity of time-honored virtue, since they are struggling to defend religion, and chiefly against the faction banded together to attack Christianity with extreme daring and without tiring, and to pursue with incessant hostility the Sovereign Pontiff, fallen into their power. But men of this high character maintain without wavering the love of obedience, nor are they wont to undertake anything upon their own authority. Now, since a like resolve to obey, combined with constancy and sturdy courage, is needful, so that whatever trials the pressure of events may bring about, they may be *deficient in nothing*,[1] We greatly desire to fix deep in the minds of each one that which Paul calls the *wisdom of the spirit*,[2] for in controlling human actions this wisdom follows the excellent rule of moderation, with the happy result that no one either timidly despairs through lack of courage or presumes over-much from want of prudence. There is, however, a difference between the political prudence that relates to the general good and that which concerns the good of individuals. This latter is shown forth in the case of private persons who obey the prompting of right reason in the direction of their own conduct; while the former is the characteristic of those who are set over others, and chiefly of rulers of the State, whose duty it is to exercise the power of command, so that the political prudence of private individuals would seem to consist wholly in carrying out faithfully the orders issued by lawful authority.[3]

[1] James i. 4.

[2] Rom. viii. 6.

[3] "Prudence proceeds from reason, and to reason it specially pertains to guide and govern. Whence it follows that insomuch as any one takes part in the control and government of affairs, in so far ought he to be gifted with reason and prudence. But it is

The like disposition and the same order should prevail in every Christian State by so much the more that the political prudence of the Pontiff embraces diverse and multiform things; for it is his charge not only to rule the Church, but generally so to regulate the actions of Christian citizens that these may be in apt conformity to their hope of gaining eternal salvation. Whence it is clear that in addition to the complete accordance of thought and deed, the faithful should imitate the practical political wisdom of the ecclesiastical authority. Now the administration of Christian affairs immediately under the Roman Pontiff appertains to the bishops, who, although they attain not to the summit of pontifical power, are nevertheless truly princes in the ecclesiastical hierarchy; and as each one of them administers a particular church, they are "as master-workers . . . in the spiritual edifice,"[1] and they have members of the clergy to share their duties and carry out their decisions. Every one has to regulate his mode of conduct according to this constitution of the Church, which it is not in the power of any man to change. Consequently, just as in the exercise of their episcopal authority the bishops ought to be united with the Apostolic See, so should the members of the clergy and the laity live in close union with their bishops. Among the prelates, indeed, one or other there may be affording scope to

evident that the subject, so far as subject, and the servant, so far as servant, ought neither to control nor govern, but rather to be controlled and governed. Prudence, then, is not the special virtue of the servant, so far as servant, nor of the subject, so far as subject. But because any man, on account of his character of a reasonable being, may have some share in the government according to the degree which reason determines, it is fitting that in such proportion he should possess the virtue of prudence. Whence it manifestly results that prudence exists in the ruler, as it exists in the architect with regard to the building he has to construct, just as is expressed in the sixth Book of Morals, and that it exists in the subject, as it exists in the workman employed in the construction."— St. Thomas, 2a 2æ, Q. ii. 2, 4, 7, art. 12.

[1] St. Thomas, Quodlib. 1, xiv.

criticism either in regard to personal conduct or in reference to opinions by him entertained about points of
doctrine; but no private person may arrogate to himself
the office of judge which Christ our Lord has bestowed on
that one alone whom He placed in charge of His lambs
and of His sheep. Let every one bear in mind that most
wise teaching of Gregory the Great: "Subjects should be
admonished not rashly to judge their prelates, even if they
chance to see them acting in a blameworthy manner, lest
reproving what is wrong, they be led by pride into greater
wrong. They are to be warned against the danger of
setting themselves up in audacious opposition to the
superiors whose shortcomings they may notice. Should,
therefore, the superiors really have committed grievous
sins, their inferiors, penetrated with the fear of God,
ought not to refuse them respectful submission. The
actions of superiors should not be smitten by the sword
of the word, even when they are rightly judged to have
deserved censure." [1]

However, all endeavors will avail but little unless our
life be regulated conformably with the discipline of the
Christian virtues. Let us call to mind what Holy Scripture records concerning the Jewish nation: *As long as they
sinned not in the sight of their God, it was well with them:
for their God hateth iniquity. And even . . . when they
had revolted from the way that God had given them to walk
therein, they were destroyed in battles by many nations.*[2]
Now the nation of the Jews bore an inchoate semblance to
the Christian people, and the vicissitudes of their history
in olden times have often foreshadowed the truth that was
to come, saving that God in His goodness has enriched
and loaded us with far greater benefits, and on this account
the sins of Christians are much greater, and bear the stamp
of more shameful and criminal ingratitude.

The Church, it is certain, at no time and in no particular is deserted by God; hence there is no reason why she

[1] Reg. Pastor. p. iii. cap. iv.   [2] Judith v 21, 22.

should be alarmed at the wickedness of men; but in the case of nations falling away from Christian virtue there is not a like ground of assurance, *for sin maketh nations miserable.*[1] If every bygone age has experienced the force of this truth, wherefore should not our own? There are in truth very many signs which proclaim that just punishments are already menacing, and the condition of modern States tends to confirm this belief, since we perceive many of them in sad plight from intestine disorders, and not one entirely exempt. But should those leagued together in wickedness hurry onward in the road they have boldly chosen, should they increase in influence and power in proportion as they make headway in their evil purposes and crafty schemes, there will be ground to fear lest the very foundations nature has laid for States to rest upon be utterly destroyed. Nor can such misgivings be removed by any mere human effort, especially as a vast number of men, having rejected the Christian faith, are on that account justly incurring the penalty of their pride, since blinded by their passions they search in vain for truth, laying hold on the false for the true, and thinking themselves wise when they call *evil good, and good evil,* and put *darkness in the place of light, and light in the place of darkness.*[2] It is therefore necessary that God come to the rescue, and that, mindful of His mercy, He turn an eye of compassion on human society. Hence, We renew the urgent entreaty We have already made, to redouble zeal and perseverance, when addressing humble supplications to our merciful God, so that the virtues whereby a Christian life is perfected may be reawakened. It is, however, urgent before all, that charity, which is the main foundation of the Christian life, and apart from which the other virtues exist not or remain barren, should be quickened and maintained. Therefore is it that the Apostle St. Paul, after having exhorted the Colossians to flee all vice and cultivate all virtue, adds: *Above all things*

[1] Prov. xiv. 34.   [2] Isa. v. 20.

have charity, which is the bond of perfection.[1] Yea, truly, charity is the bond of perfection, for it binds intimately to God those whom it has embraced and with loving tenderness, causes them to draw their life from God, to act with God, to refer all to God. Howbeit the love of God should not be severed from the love of our neighbor, since men have a share in the infinite goodness of God and bear in themselves the impress of His image and likeness. *This commandment we have from God, that he who loveth God, love also his brother.*[2] *If any man say I love God, and he hateth his brother, he is a liar.*[3] And this commandment concerning charity its divine proclaimer styled *new,* not in the sense that a previous law, or even nature itself, had not enjoined that men should love one another, but because the Christian precept of loving each other in that manner was truly new, and quite unheard of in the memory of man. For that love with which Jesus Christ is beloved by His Father and with which He Himself loves men, He obtained for His disciples and followers, that they might be of one heart and of one mind in Him by charity, as He Himself and His Father are one by their nature. No one is unaware how deeply and from the very beginning that precept has been implanted in the breast of Christians, and what abundant fruits of concord, mutual benevolence, piety, patience, and fortitude it has produced. Why, then, should we not devote ourselves to imitate the examples set by our fathers? The very times in which we live should afford sufficient motives for the practice of charity. Since impious men are bent on giving fresh impulse to their hatred against Jesus Christ, Christians should be quickened anew in piety; and charity, which is the inspirer of lofty deeds, should be imbued with new life. Let dissensions therefore, if there be any, wholly cease; let those strifes which waste the strength of those engaged in the fight, without any advantage resulting to religion, be scattered to the winds; let all minds be united in

[1] Coloss. iii. 14.   [2] 1 John iv. 21.   [3] Ibid. iv. 20.

faith and all hearts in charity, so that, as it behooves, life may be spent in the practice of the love of God and the love of men.

This is a suitable moment for us to exhort especially heads of families to govern their households according to these precepts, and to be solicitous without failing for the right training of their children. The family may be regarded as the cradle of civil society, and it is in great measure within the circle of family life that the destiny of the State is fostered. Whence it is that they who would break away from Christian discipline are working to corrupt family life, and to destroy it utterly, root and branch. From such an unholy purpose they allow not themselves to be turned aside by the reflection that it cannot, even in any degree, be carried out without inflicting cruel outrage on the parents. These hold from nature their right of training the children to whom they have given birth, with the obligation superadded of shaping and directing the education of their little ones to the end for which God vouchsafed the privilege of transmitting the gift of life. It is then incumbent on parents to strain every nerve to ward off such an outrage, and to strive manfully to have and to hold exclusive authority to direct the education of their offspring, as is fitting, in a Christian manner; and first and foremost to keep them away from schools where there is risk of their drinking in the poison of impiety. Where the right education of youth is concerned, no amount of trouble or labor can be undertaken, how great soever, but that even greater still may not be called for. In this regard indeed there are to be found in many countries Catholics worthy of general admiration, who incur considerable outlay and bestow much zeal in founding schools for the education of youth. It is highly desirable that such noble example may be generously followed, where time and circumstances demand; yet all should be intimately persuaded that the minds of children are most influenced by the training they receive at home.

If in their early years they find within the walls of their homes the rule of an upright life and the discipline of Christian virtues, the future welfare of the State will in great measure be guaranteed.

And now We seem to have touched upon those matters which Catholics ought chiefly nowadays to follow, or mainly to avoid. It rests with you, Venerable Brothers, to take measures that Our voice may reach everywhere, and that one and all may understand how urgent it is to reduce to practice the teachings set forth in this Our Letter. The observance of these duties cannot be troublesome or onerous, for the yoke of Jesus Christ is sweet, and His burden is light. If anything, however, appear too difficult of accomplishment, you will afford aid by the authority of your example, so that each one of the faithful may make more strenuous endeavor, and display a soul unconquered by difficulties. Bring it home to their minds, as We have ourselves oftentimes conveyed the warning, that matters of the highest moment and worthy of all honor are at stake, for the safeguarding of which every most toilsome effort should be readily endured; and that a sublime reward is in store for the labors of a Christian life. On the other hand, to refrain from doing battle for Jesus Christ, amounts to fighting against him; He Himself assures us *He will deny before His Father in Heaven, those who shall have refused to confess Him on earth.*[1] As for Ourselves and you all, never assuredly, so long as life lasts, shall We allow Our authority, Our counsels, and Our solicitude to be in any wise lacking in the conflict. Nor is it to be doubted but that especial aid of the great God will be vouchsafed, so long as the struggle endures, to the flock alike and to the pastors.

Sustained by this confidence, as a pledge of heavenly gifts, and of Our loving-kindness in the Lord to you, Venerable Brothers, to your clergy and to all your people, We accord the Apostolic Benediction.

[1] Luke ix. 26.

THE CONDITION OF THE WORKING CLASSES.

Encyclical Letter Rerum Novarum, May 15, 1891.

THAT the spirit of revolutionary change, which has long been disturbing the nations of the world, should have passed beyond the sphere of politics and made its influence felt in the cognate sphere of practical economics is not surprising. The elements of the conflict now raging are unmistakable in the vast expansion of industrial pursuits and the marvellous discoveries of science; in the changed relations between masters and workmen; in the enormous fortunes of some few individuals, and the utter poverty of the masses; in the increased self-reliance and closer mutual combination of the working classes; as also, finally, in the prevailing moral degeneracy. The momentous gravity of the state of things now obtaining fills every mind with painful apprehension; wise men are discussing it; practical men are proposing schemes; popular meetings, legislatures, and rulers of nations are all busied with it—and actually there is no question which has taken a deeper hold on the public mind.

Therefore, Venerable Brethren, as on former occasions when it seemed opportune to refute false teaching, We have addressed you in the interests of the Church and of the commonweal, and have issued Letters bearing on "Political Power," "Human Liberty," "The Christian Constitution of the State," and like matters, so have We thought it expedient now to speak on THE CONDITION OF THE WORKING CLASSES. It is a subject on which We have already touched more than once, incidentally. But in the present Letter, the responsibility of the Apostolic office urges us to treat the question of set purpose and in detail, in order that no misapprehension may exist as to the principles which truth and justice dictate for its settlement. The discussion is not easy, nor is it void of danger. It is no easy matter to define the relative rights and mutual duties of the rich and of the poor, of capital and of labor. And the danger lies in this, that crafty agitators are intent on making use of these differences of opinion to pervert men's judgments and to stir up the people to revolt.

But all agree, and there can be no question whatever, that some remedy must be found, and found quickly, for the misery and wretchedness pressing so heavily and unjustly at this moment on the vast majority of the working classes.

For the ancient workingmen's guilds were abolished in the last century, and no other organization took their place. Public institutions and the very laws have set aside the ancient religion. Hence by degrees it has come to pass that workingmen have been surrendered, all isolated and helpless, to the hard-heartedness of employers and the greed of unchecked competition. The mischief has been increased by rapacious usury, which, although more than once condemned by the Church, is nevertheless, under a different guise, but with the like injustice, still practised by covetous and grasping men. To this must be added the custom of working by contract, and the concentration of so many branches of trade in the hands of a few individuals; so that a small number of very rich men have been able to lay upon the teeming masses of the laboring poor a yoke little better than that of slavery itself.

To remedy these wrongs the Socialists, working on the poor man's envy of the rich, are striving to do away with private property, and contend that individual possessions should become the common property of all, to be administered by the State or by municipal bodies. They hold that by thus transferring property from private individuals to the community, the present mischievous state of things will be set to rights, inasmuch as each citizen will then get his fair share of whatever there is to enjoy.   But their contentions are so clearly powerless to end the controversy that were they carried into effect the workingman himself would be among the first to suffer.   They are, moreover, emphatically unjust, because they would rob the lawful possessor, bring State action into a sphere not within its competence, and create utter confusion in the community.

It is surely undeniable that, when a man engages in remunerative labor, the impelling reason and motive of his work is to obtain property, and thereafter to hold it as his very own.   If one man hires out to another his strength or skill, he does so for the purpose of receiving in return what is necessary for sustenance and education; he therefore expressly intends to acquire a right full and real, not only to the remuneration, but also to the disposal of such remuneration, just as he pleases.   Thus, if he lives sparingly, saves money, and, for greater security, invests his savings in land, the land, in such case, is only his wages under another form; and, consequently, a workingman's little estate thus purchased should be as completely at his full disposal as are the wages he receives for his labor.   But it is precisely in such power of disposal that ownership obtains, whether the property consist of land or chattels. Socialists, therefore, by endeavoring to transfer the possessions of individuals to the community at large, strike at the interests of every wage-earner, since they would deprive him of the liberty of disposing of his wages, and thereby of all hope and possibility of increasing his stock and of bettering his condition in life.

What is of far greater moment, however, is the fact that the remedy they propose is manifestly against justice.   For every man has by nature the right to possess property as his own.   This is one of the chief points of distinction between man and the animal creation, for the brute has no

power of self-direction, but is governed by two main instincts, which keep his powers on the alert, impel him to
develop them in a fitting manner, and stimulate and determine him to action without any power of choice. One of
these instincts is self-preservation, the other the propagation of the species. Both can attain their purpose by means
of things which lie within range; beyond their verge the
brute creation cannot go, for they are moved to action by
their senses only, and in the special direction which these
suggest. But with man it is wholly different. He possesses, on the one hand, the full perfection of the animal
being, and hence enjoys, at least as much as the rest of
the animal kind, the fruition of things material. But
animal nature, however perfect, is far from representing
the human being in its completeness, and is in truth but
humanity's humble handmaid, made to serve and to obey.
It is the mind, or reason, which is the predominant element
in us who are human creatures; it is this which renders a
human being human, and distinguishes him essentially
and generically from the brute. And on this very account
—that man alone among the animal creation is endowed
with reason—it must be within his right to possess things
not merely for temporary and momentary use, as other
living things do, but to have and to hold them in stable
and permanent possession; he must have not only things
that perish in the use of them, but those also which,
though they have been reduced into use, remain his
own for further use.

This becomes still more clearly evident if man's nature
be considered a little more deeply. For man, fathoming by
his faculty of reason matters without number, and linking
the future with the present, becoming, furthermore, by
taking enlightened forethought, master of his own acts,
guides his ways under the eternal law and the power of God,
whose providence governs all things. Wherefore it is in
his power to exercise his choice not only as to matters that
regard his present welfare, but also about those which he

deems may be for his advantage in time yet to come. Hence man not only can possess the fruits of the earth, but also the very soil, inasmuch as from the produce of the earth he has to lay by provision for the future.   Man's needs do not die out, but recur; although satisfied to-day they demand fresh supplies for to-morrow.   Nature accordingly owes to man a storehouse that shall never fail, affording the daily supply for his daily wants.   And this he finds solely in the inexhaustible fertility of the earth.

Neither do we, at this stage, need to bring into action the interference of the State.   Man precedes the State, and possesses, prior to the formation of any State, the right of providing for the sustenance of his body.   Now to affirm that God has given the earth for the use and enjoyment of the whole human race is not to deny that private property is lawful.   For God has granted the earth to mankind in general, not in the sense that all without distinction can deal with it as they like, but rather that no part of it has been assigned to any one in particular, and that the limits of private possession have been left to be fixed by man's own industry, and by the laws of individual races.   Moreover, the earth, even though apportioned among private owners, ceases not thereby to minister to the needs of all, inasmuch as there is no one who does not sustain life from what the land produces.   Those who do not possess the soil, contribute their labor; hence it may truly be said that all human subsistence is derived either from labor on one's own land, or from some toil, some calling which is paid for either in the produce of the land itself, or in that which is exchanged for what the land brings forth.

Here, again, we have further proof that private owner-ship is in accordance with the law of nature.   Truly, that which is required for the preservation of life, and for life's well-being, is produced in great abundance from the soil, but not until man has brought it into cultivation and expended upon it his solicitude and skill.   Now, when man thus turns the activity of his mind and the strength of his body towards procuring the fruits of nature, by such act he makes his own that portion of nature's field which he cultivates—that portion on which he leaves, as it were, the impress of his individuality; and it cannot but be just that he should possess that portion as his very own, and have a right to hold it without any one being justified in violating that right.

So strong and convincing are these arguments, that it seems amazing that some should now be setting up anew certain obsolete opinions in opposition to what is here laid down. They assert that it is right for private persons to have the use of the soil and its various fruits, but that it is unjust for any one to possess outright either the land on which he has built, or the estate which he has brought under cultivation. But those who deny these rights do not perceive that they are defrauding man of what his own labor has produced. For the soil which is tilled and cultivated with toil and skill utterly changes its conditions: it was wild before, now it is fruitful; was barren, but now brings forth in abundance. That which has thus altered and improved the land becomes so truly part of itself as to be in great measure indistinguishable and inseparable from it. Is it just that the fruit of a man's own sweat and labor should be possessed and enjoyed by any one else? As effects follow their cause, so is it just and right that the results of labor should belong to those who have bestowed their labor.

With reason, then, the common opinion of mankind, little affected by the few dissentients who have contended for the opposite view, has found in the careful study of nature, and in the laws of nature, the foundations of the division of property, and the practice of all ages has consecrated the principle of private ownership, as being pre-eminently in conformity with human nature, and as conducing in the most unmistakable manner to the peace and tranquillity of human existence. The same principle is confirmed and enforced by the civil laws—laws which, so long as they are just, derive from the law of nature their binding force. The authority of the divine law adds its sanction, forbidding us in severest terms even to covet that which is another's:—*Thou shalt not covet thy neighbor's wife; nor his house, nor his field, nor his man-servant, nor his maid-servant, nor his ox, nor his ass, nor anything which is his.*[1]

The rights here spoken of, belonging to each individual man, are seen in much stronger light when considered in relation to man's social and domestic obligations. In choosing a state of life, it is indisputable that all are at full liberty to follow the counsel of Jesus Christ as to observing virginity, or to bind themselves by the marriage tie. No human law can abolish the natural and original right of marriage, nor in any way limit the chief and principal purpose of marriage, ordained by God's authority from the beginning. *Increase and multiply.*[2] Hence we have the family; the "society" of a man's house— a society limited indeed in numbers, but no less a true "society," anterior to every kind of State or nation, invested with rights and duties of its own, totally independent of the civil community.

That right of property, therefore, which has been proved to belong naturally to individual persons, must in like wise belong to a man in his capacity of head of a family; nay, such person must possess this right so much the more clearly in proportion as his position multiplies his duties. For it is a most sacred law of nature that a father should provide food and all necessaries for those whom he has begotten; and, similarly, nature dictates that a man's children, who carry on, so to speak, and continue his own personality, should be by him provided with all that is needful to enable them to keep themselves honorably from want and misery amid the uncertainties of this mortal life. Now in no other way can a father effect this except

[1] Deuteronomy v. 21.   [2] Genesis i. 28.

by the ownership of lucrative property, which he can transmit to his children by inheritance. A family, no less than a State, is, as we have said, a true society, governed by a power within its sphere, that is to say, by the father. Provided, therefore, the limits which are prescribed by the very purposes for which it exists be not trangressed, the family has at least equal rights with the State in the choice and pursuit of the things needful to its preservation and its just liberty.

We say, at least equal rights; for inasmuch as the domestic household is antecedent, as well in idea as in fact, to the gathering of men into a community, the family must necessarily have rights and duties which are prior to those of the Community, and founded more immediately in nature. If the citizens of a State—in other words the families—on entering into association and fellowship, were to experience at the hands of the State hindrance instead of help, and were to find their rights attacked instead of being upheld, such association should be held in detestation, rather than be an object of desire.

The contention, then, that the civil government should at its option intrude into and exercise intimate control over the family and the household, is a great and pernicious error. True, if a family finds itself in exceeding distress, utterly deprived of the counsel of friends, and without any prospect of extricating itself, it is right that extreme necessity be met by public aid, since each family is a part of the commonwealth. In like manner, if within the precincts of the household there occur grave disturbance of mutual rights, public authority should intervene to force each party to yield to the other its proper due; for this is not to deprive citizens of their rights, but justly and properly to safeguard and strengthen them. But the rulers of the State must go no further: here nature bids them stop. Paternal authority can be neither abolished nor absorbed by the State; for it has the same source as human life itself. "The child belongs to the father," and is, as it were, the continuation of the father's personality; and, speaking strictly, the child takes its place in civil society, not of its own right, but in its quality as member of the family in which it is born. And for the very reason that "the child belongs to the father," it is, as St. Thomas of Aquin says, "before it attains the use of free-will, under power and charge of its parents." [1] The Socialists, therefore, in setting aside the parent and setting up a State supervision, act *against natural justice,* and break into pieces the stability of all family life.

And not only is such interference unjust, but it is quite certain to harass and worry all classes of citizens, and subject them to odious and intolerable bondage. It would throw open the door to envy, to mutual invective, and to discord; the sources of wealth themselves would run dry, for no one would have any interest in exerting his talents or his industry; and that ideal equality about which they entertain pleasant dreams would be in reality the levelling down of all to a like condition of misery and degradation.

Hence it is clear that the main tenet of Socialism, community of goods, must be utterly rejected, since it only injures those whom it would seem meant to benefit, is directly contrary to the natural rights of mankind, and would introduce confusion and disorder into the commonweal. The first and most fundamental principle, therefore, if one would undertake to alleviate the condition of the masses, must be the inviolability of private property. This being established, we proceed to show where the remedy sought for must be found.

We approach the subject with confidence, and in the exercise of the rights which manifestly appertain to us, for no practical solution of this question will be found apart from the intervention of Religion and of the Church. It is We who are the chief guardian of Religion and the chief dispenser of what pertains to the Church, and We must

[1] St. Thomas, Summa Theologica, 2a 2æ Q. x. Art. 12.

not by silence neglect the duty incumbent on Us. Doubt-less this most serious question demands the attention and the efforts of others besides ourselves—to wit, of the rulers of States, of employers of labor, of the wealthy, aye, of the working classes themselves, for whom We are pleading. But We affirm without hesitation that all the striving of men will be vain if they leave out the Church. It is the Church that insists, on the authority of the Gospel, upon those teachings whereby the conflict can be brought to an end, or rendered, at least, far less bitter; the Church uses her efforts not only to enlighten the mind but to direct by her precepts the life and conduct of each and all; the Church improves and betters the condition of the workingman by means of numerous useful organizations; does her best to enlist the services of all ranks in discussing and endeavoring to meet, in the most practical way, the claims of the working classes; and acts from the positive view that for these purposes recourse should be had, in due measure and degree, to the intervention of the law and of State authority.

Let it, then, be taken as granted, in the first place, that the condition of things human must be endured, for it is impossible to reduce civil society to one dead level. Socialists may in that intent do their utmost, but all striving against nature is in vain. There naturally exist among mankind manifold differences of the most important kind; people differ in capacity, skill, health, strength; and unequal fortune is a necessary result of unequal condition. Such inequality is far from being disadvantageous either to individuals or to the community. Social and public life can only be maintained by means of various kinds of capacity for business and the playing of many parts; and each man, as a rule, chooses the part which suits his own peculiar domestic condition. As regards bodily labor, even had man never fallen from *the state of innocence*, he would not have remained wholly unoccupied; but that which would then have been his free choice and his delight became afterwards compulsory, and the painful expiation for his disobedience. *Cursed be the earth in thy work; in thy labor thou shalt eat of it all the days of thy life.*[1]   In like manner, the other pains and hardships of life will have no end or cessation on earth; for the consequences of sin are bitter and hard to bear, and they must accompany man so long as life lasts.   To suffer and to endure, therefore, is the lot of humanity; let them strive as they may, no strength and no artifice will ever succeed in banishing from human life the ills and troubles which beset it.   If any there are who pretend differently— who hold out to a hard-pressed people the boon of freedom from pain and trouble, an undisturbed repose, and constant enjoyment—they delude the people and impose upon them, and their lying promises will only one day bring forth evils worse than the present.   Nothing is more useful than to look upon the world as it really is— and at the same time to seek elsewhere, as we have said, for the solace to its troubles.

The great mistake made in regard to the matter now under consideration is to take up with the notion that class is naturally hostile to class, and that the wealthy and the workingmen are intended by nature to live in mutual conflict.   So irrational and so false is this view, that the direct contrary is the truth.   Just as the symmetry of the human frame is the resultant of the disposition of the bodily members, so in a State is it ordained by nature that these two classes should dwell in harmony and agreement, and should, as it were, groove into one another, so as to maintain the balance of the body politic.   Each needs the other: Capital cannot do without Labor, nor Labor without Capital.   Mutual agreement results in pleasantness of life and the beauty of good order; while perpetual conflict necessarily produces confusion and savage barbarity.   Now, in preventing such strife as this, and in uprooting it, the efficacy

---

[1] Genesis iii. 17.

of Christian institutions is marvellous and manifold. First of all, there is no intermediary more powerful than Religion (whereof the Church is the interpreter and guardian) in drawing the rich, and the poor bread-winners, together, by reminding each class of its duties to the other, and especially of the obligations of justice. Thus Religion teaches the laboring man and the artisan to carry out honestly and fairly all equitable agreements freely entered into; never to injure the property, nor to outrage the person, of an employer; never to resort to violence in defending their own cause, nor to engage in riot or disorder; and to have nothing to do with men of evil principles, who work upon the people with artful promises, and excite foolish hopes which usually end in useless regrets, followed by insolvency. Religion teaches the wealthy owner and the employer that their work-people are not to be accounted their bondsmen; that in every man they must respect his dignity and worth as a man and as a Christian; that labor is not a thing to be ashamed of, if we lend ear to right reason and to Christian philosophy, but is an honorable calling, enabling a man to sustain his life in a way upright and creditable; and that it is shameful and inhuman to treat men like chattels to make money by, or to look upon them merely as so much muscle or physical power. Again, therefore, the Church teaches that, as Religion and things spiritual and mental are among the workingman's main concerns, the employer is bound to see that the worker has time for his religious duties; that he be not exposed to corrupting influences and dangerous occasions; and that he be not led away to neglect his home and family, or to squander his earnings. Furthermore, the employer must never tax his work-people beyond their strength, or employ them in work unsuited to their sex or age. His great and principal duty is to give every one a fair wage. Doubtless, before deciding whether wages are adequate, many things have to be considered; but wealthy owners and all masters of labor should be mindful of this—that to exercise pressure upon the indigent and the destitute for the sake of gain, and to gather one's profit out of the need of another, is condemned by all laws, human and divine. To defraud any one of wages that are his due is a crime which cries to the avenging anger of Heaven. *Behold, the hire of the laborers . . . which by fraud hath been kept back by you, crieth aloud; and the cry of them hath entered into the ears of the Lord of Sabaoth.*[1] Lastly, the rich must religiously refrain from cutting down the workmen's earnings, whether by force, by fraud, or by usurious dealing; and with all the greater reason because the laboring man is, as a rule, weak and unprotected, and because his slender means should in proportion to their scantiness be accounted sacred.

Were these precepts carefully obeyed and followed out, would they not be sufficient of themselves to keep under all strife and all its causes?

But the Church, with Jesus Christ as her Master and Guide, aims higher still. She lays down precepts yet more perfect, and tries to bind class to class in friendliness and good feeling. The things of earth cannot be understood or valued aright without taking into consideration the life to come, the life that will know no death. Exclude the idea of futurity, and forthwith the very notion of what is good and right would perish; nay, the whole scheme of the universe would become a dark and unfathomable mystery. The great truth which we learn from Nature herself is also the grand Christian dogma on which Religion rests as on its foundation—that when we have given up this present life, then shall we really begin to live. God has not created us for the perishable and transitory things of earth, but for things heavenly and everlasting; He has given us this world as a place of exile, and not as our abiding-place. As for riches and the other things which men call good and desirable, whether we have them in abundance, or lack them altogether—so far as eternal

[1] St. James v. 4.

happiness is concerned—it matters little; the only important thing is to use them aright. Jesus Christ, when He redeemed us with *plentiful redemption*, took not away the pains and sorrows which in such large proportion are woven together in the web of our mortal life. He transformed them into motives of virtue and occasions of merit: and no man can hope for eternal reward unless he follow in the blood-stained footprints of his Saviour. *If we suffer with Him, we shall also reign with Him.* [1] Christ's labors and sufferings, accepted of His own free-will, have marvellously sweetened all suffering and all labor. And not only by His example, but by His grace and by the hope held forth of everlasting recompense, has He made pain and grief more easy to endure; *for that which is at present momentary and light of our tribulation, worketh for us above measure exceedingly an eternal weight of glory.* [2]

Therefore those whom fortune favors are warned that freedom from sorrow and abundance of earthly riches are no warrant for the bliss that shall never end, but rather are obstacles; [3] that the rich should tremble at the threatenings of Jesus Christ—threatenings so unwonted in the mouth of Our Lord [4]—and that a most strict account must be given to the Supreme Judge for all we possess. The chief and most excellent rule for the right use of money is one which the heathen philosophers hinted at, but which the Church has traced out clearly, and has not only made known to men's minds, but has impressed upon their lives. It rests on the principle that it is one thing to have a right to the possession of money, and another to have a right to use money as one wills. Private ownership, as we have seen, is the natural right of man; and to exercise that right, especially as members of society, is not only lawful, but absolutely necessary. "It is lawful," says St. Thomas of Aquin, "for a man to hold private property; and it is also necessary for the carrying on of

---

[1] 2 Tim. ii. 12.
[2] 2 Cor. iv. 17.
[3] St. Matt. xix. 23, 24.
[4] St. Luke vi. 24, 25.

human existence." [1]　But if the question be asked, How must one's possessions be used? the Church replies without hesitation in the words of the same holy Doctor: "Man should not consider his outward possessions as his own, but as common to all, so as to share them without hesitation when others are in need. Whence the Apostle saith, Command the rich of this world . . . to offer with no stint, to apportion largely." [2]　True, no one is commanded to distribute to others that which is required for his own needs and those of his household; nor even to give away what is reasonably required to keep up becomingly his condition in life; "for no one ought to live other than becomingly." [3]　But when what necessity demands has been supplied, and one's standing fairly taken thought for, it becomes a duty to give to the indigent out of what remains over. *Of that which remaineth, give alms.*[4]　It is a duty, not of justice (save in extreme cases), but of Christian charity—a duty not enforced by human law. But the laws and judgments of men must yield place to the laws and judgments of Christ the true God, who in many ways urges on His followers the practice of almsgiving—*It is more blessed to give than to receive;*[5]　and who will count a kindness done or refused to the poor as done or refused to Himself—*As long as you did it to one of My least brethren, you did it to Me.*[6]　To sum up, then, what has been said: Whoever has received from the divine bounty a large share of temporal blessings, whether they be external and corporeal, or gifts of the mind, has received them for the purpose of using them for the perfecting of his own nature, and, at the same time, that he may employ them, as the steward of God's providence, for the benefit of others. "He that hath a talent," says St. Gregory the Great, "let him see that he hide it not; he that hath abundance, let him quicken himself to mercy and generosity; he that hath

---

[1] 2a 2æ Q. lxvi. Art. 2.
[2] Ibid. Q. lxv. Art. 2.
[3] Ibid. Q. xxxii. Art. 6.
[4] St. Luke xi. 41.
[5] Acts xx. 35.
[6] St. Matt. xxv. 40.

art and skill, let him do his best to share the use and the utility thereof with his neighbor." [1]

As for those who possess not the gifts of fortune, they are taught by the Church that in God's sight poverty is no disgrace, and that there is nothing to be ashamed of in seeking one's bread by labor. This is enforced by what we see in Christ Himself, who *whereas He was rich, for our sakes became poor;* [2] and who, being the Son of God, and God Himself, chose to seem and to be considered the son of a carpenter—nay, did not disdain to spend a great part of His life as a carpenter Himself. *Is not this the carpenter, the son of Mary?* [3] From contemplation of this divine exemplar, it is more easy to understand that the true worth and nobility of man lies in his moral qualities, that is, in virtue; that virtue is moreover the common inheritance of men, equally within the reach of high and low, rich and poor; and that virtue, and virtue alone, wherever found, will be followed by the rewards of everlasting happiness. Nay, God Himself seems to incline rather to those who suffer misfortune; for Jesus Christ calls the poor "blessed"; [4] He lovingly invites those in labor and grief to come to Him for solace; [5] and He displays the tenderest charity towards the lowly and the oppressed. These reflections cannot fail to keep down the pride of those who are well to do, and to embolden the spirit of the afflicted; to incline the former to generosity and the latter to meek resignation. Thus the separation which pride would set up tends to disappear, nor will it be difficult to make rich and poor join hands in friendly concord.

But, if Christian precepts prevail, the respective classes

---

[1] St. Gregory the Great, Hom. ix. in Evangel. n. 7.

[2] 2 Cor. viii. 9

[3] St. Mark vi. 3.

[4] St. Matt. v. 3: Blessed are the poor in spirit.

[5] St. Matt. xi. 28: Come to Me all you that labor and are burdened, and I will refresh you.

will not only be united in the bonds of friendship, but also in those of brotherly love. For they will understand and feel that all men are children of the same common Father, who is God; that all have alike the same last end, which is God Himself, who alone can make either men or angels absolutely and perfectly happy; that each and all are redeemed and made sons of God, by Jesus Christ, *the first-born among many brethren;* that the blessings of nature and the gifts of grace belong to the whole human race in common, and that from none except the unworthy is withheld the inheritance of the kingdom of heaven. *If sons, heirs also; heirs indeed of God, and co-heirs of Christ.*[1]

Such is the scheme of duties and of rights which is shown forth to the world by the Gospel. Would it not seem that, were society penetrated with ideas like these, strife must quickly cease?

But the Church, not content with pointing out the remedy, also applies it. For the Church does her utmost to teach and to train men, and to educate them; and by the intermediary of her bishops and clergy diffuses her salutary teachings far and wide. She strives to influence the mind and the heart so that all may willingly yield themselves to be formed and guided by the commandments of God. It is precisely in this fundamental and momentous matter, on which everything depends, that the Church possesses a power peculiarly her own. The agencies which she employs are given to her by Jesus Christ Himself for the very purpose of reaching the hearts of men, and derive their efficiency from God. They alone can reach the innermost heart and conscience, and bring men to act from a motive of duty, to resist their passions and appetites, to love God and their fellow-men with a love that is singular and supreme, and to break down courageously every barrier which impedes the way of a life of virtue.

[1] Rom. viii. 17.

On this subject we need but recall for one moment the examples recorded in history. Of these facts there cannot be any shadow of doubt: for instance, that civil society was renovated in every part by the teachings of Christianity; that in the strength of that renewal the human race was lifted up to better things—nay, that it was brought back from death to life, and to so excellent a life that nothing more perfect had been known before, or will come to be known in the ages that have yet to be. Of this beneficent transformation Jesus Christ was at once the First Cause and the final end; as from Him all came, so to Him was all to be brought back. For when the human race, by the light of the Gospel message, came to know the grand mystery of the Incarnation of the Word and the redemption of man, at once the life of Jesus Christ, God and Man, pervaded every race and nation, and interpenetrated them with His faith, His precepts and His laws. And if society is to be healed now, in no other way can it be healed save by a return to Christian life and Christian institutions. When a society is perishing, the wholesome advice to give to those who would restore it is to recall it to the principles from which it sprang; for the purpose and perfection of an association is to aim at and to attain that for which it was formed; and its efforts should be put in motion and inspired by the end and object which originally gave it being. Hence to fall away from its primal constitution implies disease; to go back to it, recovery. And this may be asserted with utmost truth both of the State in general and of that body of its citizens—by far the great majority—who sustain life by their labor.

Neither must it be supposed that the solicitude of the Church is so preoccupied with the spiritual concerns of her children as to neglect their temporal and earthly interests. Her desire is that the poor, for example, should rise above poverty and wretchedness, and better their condition in life; and for this she makes a strong endeavor. By the very fact that she calls men to virtue and forms them to its practice, she promotes this in no slight degree. Christian morality, when adequately and completely practised, leads of itself to temporal prosperity, for it merits the blessing of that God who is the source of all blessings; it powerfully restrains the greed of possession and the thirst for pleasure—twin plagues, which too often make a man who is void of self-restraint miserable in the midst of abundance;[1] it makes men supply for the lack of means through economy, teaching them to be content with frugal living, and further, keeping them out of the reach of those vices which devour not small incomes merely, but large fortunes, and dissipate many a goodly inheritance.

The Church, moreover, intervenes directly in behalf of the poor by setting on foot and maintaining many associations which she knows to be efficient for the relief of poverty. Herein again she has always succeeded so well as to have even extorted the praise of her enemies. Such was the ardor of brotherly love among the earliest Christians that numbers of those who were in better circumstances despoiled themselves of their possessions in order to relieve their brethren; whence *neither was there any one needy among them.*[2] To the order of Deacons, instituted in that very intent, was committed by the apostles the charge of the daily doles; and the Apostle Paul, though burdened with the solicitude of all the churches, hesitated not to undertake laborious journeys in order to carry the alms of the faithful to the poorer Christians. Tertullian calls these contributions, given voluntarily by Christians in their assemblies, deposits of piety; because, to cite his own words, they were employed "in feeding the needy, in burying them, in the support of youths and maidens destitute of means and deprived of their parents, in the care of the aged, and the relief of the shipwrecked."[3]

Thus by degrees came into existence the patrimony

[1] The desire of money is the root of all evils.—1 Tim. vi. 10.
[2] Acts iv. 34.
[3] Apologia Secunda, xxxix.

which the Church has guarded with religious care as the inheritance of the poor. Nay, to spare them the shame of begging, the common mother of rich and poor has exerted herself to gather together funds for the support of the needy. The Church has aroused everywhere the heroism of charity, and has established congregations of religious and many other useful institutions for help and mercy, so that hardly any kind of suffering could exist which was not afforded relief. At the present day many there are who, like the heathen of old, seek to blame and condemn the Church for such eminent charity. They would substitute in its stead a system of relief organized by the State. But no human expedients will ever make up for the devotedness and self-sacrifice of Christian charity. Charity, as a virtue, pertains to the Church; for virtue it is not, unless it be drawn from the Sacred Heart of Jesus Christ; and whosoever turns his back on the Church cannot be near to Christ.

It cannot, however, be doubted that to attain the purpose we are treating of, not only the Church but all human agencies must concur. All who are concerned in the matter should be of one mind and according to their ability act together. It is with this, as with the Providence that governs the world: the results of causes do not usually take place save where all the causes co-operate.

It is sufficient, therefore, to inquire what part the State should play in the work of remedy and relief.

By the State we here understand, not the particular form of government prevailing in this or that nation, but the State as rightly apprehended; that is to say, any government conformable in its institutions to right reason and natural law, and to those dictates of the divine wisdom which we have expounded in the Encyclical on "The Christian Constitution of the State." The foremost duty, therefore, of the rulers of the State should be to make sure that the laws and institutions, the general character and administration of the commonwealth, shall be such as of themselves to realize public well-being and private pros-

perity.   This is the proper scope of wise statesmanship
and is the work of the heads of the State.   Now, a State
chiefly prospers and thrives through moral rule, well-
regulated family life, respect for religion and justice, the
moderation and equal allocation of public taxes, the progress of the arts and of trade, the abundant yield of the
land—through everything, in fact, which makes the citizens better and happier.   Hereby, then, it lies in the power
of a ruler to benefit every class in the State, and amongst
the rest to promote to the utmost the interests of the poor;
and this in virtue of his office, and without being open to
any suspicion of undue interference—since it is the province of the State to consult the common good.   And
the more that is done for the benefit of the working classes
by the general laws of the country, the less need will there
be to seek for special means to relieve them.

There is another and deeper consideration which must
not be lost sight of.   As regards the State, the interests
of all, whether high or low, are equal.   The poor are
members of the national community equally with the
rich; they are real component living members which
constitute, through the family, the living body; and it
need hardly be said that they are in every State very largely
in the majority. It would be irrational to neglect one portion of the citizens and favor another; and, therefore, the
public administration must duly and solicitously provide
for the welfare and the comfort of the working classes;
otherwise that law of justice will be violated which ordains
that each man shall have his due.   To cite the wise words
of St. Thomas of Aquin: "As the part and the whole
are in a certain sense identical, the part may in some
sense claim what belongs to the whole." [1]   Among the
many and grave duties of rulers who would do their best for
the people, the first and chief is to act with strict justice—
with that justice which is called by the schoolmen *distrib-
utive*—towards each and every class alike.

[1] 2a 2æ Q. lxi.   Art. 1 ad 2.

But although all citizens, without exception, can and ought to contribute to that common good in which individuals share so advantageously to themselves, yet it should not be supposed that all can contribute in the like way and to the same extent. No matter what changes may occur in forms of government, there will ever be differences and inequalities of condition in the State. Society cannot exist or be conceived of without them. Some there must be who devote themselves to the work of the commonwealth, who make the laws or administer justice, or whose advice and authority govern the nation in times of peace and defend it in war. Such men clearly occupy the foremost place in the State, and should be held in highest estimation, for their work concerns most nearly and effectively the general interests of the community. Those who labor at a trade or calling do not promote the general welfare in such measure as this; but they benefit the nation, if less directly, in a most important manner. Still we have insisted that, since the end of society is to make men better, the chief good that society can possess is virtue. Nevertheless, in all well-constituted States it is in no wise a matter of small moment to provide those bodily and external commodities *the use of which is necessary to virtuous action.* [1] And in order to provide such material well-being, the labor of the poor— the exercise of their skill, and the employment of their strength, in the culture of the land and in the workshops of trade—is of great account and quite indispensable. Indeed, their co-operation is in this respect so important that it may be truly said that it is only by the labor of workingmen that States grow rich. Justice, therefore, demands that the interests of the poorer classes should be carefully watched over by the administration, so that they who contribute so largely to the advantage of the community may themselves share in the benefits which

[1] St. Thomas of Aquin, De Regimine Principum, i. 15.

they create—that being housed, clothed, and enabled to sustain life, they may find their existence less hard and more endurable. It follows that whatever shall appear to prove conducive to the well-being of those who work should obtain favorable consideration. Let it not be feared that solicitude of this kind will be harmful to any interest; on the contrary, it will be to the advantage of all; for it cannot but be good for the commonwealth to shield from misery those on whom it so largely depends.

We have said that the State must not absorb the individual or the family; both should be allowed free and untrammelled action so far as is consistent with the common good and the interests of others. Rulers should, nevertheless, anxiously safeguard the community and all its members: the community, because the conservation thereof is so emphatically the business of the supreme power that the safety of the commonwealth is not only the first law, but it is a government's whole reason of existence; and the members, because both philosophy and the Gospel concur in laying down that the object of the government of the State should be, not the advantage of the ruler, but the benefit of those over whom he is placed. The gift of authority derives from God, and is, as it were, a participation in the highest of all sovereignties; and should be exercised as the power of God is exercised— with a fatherly solicitude which not only guides the whole but reaches also to details.

Whenever the general interest or any particular class suffers, or is threatened with mischief which can in no other way be met or prevented, the public authority must step in to deal with it. Now, it interests the public, as well as the individual, that peace and good order should be maintained; that family life should be carried on in accordance with God's laws and those of nature; that religion should be reverenced and obeyed; that a high standard of morality should prevail, both in public and private life; that the sanctity of justice should be respected, and that no one should injure another with impunity; that the members of the commonwealth should grow up to man's estate strong and robust, and capable, if need be, of guarding and defending their country. If by a strike, or other combination of workmen, there should be imminent danger of disturbance to the public peace; or if circumstances were such as that among the laboring population the ties of family life were relaxed; if religion were found to suffer through the operatives not having time and opportunity afforded them to practise its duties; if in workshops and factories there were danger to morals through the mixing of the sexes or from other harmful occasions of evil; or if employers laid burdens upon their workmen which were unjust, or degraded them with conditions repugnant to their dignity as human beings; finally, if health were endangered by excessive labor, or by work unsuited to sex or age—in such cases, there can be no question but that, within certain limits, it would be right to invoke the aid and authority of the law. The limits must be determined by the nature of the occasion which calls for the law's interference—the principle being that the law must not undertake more, nor proceed further, than is required for the remedy of the evil or the removal of the mischief.

Rights must be religiously respected wherever they exist; and it is the duty of the public authority to prevent and to punish injury, and to protect every one in the possession of his own. Still, when there is a question of defending the rights of individuals, the poor and helpless have a claim to especial consideration. The richer class have many ways of shielding themselves, and stand less in need of help from the State; whereas those who are badly off have no resources of their own to fall back upon, and must chiefly depend upon the assistance of the State. And it is for this reason that wage-earners, who are undoubtedly among the weak and necessitous, should be specially cared for and protected by the Government.

Here, however, it is expedient to bring under special notice certain matters of moment. It should ever be borne in mind that the chief thing to be realized is the safeguarding of private property by legal enactment and public policy. Most of all it is essential, amid such a fever of excitement, to keep the multitude within the line of duty; for if all may justly strive to better their condition, neither justice nor the common good allows any individual to seize upon that which belongs to another, or, under the futile and shallow pretext of equality, to lay violent hands on other people's possessions. Most true it is that by far the larger part of the workers prefer to better themselves by honest labor rather than by doing any wrong to others. But there are not a few who are imbued with evil principles and eager for revolutionary change, whose main purpose is to stir up tumult and bring about measures of violence. The authority of the State should intervene to put restraint upon such firebrands, to save the working classes from their seditious arts, and protect lawful owners from spoliation.

When working men have recourse to a strike, it is frequently because the hours of labor are too long, or the work too hard, or because they consider their wages insufficient. The grave inconvenience of this not uncommon occurrence should be obviated by public remedial measures; for such paralyzing of labor not only affects the masters and their work-people alike, but is extremely injurious to trade and to the general interests of the public; moreover, on such occasions, violence and disorder are generally not far distant, and thus it frequently happens that the public peace is imperilled. The laws should forestall and prevent such troubles from arising; they should lend their influence and authority to the removal in good time of the causes which lead to conflicts between employers and employed.

But if owners of property should be made secure, the workingman, in like manner, has property and belongings

in respect to which he should be protected; and foremost
of all, his soul and mind. Life on earth, however good
and desirable in itself, is not the final purpose for which
man is created; it is only the way and the means to that
attainment of truth and that practice of goodness in
which the full life of the soul consists. It is the soul
which is made after the image and likeness of God; it is
in the soul that the sovereignty resides in virtue whereof
man is commanded to rule the creatures below him and
to use all the earth and the ocean for his profit and advantage. *Fill the earth and subdue it; and rule over the fishes
of the sea, and the fowls of the air, and all living creatures
which move upon the earth.*[1] In this respect all men are
equal; there is no difference between rich and poor,
master and servant, ruler and ruled, *for the same is Lord
over all.*[2] No man may with impunity outrage that
human dignity which God Himself treats *with reverence,*
nor stand in the way of that higher life which is the preparation for the eternal life of heaven. Nay, more: no man
has in this matter power over himself. To consent to any
treatment which is calculated to defeat the end and
purpose of his being is beyond his right; he cannot give
up his soul to servitude; for it is not man's own rights
which are here in question, but the rights of God, the
most sacred and inviolable of rights.

From this follows the obligation of the cessation from
work and labor on Sundays and certain holy days. The
rest from labor is not to be understood as mere giving
way to idleness; much less must it be an occasion for
spending money and for vicious indulgence, as many
would have it to be; but it should be rest from labor,
hallowed by religion. Rest (combined with religious observances), disposes man to forget for a while the business of
his every-day life, to turn his thoughts to things heavenly,
and to the worship which he so strictly owes to the Eter-

---

[1] Genesis i. 28. [2] Rom. x. 12.

nal Godhead. It is this, above all, which is the reason and motive of Sunday rest; a rest sanctioned by God's great law of the ancient covenant—*Remember thou keep holy the Sabbath day*,[1] and taught to the world by His own mysterious "rest" after the creation of man: *He rested on the seventh day from all His work which He had done.*[2]

If we turn now to things external and corporeal, the first concern of all is to save the poor workers from the cruelty of greedy speculators, who use human beings as mere instruments of money-making. It is neither just nor human so to grind men down with excessive labor as to stupefy their minds and wear out their bodies. Man's powers, like his general nature, are limited, and beyond these limits he cannot go. His strength is developed and increased by use and exercise, but only on condition of due intermission and proper rest. Daily labor, therefore, should be so regulated as not to be protracted over longer hours than strength admits. How many and how long the intervals of rest should be must depend on the nature of the work, on circumstances of time and place, and on the health and strength of the workmen. Those who work in mines and quarries, and extract coal, stone, and metals from the bowels of the earth, should have shorter hours in proportion as their labor is more severe and trying to health. Then, again, the season of the year should be taken into account; for not infrequently a kind of labor is easy at one time which at another is intolerable or exceedingly difficult. Finally, work which is quite suitable for a strong man cannot reasonably be required from a woman or a child. And, in regard to children, great care should be taken not to place them in workshops and factories until their bodies and minds are sufficiently developed. For just as very rough weather destroys the buds of spring, so does too early an experience of life's hard toil blight the young promise of a child's faculties,

---

[1] Exod. xx. 8.   [2] Genesis ii. 2.

and render any true education impossible. Women, again, are not suited for certain occupations; a woman is by nature fitted for home work, and it is that which is best adapted at once to preserve her modesty and to promote the good bringing up of children and the well-being of the family. As a general principle it may be laid down that a workman ought to have leisure and rest proportionate to the wear and tear of his strength; for waste of strength must be repaired by cessation from hard work.

In all agreements between masters and work-people there is always the condition, expressed or understood, that there should be allowed proper rest for soul and body. To agree in any other sense would be against what is right and just; for it can never be just or right to require on the one side, or to promise on the other, the giving up of those duties which a man owes to his God and to himself.

We now approach a subject of great and urgent importance, and one in respect of which, if extremes are to be avoided, right notions are absolutely necessary. Wages, as we are told, are regulated by free consent, and therefore the employer, when he pays what was agreed upon, has done his part and seemingly is not called upon to do anything beyond. The only way, it is said, in which injustice might occur would be if the master refused to pay the whole of the wages, or if the workman should not complete the work undertaken; in such cases the State should intervene, to see that each obtains his due—but not under any other circumstances.

This mode of reasoning is, to a fair-minded man, by no means convincing, for there are important considerations which it leaves out of account altogether. To labor is to exert one's self for the sake of procuring what is necessary for the purposes of life, and chief of all for self-preservation. *In the sweat of thy brow thou shalt eat thy bread.*[1]

[1] Genesis iii. 19.

Hence a man's labor bears two notes or characters. First of all, it is *personal,* inasmuch as the exertion of individual strength belongs to the individual who puts it forth, employing such strength to procure that personal advantage on account of which it was bestowed. Secondly, man's labor is *necessary;* for without the result of labor a man cannot live; and self-preservation is a law of nature, which it is wrong to disobey. Now, were we to consider labor so far as it is *personal* merely, doubtless it would be within the workman's right to accept any rate of wages whatsoever; for in the same way as he is free to work or not, so is he free to accept a small remuneration or even none at all. But this is a mere abstract supposition; the labor of the workingman is not only his personal attribute, but it is *necessary;* and this makes all the difference. The preservation of life is the bounden duty of one and all, and to be wanting therein is a crime. It follows that each one has a right to procure what is required in order to live; and the poor can procure it in no other way than through work and wages.

Let it be then taken for granted that workman and employer should, as a rule, make free agreements, and in particular should agree freely as to the wages; nevertheless, there underlies a dictate of natural justice more imperious and ancient than any bargain between man and man, namely, that remuneration ought to be sufficient to support a frugal and well-behaved wage-earner. If through necessity or fear of a worse evil the workman accept harder conditions because an employer or contractor will afford him no better, he is made the victim of force and injustice. In these and similar questions, however—such as, for example, the hours of labor in different trades, · the sanitary precautions to be observed in factories and workshops, etc.—in order to supersede undue interference on the part of the State, especially as circumstances, times, and localities differ so widely, it is advisable that recourse be had to societies or boards such as We shall mention presently, or to some other mode of safeguarding the interests of the wage-earners; the State being appealed to, should circumstances require, for its sanction and protection.

If a workman's wages be sufficient to enable him to maintain himself, his wife, and his children in reasonable comfort, he will not find it difficult, if he be a sensible man, to study economy; and he will not fail, by cutting down expenses, to put by some little savings and thus secure a small income. Nature and reason alike would urge him to this. We have seen that this great labor question cannot be solved save by assuming as a principle that private ownership must be held sacred and inviolable. The law, therefore, should favor ownership, and its policy should be to induce as many as possible of the humbler class to become owners.

Many excellent results will follow from this; and first of all, property will certainly become more equitably divided. For the result of civil change and revolution has been to divide society into two widely differing castes. On the one side there is the party which holds power because it holds wealth; which has in its grasp the whole of labor and trade; which manipulates for its own benefit and its own purposes all the sources of supply, and which is even represented in the councils of the State itself. On the other side there is the needy and powerless multitude, broken down and suffering, and ever ready for disturbance. If working-people can be encouraged to look forward to obtaining a share in the land, the consequence will be that the gulf between vast wealth and sheer poverty will be bridged over, and the respective classes will be brought nearer to one another. A further consequence will result in the greater abundance of the fruits of the earth. Men always work harder and more readily when they work on that which belongs to them; nay, they learn to love the very soil that yields, in response to the labor of their hands, not only food to eat but an abundance of good things for themselves and those that are dear to them. That such a spirit of willing labor would add to the produce of the earth and to the wealth of the community is self-evident. And a third advantage would spring from this: men would cling to the country in which they were born; for no one would exchange his country for a foreign land if his own afforded him the means of living a decent and happy life. These three important benefits, however, can be reckoned on only provided that a man's means be not drained and exhausted by excessive taxation. The right to possess private property is derived from nature, not from man; and the State has the right to control its use in the interests of the public good alone, but by no means to absorb it altogether. The State would therefore be unjust and cruel if under the name of taxation it were to deprive the private owner of more than is fitting.

In the last place—employers and workmen may of themselves effect much in the matter we are treating, by means of such associations and organizations as afford opportune aid to those who are in distress, and which draw the two classes more closely together. Among these may be enumerated societies for mutual help; various benevolent foundations established by private persons to provide for the workman, and for his widow or his orphans, in case of sudden calamity, in sickness, and in the event of death; and what are called "patronages," or institutions for the care of boys and girls, for young people, as well as homes for the aged.

The most important of all are workingmen's unions; for these virtually include all the rest. History attests what excellent results were brought about by the artificers' guilds of olden times. They were the means of affording not only many advantages to the workmen, but in no small degree of promoting the advancement of art, as numerous monuments remain to bear witness. Such unions should be suited to the requirements of this our age—an age of wider education, of different habits, and of far more numerous requirements in daily life. It is gratifying to know that there are actually in existence not a few associations of this nature, consisting either of workmen alone, or of workmen and employers together;' but it were greatly to be desired that they should become more numerous and more efficient. We have spoken of them more than once; yet it will be well to explain here how notably they are needed, to show that they exist of their own right, and what should be their organization and their mode of action.

The consciousness of his own weakness urges man to call in aid from without. We read in the pages of holy writ: *It is better that two should be together than one; for they have the advantage of their society. If one fall he shall be supported by the other. Woe to him that is alone, for when he falleth he hath none to lift him up.*[1] And further: *A brother that is helped by his brother is like a strong city.*[2] It is this natural impulse which binds men together in civil society; and it is likewise this which leads them to join together in associations of citizen with citizen; associations which, it is true, cannot be called societies in the full sense of the word, but which, notwithstanding, *are* societies.

These lesser societies and the society which constitutes the State differ in many respects, because their immediate purpose and aim is different. Civil society exists for the common good, and hence is concerned with the interests of all in general, albeit with individual interests also in their due place and degree. It is therefore called *public* society, because by its agency, as St. Thomas of Aquin says, "Men establish relations in common with one another in the setting up of a commonwealth."[3] But societies which are formed in the bosom of the State are styled *private*, and rightly so, since their immediate purpose

[1] Ecclesiastes iv. 9, 10.
[2] Prov. xviii. 19.
[3] Contra impugnantes Dei cultum et religionem, ii.

is the private advantage of the associates. "Now a private society," says St. Thomas again, "is one which is formed for the purpose of carrying out private objects; as when two or three enter into partnership with the view of trading in common." [1] Private societies, then, although they exist within the State, and are severally part of the State, cannot nevertheless be absolutely, and as such, prohibited by the State. For to enter into a "society" of this kind is the natural right of man; and the State is bound to protect natural rights, not to destroy them; and if it forbid its citizens to form associations, it contradicts the very principle of its own existence; for both they and it exist in virtue of the like principle, namely, the natural tendency of man to dwell in society.

There are occasions, doubtless, when it is fitting that the law should intervene to prevent association; as when men join together for purposes which are evidently bad, unlawful, or dangerous to the State. In such cases public authority may justly forbid the formation of associations, and may dissolve them if they already exist. But every precaution should be taken not to violate the rights of individuals and not to impose unreasonable regulations under pretence of public benefit. For laws only bind when they are in accordance with right reason, and hence with the eternal law of God.[2]

And here we are reminded of the confraternities, societies, and religious orders which have arisen by the Church's authority and the piety of Christian men. The annals of every nation down to our own days bear witness to what they have accomplished for the human race. It is indisputable that on grounds of reason alone such

---

[1] Contra impugnantes Dei cultum et religionem, ii.

[2] "Human law is law only by virtue of its accordance with right reason; and thus it is manifest that it flows from the eternal law. And in so far as it deviates from right reason it is called an unjust law; in such case it is no law at all, but rather a species of violence." —St. Thomas of Aquin, Summa Theologica, 1a 2æ Q. xciii. art. 3.

associations, being perfectly blameless in their objects, possess the sanction of the law of nature. In their religious aspect, they claim rightly to be responsible to the Church alone. The rulers of the State accordingly have no rights over them, nor can they claim any share in their control; on the contrary, it is the duty of the State to respect and cherish them, and, if need be, to defend them from attack. It is notorious that a very different course has been followed, more especially in our own times. In many places the State authorities have laid violent hands on these communities, and committed manifold injustice against them; it has placed them under control of the civil law, taken away their rights as corporate bodies, and despoiled them of their property. In such property the Church had her rights, each member of the body had his or her rights, and there were also the rights of those who had founded or endowed these communities for a definite purpose, and, furthermore, of those for whose benefit and assistance they had their being. Therefore We cannot refrain from complaining of such spoliation as unjust and fraught with evil results; and with all the more reason do We complain because, at the very time when the law proclaims that association is free to all, We see that Catholic societies, however peaceful and useful, are hampered in every way, whereas the utmost liberty is conceded to individuals whose purposes are at once hurtful to religion and dangerous to the State.

Associations of every kind, and especially those of workingmen, are now far more common than heretofore. As regards many of these there is no need at present to inquire whence they spring, what are their objects, or what the means they employ. There is a good deal of evidence, however, which goes to prove that many of these societies are in the hands of secret leaders, and are managed on principles ill-according with Christianity and the public well-being; and that they do their utmost to get within their grasp the whole field of labor, and force workingmen either to join them or to starve. Under these circumstances Christian workingmen must do one of two things: either join associations in which their religion will be exposed to peril, or form associations among themselves—unite their forces and shake off courageously the yoke of so unrighteous and intolerable an oppression. No one who does not wish to expose man's chief good to extreme risk will for a moment hesitate to say that the second alternative should by all means be adopted.

Those Catholics are worthy of all praise—and they are not a few—who, understanding what the times require, have striven, by various undertakings and endeavors, to better the condition of the working class without any sacrifice of principle being involved. They have taken up the cause of the workingman, and have spared no efforts to better the condition both of families and individuals; to infuse a spirit of equity into the mutual relations of employers and employed; to keep before the eyes of both classes the precepts of duty and the laws of the Gospel—that Gospel which, by inculcating self-restraint, keeps men within the bounds of moderation, and tends to establish harmony among the divergent interests, and the various classes which compose the State. It is with such ends in view that we see men of eminence meeting together for discussion, for the promotion of concerted action, and for practical work. Others, again, strive to unite workingmen of various grades into associations, help them with their advice and means, and enable them to obtain fitting and profitable employment. The bishops, on their part, bestow their ready good-will and support; and with their approval and guidance many members of the clergy, both secular and regular, labor assiduously in behalf of the spiritual and mental interests of the members of such associations. And there are not wanting Catholics blessed with affluence, who have, as it were, cast in their lot with the wage-earners, and who have spent large sums in founding and widely spreading benefit and insurance societies, by means of which the workingman may without difficulty acquire, through his labor, not only many present advantages but also the certainty of honorable support in days to come. How greatly such manifold and earnest activity has benefited the community at large is too well known to require Us to dwell upon it. We find therein grounds for most cheering hope in the future, provided always that the associations We have described continue to grow and spread, and are well and wisely administered. Let the State watch over these societies of citizens banded together for the exercise of their rights; but let it not thrust itself into their peculiar concerns and their organization; for things move and live by the spirit inspiring them, and may be killed by the rough grasp of a hand from without.

In order, then, that an association may be carried on with unity of purpose and harmony of action, its organization and government should be firm and wise. All such societies, being free to exist, have the further right to adopt such rules and organization as may best conduce to the attainment of their respective objects. We do not judge it expedient to enter into minute particulars touching the subject of organization: this must depend on national character, on practice and experience, on the nature and aim of the work to be done, on the scope of the various trades and employments, and on other circumstances of fact and of time:—all of which should be carefully considered.

To sum up, then, We may lay it down as a general and lasting law, that workingmen's associations should be so organized and governed as to furnish the best and most suitable means for attaining what is aimed at; that is to say, for helping each individual member to better his condition to the utmost in body, mind, and property. It is clear that they must pay special and chief attention to the duties of religion and morality, and that their internal discipline must be guided very strictly by these weighty considerations; otherwise they would lose wholly their special character, and end by becoming little better than those societies which take no account whatever of religion. What advantage can it be to a workingman to obtain by means of a society all that he requires, and to endanger his soul for lack of spiritual food? *What doth it profit a man if he gain the whole world and suffer the loss of his own soul?* [1] This, as Our Lord teaches, is the mark or character that distinguishes the Christian from the heathen. *After all these things do the heathens seek. . . . Seek ye first the kingdom of God and His justice, and all these things shall be added unto you.* [2] Let our associations, then, look first and before all things to God; let religious instruction have therein the foremost place, each one being carefully taught what is his duty to God, what he has to believe, what to hope for, and how he is to work out his salvation; and let all be warned and strengthened with special care against wrong principles and false teaching. Let the workingman be urged and led to the worship of God, to the earnest practice of religion, and, among other things, to the keeping holy of Sundays and holydays. Let him learn to reverence and love Holy Church, the common Mother of us all; and hence to obey the precepts of the Church, and to frequent the sacraments, since they are the means ordained by God for obtaining forgiveness of sin and for leading a holy life.

The foundations of the organization being thus laid in religion, We next proceed to make clear the relations of the members one to another, in order that they may live together in concord and go forward prosperously and with good results. The offices and charges of the society should be apportioned for the good of the society itself, and in such mode that difference in degree or standing should not interfere with unanimity and good-will. Office-

Matt. xvi. 26.   [2] Matt. vi. 32, 33.

bearers should be appointed with due prudence and discretion, and each one's charge should be carefully mapped out. Hereby no member will suffer injury. Let the common funds be administered with strict honesty, in such a way that a member may receive assistance in proportion to his necessities. The rights and duties of the employers, as compared with the rights and duties of the employed, ought to be the subject of careful consideration. Should it happen that either a master or a workman believe himself injured, nothing would be more desirable than that a committee should be appointed composed of reliable and capable members of the association, whose duty would be, conformably with the rules of the association, to settle the dispute. Among the several purposes of a society one should be to try to arrange for a continuous supply of work at all times and seasons, as well as to create a fund out of which the members may be effectually helped in their needs, not only in cases of accident but also in sickness, old age, and distress.

Such rules and regulations, if willingly obeyed by all, will sufficiently ensure the well-being of the poor; whilst such mutual associations among Catholics are certain to be productive in no small degree of prosperity to the State. It is not rash to conjecture the future from the past. Age gives way to age, but the events of one century are wonderfully like those of another; for they are directed by the providence of God, who overrules the course of history in accordance with His purposes in creating the race of man. We are told that it was cast as a reproach on the Christians in the early ages of the Church that the greater number among them had to live by begging or by labor. Yet, destitute though they were of wealth and influence, they ended by winning over to their side the favor of the rich and the good-will of the powerful. They showed themselves industrious, hard-working, assiduous, and peaceful, ruled by justice, and, above all, bound together in brotherly love. In presence of such mode of life and such example, prejudice gave way, the tongue of malevolence was silenced, and the lying legends of ancient superstition little by little yielded to Christian truth.

At the time being, the condition of the working classes is the pressing question of the hour; and nothing can be of higher interest to all classes of the State than that it should be rightly and reasonably adjusted. But it will be easy for Christian workingmen to decide it aright if they will form associations, choose wise guides, and follow on the path which with so much advantage to themselves and the commonweal was trodden by their fathers before them. Prejudice, it is true, is mighty, and so is the greed of money; but if the sense of what is just and rightful be not debased through depravity of heart, their fellow-citizens are sure to be won over to a kindly feeling towards men whom they see to be in earnest as regards their work and who prefer so unmistakably right dealing to mere lucre, and the sacredness of duty to every other consideration.

And further great advantage would result from the state of things We are describing; there would exist so much more ground for hope, and likelihood even, of recalling to a sense of their duty those workingmen who have either given up their faith altogether, or whose lives are at variance with its precepts. Such men feel in most cases that they have been fooled by empty promises and deceived by false pretexts. They cannot but perceive that their grasping employers too often treat them with great inhumanity and hardly care for them outside the profit their labor brings; and if they belong to any union, it is probably one in which there exists, instead of charity and love, that intestine strife which ever accompanies poverty when unresigned and unsustained by religion. Broken in spirit and worn down in body, how many of them would gladly free themselves from such galling bondage! But human respect, or the dread of starvation, makes them tremble to take the step. To such as these

Catholic associations are of incalculable service, by helping them out of their difficulties, inviting them to com-
panionship, and receiving the returning wanderers to a
haven where they may securely find repose.

We have now laid before you, Venerable Brethren,
both who are the persons and what are the means whereby this most arduous question must be solved. Every
one should put his hand to the work which falls to his
share, and that at once and straightway, lest the evil which
is already so great become through delay absolutely beyond
remedy. Those who rule the State should avail them
of the laws and institutions of the country; masters and
wealthy owners must be mindful of their duty; the poor,
whose interests are at stake, should make every lawful
and proper effort; and since religion alone, as We said
at the beginning, can avail to destroy the evil at its root,
all men should rest persuaded that the main thing needful is to return to real Christianity, apart from which all
the plans and devices of the wisest will prove of little
avail.

In regard to the Church, her co-operation will never be
found lacking, be the time or the occasion what it may; and
she will intervene with all the greater effect in proportion
as her liberty of action is the more unfettered. Let this be
carefully taken to heart by those whose office it is to safeguard the public welfare. Every minister of holy religion
must bring to the struggle the full energy of his mind and
all his power of endurance. Moved by your authority,
Venerable Brethren, and quickened by your example, they
should never cease to urge upon men of every class, upon
the high-placed as well as the lowly, the Gospel doctrines of
Christian life; by every means in their power they must
strive to secure the good of the people; and above all must
earnestly cherish in themselves, and try to arouse in others,
charity, the mistress and the queen of virtues. For the
happy results we all long for must be chiefly brought about
by the plenteous outpouring of charity; of that true Chris-

tian charity which is the fulfilling of the whole Gospel law, which is always ready to sacrifice itself for others' sake, and is man's surest antidote against worldly pride and immoderate love of self; that charity whose office is described and whose Godlike features are outlined by the Apostle St. Paul in these words: *Charity is patient, is kind,* . . . *seeketh not her own,* . . . . *suffereth all things,* . . . *endureth all things.* [1]

On each one of you, Venerable Brothers, and on your clergy and people, as an earnest of God's mercy and a mark of Our affection, We, lovingly in the Lord, bestow the Apostolic Benediction.

[1] 1 Cor. xiii. 4–7.

ALLEGIANCE TO THE REPUBLIC.

Encyclical Letter Au Milieu des Sollicitudes, February **16,**
1892.

To the Bishops and Faithful of France:
Amid the cares of the universal Church We have many
times, in the course of Our Pontificate, been pleased to
testify Our affection for France and her noble people,
and in one of Our Encyclicals, still within the memory of
all, We endeavored solemnly to express the innermost
feelings of Our soul on this subject. It is precisely this
affection that has caused Us to watch with deep interest
and then to revolve in Our mind the succession of events,
sometimes sad, sometimes consoling, which, of late years,
has taken place in your midst.

Again, at present, when contemplating the depths of
the vast conspiracy that certain men have formed for
the annihilation of Christianity in France and the animosity
with which they pursue the realization of their design,
trampling under foot the most elementary notions of
liberty and justice for the sentiment of the greater part
of the nation, and of respect for the inalienable rights of
the Catholic Church, how can We but be stricken with
deepest grief? And when We behold, one after another,
the dire consequences of these sinful attacks which conspire to ruin morals, religion, and even political interests,
wisely understood, how express the bitterness that overwhelms Us and the apprehensions that beset Us?

On the other hand, We feel greatly consoled when We
see this same French people increasing its zeal and affection for the Holy See in proportion as that See is

abandoned—We should rather say warred with upon earth. Moved by deeply religious and patriotic sentiments, representatives of all the social classes have repeatedly come to Us from France, happy to aid the Church in her incessant needs and eager to ask Us for light and counsel, so as to be sure that amid present tribulations they would in nowise deviate from the teachings of the Head of the Faithful. And We, in Our turn, either in writing or by word of mouth, have openly told Our sons what they had a right to demand of their Father, and, far from discouraging them, We have strongly exhorted them to increase their love and efforts in defence of the Catholic faith and likewise of their native land: two duties of paramount importance, and from which, in this life, no man can exempt himself.

Now We deem it opportune, nay, even necessary, once again to raise Our voice entreating still more earnestly, We shall not say Catholics only, but all upright and intelligent Frenchmen, utterly to disregard all germs of political strife in order to devote their efforts solely to the pacification of their country. All understand the value of this pacification; all continue to desire it more and more. And We who crave it more than any one, since We represent on earth the God of peace, urge by these present Letters all righteous souls, all generous hearts, to assist Us in making it stable and fruitful.

First of all, let us take as a starting-point a well-known truth admitted by all men of good sense and loudly proclaimed by the history of all peoples; namely, that religion, and religion only, can create the social bond; that it alone maintains the peace of a nation on a solid foundation. When different families, without giving up the rights and duties of domestic society, unite under the inspiration of nature, in order to constitute themselves members of another larger family circle called civil society, their object is not only to find therein the means of providing for their material welfare, but, above all, to draw thence the boon of moral improvement. Otherwise society would rise but little above the level of an aggregation of beings devoid of reason, and whose whole life would consist in the satisfaction of sensual instincts. Moreover, without this moral improvement it would be difficult to demonstrate that civil society was an advantage rather than a detriment to man, as man.

Now, morality, in man, by the mere fact that it should establish harmony among so many dissimilar rights and duties, since it enters as an element into every human act, necessarily supposes God, and with God, religion, that sacred bond whose privilege is to unite, anteriorly to all other bonds, man to God. Indeed, the idea of morality signifies, above all, an order of dependence in regard to truth which is the light of the mind; in regard to good which is the object of the will; and without truth and good there is no morality worthy of the name. And what is the principal and essential truth, that from which all truth is derived? It is God. What, therefore, is the supreme good from which all other good proceeds? God. Finally, who is the creator and guardian of our reason, our will, our whole being, as well as the end of our life? God; always God. Since, therefore, religion is the interior and exterior expression of the dependence which, in justice, we owe to God, there follows a grave obligation. All citizens are bound to unite in maintaining in the nation true religious sentiment, and to defend it in case of need, if ever, despite the protestations of nature and of history, an atheistical school should set about banishing God from society, thereby surely annihilating the moral sense even in the depths of the human conscience. Among men who have not lost all notion of integrity there can exist no difference of opinion on this point.

In French Catholics the religious sentiment should be even deeper and more universal because they have the happiness of belonging to the true religion. If, indeed, religious beliefs were, always and everywhere, given as a basis of the morality of human actions and the existence of all well-ordained society, it is evident that the Catholic religion, by the mere fact that it is the true Church of Jesus Christ, possesses, more than any other, the efficacy required for the regulation of life in society and in the individual. Would you have a brilliant example of this? France herself furnishes the same. . . . In proportion as France progressed in the Christian faith she was seen to rise gradually to the moral greatness which she attained as a political and military power. To the natural generosity of her heart Christian charity came and added an abundant source of new energy; her wonderful activity received still greater impetus from contact with the light that guides and is the pledge of constancy, the Christian faith, which, by the hand of France, traced such glorious pages in the history of mankind. And even to-day does not her faith continue to add new glories to those of the past? We behold France, inexhaustible in her genius and resources, multiplying works of charity at home; we admire her enterprises in foreign lands where, by means of her gold and the labors of her missionaries who work even at the price of their blood, she simultaneously propagates her own renown and the benefits of the Catholic religion. No Frenchman, whatever his convictions in other respects, would dare to renounce glory such as this, for to do so would be to deny his native land.

Now the history of a nation reveals in an incontestable way the generating and preserving element of its moral greatness, and should this element ever be missing, neither a superabundance of gold nor even force of arms could save it from moral decadence and perhaps death. Who then but understands that for all Frenchmen professing the Catholic religion the great anxiety should be to insure its preservation, and that with all the more devotedness since in their midst the sects are making Christianity an object of implacable hostility. Therefore, on this ground, they can afford neither indolence of action nor party divisions; the one would bespeak cowardice unworthy of a Christian, the other would bring about disastrous weakness.

And now, before going any further, We must indicate a craftily circulated calumny making most odious imputations against Catholics, and even against the Holy See itself. It is maintained that that vigor of action inculcated in Catholics for the defence of their faith has for a secret motive much less the safeguarding of their religious interests than the ambition of securing to the Church *political domination over the State.* Truly this is the revival of a very ancient calumny, as its invention belongs to the first enemies of Christianity. Was it not first of all formulated against the adorable person of the Redeemer? Yes, when He illuminated souls by His preaching and alleviated the corporal or spiritual sufferings of the unfortunate with the treasures of His divine bounty, he was accused of having political ends in view. "We have found this man perverting our nation, and forbidding to give tribute to Cæsar, and saying that he is Christ, the king. . . . If thou release this man, thou are not Cæsar's friend. For whomsoever maketh himself a king, speaketh against Cæsar. . . . We have no king but Cæsar."

It was these threatening calumnies which drew from Pilate the sentence of death against Him whom he had repeatedly declared innocent. And the authors of these lies, or of others of equal strength, omitted nothing that would aid their emissaries in propagating them far and wide; and thus did St. Justin, martyr, rebuke the Jews of his time: "Far from repenting when you had learned of His resurrection from the dead, you sent to Jerusalem shrewdly chosen men to announce that a heresy and an impious sect had been started by a certain seducer called Jesus of Galilee."

In so audaciously defaming Christianity its enemies know well what they did; their plan was to raise against its propagation a formidable adversary, the Roman

Empire. The calumny made headway; and in their credulity the pagans called the first Christians "*useless creatures, dangerous citizens, factionists, enemies of the Empire and the Emperors.* But in vain did the apologists of Christianity by their writings, and Christians by their splendid conduct, endeavor to demonstrate the absurdity and criminality of these qualifications: they were not heeded. Their very name was equivalent to a declaration of war; and Christians, by the mere fact of their being such, and for no other reason, were forced to choose between apostasy and martyrdom, being allowed no alternative. During the following centuries the same grievances and the same severity prevailed to a greater or less extent, whenever governments were unreasonably jealous of their power and maliciously disposed against the Church. They never failed to call public attention to the pretended encroachment of the Church upon the State, in order to furnish the State with some apparent right to violently attack the Catholic religion.

We have expressly recalled some features of the past that Catholics might not be dismayed by the present. Substantially the struggle is ever the same: Jesus Christ is always exposed to the contradictions of the world, and the same means are always used by modern enemies of Christianity means old in principle and scarcely modified in form; but the same means of defence are also clearly indicated to Christians of the present day by our apologists, our doctors and our martyrs. What they have done it is incumbent upon us to do in our turn. Let us therefore place above all else the glory of God and of His Church; let us work for her with an assiduity at once constant and effective, and leave all care of success to Jesus Christ, who tells us: "In the world you shall have distress: but have confidence, I have overcome the world."

To attain this We have already remarked that a great union is necessary, and if it is to be realized, it is indisspensable that all preoccupation capable of diminishing its strength and efficacy must be abandoned. Here We intend alluding principally to the political differences among the French in regard to the actual republic—a question We would treat with the clearness which the gravity of the subject demands, beginning with the principles and descending thence to practical results.

Various political governments have succeeded one another in France during the last century, each having its own distinctive form: the Empire, the Monarchy, and the Republic. By giving one's self up to abstractions, one could at length conclude which is the best of these forms, considered in themselves; and in all truth it may be affirmed that each of them is good, provided it lead straight to its end—that is to say, to the common good for which social authority is constituted; and finally, it may be added that, from a relative point of view, such and such a form of government may be preferable because of being better adapted to the character and customs of such or such a nation. In this order of speculative ideas, Catholics, like all other citizens, are free to prefer one form of government to another precisely because no one of these social forms is, in itself, opposed to the principles of sound reason nor to the maxims of Christian doctrine. What amply justifies the wisdom of the Church is that in her relations with political powers she makes abstraction of the forms which differentiate them and treats with them concerning the great religious interests of nations, knowing that hers is the duty to undertake their tutelage above all other interests. Our preceding Encyclicals have already exposed these principles, but it was nevertheless necessary to recall them for the development of the subject which occupies Us to-day.

In descending from the domain of abstractions to that of facts, we must beware of denying the principles just established: they remain fixed. However, becoming incarnated in facts, they are clothed with a contingent character, determined by the centre in which their application is produced. Otherwise said, if every political form is good by itself and may be applied to the government of nations, the fact still remains that political power is not found in all nations under the same form; each has its own. This form springs from a combination of historical or national, though always human, circumstances which, in a nation, give rise to its traditional and even fundamental laws, and by these is determined the particular form of government, the basis of transmission of supreme power.

It were useless to recall that all individuals are bound to accept these governments and not to attempt their overthrow or a change in their form. Hence it is that the Church, the guardian of the truest and highest idea of political sovereignty, since she has derived it from God, has always condemned men who rebelled against legitimate authority and disapproved their doctrines. And that too at the very time when the custodians of power used it against her, thereby depriving themselves of the strongest support given their authority and of efficacious means of obtaining from the people obedience to their laws. And apropos of this subject, We cannot lay too great stress upon the precepts given to the first Christians by the Prince of the apostles in the midst of persecutions: "Honor all men: love the brotherhood: fear God: honor the king"; and those of St. Paul: "I desire, therefore, first of all, that supplications, prayers, intercessions, and thanksgivings be made for all men: For kings and for all who are in high station, that we may lead a quiet and peaceable life, in all piety and chastity. For this is good and acceptable in the sight of God, our Saviour."

However, here it must be carefully observed that whatever be the form of civil power in a nation, it cannot be considered so definitive as to have the right to remain immutable, even though such were the intention of those who, in the beginning, determined it. . . . Only the Church of Jesus Christ has been able to preserve, and surely will preserve unto the consummation of time, her form of government. Founded by Him who *was*, who *is*, and who *will be forever*, she has received from Him, since her very origin, all that she requires for the pursuing of her divine mission across the changeable ocean of human affairs. And, far from wishing to transform her essential constitution, she has not the power even to relinquish the conditions of true liberty and sovereign independence with which Providence has endowed her in the general interest of souls. . . . But, in regard to purely human societies, it is an oft-repeated historical fact that time, that great transformer of all things here below, operates great changes in their political institutions. On some occasions it limits itself to modifying something in the form of the established government; or, again, it will go so far as to substitute other forms for the primitive ones— forms totally different, even as regards the mode of transmitting sovereign power.

And how are these political changes of which We speak produced? They sometimes follow in the wake of violent crises, too often of a bloody character, in the midst of which pre-existing governments totally disappear; then anarchy holds sway, and soon public order is shaken to its very foundations and finally overthrown. From that time onward a *social need* obtrudes itself upon the nation; it must provide for itself without delay. Is it not its privilege—or, better still, its duty—to defend itself against a state of affairs troubling it so deeply, and to re-establish public peace in the tranquillity of order? Now, this social need justifies the creation and the existence of new governments, whatever form they take; since, in the hypothesis wherein we reason, these new governments are a requisite to public order, all public order being impossible without a government. Thence it follows that, in similar junctures, all the novelty is limited to the political form of civil power, or to its mode of transmission; it in no wise affects the power considered in itself. This continues to be immutable and worthy of respect, as, considered in its nature, it is constituted to provide for the common good, the supreme end which gives human society its origin. To put it otherwise, in all hypotheses, civil power, considered as such, is from God, always from God: "For there is no power but from God."

Consequently, when new governments representing this immutable power are constituted, their acceptance is not only permissible but even obligatory, being imposed by the need of the social good which has made and which upholds them. This is all the more imperative because an insurrection stirs up hatred among citizens, provokes civil war, and may throw a nation into chaos and anarchy, and this great duty of respect and dependence will endure as long as the exigencies of the common good shall demand it, since this good is, after God, the first and last law in society.

Thus the wisdom of the Church explains itself in the maintenance of her relations with the numerous governments which have succeeded one another in France in less than a century, each change causing violent shocks. Such a line of conduct would be the surest and most salutary for all Frenchmen in their civil relations with the republic, which is the actual government of their nation. Far be it from them to encourage the political dissensions which divide them; all their efforts should be combined to preserve and elevate the moral greatness of their native land.

But a difficulty presents itself. "This Republic," it is said, "is animated by such anti-Christian sentiments that honest men, Catholics particularly, could not conscientiously accept it." This, more than anything else, has given rise to dissensions, and in fact aggravated them. . . . These regrettable differences would have been avoided if the very considerable distinction between *constituted power* and *legislation* had been carefully kept in view. In so much does legislation differ from political power and its form, that under a system of government

most excellent in form legislation could be detestable;
while quite the opposite under a régime most imperfect in
form, might be found excellent legislation. It were an
easy task to prove this truth, history in hand, but what
would be the use? All are convinced of it. And who,
better than the Church, is in position to know it—she
who has striven to maintain habitual relations with all
political governments? Assuredly she, better than any
other power, could tell the consolation or sorrow oc-
casioned her by the laws of the various governments
by which nations have been ruled from the Roman Empire
down to the present.

If the distinction just established has its major importance, it is likewise manifestly reasonable: Legislation
is the work of men invested with power, and who, in fact,
govern the nation; therefore it follows that, practically,
the quality of the laws depends more upon the quality
of these men than upon the form of power. The laws
will be good or bad accordingly as the minds of the legislators are imbued with good or bad principles, and as
they allow themselves to be guided by political prudence
or by passion.

That several years ago different important acts of
legislation in France proceeded from a tendency hostile
to religion, and therefore to the interests of the nation,
is admitted by all, and unfortunately confirmed by the
evidence of facts. We Ourselves, in obedience to a sacred
duty, made earnest appeals to him who was then at the
head of the republic, but these tendencies continued to
exist; the evil grew, and it was not surprising that the
members of the French Episcopate chosen by the Holy
Ghost to rule over their respective illustrious churches
should even quite recently have considered it an obligation publicly to express their grief concerning the condition of affairs in France in regard to the Catholic religion. Poor France! God alone can measure the abyss
of evil into which she will sink if this legislation, instead

of improving, will stubbornly continue in a course which must end in plucking from the minds and hearts of Frenchmen the religion which has made them so great.

And here is precisely the ground on which, political dissensions aside, upright men should unite as one to combat, by all lawful and honest means, these progressive abuses of legislation. The respect due to constituted power cannot prohibit this: unlimited respect and obedience cannot be yielded to all legislative measures, of no matter what kind, enacted by this same power. Let it not be forgotten that law is a precept ordained according to reason and promulgated for the good of the community by those who, for this end, have been entrusted with power. . . . Accordingly, such points in legislation as are hostile to religion and to God should never be approved; to the contrary, it is a duty to disapprove them. It was this that St. Augustine, the great Bishop of Hippo, brought out so strongly in his eloquent reasoning: "Sometimes the powerful ones of earth are good and fear God; at other times they fear Him not. Julian was an emperor unfaithful to God, an apostate, a pervert, an idolator. Christian soliders served this faithless emperor, but as soon as there was question of the cause of *Jesus Christ* they recognized only Him who was in heaven. Julian commanded them to honor idols and offer them incense, but they put God above the prince. However, when he made them form into ranks and march against a hostile nation, they obeyed instantly. They distinguished the eternal from the temporal master and still in view of the eternal Master they submitted to such a temporal master."

We know that, by a lamentable abuse of his reason, and still more so of his will, the atheist denies these principles. But, in a word, atheism is so monstrous an error that it could never, be it said to the honor of humanity, annihilate in it the consciousness of God's claims and substitute them with idolatry of the State.

The principles which should regulate our conduct towards God and towards human governments being thus defined, no unprejudiced man can censure French Catholics if, sparing themselves neither fatigue nor sacrifice, they labor to preserve a condition essential to their country's salvation, one which embodies so many glorious traditions registered by history, and which every Frenchman is in duty bound not to forget

Before closing Our Letter, We wish to touch upon two points bearing an affinity to each other and which, because so closely connected with religious interests, have stirred up some division among Catholics. . . . One of them is the *Concordat*, which for so many years has facilitated in France the harmony between the government of the Church and that of the State. On the observance of this solemn, bi-lateral compact, always faithfully kept by the Holy See, the enemies of the Catholic religion do not themselves agree. . . . The more violent among them desire its abolition, that the State may be entirely free to molest the Church of JESUS CHRIST. . . . On the contrary, others, being more astute, wish, or rather claim to wish, the preservation of the Concordat: not because they agree that the State should fulfil toward the Church the subscribed engagements, but solely that the State may be benefited by the concessions made by the Church; as if one could, at will, separate engagements entered into from concessions obtained, when both of these things form a substantial part of one whole. For them the Concordat would amount to no more than a chain forged to fetter the liberty of the Church, that holy liberty to which she has a divine and inalienable right. Of these two opinions which will prevail? We know not. We desired to recall them only to recommend Catholics not to provoke a secession by interfering in a matter with which it is the business of the Holy See to deal.

We shall not hold to the same language on another point, concerning the principle of the separation of the

State and Church, which is equivalent to the separation of human legislation from Christian and divine legislation. We do not care to interrupt Ourselves here in order to demonstrate the absurdity of such a separation; each one will understand for himself. As soon as the State refuses to give to God what belongs to God, by a necessary consequence it refuses to give to citizens that to which, as men, they have a right; as, whether agreeable or not to accept, it cannot be denied that man's rights spring from his duty toward God. Whence it follows that the State, by missing in this connection the principal object of its institution, finally becomes false to itself by denying that which is the reason of its own existence. These superior truths are so clearly proclaimed by the voice of even natural reason, that they force themselves upon all who are not blinded by the violence of passion; therefore Catholics cannot be too careful in defending themselves against such a separation. In fact, to wish that the State would separate itself from the Church would be to wish, by a logical sequence, that the Church be reduced to the liberty of living according to the law common to all citizens. . . . It is true that in certain countries this state of affairs exists. It is a condition which, if it have numerous and serious inconveniences, also offers some advantages—above all when, by a fortunate inconsistency, the legislator is inspired by Christian principles—and, though these advantages cannot justify the false principle of separation nor authorize its defence, they nevertheless render worthy of toleration a situation which, practically, might be worse.

But in France, a nation Catholic in her traditions and by the present faith of the great majority of her sons, the Church should not be placed in the precarious position to which she must submit among other peoples; and the better that Catholics understand the aim of the enemies who desire this separation, the less will they favor it. To these enemies, and they say it clearly enough, this separation means that political legislation be entirely independent of religious legislation; nay, more, that Power be absolutely indifferent to the interests of Christian society, that is to say, of the Church; in fact, that it deny her very existence. But they make a reservation formulated thus: As soon as the Church, utilizing the resources which common law accords to the least among Frenchmen, will, by redoubling her native activity, cause her work to prosper, then the State intervening, can and will put French Catholics outside the common law itself. . . . In a word: the ideal of these men would be a return to paganism: the State would recognize the Church only when it would be pleased to persecute her.

We have explained, Venerable Brethren, in an abridged though clear way, some if not all the points upon which French Catholics and all intelligent men should be at peace and unity, so as to remedy, in so far as still remains possible, the evils with which France is afflicted, and to elevate its moral greatness. The points in question are: Religion and country, political power and legislation, the conduct to be observed in regard to this power and legislation, the Concordat, the separation of Church and State. . . . We cherish the hope and the confidence that the elucidation of these points will dissipate the prejudices of many honest, well-meaning men, facilitate the pacification of minds, and thereby cement the union of all Catholics for the sustaining of the great cause of *Christ, who loves the Franks.*

How consoling to Our heart to encourage you all in this way and to behold you all responding with docility to Our appeal! You, Venerable Brethren, by your authority and with the enlightened zeal for Church and Fatherland which so distinguishes you, will give able support to this peace-making work. We delight in the hope that those who are in power will appreciate Our words, which aim at the happiness and prosperity of France.

Meanwhile, as a pledge of Our paternal affection, We bestow upon you, Venerable Brethren, upon your clergy and also upon all the Catholics of France, the apostolic blessing.

THE POPE AND THE COLUMBUS TER= CENTENARY.

Encyclical Quarto Abrupto Sœculo, July 16, 1902.

Now that four centuries have sped since a Ligurian first, under God's guidance, touched shores unknown beyond the Atlantic, the whole world is eager to celebrate the memory of the event, and glorify its author. Nor could a worthier reason be found wherethrough zeal should be kindled. For the exploit is in itself the highest and grandest which any age has ever seen accomplished by man; and he who achieved it, for the greatness of his mind and heart, can be compared to but few in the history of humanity. By his toil another world emerged from the unsearched bosom of the ocean: hundreds of thousands of mortals have, from a state of blindness been raised to the common level of the human race, reclaimed from savagery to gentleness and humanity; and, greatest of all, by the acquisition of those blessings of which Jesus Christ is the author, they have been recalled from destruction to eternal life. Europe, indeed, overpowered at the time by the novelty and strangeness of the discovery, presently came to recognize what was due to Columbus, when, through the numerous colonists shipped to America, through the constant intercourse and interchange of business and the ocean-trade, an incredible addition was made to our knowledge of nature, and to the commonwealth; whilst at the same time the prestige of the European name was marvellously increased. Therefore, amidst so lavish a display of honor, so unanimous a tribute of congratulations, it is fitting that the Church should not be altogether silent; since she, by custom and precedent, willingly approves and endeavors to forward whatsoever she sees, and wherever she sees it, that is honorable and praiseworthy. It is true she reserves her special and greatest honors for virtues that most signally proclaim a high morality, for these are directly associated with the salvation of souls; but she does not, therefore, despise or lightly estimate virtues of other kinds. On the contrary, she has ever highly favored and held in honor those who have deserved well of men in civil society, and have thus attained a lasting name among posterity. For God, indeed, is especially wonderful in His saints—*mirabilis in Sanctis suis;* but the impress of His divine virtue also appears in those who shine with excellent power of mind and spirit, since high intellect and greatness of spirit can be the property of men only through their parent and creator, God. But there is, besides, another reason, a unique one, why We consider that this immortal achievement should be recalled by Us with memorial words. For Columbus is ours; since if a little consideration be given to the particular reason of his design in exploring the *mare tenebrosum,* and also the manner in which he endeavored to execute the design, it is indubitable that the Catholic faith was the strongest motive for the inception and prosecution of the design; so that for this reason also the whole human race owes not a little to the Church. For we have the record of not a few brave and experienced men, both before and after Christopher Columbus, who with stubbornness and zeal explored unknown lands and seas yet more unknown. And the memory of these, man, mindful of benefits, rightly holds, and will hold in honor; because they advanced the ends of knowledge and humanity, and increased the common prosperity of the race, not by light labor, but by supreme exertion, often accompanied by great dangers. But there is, nevertheless, between these and him of whom We speak, a generous difference. He was distinguished by this unique note, that in his work of traversing and retraversing immense tracts of ocean, he looked for a something greater and higher than did these others. We say not that he was unmoved by perfectly honorable aspirations after knowledge, and deserving well of human society; nor did he despise glory, which is a most engrossing ideal to great souls; nor did he altogether scorn a hope of advantages to himself; but to him far before all these human considerations was the consideration of his ancient faith, which questionless dowered him with strength of mind and will, and often strengthened and consoled him in the midst of the greatest difficulties. This view and aim is known to have possessed his mind above all; namely, to open a way for the Gospel over new lands and seas.

This, indeed, may seem of small likelihood to such as confine their whole thought and care to the evidence of the senses, and refuse to look for anything higher. But great intellects, on the contrary, are usually wont to cherish higher ideals; for they, of all men, are most excellently fitted to receive the intuitions and breathings of divine faith. Columbus certainly had joined to the study of nature the study of religion, and had trained his mind on the teachings that well up from the most intimate depths of the Catholic faith. For this reason, when he learned from the lessons of astronomy and the record of the ancients, that there were great tracts of land lying towards the West, beyond the limits of the known world, lands hitherto explored by no man, he saw in spirit a mighty multitude, cloaked in miserable darkness, given over to evil rites, and the superstitious worship of vain gods. Miserable it is to live in a barbarous state and with savage manners: but more miserable to lack the knowledge of that which is highest, and to dwell in ignorance of the one true God. Considering these things, therefore, in his mind, he sought first of all to extend the

Christian name and the benefits of Christian charity to the West, as is abundantly proved by the history of the whole undertaking. For when he first petitioned Ferdinand and Isabella, the sovereigns of Spain, for fear lest they should be reluctant to encourage the undertaking, he clearly explained its object: "That their glory would grow to immortality, if they resolved to carry the name and doctrine of Jesus Christ into regions so distant." And in no long time having obtained his desires, he bears witness: "That he implores of God that, through His divine aid and grace, the sovereigns may continue steadfast in their desire to fill these new missionary shores with the truths of the Gospel." He hastens to seek missionaries from Pope Alexander VI., through a letter in which this sentence occurs: "I trust that, by God's help, I may spread the Holy Name and Gospel of Jesus Christ as widely as may be." He was carried away, as we think, with joy, when on his first return from the Indies he wrote to Raphael Sanchez: "That to God should be rendered immortal thanks, who had brought his labors such prosperous issues; that Jesus Christ rejoices and triumphs on earth no less than in heaven, at the approaching salvation of nations innumerable, who were before hastening to destruction." And if he moved Ferdinand and Isabella to decree that only Catholic Christians should be suffered to approach the New World and trade with the natives, he brought forward as reason, "that he sought nothing from his enterprise and endeavor but the increase and glory of the Christian religion." And this was well known to Isabella, who better than any had understood the great man's mind; indeed it is evident that it had been clearly laid before that most pious, masculine-minded, and great-souled woman. For she had declared of Columbus that he would boldly thrust himself upon the vast ocean, "to achieve a most signal thing, for the sake of the divine glory." And to Columbus himself, on his second return, she writes: "That the expenses she had incurred, and was about to incur, for the Indian expeditions, had been well bestowed; for thence would ensure a spreading of Catholicism."

In truth, except for a divine cause, whence was he to draw constancy and strength of mind to bear those sufferings which to the last he was obliged to endure? We allude to the adverse opinions of the learned, the rebuffs of the great, the storms of a raging ocean, and those assiduous vigils by which he more than once lost the use of his sight. Then, in addition, were fights with savages, the infidelity of friends and companions, criminal conspiracies, the perfidy of the envious, and the calumnies of detractors. He must needs have succumbed under labors so vast and overwhelming if he had not been sustained by the consciousness of a nobler aim, which he knew would bring much glory to the Christian name, and salvation to an infinite multitude. And indeed the circumstances of the time illustrate his achievement with wonderful effect. Columbus threw open America at the time when a great storm was about to break over the Church. As far, therefore, as it is lawful for man to divine from events the ways of divine Providence, he seemed to have truly been born, by a singular provision of God, to remedy those losses which were awaiting the Catholic Church on the side of Europe. To persuade the Indian people to Christianity was, indeed, the duty and work of the Church, and upon that duty she entered from the beginning, and continued, and still continues, to pursue in continuous charity, reaching finally the furthest limits of Patagonia. Columbus resolved to go before and prepare the ways for the Gospel, and, deeply absorbed in this idea, gave all his energies to it, attempting hardly anything without religion for his guide and piety for his companion. We mention what is indeed well known, but is also characteristic of the man's mind and soul. For being compelled by the Portuguese and Genoese to leave his object unachieved, when he had reached Spain, within the walls of a religious house he matured his great design of meditated exploration, having for confidant and adviser a religious—a disciple of Francis of Assisi. Being at length about to depart for the sea, he attended to all that which concerned the welfare of his soul on the eve of his enterprise. He implored the Queen of heaven to assist his efforts and direct his course; and he ordered that no sail should be hoisted until the name of the Trinity had been invoked. When he had put out to sea, and the waves were now growing tempestuous, and the sailors were filled with terror, he kept a tranquil constancy of mind, relying on God. The very names he gave to the newly discovered islands tell the purposes of the man. At each disembarkation he offered up prayers to Almighty God, nor did he take possession save "in the Name of Jesus Christ." Upon whatsoever shores he might be driven, his first act was to set upon the shore the standard of the holy cross: and the name of the divine Redeemer, which he had so often sung on the open sea to the sound of the murmuring waves, he conferred upon the new islands. Thus at Hispaniola he began to build from the ruins of the temple, and all popular celebrations were preceded by the most sacred ceremonies.

This, then, was the object, this the end Columbus had in view in traversing such a vast extent of land and water to discover those countries hitherto uncultivated and inaccessible, but which, afterwards, as we have seen, have made such rapid strides in civilization and wealth and fame. And in truth the magnitude of the undertaking as well as the importance and variety of the benefits that arose from it, call for some fitting and honorable commemoration of it among men. And, above all, it is fitting that we should confess and celebrate in an especial manner the will and designs of the Eternal Wisdom, under whose guidance the discoverer of the New World placed himself with a devotion so touching.

In order, therefore, that the commemoration of Columbus may be worthily observed, religion must give her assistance to the secular ceremonies. And as at the time of the first news of the discovery public thanksgiving was offered by the command of the Sovereign Pontiff to Almighty God, so now we have resolved to act in like manner in celebrating the anniversary of this auspicious event.

We decree, therefore, that on October 12, or on the following Sunday, if the Ordinary should prefer it, in all the cathedral churches and convent chapels throughout Spain, Italy, and the two Americas, after the office of the day there shall be celebrated a Solemn Mass of the Most Holy Trinity. Moreover, besides the above-mentioned countries, We feel assured that the other nations, prompted to it by the counsel of their bishops will likewise join in the celebration, since it is fitting that an event from which all have derived benefit should be piously and gratefully commemorated by all.

Meanwhile, as a pledge of heavenly favors and of Our own paternal good-will, we lovingly bestow the Apostolic Benediction in Our Lord upon you, Venerable Brethren, and upon your clergy and people.

THE STUDY OF HOLY SCRIPTURE.

Encyclical Letter Providentissimus Deus, November **18,**
1893.

THE God of all providence, who in the adorable designs
of His love at first elevated the human race to the participation of the divine nature, and afterwards delivered it
from universal guilt and ruin, restoring it to its primitive
dignity, has, in consequence, bestowed upon man a splendid gift and safeguard—making known to him, by supernatural means, the hidden mysteries of His divinity, His
wisdom and His mercy.   For although in divine revelation
there are contained some things which are not beyond the
reach of unassisted reason, and which are made the objects
of such revelation in order "that all may come to know
them with facility, certainty, and safety from error, yet
not on this account can supernatural revelation be said to
be absolutely necessary; it is only necessary because God
has ordained man to a supernatural end." [1]   This supernatural revelation, according to the belief of the universal
Church, is contained both in unwritten tradition and in
written books, which are, therefore, called sacred and
canonical because, "being written under the inspiration of
the Holy Ghost, they have God for their author, and as such
have been delivered to the Church." [2]   This belief has
been perpetually held and professed by the Church in regard to the Books of both Testaments; and there are well-
known documents of the gravest kind, coming down to us
from the earliest times, which proclaim that God, who

---

[1] Conc. Vat. sess iii. cap. ii. de revel.   [2] Ibid.

spoke first by the prophets, then by His own mouth, and lastly by the apostles, composed also the canonical Scriptures,[1] and that these are His own oracles and words [2]— a Letter written by our Heavenly Father and transmitted by the sacred writers to the human race in its pilgrimage so far from its heavenly country.[3]   If, then, such and so great is the excellence and dignity of the Scriptures, that God Himself has composed them, and that they treat of God's marvellous mysteries, counsels and works, it follows that the branch of sacred theology which is concerned with the defence and elucidation of these divine books must be excellent and useful in the highest degree.

Now We, who by the help of God, and not without fruit, have by frequent Letters and exhortation endeavored to promote other branches of study which seem capable of advancing the glory of God and contributing to the salvation of souls, have for a long time cherished the desire to give an impulse to the noble science of Holy Scripture, and to impart to Scripture study a direction suitable to the needs of the present day.   The solicitude of the apostolic office naturally urges, and even compels us, not only to desire that this grand source of Catholic revelation should be made safely and abundantly accessible to the flock of Jesus Christ, but also not to suffer any attempt to defile or corrupt it, either on the part of those who impiously or openly assail the Scriptures, or of those who are led astray into fallacious and imprudent novelties.   We are not ignorant, indeed, Venerable Brethren, that there are not a few Catholics, men of talent and learning, who do devote themselves with ardor to the defence of the sacred writings and to making them known and better understood.   But whilst giving to these the commendation they deserve, We cannot but earnestly exhort others also, from whose skill

[1] S. Aug. de civ. Dei. xi. 3.

[2] S. Clem. Rom. 1 ad. Cor. 45; S. Polycarp. ad Phil. 7; S. Iren. c. haer. ii. 28, 2.

[3] S. Chrys. in Gen. hom. 2, 2; S. Aug. in Ps. xxx., serm., 2, 1; S. Greg. M. ad Theo. ep. iv. 31.

and piety and learning we have a right to expect good results, to give themselves to the same most praiseworthy work. It is Our wish and fervent desire to see an increase in the number of the approved and persevering laborers in the cause of Holy Scripture; and more especially that those whom divine grace has called to holy orders should, day by day, as their state demands, display greater diligence and industry in reading, meditating, and explaining it.

Among the reasons for which the Holy Scripture is so worthy of commendation—in addition to its own excellence and to the homage which we owe to God's Word—the chief of all is, the innumerable benefits of which it is the source; according to the infallible testimony of the Holy Ghost Himself, who says: *All Scripture inspired of God is profitable to teach, to reprove, to correct, to instruct in justice: that the man of God may be perfect, furnished to every good work.*[1] That such was the purpose of God in giving the Scripture to men is shown by the example of Christ our Lord and of His apostles. For He Himself who "obtained authority by miracles, merited belief by authority, and by belief drew to himself the multitude"[2] was accustomed, in the exercise of His divine mission, to appeal to the Scriptures. He uses them at times to prove that He is sent by God, and is God Himself. From them He cites instructions for His disciples and confirmation of His doctrine. He vindicates them from the calumnies of objectors; He quotes them against Sadducees and Pharisees and retorts from them upon Satan himself when he dares to tempt Him. At the close of His life His utterances are from the Holy Scripture, and it is the Scripture that He expounds to His disciples after His resurrection, until He ascends to the glory of His Father. Faithful to His precepts, the apostles, although He Himself granted *signs and wonders to be done by their hands,*[3] nevertheless used with the greatest effect the sacred writings, in order to

---

[1] 2 Tim. iii. 16, 17.   [2] S. Aug. de util. cred. xiv. 32.
[3] Act xiv. 3.

persuade the nations everywhere of the wisdom of Christianity, to conquer the obstinacy of the Jews, and to suppress the outbreak of heresy. This is plainly seen in their discourses, especially in those of St. Peter; these were often little less than a series of citations from the Old Testament making in the strongest manner for the new dispensation. We find the same things in the Gospels of St. Matthew and St. John and in the Catholic Epistles; and, most remarkable of all, in the words of him who "boasts that he learned the law at the feet of Gamaliel, in order that, being armed with spiritual weapons, he might afterwards say with confidence, 'the arms of our warfare are not carnal but mighty unto God.'" [1] Let all, therefore, especially the novices of the ecclesiastical army, understand how deeply the sacred books should be esteemed, and with what eagerness and reverence they should approach this great arsenal of heavenly arms. For those whose duty it is to handle Catholic doctrine before the learned or the unlearned will nowhere find more ample matter or more abundant exhortation, whether on the subject of God, the supreme Good and the all-perfect Being, or the works which display His glory and His love. Nowhere is there anything more full or more express on the subject of the Saviour of the world than is to be found in the whole range of the Bible. As St. Jerome says, *to be ignorant of the Scripture is not to know Christ*.[2] In its pages His Image stands out, living and breathing; diffusing everywhere around consolation in trouble, encouragement to virtue, and attraction to the love of God. And as to the Church, her institutions, her nature, her office and her gifts, we find in Holy Scripture so many references and so many ready and convincing arguments that, as St. Jerome again most truly says, "A man who is well grounded in the testimonies of the Scripture is the bulwark of the Church." [3] And if we come to morality and disci-

---

[1] St. Hier. de stud. Script. ad Paulin. ep. liii. 3.
[2] in Isaiam. Prol.   [3] in Isaiam liv. 12.

pline, an apostolic man finds in the sacred writings abundant and excellent assistance; most holy precepts, gentle and strong exhortation, splendid examples of every virtue, and finally the promise of eternal reward and the threat of eternal punishment, uttered in terms of solemn import, in God's name and in God's own words.

And it is this peculiar and singular power of Holy Scripture, arising from the inspiration of the Holy Ghost, which gives authority to the sacred orator, fills him with apostolic liberty of speech, and communicates force and power to his eloquence. For those who infuse into their efforts the spirit and strength of the Word of God speak *not in word only, but in power also, and in the Holy Ghost, and in much fulness.*[1] Hence, those preachers are foolish and improvident who, in speaking of religion and proclaiming the things of God, use no words but those of human science and human prudence, trusting to their own reasonings rather than to those of God. Their discourses may be brilliant and fine, but they must be feeble and they must be cold, for they are without the fire of the utterance of God [2] and they must fall far short of that mighty power which the speech of God possesses: *for the Word of God is living and effectual, and more piercing than any two-edged sword; and reaching unto the division of the soul and the spirit.*[3] But, indeed, those who have a right to speak are agreed that there is in the Holy Scripture an eloquence that is wonderfully varied and rich and worthy of great themes. This St. Augustine thoroughly understood and has abundantly set forth.[4] This, also, is confirmed by the best preachers of all ages, who have gratefully acknowledged that they owed their repute chiefly to the assiduous use of the Bible, and to devout meditation on its pages.

The Holy Fathers well knew all this by practical experience, and they never cease to extol the sacred Scripture

[1] 1 Thess. i. 5.
[2] Jerem. xxiii. 29.
[3] Hebr. iv. 12.
[4] De doctr. Chr. iv. 6, 7.

and its fruits. In innumerable passages of their writings we find them applying to it such phrases as *an inexhaustible treasury of heavenly doctrine*,[1] or *an overflowing fountain of salvation*,[2] or putting it before us as fertile pastures and beautiful gardens in which the flock of the Lord is marvellously refreshed and delighted.[3] Let us listen to the words of St. Jerome, in his Epistle to Nepotian: "Often read the divine Scriptures; yea, let holy reading be always in thy hand; study that which thou thyself must preach. . . . Let the speech of the priest be ever seasoned with Scriptural reading."[4] St. Gregory the Great, than whom no one has more admirably described the pastoral office, writes in the same sense. "Those," he says, "who are zealous in the work of preaching must never cease the study of the written Word of God."[5] St. Augustine, however, warns us that "vainly does the preacher utter the Word of God exteriorly unless he listens to it interiorly";[6] and St. Gregory instructs sacred orators "first to find in Holy Scripture the knowledge of themselves, and then carry it to others, lest in reproving others they forget themselves."[7] Admonitions such as these had, indeed, been uttered long before by the apostolic voice which had learned its lesson from Christ Himself, who "began to do and teach." It was not to Timothy alone, but to the whole order of the clergy, that the command was addressed: *Take heed to thyself and to doctrine; be earnest in them. For in doing this thou shalt both save thyself and them that hear thee.*[8] For the saving and for the perfection of ourselves and of others

---

[1] S. Chrys. in Gen. Hom. xxi. 2; Hom. lx. 3; S. Aug. de Disc. Christ. ii.

[2] S. Athan. ep. fest. xxxix.

[3] S. Aug. serm. xxvi. 24; S. Ambr. in Ps. cxviii, serm. xix. 2.

[4] S. Hier. de vita cleric. ad Nepot.

[5] S. Greg. M. Regul. past. ii. 11 (al. 22); Moral. xvii. 26 (al. 14).

[6] S. Aug. serm. clxxix. 1.

[7] S. Greg. M. Regul. past. iii. 24 (al. 14).

[8] 1 Tim. iv. 16.

there is at hand the very best of help in the Holy Scriptures, as the Book of Psalms, among others, so constantly
insists; but those only will find it who bring to this divine
reading not only docility and attention but also piety and
an innocent life. For the sacred Scripture is not like
other books. Dictated by the Holy Ghost, it contains
things of the deepest importance, which in many instances are most difficult and obscure. To understand
and explain such things there is always required the
" coming"[1] of the same Holy Spirit; that is to say, His
light and His grace; and these, as the royal psalmist so
frequently insists, are to be sought by humble prayer
and guarded by holiness of life.

It is in this that the watchful eye of the Church shines
forth conspicuously. By admirable laws and regulations,
she has shown herself solicitous that " the celestial treasure
of the sacred books, so bountifully bestowed upon man
by the Holy Spirit, should not lie neglected."[2] She has
prescribed that a considerable portion of them shall be
read and piously reflected upon by all her ministers in the
daily office of the sacred psalmody. She has ordered that
in cathedral churches, in monasteries, and in other convents in which study can conveniently be pursued, they
shall be expounded and interpreted by capable men; and
she has strictly commanded that her children shall be
fed with the saving words of the Gospel at least on Sundays
and solemn feasts.[3] Moreover, it is owing to the wisdom
and exertions of the Church that there has always been
continued, from century to century, that cultivation of
Holy Scripture which has been so remarkable and has
borne such ample fruit.

And here, in order to strengthen Our teaching and Our
exhortations, it is well to recall how, from the beginning of
Christianity, all who have been renowned for holiness of

[1] S. Hier. in Mic. i. 10.
[2] Conc. Trid. sess. v. decret. de reform, 1.
[3] Ibid 1, 2.

life and sacred learning have given their deep and constant attention to Holy Scripture. If we consider the immediate disciples of the apostles, St. Clement of Rome, St. Ignatius of Antioch, St. Polycarp—or the apologists, such as St. Justin and St. Irenæus, we find that in their letters and books, whether in defence of the Catholic faith or in its commendation, they drew faith, strength, and unction from the Word of God. When there arose, in various sees, catechetical and theological schools, of which the most celebrated were those of Alexandria and of Antioch, there was little taught in those schools but what was contained in the reading, the interpretation, and the defence of the divine written word. From them came forth numbers of Fathers and writers whose laborious studies and admirable writings have justly merited for the three following centuries the appellation of the golden age of biblical exegesis. In the Eastern Church the greatest name of all is Origen—a man remarkable alike for penetration of genius and persevering labor; from whose numerous works and his great *Hexapla* almost all have drawn who came after him. Others who have widened the field of this science may also be named, as especially eminent; thus, Alexandria could boast of St. Clement and St. Cyril; Palestine, of Eusebius and the other St. Cyril; Cappadocia, of St. Basil the Great and the two Gregories, of Nazianzus and Nyssa; Antioch, of St. John Chrysostom, in whom the science of Scripture was rivalled by the splendor of his eloquence. In the Western Church there are as many names as great: Tertullian, St. Cyprian, St. Hilary, St. Ambrose, St. Leo the Great, St. Gregory the Great; most famous of all, St. Augustine and St. Jerome, of whom the former was so marvellously acute in penetrating the sense of God's Word and so fertile in the use that he made of it for the promotion of the Catholic truth, and the latter has received from the Church, by reason of his pre-eminent knowledge of Scripture and his labors in promoting its use, the name of the "great Doctor."[1] From this period down to the eleventh century, although biblical studies did not flourish with the same vigor and the same fruitfulness as before, yet they did flourish, and principally by the instrumentality of the clergy. It was their care and solicitude that selected the best and most useful things that the ancients had left, arranged them in order, and published them with additions of their own—as did St. Isidore of Seville, Venerable Bede, and Alcuin, among the most prominent; it was they who illustrated the sacred pages with "glosses" or short commentaries, as we see in Walafrid Strabo and St. Anselm of Laon, or expended fresh labor in securing their integrity, as did St. Peter Damian and Blessed Lanfranc. In the twelfth century many took up, with great success, the allegorical exposition of Scripture. In this kind, St. Bernard is preeminent; and his writings, it may be said, are Scripture all through. With the age of the scholastics came fresh and welcome progress in the study of the Bible. That the scholastics were solicitous about the genuineness of the Latin version is evident from the *Correctoria Biblica,* or list of emendations, which they have left. But they expended their labors and industry chiefly on interpretation and explanation. To them we owe the accurate and clear distinction, such as had not been given before, of the various senses of the sacred words; the assignment of the value of each "sense" in theology; the division of books into parts, and the summaries of the various parts; the investigation of the objects of the writers; the demonstration of the connection of sentence with sentence, and clause with clause; all of which is calculated to throw much light on the more obscure passages of the sacred volume. The valuable work of the scholastics in Holy Scripture is seen in their theological treatises and in their Scripture commentaries; and in this respect the greatest name among them all is St. Thomas Aquinas.

[1] See the Collect on his feast, September 30.

When Our predecessor, Clement V., established chairs of Oriental literature in the Roman College and in the principal universities of Europe, Catholics began to make more accurate investigation on the original text of the Bible as well as on the Latin version. The revival amongst us of Greek learning, and, much more, the happy invention of the art of printing, gave a strong impetus to biblical studies. In a brief space of time, innumerable editions, especially of the Vulgate, poured from the press and were diffused throughout the Catholic world; so honored and loved was Holy Scripture during that very period against which the enemies of the Church direct their calumnies Nor must we forget how many learned men there were, chiefly among the religious orders, who did excellent work for the Bible between the Council of Vienna and that of Trent; men who, by the employment of modern means and appliances, and by the tribute of their own genius and learning, not only added to the rich store of ancient times but prepared the way for the succeeding century, the century which followed the Council of Trent, when it almost seemed that the great age of the Fathers had returned. For it is well known, and We recall it with pleasure, that Our predecessors, from Pius IV. to Clement VIII., caused to be prepared the celebrated editions of the Vulgate and the Septuagint, which, having been published by the command and authority of Sixtus V., and of the same Clement, are now in common use. At this time, moreover, were carefully brought out various other ancient versions of the Bible, and the Polyglots of Antwerp and of Paris, most important for the investigation of the true meaning of the text; nor is there any one book of either Testament which did not find more than one expositor, nor any grave question which did not profitably exercise the ability of many inquirers, among whom there are not a few—more especially of those who made most use of the Fathers—who have acquired great reputation. From that time downwards the labor and solicitude of Catholics have never been wanting; for, as time went on, eminent scholars have carried on biblical studies with success, and have defended Holy Scripture against *rationalism* with the same weapons of philology and kindred sciences with which it had been attacked. The calm and fair consideration of what has been said will clearly show that the Church has never failed in taking due measures to bring the Scriptures within reach of her children, and that she has ever held fast and exercised profitably that guardianship conferred upon her by Almighty God for the protection and glory of His Holy Word; so that she has never required, nor does she now require, any stimulation from without.

We must now, Venerable Brethren, as Our purpose demands, impart to you such counsels as seem best suited for carrying on successfully the study of biblical science.

But first it must be clearly understood whom we have to oppose and contend against, and what are their tactics and their arms. In earlier times the contest was chiefly with those who, relying on private judgment and repudiating the divine traditions and teaching office of the Church, held the Scriptures to be the one source of revelation and the final appeal in matters of faith. Now we have to meet the rationalists, true children and inheritors of the older heretics, who, trusting in their turn to their own way of thinking, have rejected even the scraps and remnants of Christian belief which had been handed down to them. They deny that there is any such thing as revelation or inspiration, or Holy Scripture at all; they see, instead, only the forgeries and falsehoods of men; they set down the Scripture narratives as stupid fables and lying stories: the prophecies and oracles of God are to them either predictions made up after the event or forecasts formed by the light of nature; the miracles and wonders of God's power are not what they are said to be, but the startling effects of natural law, or else mere tricks and myths; and the apostolic Gospels and writings are not the work of the apostles at all. These detestable errors, whereby they think they destroy the truth of the divine books, are obtruded on the world as the peremptory pronouncements of a newly invented *free science;* a science, however, which is so far from final that they are perpetually modifying and supplementing it. And there are some of them who, notwithstanding their impious opinions and utterances about God, and Christ, the Gospels and the rest of Holy Scripture, would fain be considered both theologians and Christians and men of the Gospel, and who attempt to disguise by such honorable names their rashness and their pride. To them we must add not a few professors of other sciences who approve their views and give them assistance, and are urged to attack the Bible by a similar intolerance of revelation. And it is deplorable to see these attacks growing every day more numerous and more severe. It is sometimes men of learning and judgment who are assailed; but these have little difficulty in defending themselves from evil consequences. The efforts and arts of the enemy are chiefly directed against the more ignorant masses of the people. They diffuse their deadly poison by means of books, pamphlets, and newspapers; they spread it by addresses and by conversation; they are found everywhere; and they are in possession of numerous schools, taken by violence from the Church, in which, by ridicule and scurrilous jesting, they pervert the credulous and unformed minds of the young to the contempt of Holy Scripture. Should not these things, Venerable Brethren, stir up and set on fire the heart of every pastor, so that to this *knowledge, falsely so-called,*[1] may be opposed the ancient and true science which the Church, through the apostles, has received from Christ, and that Holy Scripture may find the champions that are needed in so momentous a battle?

Let our first care, then, be to see that in seminaries and

[1] 1 Tim. iv. 20.

academical institutions the study of Holy Scripture is placed on such a footing as its own importance and the circumstances of the time demand. With this view, the first thing which requires attention is the wise choice of professors. Teachers of sacred Scripture are not to be appointed at haphazard out of the crowd; but they must be men whose character and fitness are proved by their love of, and their long familiarity with, the Bible, and by suitable learning and study.

It is a matter of equal importance to provide in time for a continuous succession of such teachers; and it will be well, wherever this can be done, to select young men of good promise who have successfully accomplished their theological course, and to set them apart exclusively for Holy Scripture, affording them facilities for full and complete studies. Professors thus chosen and thus prepared may enter with confidence on the task that is appointed for them; and that they may carry out their work well and profitably, let them take heed to the instructions We now proceed to give.

At the commencement of a course of Holy Scripture, let the professor strive earnestly to form the judgment of the young beginners so as to train them equally to defend the sacred writings and to penetrate their meaning. This is the object of the treatise which is called "Introduction." Here the student is taught how to prove the integrity and authority of the Bible, how to investigate and ascertain its true sense, and how to meet and refute objections. It is needless to insist upon the importance of making these preliminary studies in an orderly and thorough fashion, with the accompaniment and assistance of theology; for the whole subsequent course must rest on the foundation thus laid and make use of the light thus acquired. Next, the teacher will turn his attention to that more fruitful division of Scripture science which has to do with interpretation, wherein is imparted the method of using the Word of God for the advantage of religion and piety. We recognize, without hesitation, that neither the extent of the matter nor the time at disposal allows each single book of the Bible to be separately gone through. But the teaching should result in a definite and ascertained method of interpretation—and, therefore, the professor should equally avoid the mistake of giving a mere taste of every book, and of dwelling at too great a length on a part of one book. If most schools cannot do what is done in large institutions—take the students through the whole of one or two books continuously and with a certain development—yet at least those parts which are selected should be treated with suitable fulness, in such a way that the students may learn from the sample that is put before them to love and use the remainder of the sacred book during the whole of their lives. The professor, following the tradition of antiquity, will make use of the Vulgate as his text; for the Council of Trent decreed that "in public lectures, disputations, preaching, and exposition," [1] the Vulgate is the "authentic" version; and this is the existing custom of the Church. At the same time, the other versions, which Christian antiquity has approved, should not be neglected, more especially the more ancient MSS. For, although the meaning of the Hebrew and Greek is substantially rendered by the Vulgate, nevertheless, wherever there may be ambiguity or want of clearness, the "examination of older tongues," [2] to quote St. Augustine, will be useful and advantageous. But in this matter we need hardly say that the greatest prudence is required, for the "office of a commentator," as St. Jerome says, "is to set forth not what he himself would prefer but what his author says." [3] The question of "reading" having been, when necessary, carefully discussed, the next thing is to investigate and expound the meaning. And the first counsel to be given is this: that

---

[1] Sess. iv. decr. de edit. et usu sacr. libror.
[2] De doctr. chr. iii. 4.
[3] Ad Pammachium.

the more our adversaries contend to the contrary, so much the more solicitously should we adhere to the received and approved canons of interpretation. Hence, whilst weighing the meaning of words, the connection of ideas, the parallelism of passages, and the like, we should by all means make use of such illustrations as can be drawn from opposite erudition of an external sort; but this should be done with caution, so as not to bestow on questions of this kind more labor and time than are spent on the sacred books themselves, and not to overload the minds of the students with a mass of information that will be rather a hindrance than a help.

The professor may now safely pass on to the use of Scripture in matters of theology. On this head it must be observed that, in addition to the usual reasons which make ancient writings more or less difficult to understand, there are some which are peculiar to the Bible. For the language of the Bible is employed to express, under the inspiration of the Holy Ghost, many things which are beyond the power and scope of the reason of man—that is to say, divine mysteries and all that is related to them. There is sometimes in such passages a fulness and a hidden depth of meaning which the letter hardly expresses and which the laws of interpretation hardly warrant. Moreover, the literal sense itself frequently admits other senses, adapted to illustrate dogma or to confirm morality. Wherefore, it must be recognized that the sacred writings are wrapped in a certain religious obscurity, and that no one can enter into their interior without a guide;[1] God so disposing, as the holy Fathers commonly teach, in order that men may investigate them with greater ardor and earnestness, and that what is attained with difficulty may sink more deeply into the mind and heart, and, most of all, that they may understand that God has delivered the Holy Scripture to the Church, and that in

[1] S. Hier. ad Paulin. de studio Script. ep. liii. 4.

reading and making use of His Word they must follow the Church as their guide and their teacher. St. Irenæus long since laid down that where the *chrismata* of God were, there the truth was to be learned, and the Holy Scripture was safely interpreted by those who had the apostolic succession.[1] His teaching and that of other holy Fathers is taken up by the Council of the Vatican, which in renewing the decree of Trent declared its "mind" to be this—that "in things of faith and morals, belonging to the building up of Christian doctrine, that it is to be considered the true sense of Holy Scripture, which has been held and is held by our Holy Mother the Church, whose place it is to judge of the true sense and interpretation of the Scriptures; and, therefore, that it is permitted to no one to interpret Holy Scripture against such sense or also against the unanimous agreement of the Fathers."[2] By this most wise decree the Church by no means prevents or restrains the pursuit of biblical science, but rather protects it from error, and largely assists its real progress. A wide field is still left open to the private student, in which his hermeneutical skill may display itself with signal effect and to the advantages of the Church. On the one hand, in those passages of Holy Scripture which have not as yet received a certain and definite interpretation, such labors may, in the benignant providence of God, prepare for and bring to maturity the judgment of the Church; on the other, in passages already defined, the private student may do work equally valuable, either by setting them forth more clearly to the flock or more skilfully to the scholars, or by defending them more powerfully from hostile attack. Wherefore the first and dearest object of the Catholic commentator should be to interpret those passages which have received an authentic interpretation either from the sacred writers

[1] C. haer. iv. 26, 5.
[2] Sess. iii. cap. ii. de revel.; cf. Conc. Trid. sess. iv. decret de edit. et usu sacr. libror.

themselves, under the inspiration of the Holy Ghost (as in many places of the New Testament), or from the Church, under the assistance of the same Holy Spirit, whether by her solemn judgment or by her ordinary and universal *magisterium* [1]—to interpret these passages in that identical sense, and to prove by all the resources of science that sound hermeneutical laws admit of no other interpretation. In the other passages the analogy of faith should be followed, and Catholic doctrine, as authoritatively proposed by the Church, should be held as the supreme law; for, seeing that the same God is the author both of the sacred books and of the doctrine committed to the Church, it is clearly impossible that any teaching can, by legitimate means, be extracted from the former which shall, in any respect, be at variance with the latter. Hence it follows that all interpretation is foolish or false which either makes the sacred writers disagree one with another, or is opposed to the doctrine of the Church. The professor of Holy Scripture, therefore, amongst other recommendations, must be well acquainted with the whole circle of theology and deeply read in the commentaries of the holy Fathers and Doctors, and in other interpreters of mark.[2] This is inculcated by St. Jerome, and still more frequently by St. Augustine, who thus justly complains: "If there is no branch of teaching, however humble and easy to learn, which does not require a master, what can be a greater sign of rashness and pride than to refuse to study the books of the divine mysteries by the help of those who have interpreted them?"[3] The other Fathers have said the same, and have confirmed it by their example, for they "endeavored to acquire the understanding of the Holy Scriptures not by their own lights and ideas but from the writing and authority of the ancients, who, in their turn, as we know, received the rule of interpretation in direct line from the apostles."[4] The holy Fathers

[1] Conc. Vat. sess. iii. cap. ii. de fide.   [2] Ibid.
[3] Ad Honorat de util. cred. xvii. 35. [4] Rufinus Hist. eccl. li. 9.

"to whom, after the apostles, the Church owes its growth —who have planted, watered, built, governed, and cherished it";[1] the holy Fathers, We say, are of supreme authority, whenever they all interpret in one and the same manner any text of the Bible, as pertaining to the doctrine of faith and morals; for their unanimity clearly evinces that such interpretation has come down from the apostles as a matter of Catholic faith. The opinion of the Fathers is also of very great weight when they treat of these matters in their capacity of Doctors unofficially; not only because they excel in their knowledge of revealed doctrine and in their acquaintance with many things which are useful in understanding the apostolic books, but because they are men of eminent sanctity and of ardent zeal for the truth, on whom God has bestowed a more ample measure of His light. Wherefore the expositor should make it his duty to follow their footsteps with all reverence, and to use their labors with intelligent appreciation.

But he must not on that account consider that it is forbidden, when just cause exists, to push inquiry and exposition beyond what the Fathers have done; provided he carefully observes the rule so wisely laid down by St. Augustine—not to depart from the literal and obvious sense, except only where reason makes it untenable or necessity requires; [2] a rule to which it is the more necessary to adhere strictly in these times, when the thirst for novelty and the unrestrained freedom of thought make the danger of error most real and proximate. Neither should those passages be neglected which the Fathers have understood in an allegorical or figurative sense, more especially when such interpretation is justified by the literal, and when it rests on the authority of many. For this method of interpretation has been received by the Church from the apostles, and has been approved by her own practice, as the holy Liturgy attests; although it is true that the holy Fathers did not

[1] S. Aug. c. Julian. ii. 10, 37.
[2] De Gen. ad litt. lviii. c. 7, 13.

thereby pretend directly to demonstrate dogmas of faith, but used it as a means of promoting virtue and piety, such as, by their own experience, they knew to be most valuable. The authority of other Church interpreters is not so great; but the study of Scripture has always continued to advance in the Church, and, therefore, these commentaries also have their own honorable place, and are serviceable in many ways for the refutation of assailants and the explanation of difficulties. But it is most unbecoming to pass by, in ignorance or contempt, the excellent work which Catholics have left in abundance, and to have recourse to the work of non-Catholics—and to seek in them, to the detriment of sound doctrine and often to the peril of faith, the explanation of passages on which Catholics long ago have successfully employed their talent and their labor. For although the studies of non-Catholics, used with prudence, may sometimes be of use to the Catholic student, he should, nevertheless, bear well in mind—as the Fathers also teach in numerous passages [1]—that the sense of Holy Scripture can nowhere be found incorrupt outside the Church, and cannot be expected to be found in writers who, being without the true faith, only know the bark of sacred Scripture, and never attain its pith.

Most desirable is it, and most essential, that the whole teaching of theology should be pervaded and animated by the use of the divine Word of God. That is what the Fathers and the greatest theologians of all ages have desired and reduced to practice. It is chiefly out of the sacred writings that they endeavored to proclaim and establish the Articles of Faith and the truths therewith connected, and it was in them, together with divine tradition, that they found the refutation of heretical error, and the reasonableness, the true meaning, and the mutual relation of the truths of Catholicism. Nor will any one wonder at this who considers that the sacred books hold

[1] Cfr. Clem. Alex. Strom. vii. 16; Orig. de princ. iv. 8; in Levit. hom. 48; Tertull. de praescr. 15, seqq.; S. Hilar. Pict. in Matth. 13, 1.

such an eminent position among the sources of revelation that without their assiduous study and use theology cannot be placed on a true footing, or treated as its dignity demands. For although it is right and proper that students in academies and schools should be chiefly exercised in acquiring a scientific knowledge of dogma, by means of reasoning from the Articles of Faith to their consequences, according to the rules of approved and sound philosophy—nevertheless the judicious and instructed theologian will by no means pass by that method of doctrinal demonstration which draws its proof from the authority of the Bible; "for theology does not receive her first principles from any other science, but immediately from God by revelation. And, therefore, she does not receive of other sciences as from a superior, but uses them as her inferiors or handmaids." [1]　It is this view of doctrinal teaching which is laid down and recommended by the prince of theologians, St. Thomas of Aquin; [2] who moreover shows—such being the essential character of Christian theology—how she can defend her own principles against attack: "If the adversary," he says, "do but grant any portion of the divine revelation, we have an argument against him; thus, against a heretic we can employ Scripture authority, and against those who deny one article we can use another. But if our opponent reject divine revelation entirely, there is no way left to prove the Articles of Faith by reasoning; we can only solve the difficulties which are raised against them." [3]　Care must be taken, then, that beginners approach the study of the Bible well prepared and furnished; otherwise, just hopes will be frustrated, or, perchance, what is worse, they will unthinkingly risk the danger of error, falling an easy prey to the sophisms and labored erudition of the rationalists. The best preparation will be a conscientious application to philosophy and theology

[1] S. Greg. M. Moral xx. 9 (al. 11).
[2] Summ. Theol. p. i. q. i. a. 5 ad 2.
[3] Ibid. a. 8.

under the guidance of St. Thomas of Aquin, and a thorough training therein—as We Ourselves have elsewhere pointed out and directed. By this means, both in biblical studies and in that part of theology which is called *positive*, they will pursue the right path and make satisfactory progress.

To prove, to expound, to illustrate Catholic doctrine by the legitimate and skilful interpretation of the Bible is much; but there is a second part of the subject of equal importance and equal difficulty—the maintenance in the strongest possible way of its full authority. This cannot be done completely or satisfactorily except by means of the living and proper *magisterium* of the Church. The Church, by reason of her wonderful propagation, her distinguished sanctity, and inexhaustible fecundity in good, her Catholic unity, and her unshaken stability, is herself a great and perpetual motive of credibility, and an unassailable testimony to her own divine mission." [1] But, since the divine and infallible *magisterium* of the Church rests also on Holy Scripture. the first thing to be done is to vindicate the trustworthiness of sacred records, at least as human documents from which can be clearly proved, as from primitive and authentic testimony, the divinity and the mission of Christ our Lord, the institution of a hierarchical Church and the primacy of Peter and his successors. It is most desirable, therefore, that there should be numerous members of the clergy well prepared to enter on a contest of this nature, and to repulse hostile assaults, chiefly trusting in the armor of God recommended by the Apostle,[2] but also not unaccustomed to modern methods of attack. This is beautifully alluded to by St. John Chrysostom, when describing the duties of priests: "We must use every endeavor that the 'Word of God may dwell in us abundantly';[3] not merely for one kind of a fight must we be prepared—for the contest is many-sided and the enemy is of every sort;

---

[1] Conc. Vat. sess iii. c. ii. de fide.   [2] Eph. vi. 13, seqq.
[3] Cfr. Coloss. iii. 16.

and they do not all use the same weapons nor make their onset in the same way. Wherefore it is needful that the man who has to contend against all should be acquainted with the engines and the arts of all—that he should be at once archer and slinger, commandant and officer, general and private soldier, foot-soldier and horseman, skilled in sea-fight and in siege; for unless he knows every trick and turn of war, the devil is well able, if only a single door be left open, to get in his fierce bands and carry off the sheep." [1] The sophisms of the enemy and his manifold arts of attack we have already touched upon. Let us now say a word of advice on the means of defence. The first means is the study of the Oriental languages and of the art of criticism. These two acquirements are in these days held in high estimation, and, therefore, the clergy, by making themselves fully acquainted with them as time and place may demand, will the better be able to discharge their office with becoming credit; for they must make themselves *all to all,*[2] always *ready to satisfy every one that asketh them a reason for the hope that is in them.*[3]   Hence it is most proper that professors of sacred Scripture and theologians should master those tongues in which the sacred books were originally written; and it would be well that Church students also should cultivate them, more especially those who aspire to academic degrees. And endeavors should be made to establish in all academic institutions—as has already been laudably done in many—chairs of the other ancient languages, especially the Semitic, and of subjects connected therewith, for the benefit, principally, of those who are intended to profess sacred literature. These latter, with a similar object in view, should make themselves well and thoroughly acquainted with the art of true criticism. There has arisen, to the great detriment of religion, an inept method, dignified by the name of the "higher criticism," which pretends to judge the origin,

---

[1] De Sacerdotio iv. 4.   [2] 1 Cor. ix. 22.   [3] 1 Peter iii. 15.

integrity and authority of each book from internal indications alone. It is clear, on the other hand, that in historical
questions, such as the origin and handing down of writings,
the witness of history is of primary importance, and that
historical investigation should be made with the utmost
care; and that in this manner internal evidence is seldom
of great value, except as confirmation. To look upon it
in any other light will be to open the door to many evil
consequences. It will make the enemies of religion much
more bold and confident in attacking and mangling the
sacred books; and this vaunted "higher criticism" will
resolve itself into the reflection of the bias and the prejudice of the critics. It will not throw on the Scripture the
light which is sought, or prove of any advantage to doctrine; it will only give rise to disagreement and dissension,
those sure notes of error which the critics in question so
plentifully exhibit in their own persons; and seeing that
most of them are tainted with false philosophy and rationalism, it must lead to the elimination from the sacred
writings of all prophecy and miracle, and of everything
else that is outside the natural order.

In the second place, we have to contend against those
who, making an evil use of physical science, minutely
scrutinize the sacred book in order to detect the writers in
a mistake, and to take occasion to vilify its contents. Attacks of this kind, bearing as they do on matters of sensible
experience, are peculiarly dangerous to the masses, and
also to the young who are beginning their literary studies;
for the young, if they lose their reverence for the Holy
Scripture on one or more points, are easily led to give up
believing in it altogether. It need not be pointed out how
the nature of science, just as it is so admirably adapted to
show forth the glory of the Great Creator, provided it is
taught as it should be, so, if it be perversely imparted to
the youthful intelligence, it may prove most fatal in destroying the principles of true philosophy and in the corruption of morality. Hence, to the professor of sacred

Scripture a knowledge of natural science will be of very great assistance in detecting such attacks on the sacred books, and in refuting them.   There can never, indeed, be any real discrepancy between the theologian and the physicist, as long as each confines himself within his own lines, and both are careful, as St. Augustine warns us, "not to make rash assertions, or to assert what is not known as known." [1] If dissension should arise between them, here is the rule also laid down by St. Augustine, for the theologian: "Whatever they can really demonstrate to be true of physical nature we must show to be capable of reconciliation with our Scriptures; and whatever they assert in their treatises which is contrary to these Scriptures of ours, that is to Catholic faith, we must either prove it as well as we can to be entirely false, or at all events we must, without the smallest hesitation, believe it to be so." [2] To understand how just is the rule here formulated we must remember, first, that the sacred writers, or, to speak more accurately, the Holy Ghost "who spoke by them, did not intend to teach men these things (that is to say, the essential nature of the things of the visible universe), things in no way profitable unto salvation." [3] Hence they did not seek to penetrate the secrets of nature, but rather described and dealt with things in more or less figurative language, or in terms which were commonly used at the time, and which in many instances are in daily use at this day, even by the most eminent men of science. Ordinary speech primarily and properly describes what comes under the senses; and somewhat in the same way the sacred writers—as the Angelic Doctor also reminds us—"went by what sensibly appeared," [4] or put down what God, speaking to men, signified, in the way men could understand and were accustomed to.

[1] In. Gen. op. imperf. ix. 30.
[2] De Gen. ad litt. i. 21, 41.
[3] S. Aug. ib. ii. 9, 20.
[4] Summa Theol. p. i. q. lxxx. a. 1 ad 3.

The unshrinking defence of the Holy Scripture, however, does not require that we should equally uphold all the opinions which each of the Fathers or the more recent interpreters have put forth in explaining it; for it may be that, in commenting on passages where physical matters occur, they have sometimes expressed the ideas of their own times, and thus made statements which in these days have been abandoned as incorrect. Hence, in their interpretations, we must carefully note what they lay down as belonging to faith, or as intimately connected with faith—what they are unanimous in. For "in those things which do not come under the obligation of faith, the saints were at liberty to hold divergent opinions, just as we ourselves are,"[1] according to the saying of St. Thomas. And in another place he says most admirably: "When philosophers are agreed upon a point, and it is not contrary to our faith, it is safer, in my opinion, neither to lay down such a point as a dogma of faith, even though it is perhaps so presented by the philosophers, nor to reject it as against faith, lest we thus give to the wise of this world an occasion of despising our faith."[2] The Catholic interpreter, although he should show that those facts of natural science which investigators affirm to be now quite certain are not contrary to the Scripture rightly explained, must, nevertheless, always bear in mind that much which has been held and proved as certain has afterwards been called in question and rejected. And if writers on physics travel outside the boundaries of their own branch, and carry their erroneous teaching into the domain of philosophy, let them be handed over to philosophers for refutation.

The principles here laid down will apply to cognate sciences, and especially to history. It is a lamentable fact that there are many who with great labor carry out and publish investigations on the monuments of antiquity, the manners and institutions of nations, and other illustrative

[1] In Sent. ii. Dist. q. i. a. 3.   [2] Opusc. x.

subjects, and whose chief purpose in all this is to find mistakes in the sacred writings and so to shake and weaken their authority. Some of these writers display not only extreme hostility but the greatest unfairness; in their eyes a profane book or ancient document is accepted without hesitation, whilst the Scripture, if they only find in it a suspicion of error, is set down with the slightest possible discussion as quite untrustworthy. It is true, no doubt, that copyists have made mistakes in the text of the Bible; this question, when it arises, should be carefully considered on its merits, and the fact not too easily admitted, but only in those passages where the proof is clear. It may also happen that the sense of a passage remains ambiguous, and in this case good hermeneutical methods will greatly assist in clearing up the obscurity. But it is absolutely wrong and forbidden either to narrow inspiration to certain parts only of Holy Scripture or to admit that the sacred writer has erred. For the system of those who, in order to rid themselves of those difficulties, do not hesitate to concede that divine inspiration regards the things of faith and morals, and nothing beyond, because (as they wrongly think) in a question of the truth or falsehood of a passage we should consider not so much what God has said as the reason and purpose which He had in mind when saying it—this system cannot be tolerated. For all the books which the Church receives as sacred and canonical are written wholly and entirely, with all their parts, at the dictation of the Holy Ghost; and so far is it from being possible that any error can co-exist with inspiration, that inspiration not only is essentially incompatible with error, but excludes and rejects it as absolutely and necessarily as it is impossible that God Himself, the Supreme Truth, can utter that which is not true. This is the ancient and unchanging faith of the Church, solemnly defined in the Councils of Florence and of Trent, and finally confirmed and more expressly formulated by the Council of the Vatican. These are the words of the last: "The books of the Old and New

Testament, whole and entire, with all their parts, as enumerated by the decree of the same Council (Trent) and in the ancient Latin Vulgate, are to be received as sacred and canonical. And the Church holds them as sacred and canonical not because, having been composed by human industry, they were afterwards approved by her authority, nor only because they contain revelation without error, but because, having been written under the inspiration of the Holy Ghost, they have God for their Author." [1] Hence, because the Holy Ghost employed men as His instruments, we cannot, therefore, say that it was these inspired instruments who, perchance, have fallen into error, and not the primary author. For, by supernatural power, He so moved and impelled them to write—He was so present to them—that the things which He ordered, and those only, they, first, rightly understood, then willed faithfully to write down, and finally expressed in apt words and with infallible truth. Otherwise, it could not be said that He was the Author of the entire Scripture. Such has always been the persuasion of the Fathers. "Therefore," says St. Augustine, "since they wrote the things which He showed and uttered to them, it cannot be pretended that He is not the writer; for His members executed what their head dictated." [2] And St. Gregory the Great thus pronounces: "Most superfluous it is to inquire who wrote these things—we loyally believe the Holy Ghost to be the author of the Book. He wrote it who dictated it for writing; He wrote it who inspired its execution." [3]

It follows that those who maintain that an error is possible in any genuine passage of the sacred writings either pervert the Catholic notion of inspiration or make God the author of such error. And so emphatically were all the Fathers and Doctors agreed that the divine writings, as left by the hagiographers, are free from all error, that

---

[1] Sess. iii. c. ii. de Rev.   [2] De consensu Evangel l. 1, c. 35.
[3] Praef. in Job, n. 2.

they labored earnestly, with no less skill than reverence, to reconcile with each other those numerous passages which seem at variance—the very passages which in a great measure have been taken up by the "higher criticism"; for they were unanimous in laying it down that those writings, in their entirety and in all their parts were equally from the *afflatus* of Almighty God, and that God, speaking by the sacred writers, could not set down anything that was not true.   The words of St. Augustine to St. Jerome may sum up what they taught: "On my own part I confess to your charity that it is only to those books of Scripture which are now called canonical that I have learned to pay such honor and reverence as to believe most firmly that none of their writers has fallen into any error.   And if in these books I meet anything which seems contrary to truth I shall not hesitate to conclude either that the text is faulty, or that the translator has not expressed the meaning of the passage, or that I myself do not understand." [1]

But to undertake fully and perfectly, and with all the weapons of the best science, the defence of the Holy Bible is far more than can be looked for from the exertions of commentators and theologians alone.   It is an enterprise in which we have a right to expect the co-operation of all those Catholics who have acquired reputation in any branch of learning whatever.   As in the past, so at the present time, the Church is never without the graceful support of her accomplished children; may their service to the Faith grow and increase!   For there is nothing which We believe to be more needful than that truth should find defenders more powerful and more numerous than the enemies it has to face; nor is there anything which is better calculated to impress the masses with respect for truth than to see it boldly proclaimed by learned and distinguished men.   Moreover, the bitter tongues of objectors will be silenced, or at least they will not dare to insist so

---

[1] Ep. lxxvii. 1, et crebrius alibi.

shamelessly that faith is the enemy of science, when they see that scientific men of eminence in their profession show towards faith the most marked honor and respect. Seeing, then, that those can do so much for the advantage of religion on whom the goodness of Almighty God has bestowed, together with the grace of the faith, great natural talent, let such men, in this bitter conflict of which the Holy Scripture is the object, select each of them the branch of study most suitable to his circumstances, and endeavor to excel therein, and thus be prepared to repulse with credit and distinction the assaults on the Word of God. And it is Our pleasing duty to give deserved praise to a work which certain Catholics have taken up—that is to say, the formation of societies and the contribution of considerable sums of money for the purpose of supplying studios and learned men with every kind of help and assistance in carrying out complete studies. Truly an excellent fashion of investing money, and well suited to the times in which we live! The less hope of public patronage there is for Catholic study, the more ready and the more abundant should be the liberality of private persons —those to whom God has given riches thus willingly making use of their means to safeguard the treasure of His revealed doctrine.

In order that all these endeavors and exertions may really prove advantageous to the cause of the Bible, let scholars keep steadfastly to the principles which We have in this Letter laid down. Let them loyally hold that God, the Creator and Ruler of all things, is also the Author of the Scriptures—and that, therefore, nothing can be proved either by physical science or archæology which can really contradict the Scriptures. If, then, apparent contradiction be met with, every effort should be made to remove it. Judicious theologians and commentators should be consulted as to what is the true or most probable meaning of the passage in discussion, and hostile arguments should be carefully weighed. Even if the difficulty is after all not cleared up and the discrepancy seems to remain, the contest must not be abandoned; truth cannot contradict truth, and we may be sure that some mistake has been made either in the interpretation of the sacred words or in the polemical discussion itself; and if no such mistake can be detected, we must then suspend judgment for the time being. There have been objections without number perseveringly directed against the Scripture for many a long year, which have been proved to be futile and are now never heard of; and not infrequently interpretations have been placed on certain passages of Scripture (not belonging to the rule of faith or morals) which have been rectified by more careful investigations. As time goes on, mistaken views die and disappear; but *truth remaineth and groweth stronger forever and ever.*[1] Wherefore, as no one should be so presumptuous as to think that he understands the whole of the Scripture, in which St. Augustine himself confessed that there was more that he did not know than that he knew,[2] so, if he should come on anything that seems incapable of solution, he must take to heart the cautious rule of the same holy doctor: "It is better even to be oppressed by unknown but useful signs than to interpret them uselessly, and thus to throw off the yoke only to be caught in the trap of error." [3]

As to those who pursue the subsidiary studies of which We have spoken, if they honestly and modestly follow the counsels We have given—if by their pen and their voice they make their studies profitable against the enemies of truth, and useful in saving the young from the loss of their faith—they may justly congratulate themselves on their worthy service to the sacred writings, and on affording to Catholicism that assistance which the Church has a right to expect from the piety and learning of her children.

Such, Venerable Brethren, are the admonitions and the instructions which, by the help of God, We have thought

[1] 3 Esdr. iv. 38.   [2] Ad Ianuar. ep. lv. 21.
[3] De doctr. chr. iii. 9, 18.

it well, at the present moment, to offer to you on the study of Holy Scripture. It will now be your province to see that what We have said be observed and put in practice with all due reverence and exactness; that so We may prove our gratitude to God for the communication to man of the words of His wisdom, and that all the good results so much to be desired may be realized, especially as they affect the training of the students of the Church, which is our own great solicitude and the Church's hope. Exert yourselves with willing alacrity, and use your authority and your persuasion in order that these studies may be held in just regard and may flourish in seminaries and in educational institutions which are under your jurisdiction. Let them flourish in completeness and in happy success, under the direction of the Church, in accordance with the salutary teaching and example of the holy Fathers, and the laudable traditions of antiquity; and, as time goes on, let them be widened and extended as the interests and glory of truth may require—the interests of that Catholic truth which comes from above, the never-failing source of man's salvation. Finally, We admonish with paternal love all students and ministers of the Church always to approach the sacred writings with reverence and piety; for it is impossible to attain to the profitable understanding thereof unless the arrogance of "earthly" science be laid aside, and there be excited in the heart the holy desire for that wisdom "which is from above." In this way the intelligence which is once admitted to these sacred studies, and thereby illuminated and strengthened, will acquire a marvellous facility in detecting and avoiding the fallacies of human science, and in gathering and using for eternal salvation all that is valuable and precious; whilst, at the same time, the heart will grow warm, and will strive, with ardent longing, to advance in virtue and in divine love. *Blessed are they who examine His testimonies; they shall seek Him with their whole heart.*[1]

[1] Ps. cxviii. 2.

And now, filled with hope in the divine assistance, and trusting to your pastoral solicitude—as a pledge of heavenly grace, and a sign of Our special good-will—to you all, and to the clergy, and to the whole flock entrusted to you, We lovingly impart in Our Lord the Apostolic Benediction.

THE REUNION OF CHRISTENDOM.

Encyclical Letter Præclara Gratulationis Publicæ, June 20, 1894.

THE splendid tokens of public rejoicing which have come to Us from all sides in the whole course of last year, to commemorate Our Episcopal Jubilee, and which were lately crowned by the remarkable devotion of the Spanish nation, have afforded Us special joy, inasmuch as the unity of the Church and the admirable adhesion of her members to the Sovereign Pontiff have shone forth in this perfect agreement of concurring sentiments. During those days it seemed as if the Catholic world, forgetful of everything else, had centred its gaze and all its thoughts upon the Vatican.

The special missions sent by kings and princes, the many pilgrimages, the letters We received so full of affectionate feeling, the sacred services—everything clearly brought out the fact that all Catholics are of one mind and of one heart in their veneration for the Apostolic See. And this was all the more pleasing and agreeable to Us, that it is entirely in conformity with Our intent and with Our endeavors. For, indeed, well acquainted with Our times, and mindful of the duties of Our ministry, We have constantly sought during the whole course of Our Pontificate and striven, as far as it was possible, by teaching and action, to bind every nation and people more closely to Us, and make manifest everywhere the salutary influence of the See of Rome. Therefore do We most earnestly offer thanks in the first place to the goodness of God, by whose help and bounty We have been preserved to attain

303

Our great age; and then, next, to all the princes and rulers, to the bishops and clergy, and to as many as have co-operated by such repeated tokens of piety and reverence to honor Our character and office, while affording Us personally such seasonable consolation.

A great deal, however, has been wanting to the entire fulness of that consolation. Amidst these very manifestations of public joy and reverence Our thoughts went out towards the immense multitude of those who are strangers to the gladness that filled all Catholic hearts: some because they lie in absolute ignorance of the Gospel; others because they dissent from the Catholic belief, though they bear the name of Christians.

This thought has been, and is, a source of deep concern to Us; for it is impossible to think of such a large portion of mankind deviating, as it were, from the right path, as they move away from Us, and not experience a sentiment of innermost grief.

But since We hold upon this earth the place of God Almighty, who will have all men to be saved and to come to the knowledge of the truth, and now that Our advanced age and the bitterness of anxious cares urge Us on towards the end common to every mortal, We feel drawn to follow the example of Our Redeemer and Master, Jesus Christ, who, when about to return to heaven, implored of God, His Father, in earnest prayer, that His disciples and folfowers should be of one mind and of one heart: *I pray . . . that they all may be one, as thou Father in Me, and I in Thee: that they also may be one in Us.* And as this divine prayer and supplication does not include only the souls who then believed in Jesus Christ, but also every one of those who were henceforth to believe in Him, this prayer holds out to Us no indifferent reason for confidently expressing Our hopes, and for making all possible endeavors in order that the men of every race and clime should be called and moved to embrace the unity of divine faith.

Pressed on to Our intent by charity, that hastens fastest there where the need is greatest, We direct Our first thoughts to those most unfortunate of all nations who have never received the light of the Gospel, or who, after having possessed it, have lost it through neglect or the vicissitudes of time: hence do they ignore God, and live in the depths of error. Now, as all salvation comes from Jesus Christ—*for there is no other name under heaven given to men whereby we must be saved*—Our ardent desire is that the most holy name of Jesus should rapidly pervade and fill every land.

And here, indeed, is a duty which the Church, faithful to the divine mission entrusted to her, has never neglected. What has been the object of her labors for more than nineteen centuries? Is there any other work she has undertaken with greater zeal and constancy than that of bringing the nations of the earth to the truth and principles of Christianity? To-day, as ever, by Our authority, the heralds of the Gospel constantly cross the seas to reach the farthest corners of the earth; and We pray God daily that in His goodness He may deign to increase the number of His ministers who are really worthy of this apostolate, and who are ready to sacrifice their convenience, their health, and their very life, if need be, in order to extend the frontiers of the kingdom of Christ.

Do Thou, above all, O Saviour and Father of mankind, Christ Jesus, hasten and do not delay to bring about what Thou didst once promise to do—that when lifted up from the earth Thou wouldst draw all things to Thyself. Come, then, at last, and manifest Thyself to the immense multitude of souls who have not felt, as yet, the ineffable blessings which Thou hast earned for men with Thy blood; rouse those who are sitting in darkness and in the shadow of death, that, enlightened by the rays of Thy wisdom and virtue, in Thee and by Thee "they may be made perfect in one."

As We consider the mystery of this unity We see before

Us all the countries which have long since passed, by the mercy of God, from timeworn error to the wisdom of the Gospel. Nor could We, indeed, recall anything more pleasing or better calculated to extol the work of divine Providence than the memory of the days of yore, when the faith that had come down from heaven was looked upon as the common inheritance of one and all; when civilized nations, separated by distance, character and habits, in spite of frequent disagreements and warfare on other points, were united by Christian faith in all that concerned religion. The recollection of that time causes Us to regret all the more deeply that as the ages rolled by the waves of suspicion and hatred arose, and great and flourishing nations were dragged away, in an evil hour, from the bosom of the Roman Church. In spite of that, however, We trust in the mercy of God's almighty power, in Him who alone can fix the hour of His benefits and who has power to incline man's will as He pleases; and We turn to those same nations, exhorting and beseeching them with fatherly love to put an end to their dissensions and return again to unity.

First of all, then, We cast an affectionate look upon the East, from whence in the beginning came forth the salvation of the world. Yes, and the yearning desire of Our heart bids us conceive and hope that the day is not far distant when the Eastern Churches, so illustrious in their ancient faith and glorious past, will return to the fold they have abandoned. We hope it all the more, that the distance separating them from Us is not so great: nay, with some few exceptions, we agree so entirely on other heads that, in defence of the Catholic faith, we often have recourse to reasons and testimony borrowed from the teaching, the rites, and customs of the East.

The principal subject of contention is the primacy of the Roman Pontiff. But let them look back to the early years of their existence, let them consider the sentiments entertained by their forefathers, and examine what the oldest traditions testify, and it will, indeed, become evident to them that Christ's divine utterance, *Thou art Peter, and upon this rock I will build My Church,* has undoubtedly been realized in the Roman Pontiffs. Many of these latter in the first ages of the Church were chosen from the East, and foremost among them Anacletus, Evaristus, Anicetus, Eleutherius, Zosimus, and Agatho; and of these a great number, after governing the Church in wisdom and sanctity, consecrated their ministry with the shedding of their blood. The time, the reasons, the promoters of the unfortunate division, are well known. Before the day when man separated what God had joined together, the name of the Apostolic See was held in reverence by all the nations of the Christian world: and the East, like the West, agreed without hesitation in its obedience to the Pontiff of Rome, as the legitimate successor of St. Peter, and, therefore, the Vicar of Christ here on earth.

And, accordingly, if we refer to the beginning of the dissension, we shall see that Photius himself was careful to send his advocates to Rome on the matters that concerned him; and Pope Nicholas I. sent his legates to Constantinople from the Eternal City, without the slightest opposition, "in order to examine the case of Ignatius the Patriarch with all diligence, and to bring back to the Apostolic See a full and accurate report"; so that the history of the whole negotiation is a manifest confirmation of the primacy of the Roman See with which the dissension then began. Finally, in two great Councils, the second of Lyons and that of Florence, Latins and Greeks, as is notorious, easily agreed, and all unanimously proclaimed as dogma the supreme power of the Roman Pontiffs.

We have recalled these things intentionally, for they constitute an invitation to peace and reconciliation; and with all the more reason that in Our own days it would seem as if there were a more conciliatory spirit towards Catholics on the part of the Eastern Churches, and even some degree of kindly feeling. To mention an instance, those sentiments were lately made manifest when some of Our faithful travelled to the East on a holy enterprise, and received so many proofs of courtesy and good-will.

Therefore, *Our mouth is open to you,* to you all of Greek or other Oriental rites who are separated from the Catholic Church. We earnestly desire that each and every one of you should meditate upon the words, so full of gravity and love, addressed by Bessarion to your forefathers: "What answer shall we give to God when He comes to ask why we have separated from our brethren: to Him who, to unite us and bring us into one fold, came down from heaven, was incarnate, and was crucified? What will our defence be in the eyes of posterity? Oh, my Venerable Fathers, we must not suffer this to be, we must not entertain this thought, we must not thus so ill provide for ourselves and for our brethren."

Weigh carefully in your minds and before God the nature of Our request. It is not for any human motive, but impelled by divine charity and a desire for the salvation of all, that We advise the reconciliation and union with the Church of Rome; and We mean a perfect and complete union, such as could not subsist in any way if nothing else was brought about but a certain kind of agreement in the tenets of belief and an intercourse of fraternal love. The true union between Christians is that which Jesus Christ, the Author of the Church, instituted and desired, and which consists in a unity of faith and a unity of government.

Nor is there any reason for you to fear on that account that We or any of Our successors will ever diminish your rights, the privileges of your patriarchs, or the established ritual of any one of your churches. It has been and always will be the intent and tradition of the Apostolic See, to make a large allowance, in all that is right and good, for the primitive traditions and special customs of every nation. On the contrary, if you re-establish union with Us, you will see how, by God's bounty, the glory and dignity of your churches will be remarkably increased. May God, then, in His goodness, hear the prayer that you yourselves address to Him: "Make the schisms of the churches cease," and "Assemble those who are dispersed, bring back those who err, and unite them to Thy Holy Catholic and Apostolic Church." May you thus return to that one holy Faith which has been handed down both to Us and to you from time immemorial; which your forefathers preserved untainted, and which was enhanced by the rival splendor of the virtues, the great genius, and the sublime learning of St. Athanasius and St. Basil, St. Gregory of Nazianzum and St. John Chrysostom, the two saints who bore the name of Cyril, and so many other great men whose glory belongs as a common inheritance to the East and to the West.

Suffer that We should address you more particularly, nations of the Slavonic race, you whose glorious name and deeds are attested by many an ancient record. You know full well how much the Slavs are indebted to the merits of St. Cyril and St. Methodius, to whose memory We Ourselves have rendered due honor only a few years ago. Their virtues and their labors were to great numbers of your race the source of civilization and salvation. And hence the admirable interchange, which existed for so long between the Slavonic nations and the Pontiffs of Rome, of favors on the one side and of filial devotion on the other. If in unhappy times many of your forefathers were separated from the Faith of Rome, consider now what priceless benefits a return of unity would bring to you. The Church is anxious to welcome you also to her arms, that she may give you manifold aids to salvation, prosperity, and grandeur.

With no less affection do We now look upon the nations who, at a more recent date, were separated from the Roman Church by an extraordinary revolution of things and circumstances. Let them forget the various events of times gone by, let them raise their thoughts far above all that is human, and seeking only truth and salvation, reflect within their hearts upon the Church as it was constituted by Christ. If they will but compare that Church with their own communions, and consider what the actual state of religion is in these, they will easily acknowledge that, forgetful of their early history, they have drifted away, on many and important points, into the novelty of various errors; nor will they deny that of what may be called the patrimony of truth, which the authors of those innovations carried away with them in their desertion, there now scarcely remains to them any article of belief that is really certain and supported by authority.

Nay, more, things have already come to such a pass that many do not even hesitate to root up the very foundation upon which alone rests all religion, and the hope of men, to wit, the divine nature of Jesus Christ, our Saviour. And again, whereas formerly they used to assert that the books of the Old and the New Testament were written under the inspiration of God, they now deny them that authority: this, indeed, was an inevitable consequence when they granted to all the right of private interpretation. Hence, too, the acceptance of individual conscience as the sole guide and rule of conduct to the exclusion of any other: hence those conflicting opinions and numerous sects that fall away so often into the doctrines of Naturalism and Rationalism.

Therefore it is, that having lost all hope of an agreement in their persuasions, they now proclaim and recommend a union of brotherly love. And rightly, too, no doubt, for we should all be united by the bond of mutual charity. Our Lord Jesus Christ enjoined it most emphatically, and wished that this love of one another should be the mark of His disciples. But how can hearts be united in perfect charity where minds do not agree in faith?

It is on this account that many of those We allude to

men of sound judgment and seeking after truth, have looked to the Catholic Church for the sure way of salvation; for they clearly understand that they could never be united to Jesus Christ as their head if they were not members of His body, which is the Church; nor really acquire the true Christian faith if they rejected the legitimate teaching confided to Peter and his successors. Such men as these have recognized in the Church of Rome the form and image of the true Church, which is clearly made manifest by the marks that God, her Author, placed upon her: and not a few who were possessed with penetrating judgment and a special talent for historical research, have shown forth in their remarkable writings the uninterrupted succession of the Church of Rome from the apostles, the integrity of her doctrine, and the consistency of her rule and discipline.

With the example of such men before you, Our heart appeals to you even more than Our words: to you, Our Brethren, who for three centuries and more differ from Us on Christian faith; and to you all likewise, who in later times, for any reason whatsoever, have turned away from Us: *Let us all meet in the unity of faith and of the knowledge of the Son of God.* Suffer that We should invite you to the unity which has ever existed in the Catholic Church and can never fail; suffer that We should lovingly hold out Our hand to you. The Church, as the common mother of all, has long been calling you back to her; the Catholics of the world await you with brotherly love, that you may render holy worship to God together with us, united in perfect charity by the profession of one Gospel, one faith, and one hope.

To complete the harmony of this most desired unity, it remains for Us to address all those throughout the world whose salvation has long been the object of Our thoughts and watchful cares; We mean Catholics, whom the profession of the Roman faith, while it renders them obedient to the Apostolic See, preserves in union with Jesus Christ.

There is no need to exhort them to true and holy unity, since through the divine goodness they already possess it; nevertheless, they must be admonished, lest under pressure of the growing perils on all sides around them, through negligence or indolence they should lose this great blessing of God. For this purpose, let them take this rule of thought and action, as the occasion may require, from those instructions which at other times We have addressed to Catholic peoples, either collectively or individually; and above all, let them lay down for themselves as a supreme law, to yield obedience in all things to the teaching and authority of the Church, in no narrow or mistrustful spirit, but with their whole soul and promptitude of will.

On this account let them consider how injurious to Christian unity is that error, which in various forms of opinion has ofttimes obscured, nay, even destroyed the true character and idea of the Church. For by the will and ordinance of God, its Founder, it is a society perfect in its kind, whose office and mission it is to school mankind in the precepts and teachings of the Gospel, and by safeguarding the integrity of moral and the exercise of Christian virtue, to lead men to that happiness which is held out to every one in heaven. And since it is, as we have said, a perfect society, therefore it is endowed with a living power and efficacy which is not derived from any external source, but in virtue of the ordinance of God and its own constitution, inherent in its very nature; for the same reason it has an inborn power of making laws, and justice requires that in its exercise it should be dependent on no one; it must likewise have freedom in other matters appertaining to its rights.

But this freedom is not of a kind to occasion rivalry or envy, for the Church does not covet power, nor is she urged on by any selfish desire; but this one thing she does wish, this only does she seek, to preserve amongst men the duties which virtue imposes, and by this means and in this way to provide for their everlasting welfare.

Therefore is she wont to be yielding and indulgent as a mother; yea, it not unfrequently happens that in making large concessions to the exigencies of States, she refrains from the exercise of her own rights, as the compacts often concluded with civil governments abundantly testify.

Nothing is more foreign to her disposition than to encroach on the rights of civil power; but the civil power in its turn must respect the rights of the Church, and beware of arrogating them in any degree to itself. Now, what is the ruling spirit of the times when actual events and circumstances are taken into account? No other than this: it has been the fashion to regard the Church with suspicion, to despise and hate and spitefully calumniate her; and, more intolerable still, men strive with might and main to bring her under the sway of civil governments. Hence it is that her property has been plundered and her liberty curtailed: hence again, that the training of her priesthood has been beset with difficulties; that laws of exceptional rigor have been passed against her clergy; that religious orders, those excellent safeguards of Christianity, have been suppressed and placed under a ban; in a word, the principles and practice of the regalists have been renewed with increased virulence.

Such a policy is a violation of the most sacred rights of the Church, and it breeds enormous evils to States, for the very reason that it is in open conflict with the purposes of God. When God, in His most wise providence, placed over human society both temporal and spiritual authority, He intended them to remain distinct indeed, but by no means disconnected and at war with each other. On the contrary, both the will of God and the common weal of human society imperatively require that the civil power should be in accord with the ecclesiastical in its rule and administration.

Hence the State has its own peculiar rights and duties, the Church likewise has hers; but it is necessary that each should be united with the other in the bonds of concord. Thus will it come about that the close mutual relations of Church and State will be freed from the present turmoil, which for manifold reasons is ill-advised and most distressing to all well-disposed persons; furthermore, it will be brought to pass that, without confusion or separation of the peculiar interests of each, the people will *render to Cæsar the things that are Cæsar's, and to God the things that are God's.*

There is likewise a great danger threatening unity on the part of that association which goes by the name of the society of Freemasons, whose fatal influence for a long time past oppresses Catholic nations in particular. Favored by the agitations of the times, and waxing insolent in its power and resources and success, it strains every nerve to consolidate its sway and enlarge its sphere. It has already sallied forth from its hiding-places, where it hatched its plots, into the throng of cities, and as if to defy the Almighty, has set up its throne in this very city of Rome, the capital of the Catholic world. But what is most disastrous is, that wherever it has set its foot it penetrates into all ranks and departments of the commonwealth, in the hope of obtaining at last supreme control. This is, indeed, a great calamity: for its depraved principles and iniquitous designs are well known. Under the pretence of vindicating the rights of man and of reconstituting society, it attacks Christianity; it rejects revealed doctrine, denounces practices of piety, the divine sacraments, and every sacred thing as superstition; it strives to eliminate the Christian character from marriage and the family and the education of youth, and from every form of instruction, whether public or private, and to root out from the minds of men all respect for authority, whether human or divine. On its own part, it preaches the worship of nature, and maintains that by the principles of nature are truth and probity and justice to be measured and regulated. In this way, as is quite evident, man is being driven to adopt customs and habits of life akin to those of the heathen, only more corrupt in proportion as the incentives to sin are more numerous.

Although We have spoken on this subject in the strongest terms before, yet We are led by Our Apostolic watchfulness to urge it once more, and We repeat Our warning again and again, that in face of such an eminent peril, no precaution, howsoever great, can be looked upon as sufficient. May God in His mercy bring to naught their impious designs; nevertheless, let all Christians know and understand that the shameful yoke of Freemasonry must be shaken off once and for all; and let them be the first to shake it off who are most galled by its oppression—the men of Italy and of France. With what weapons and by what method this may best be done We Ourselves have already pointed out: the victory cannot be doubtful to those who trust in that leader whose divine words still remain in all their force: *I have overcome the world.*

Were this twofold danger averted, and government and States restored to the unity of faith, it is wonderful what efficacious remedies for evils and abundant store of benefits would ensue. We will touch upon the principal ones.

The first regards the dignity and office of the Church. She would receive that honor which is her due and she would go on her way, free from envy and strong in her liberty, as the minister of Gospel truth and grace to the notable welfare of States. For as she has been given by God as a teacher and guide to the human race, she can contribute assistance which is peculiarly adapted to direct even the most radical transformations of time to the common good, to solve the most complicated questions, and to promote uprightness and justice, which are the most solid foundations of the commonwealth.

Moreover there would be a marked increase of union among the nations, a thing most desirable to ward off the horrors of war.

We behold the condition of Europe. For many years

past peace has been rather an appearance than a reality. Possessed with mutual suspicions, almost all the nations are vying with one another in equipping themselves with military armaments. Inexperienced youths are removed from parental direction and control, to be thrown amid the dangers of the soldier's life; robust young men are taken from agriculture or ennobling studies or trade or the arts to be put under arms. Hence the treasures of States are exhausted by the enormous expenditure, the national resources are frittered away, and private fortunes impaired; and this, as it were, armed peace, which now prevails, cannot last much longer. Can this be the normal condition of human society? Yet we cannot escape from this situation, and obtain true peace, except by the aid of Jesus Christ. For to repress ambition and covetousness and envy—the chief instigators of war—nothing is more fitted than the Christian virtues and, in particular, the virtue of justice; for, by its exercise, both the law of nations and the faith of treaties may be maintained inviolate, and the bonds of brotherhood continue unbroken, if men are but convinced that *justice exalteth a nation.*

As in its external relations, so in the internal life of the State itself, the Christian virtues will provide a guarantee of the commonweal much more sure and stronger far than any which laws or armies can afford. For there is no one who does not see that the dangers to public security and order are daily on the increase, since seditious societies continue to conspire for the overthrow and ruin of States, as the frequency of their atrocious outrages testifies.

There are two questions, forsooth—the one called the *social,* and other the *political* question—which are discussed with the greatest vehemence. Both of them, without doubt, are of the last importance, and, though praiseworthy efforts have been put forth, in studies and measures and experiments for their wise and just solution, yet nothing could contribute more to this purpose than that the minds of men in general should be imbued with right sentiments of duty from the internal principle of Christian faith. We treated expressly of the social question in this sense a short time ago, from the standpoint of principles drawn from the Gospel and natural reason.

As regards the political question, which aims at reconciling liberty with authority—two things which many confound in theory, and separate too widely in practice—most efficient aid may be derived from the Christian philosophy. For, when this point has been settled and recognized by common agreement, that, whatsoever the form of government, the authority is from God, reason at once perceives that in some there is a legitimate right to command, in others the corresponding duty to obey, and that without prejudice to their dignity, since obedience is rendered to God rather than to man; and God has denounced the most rigorous judgment against those in authority, if they fail to represent Him with uprightness and justice. Then the liberty of the individual can afford ground of suspicion or envy to no one; since, without injury to any, his conduct will be guided by truth and rectitude and whatever is allied to public order. Lastly, if it be considered what influence is possessed by the Church, the mother of and peacemaker between rulers and peoples, whose mission it is to help them both with her authority and counsel, then it will be most manifest how much it concerns the commonweal that all nations should resolve to unite in the same belief and the same profession of the Christian faith.

With these thoughts in Our mind and ardent yearnings in Our heart, We see from afar what would be the new order of things that would arise upon the earth, and nothing could be sweeter to Us than the contemplation of the benefits that would flow from it. It can hardly be imagined what immediate and rapid progress would be made all over the earth, in all manner of greatness and prosperity, with the establishment of tranquillity and peace, the promotion of studies, the founding and the multiplying on Christian lines according to Our directions, of associations for the cultivators of soil, for workmen and tradesmen, through whose agency rapacious usury would be put down, and a large field opened up for useful labors.

And these abundant benefits would not be confined within the limits of civilized nations, but, like an over-charged river, would flow far and wide. It must be remembered, as we observed at the outset, that an immense number of races have been waiting, all through the long ages, to receive the light of truth and civilization. Most certainly, the counsels of God with regard to the eternal salvation of peoples are far removed above the understanding of man; yet if miserable superstition still prevails in so many parts of the world, the blame must be attributed in no small measure to religious dissensions. For, as far as it is given to human reason to judge from the nature of events, this seems without doubt to be the mission assigned by God to Europe, to go on by degrees carrying Christian civilization to every portion of the earth. The beginnings and first growth of this great work, which sprang from the labors of former centuries, were rapidly receiving large development, when all of a sudden the discord of the sixteenth century broke out. Christendom was torn with quarrels and dissensions, Europe exhausted with contests and wars, and the sacred missions felt the baneful influence of the times. While the causes of dissension still remain, what wonder is it that so large a portion of mankind is held enthralled with barbarous customs and insane rites?

Let us one and all, then, for the sake of the common welfare, labor with equal assiduity to restore the ancient concord. In order to bring about this concord, and spread abroad the benefits of the Christian revelation, the present is the most seasonable time; for never before have the sentiments of human brotherhood penetrated so deeply into the souls of men, and never in any age has man been seen to seek out his fellowmen more eagerly in order to know them better and to help them. Immense tracts of land and sea are traversed with incredible rapidity, and thus extraordinary advantages are afforded not only for commerce and scientific investigations but also for the propagation of the word of God from the rising of the sun to the going down of the same.

We are well aware of the long labors involved in the restoration of that order of things which We desire; and it may be that there are those who consider that We are far too sanguine and look for things that are rather too be wished for than expected. But We unhesitatingly place all Our hope and confidence in the Saviour of mankind, Jesus Christ, well remembering what great things have been achieved in times past by the folly of the Cross and its preaching, to the astonishment and confusion of the *wisdom of the world.* We beg of princes and rulers of States, appealing to their statesmanship and earnest solicitude for the people, to weigh Our counsels in the balance of truth and second them with their authority and favor. If only a portion of the looked-for results should come about, it will cause no inconsiderable boon in the general decadence, when the intolerable evils of the present day bring with them the dread of further evils in days to come.

The last years of the past century left Europe worn out with disasters and panic-stricken with the turmoils of revolution. And why should not our present century, which is now hastening to its close, by a reversion of circumstances bequeath to mankind the pledges of concord, with the prospects of the great benefits which are bound up in the unity of the Christian faith?

May God, who *is rich in mercy, and in whose power are the times and moments,* grant Our wishes and desires, and in His great goodness, hasten the fulfilment of that divine promise of Jesus Christ: *There will be one Fold and one Shepherd.*

CATHOLICITY IN THE UNITED STATES.

Encyclical Letter Longinque Oceani, January 6, 1895.

WE traverse in spirit and thought the wide expanse of ocean; and although We have at other times addressed you in writing—chiefly when We directed Encyclical Letters to the bishops of the Catholic world—yet have We now resolved to speak to you separately, trusting that We shall be, God willing, of some assistance to the Catholic cause amongst you. To this We apply Ourselves with the utmost zeal and care; because We highly esteem and love exceedingly the young and vigorous American nation, in which We plainly discern latent forces for the advancement alike of civilization and of Christianity.

Not long ago, when your whole nation, as was fitting, celebrated, with grateful recollection and every manifestation of joy, the completion of the fourth century since the discovery of America, We, too, commemorated together with you that most auspicious event, sharing in your rejoicings with equal good-will. Nor were We on that occasion content with offering prayers at a distance for your welfare and greatness. It was Our wish to be in some manner present with you in your festivities. Hence We cheerfully sent one who should represent Our person. Not without good reason did We take part in your celebration. For when America was, as yet, but a new-born babe, uttering in its cradle its first feeble cries, the Church took it to her bosom and motherly embrace. Columbus, as We have elsewhere expressly shown, sought, as the primary fruit of his voyages and labors, to open a pathway for the Christian faith into new lands and new seas. Keeping this thought constantly in view, his first solicitude, wherever he disembarked, was to plant upon the shore the sacred emblem of the cross. Wherefore, like as the Ark of Noe, surmounting the overflowing waters, bore the seed of Israel together with the remnants of the human race, even thus did the barks launched by Columbus upon the ocean carry into regions beyond the seas as well the germs of mighty States as the principles of the Catholic religion.

This is not the place to give a detailed account of what thereupon ensued. Very rapidly did the light of the Gospel shine upon the savage tribes discovered by the Ligurian. For it is sufficiently well known how many of the children of Francis, as well as of Dominic and of Loyola, were accustomed during the two following centuries to voyage thither for this purpose; how they cared for the colonies brought over from Europe; but primarily and chiefly how they converted the natives from superstition to Christianity, sealing their labors in many instances with the testimony of their blood. The names newly given to so many of your towns and rivers and mountains and lakes teach and clearly witness how deeply your beginnings were marked with the footprints of the Catholic Church.

Nor, perchance, did the fact which We now recall take place without some design of divine Providence. Precisely at the epoch when the American colonies, having, with Catholic aid, achieved liberty and independence, coalesced into a constitutional Republic the ecclesiastical hierarchy was happily established amongst you; and at the very time when the popular suffrage placed the great Washington at the helm of the Republic, the first bishop was set by apostolic authority over the American Church. The well-known friendship and familiar intercourse which subsisted between these two men seems to be an evidence that the United States ought to be conjoined in concord and amity with the Catholic Church. And not without cause; for without morality the State cannot endure— a truth which that illustrious citizen of yours, whom We have just mentioned, with a keenness of insight worthy of his genius and statesmanship perceived and proclaimed. But the best and strongest support of morality is religion. She, by her very nature, guards and defends all the principles on which duties are founded, and, setting before us the motives most powerful to influence us, commands us to live virtuously and forbids us to transgress. Now what is the Church other than a legitimate society, founded by the will and ordinance of Jesus Christ for the preservation of morality and the defence of religion? For this reason have We repeatedly endeavored, from the summit of the pontifical dignity, to inculcate that the Church, whilst directly and immediately aiming at the salvation of souls and the beatitude which is to be attained in heaven, is yet, even in the order of temporal things, the fountain of blessings so numerous and great that they could not have been greater or more numerous had the original purpose of her institution been the pursuit of happiness during the life which is spent on earth.

That your Republic is progressing and developing by giant strides is patent to all; and this holds good in religious matters also. For even as your cities, in the course of one century, have made a marvellous increase in wealth and power, so do we behold the Church, from scant and slender beginnings, grown with rapidity to be great and exceedingly flourishing. Now if, on the one hand, the increased riches and resources of your cities are justly attributed to the talents and active industry of the American people, on the other hand, the prosperous condition of Catholicity must be ascribed, first indeed, to the virtue, the ability, and the prudence of the bishops and clergy; but in no slight measure also, to the faith and generosity of the Catholic laity. Thus, while the different classes exerted their best energies, you were enabled to erect unnumbered religious and useful institutions, sacred edifices, schools for the instruction of youth, colleges for the higher branches, homes for the poor, hospitals for the sick, and convents and monasteries. As for what more closely touches spiritual interests, which are based upon the exercise of Christian virtues, many facts have been brought to Our notice, whereby We are animated with hope and filled with joy, namely, that the numbers of the secular and regular clergy are steadily augmenting, that pious sodalities and confraternities are held in esteem, that the Catholic parochial schools, the Sunday-schools for imparting Christian doctrine, and summer schools are in a flourishing condition; moreover, associations for mutual aid, for the relief of the indigent, for the promotion of temperate living, add to all this the many evidences of popular piety.

The main factor, no doubt, in bringing things into this happy state were the ordinances and decrees of your synods, especially of those which in more recent times were convened and confirmed by the authority of the Apostolic See. But, moreover (a fact which it gives pleasure to acknowledge), thanks are due to the equity of the laws which obtain in America and to the customs of the well-ordered Republic. For the Church amongst you, unopposed by the Constitution and government of your nation, fettered by no hostile legislation, protected against violence by the common laws and the impartiality of the tribunals, is free to live and act without hindrance. Yet, though all this is true, it would be very erroneous to draw the conclusion that in America is to be sought the type of the most desirable status of the Church, or that it would be universally lawful or expedient for State and Church to be, as in America, dissevered and divorced. The fact that Catholicity with you is in good condition, nay, is even enjoying a prosperous growth, is by all means to be attributed to the fecundity with which God has endowed His Church, in virtue of which unless men or circumstances interfere, she spontaneously expands and propagates herself; but she would bring forth more abundant fruits if, in addition to liberty, she enjoyed the favor of the laws and the patronage of the public authority.

For Our part We have left nothing undone, as far as circumstances permitted, to preserve and more solidly establish amongst you the Catholic religion. With this intent, We have, as you are well aware, turned Our attention to two special objects: first, the advancement of learning; second, a perfecting of methods in the management of Church affairs. There already, indeed, existed several distinguished universities. We, however, thought it advisable that there should be one founded by authority of the Apostolic See and endowed by Us with all suitable powers, in which Catholic professors might instruct those devoted to the pursuit of learning. The design was to begin with philosophy and theology, adding, as means and circumstances would allow, the remaining branches, those particularly which the present age has introduced or perfected. An education cannot be deemed complete which takes no notice of modern sciences. It is obvious that in the existing keen competition of talents, and the widespread and, in itself, noble and praiseworthy passion for knowledge, Catholics ought to be not followers but leaders. It is necessary, therefore, that they should cultivate every refinement of learning, and zealously train their minds to the discovery of truth and the investigation, so far as it is possible, of the entire domain of nature. This in every age has been the desire of the Church; upon the enlargement of the boundaries of the sciences has she been wont to bestow all possible labor and energy. By a letter, therefore, dated the seventh day of March, in the year of Our Lord 1889, directed to you, Venerable Brethren, We established at Washington, your capital city, esteemed by a majority of you a very proper seat for the higher studies, a university for the instruction of young men desirous of pursuing advanced courses. In announcing this matter to Our Venerable Brethren, the Cardinals of the Holy Roman Church, in Consistory, We expressed the wish that it should be regarded as the fixed law of the university to unite erudition and learning with soundness of faith and to imbue its students not less with religion than with scientific culture. To the Bishops of the United States We entrusted the task of establishing a suitable course of studies and of supervising the discipline of the students; and We conferred the office and authority of Chancellor, as it is called, upon the Archbishop of Baltimore. And, by divine favor, a quite happy beginning was made. For, without any delay, whilst you were celebrating the hundredth anniversary of the establishment of your ecclesiastical hierarchy, under the brightest auspices, in the presence of Our delegate, the divinity classes were opened. From that time onward We know that theological science has been imparted by the diligence of eminent men the renown of whose talents and learning receives a fitting crown in their recognized loyalty and devotion to the Apostolic See. Nor is it long since We were apprised that, thanks to the liberality of a pious priest, a new building had been constructed, in which young men, as well cleric as lay, are to receive instruction in the natural sciences and in literature. From Our knowledge of the American character, We are fully confident that the example set by this noble man will incite others of your citizens to imitate him; they will not fail to realize that liberality exercised towards such an object will be repaid by the very greatest advantages to the public.

No one can be ignorant how powerfully similar institutions of learning, whether originally founded by the Roman Church herself from time to time or approved and promoted by her legislation, have contributed to the spread of knowledge and civilization in every part of Europe. Even in Our own day, though other instances might be given, it is enough to mention the University of Louvain, to which the entire Belgian nation ascribes its almost daily increase in prosperity and glory. Equally abundant will be the benefits proceeding from the Washington University, if the professors and students (as We doubt not they will) be mindful of Our injunctions, and, shunning party spirit and strife, conciliate the good opinion of the people and the clergy.

We wish now, Venerable Brethren, to commend to your affection and to the generosity of your people the college which Our predecessor, Pius IX., founded in this city for the ecclesiastical training of young men from North America, and which We took care to place upon a firm basis by a letter dated the twenty-fifth day of October, in the year of Our Lord 1884 We can make this appeal the more confidently, because the results obtained from this institution have by no means belied the expectations commonly entertained regarding it. You yourselves can testify that during its brief existence it has sent forth a very large number of exemplary priests, some of whom have been promoted for their virtue and learning to the highest degrees of ecclesiastical dignity. We are, therefore, thoroughly persuaded that you will continue to be solicitous to send hither select young men who are in training to become the hope of the Church. For they will carry back to their homes and utilize for the general good the wealth of intellectual attainments and moral excellence which they shall have acquired in the city of Rome.

The love which We cherish towards the Catholics of your nation moved Us, likewise, to turn Our attention at the very beginning of Our Pontificate to the convocation of a third Plenary Council of Baltimore. Subsequently, when the archbishops, at Our invitation, had come to Rome, We diligently inquired from them what they deemed most conducive to the common good. We finally, and after mature deliberation, ratified by apostolic authority the decrees of the prelates assembled at Baltimore. In truth the event has proven, and still proves, that the decrees of Baltimore were salutary and timely in the extreme. Experience has demonstrated their power for the maintenance of discipline; for stimulating the intelligence and zeal of the clergy; for defending and developing the Catholic education of youth. Wherefore, Venerable Brethren, if We make acknowledgment of your activity in these matters, if We laud your firmness tempered with prudence, We but pay tribute due to your merit; for We are fully sensible that so great a harvest of blessings could by no means have so swiftly ripened to maturity, had you not exerted yourselves, each to the utmost of his ability, sedulously and faithfully to carry into effect the statutes you had wisely framed at Baltimore.

But when the Council of Baltimore had concluded its labors, the duty still remained of putting, so to speak, a proper and becoming crown upon the work. This, We perceived, could scarcely be done in a more fitting manner than through the due establishment by the Apostolic See of an American Legation. Accordingly, as you are well aware, We have done this. By this action, as We have elsewhere intimated, We have wished, first of all, to certify that, in Our judgment and affection, America occupies the same place and rights as other States, be they ever so mighty and imperial. In addition to this We had in mind to draw more closely the bonds of duty and friendship which connect you and so many thousands of Catholics with the Apostolic See. In fact, the mass of the Catholics understood how salutary Our action was destined to be; they saw, moreover, that it accorded with the usage and policy of the Apostolic See. For it has been, from earliest antiquity, the custom of the Roman Pontiffs in the exercise of the divinely bestowed gift of the primacy in the administration of the Church of Christ to send forth legates to Christian nations and peoples.

And they did this, not by an adventitious but an inherent right. For "the Roman Pontiff, upon whom Christ has conferred ordinary and immediate jurisdiction, as well over all and singular churches, as over all and singular pastors and faithful,[1] since he cannot personally visit the different regions and thus exercise the pastoral office over the flock entrusted to him, finds it necessary, from time to time, in the discharge of the ministry imposed on him, to despatch legates into different parts of the world, according as the need arises; who, supplying his place, may correct errors, make the rough ways plain, and administer to the people confided to their care increased means of salvation."[2]

But how unjust and baseless would be the suspicion, should it anywhere exist, that the powers conferred on the legate are an obstacle to the authority of the bishops! Sacred to Us (more than to any other) are the rights of those "*whom the Holy Ghost has placed as bishops to rule the Church of God.*" That these rights should remain intact in every nation in every part of the globe, We both desire and ought to desire, the more so since the dignity of the individual bishop is by nature so interwoven with the dignity of the Roman Pontiff that any measure which benefits the one necessarily protects the other. "My honor is the honor of the Universal Church. My honor is the unimpaired vigor of My brethren. Then am I truly honored when to each one due honor is not denied."[3] Therefore, since it is the office and function of an apostolic legate, with whatsoever powers he may be vested, to execute the mandates and interpret the will of the Pontiff who sends him, thus, so far from his being of any detriment to the ordinary power of the bishops, he will rather bring an accession of stability and strength.

[1] Con. Vat. Sess., iv. c. 3.
[2] Cap. Un. Extrav. Comm. De Consuet, l. 1.
[3] S. Gregorius Epis. ad Eulog. Alex. lib. viii. ep. 30.

His authority will possess no slight weight for preserving in the multitude a submissive spirit; in the clergy discipline and due reverence for the bishops, and in the bishops mutual charity and an intimate union of souls. And since this union, so salutary and desirable, consists mainly in harmony of thought and action, he will, no doubt, bring it to pass that each one of you shall persevere in the diligent administration of his diocesan affairs; that one shall not impede another in matters of government; that one shall not pry into the counsels and conduct of another; finally, that with disagreements eradicated and mutual esteem maintained, you may all work together with combined energies to promote the glory of the American Church and the general welfare. It is difficult to estimate the good results which will flow from this concord of the bishops. Our own people will receive edification; and the force of example will have its effect on those without—who will be persuaded by this argument alone that the divine apostolate has passed by inheritance to the ranks of the Catholic episcopate.

Another consideration claims our earnest attention. All intelligent men are agreed, and We Ourselves have with pleasure intimated it above, that America seems destined for greater things. Now, it is Our wish that the Catholic Church should not only share in, but help to bring about, this prospective greatness. We deem it right and proper that she should, by availing herself of the opportunities daily presented to her, keep equal step with the Republic in the march of improvement, at the same time striving to the utmost, by her virtue and her institutions, to aid in the rapid growth of the States. Now, she will attain both these objects the more easily and abundantly, in proportion to the degree in which the future shall find her constitution perfected. But what is the meaning of the legation of which we are speaking, or what is its ultimate aim except to bring it about that the constitution of the Church shall be strengthened, her discipline better fortified? Wherefore, We ardently desire that this truth should sink day by day more deeply into the minds of Catholics—namely, that they can in no better way safeguard their own individual interests and the common good than by yielding a hearty submission and obedience to the Church. Your faithful people, however, are scarcely in need of exhortation on this point; for they are accustomed to adhere to the institutions of Catholicity with willing souls and a constancy worthy of all praise.

To one matter of the first importance and fraught with the greatest blessings it is a pleasure at this place to refer, on account of the holy firmness in principle and practice respecting it which, as a rule, rightly prevails amongst you; We mean the Christian dogma of the unity and indissolubility of marriage; which supplies the firmest bond of safety not merely to the family but to society at large. Not a few of your citizens, even of those who dissent from us in other doctrines, terrified by the licentiousness of divorce, admire and approve in this regard the Catholic teaching and the Catholic customs. They are led to this judgment not less by love of country than by the wisdom of the doctrine. For difficult it is to imagine a more deadly pest to the community than the wish to declare dissoluble a bond which the law of God has made perpetual and inseverable. Divorce "is the fruitful cause of mutable marriage contracts; it diminishes mutual affection; it supplies a pernicious stimulus to unfaithfulness; it is injurious to the care and education of children; it gives occasion to the breaking up of domestic society; it scatters the seeds of discord among families; it lessens and degrades the dignity of women, who incur the danger of being abandoned when they shall have subserved the lust of their husbands. And since nothing tends so effectually as the corruption of morals to ruin families and undermine the strength of kingdoms, it may easily be perceived that divorce is especially hostile to the prosperity of families and States." [1]

As regards civil affairs, experience has shown how important it is that the citizens should be upright and virtuous. In a free State, unless justice be generally cultivated, unless the people be repeatedly and diligently urged to observe the precepts and laws of the Gospel, liberty itself may be pernicious. Let those of the clergy, therefore, who are occupied with the instruction of the multitude, treat plainly this topic of the duties of citizens, so that all may understand and feel the necessity, in political life, of conscientiousness, self-restraint, and integrity; for that cannot be lawful in public which is unlawful in private affairs. On this whole subject there are to be found, as you know, in the encyclical letters written by Us from time to time in the course of Our pontificate, many things which Catholics should attend to and observe. In these writings and expositions We have treated of human liberty, of the chief Christian duties, of civil government, and of the Christian constitution of States, drawing Our principles as well from the teaching of the Gospels as from reason. They, then, who wish to be good citizens and discharge their duties faithfully may readily learn from Our Letters the ideal of an upright life. In like manner, let the priests be persistent in keeping before the minds of the people the enactments of the Third Council of Baltimore, particularly those which inculcate the virtue of temperance, the frequent use of the sacraments and the observance of the just laws and institutions of the Republic.

Now, with regard to entering societies, extreme care should be taken not to be ensnared by error. And We wish to be understood as referring in a special manner to the working classes, who assuredly have the right to unite in associations for the promotion of their interests; a right acknowledged by the Church and unopposed by

[1] Encyc. Arcanum.

nature. But it is very important to take heed with whom they are to associate, lest whilst seeking aid for the improvement of their condition they may be imperilling far weightier interests. The most effectual precaution against this peril is to determine with themselves at no time or in any matter to be parties to the violation of justice. Any society, therefore, which is ruled by and servilely obeys persons who are not steadfast for the right and friendly to religion is capable of being extremely prejudicial to the interests as well of individuals as of the community; beneficial it cannot be. Let this conclusion, therefore, remain firm—to shun not only those associations which have been openly condemned by the judgment of the Church, but those also which, in the opinion of intelligent men, and especially of the bishops, are regarded as suspicious and dangerous.

Nay, rather, unless forced by necessity to do otherwise, Catholics ought to prefer to associate with Catholics, a course which will be very conducive to the safeguarding of their faith. As presidents of societies thus formed among themselves, it will be well to appoint either priests or upright laymen of weight and character, guided by whose counsels they should endeavor peacefully to adopt and carry into effect such measures as may seem most advantageous to their interests, keeping in view the rules laid down by Us in Our Encyclical, *Rerum Novarum.* Let them, however, never allow this to escape their memory: that whilst it is proper and desirable to assert and secure the rights of the many, yet this is not to be done by a violation of duty; and that these are very important duties; not to touch what belongs to another; to allow every one to be free in the management of his own affairs; not to hinder any one to dispose of his services when he please and where he please. The scenes of violence and riot which you witnessed last year in your own country sufficiently admonish you that America too is threatened with the audacity and ferocity of the enemies of public order. The state of the times, therefore, bids Catholics to labor for the tranquillity of the commonwealth, and for this purpose to obey the laws, abhor violence, and seek no more than equity or justice permits.

Towards these objects much may be contributed by those who have devoted themselves to writing, and in particular by those who are engaged on the daily press. We are aware that already there labor in this field many men of skill and experience, whose diligence demands words of praise rather than of encouragement. Nevertheless, since the thirst for reading and knowledge is so vehement and widespread amongst you, and since, according to circumstances, it can be productive either of good or evil, every effort should be made to increase the number of intelligent and well-disposed writers who take religion for their guide and virtue for their constant companion. And this seems all the more necessary in America, on account of the familiar intercourse and intimacy between Catholics and those who are estranged from the Catholic name, a condition of things which certainly exacts from our people great circumspection and more than ordinary firmness. It is necessary to instruct, admonish, strengthen and urge them on to the pursuit of virtue and to the faithful observance, amid so many occasions of stumbling, of their duties towards the Church. It is, of course, the proper function of the clergy to devote their care and energies to this great work; but the age and the country require that journalists should be equally zealous in this same cause and labor in it to the full extent of their powers. Let them, however, seriously reflect that their writings, if not positively prejudicial to religion, will surely be of slight service to it unless in concord of minds they all seek the same end. They who desire to be of real service to the Church, and with their pens heartily to defend the Catholic cause, should carry on the conflict with perfect unanimity, and, as it were, with serried ranks, for they rather inflict than repel war if they waste their strength by discord. In like manner their work, instead of being profitable and fruitful, becomes injurious and disastrous whenever they presume to call before their tribunal the decisions and acts of bishops, and, casting off due reverence, cavil and find fault; not perceiving how great a disturbance of order, how many evils are thereby produced. Let them, then, be mindful of their duty, and not overstep the proper limits of moderation. The bishops, placed in the lofty position of authority, are to be obeyed, and suitable honor befitting the magnitude and sanctity of their office should be paid them. Now, this reverence, "which it is lawful to no one to neglect," should of necessity be eminently conspicuous and exemplary in Catholic journalists. For journals, naturally circulating far and wide, come daily into the hands of everybody, and exert no small influence upon the opinions and morals of the multitude.[1]

We have Ourselves, on frequent occasions, laid down many rules respecting the duties of a good writer; many of which were unanimously inculcated as well by the Third Council of Baltimore as by the archbishops in their meeting at Chicago in the year 1893. Let Catholic writers, therefore, bear impressed on their minds Our teachings on this point as well as yours; and let them resolve that their entire method of writing shall be thereby guided, if they indeed desire, as they ought to desire, to discharge their duty well.

Our thoughts now turn to those who dissent from us in matters of Christian faith; and who shall deny that, with not a few of them, dissent is a matter rather of inheritance than of will? How solicitous We are of their salvation, with what ardor of soul We wish that they should be at length restored to the embrace of the Church, the common mother of all, Our Apostolic Epistle,

[1] Ep. Cognita Nobis ad Archiepp, et Epp. Provinciarum, Taurinen. Mediolanen. et Vercellen, xxv., Jan. an, MDCCCLXXXII.

"*Praeclara*," has in very recent times declared. Nor are we destitute of all hope; for He is present and hath a care whom all things obey and who laid down His life that He might "gather in one the children of God who were dispersed." (John xi. 52.)

Surely we ought not to desert them nor leave them to their fancies; but with mildness and charity draw them to us, using every means of persuasion to induce them to examine closely every part of the Catholic doctrine, and to free themselves from preconceived notions. In this matter, if the first place belongs to the bishops and clergy, the second belongs to the laity, who have it in their power to aid the apostolic efforts of the clergy by the probity of their morals and the integrity of their lives. Great is the force of example; particularly with those who are earnestly seeking the truth, and who, from a certain inborn virtuous disposition, are striving to live an honorable and upright life, to which class very many of your fellow-citizens belong. If the spectacle of Christian virtues exerted the powerful influence over the heathens blinded, as they were, by inveterate superstition, which the records of history attest, shall we think it powerless to eradicate error in the case of those who have been initiated into the Christian religion?

Finally, We cannot pass over in silence those whose long-continued unhappy lot implores and demands succor from men of apostolic zeal; We refer to the Indians and the negroes who are to be found within the confines of America, the greatest portion of whom have not yet dispelled the darkness of superstition. How wide a field for cultivation! How great a multitude of human beings to be made partakers of the blessing derived through Jesus Christ!

Meanwhile, as a presage of heavenly graces and a testimony of Our benevolence, We most lovingly in the Lord impart to you, Venerable Brethren, and to your clergy and people, Our Apostolic Benediction.

TO THE ENGLISH PEOPLE.

Apostolical Letter Amantissima voluntatis, April 27, 1895.

SOME time since, in an apostolic letter to princes and peoples, We addressed the English in common with other nations, but We have greatly desired to do this by a special letter, and thus give to the illustrious English race a token of Our sincere affection. This wish has been kept alive by the hearty good-will We have always felt towards your people, whose great deeds in olden times the history of the Church declares. We were yet more moved by not infrequent conversations with your countrymen, who testified to the kindly feeling of the English towards Us personally, and above all to their anxiety for peace and eternal salvation through unity of faith. God is Our witness how keen is Our wish that some effort of Ours might tend to assist and further the great work of obtaining the reunion of Christendom; and We render thanks to God, who has so far prolonged Our life, that We may make an endeavor in this direction. But since, as is but right, We place Our confidence of a happy issue principally and above all in the wonderful power of God's grace, We have with full consideration determined to invite all Englishmen who glory in the Christian name to this same work, and We exhort them to lift up their hearts to God with Us, to fix their trust in Him, and to seek from Him the help necessary in such a matter by assiduous diligence in holy prayer.

The love and care of the Roman Pontiffs for England has been traditional from the days of Our holy predecessor

Gregory the Great. Religion and humanity generally, and especially the English nation, owe him a deep debt of gratitude. Although prevented, by the divine call to yet higher duty, from himself undertaking the apostolic labor "of converting the Anglo-Saxons, as he had proposed to do whilst still a monk, his mind remained intent upon this great and salutary design,"[1] nor did he rest until it was accomplished. For from that monastic family which he had formed in learning and holiness of life in his own house he sent a chosen band under the leadership of Augustine to be the messengers of grace, wisdom and civilization to those who were still buried in paganism. And relying as he did on divine help his hope grew stronger under difficulty, until at length he saw his work crowned with success. He himself writes of this in tones of triumphant joy in reply to St. Augustine, who had sent him the news of the happy result: "Glory be to God on high and on earth peace to men of good will. To Christ be the glory in whose death we live; by whose weakness we are strong, in the love of whom We seek in Britain those brethren whom We knew not; by whose mercy We have found those whom knowing not We sought. Who can tell what gladness filled the hearts of all here to know that the English race, by the workings of the grace of God Almighty, and by your labors, my brother, has been illuminated by the light of our holy faith, which expels the darkness of error, and has with free mind trodden under foot those idols to which aforetime they were subject in foolish fear."[2] And congratulating Ethelbert, King of Kent, and Bertha his Queen, in a letter full of affection, in that they imitated "Helen, of illustrious memory, and Constantine, the devout Emperor,"[3] he strengthens them and their people with salutary admonitions. Nor did he cease for the rest of his life to foster and develop

---

[1] Joann. Diac. in vita ejus, c. ii. 33.
[2] Epist. c. xi. 28, et c. ix. 58.
[3] Ib. c. xi. 66, al c. ix. 60, c. xi. 29, et c. ix. 59.

their faith in instructions dictated by holy prudence. Thus Christianity, which the Church had conveyed to Britain, and spread and defended there against rising heresy,[1] after having been blotted out by the invasion of heathen races, was now by the care of Gregory happily restored.

Having resolved to address this letter to the English people, We recall at once these great and glorious events in the annals of the Church, which must surely be remembered by them in gratitude. Moreover, it is noteworthy that this love and solicitude of Gregory was inherited by the Pontiffs who succeeded him. This is shown by their constant interposition in providing worthy pastors and capable teachers in learning, both human and divine, by their helpful counsels, and by their affording in abundant measure whatever was necessary for establishing and developing that rising Church. And very soon was such care rewarded, for in no other case perhaps did the faith take root so quickly nor was so keen and intense a love manifested towards the See of Peter. That the English race was in those days devoted to this centre of Christian unity divinely constituted in the Roman Bishops, and that in the course of ages men of all ranks were bound to them by ties of loyalty, are facts too abundantly and plainly testified by the pages of history to admit of doubt or question.

But, in the storms which devasted Catholicity throughout Europe in the sixteenth century, England, too, received a grievous wound; for it was first unhappily

---

[1] The action of St. Celestine I. was most efficacious against the Pelagian heresy which had infected Britain, as St. Prosper of Aquitaine, a writer of that time, and afterwards secretary to St. Leo the Great, records in his chronicle: ''Agricola the Pelagian, son of the Pelagian Bishop Severianus, tainted the Churches of Britain with the insinuations of his teaching. But at the instance of the deacon, Palladius, Pope Celestine sent Germanus, Bishop of Auxerre, as his vicar (*vice sua*), and led back the British people to the Catholic faith, having driven out the heretics.'' (Migne, Bibl. P. P. S. Prosp. Aquit. opp. vol. un: p. 594).

wrenched from communication with the Apostolic See, and then was bereft of that holy faith in which for long centuries it had rejoiced and found liberty. It was a sad defection; and Our predecessors, while lamenting it in their earnest love, made every prudent effort to put an end to it, and to mitigate the many evils consequent upon it. It would take long, and it is not necessary, to detail the sedulous and increasing care taken by Our predecessors in those circumstances. But by far the most valuable and effective assistance they afforded lies in their having so repeatedly urged on the faithful the practice of special prayer to God that He would look with compassion on England. In the number of those who devoted themselves to this special work of charity there were some venerable and saintly men, especially St. Charles Borromeo and St. Philip Neri, and, in the last century, Paul, the founder of the Society of the Passion of Christ, who, not without a certain divine impulse, it is said, was instant in supplication "at the throne of divine grace"; and this all the more earnestly that the times seemed less favorable to the realization of his hopes. We, indeed, long before being raised to the Supreme Pontificate, were deeply sensible also of the importance of holy prayer offered for this cause, and heartily approved of it. For, as We gladly recall, at the time when We were Nuncio in Belgium, becoming acquainted with an Englishman, Ignatius Spencer, himself a devout son of the same St. Paul of the Cross, he laid before Us the project he had already initiated for extending a society of pious people, to pray for the return of the English nation to the Church.[1]

We can hardly say how cordially We entered into this design, wholly inspired by faith and charity, and how We helped forward this cause, anticipating that the

---

[1] For this purpose he specially recommended the "Hail Mary," and obtained from the General Chapter of his Order, held in Rome in 1857, a special injunction upon its menbers.

English Church would obtain abundant assistance thereby. Although the fruits of divine grace obtained by prayer had previously manifested themselves, yet as that holy league spread they became notorious. Very many were led to follow the divine call, and among them not a few men of distinguished eminence, and many, too, who in doing so had to make personal and heroic sacrifices. Moreover, there was a wonderful drawing of hearts and minds towards Catholic faith and practice, which rose in public respect and esteem, and many a long-cherished prejudice yielded to the force of truth.

Looking at all this, We do not doubt that the united and humble supplications of so many to God are hastening the time of further manifestations of His merciful designs towards the English people when *the Word of the Lord may run and be glorified.*[1] Our confidence is strengthened by observing the legislative and other measures which, if they do not perhaps directly, still do indirectly help forward the end We have in view by ameliorating the condition of the people at large, and by giving effect to the laws of justice and charity.

We have heard with singular joy of the great attention which is being given in England to the solution of the social question, of which We have treated with much care in Our encyclicals, and of the establishment of benefit and similar societies, whereby on a legal basis the condition of the working classes is improved. And We have heard of the vigorous and persevering efforts made to preserve for the people at large an education based on religious teaching, than which there is no firmer foundation for the instruction of youth and the maintenance of domestic life and civil polity; of the zeal and energy with which so many engage in forwarding opportune measures for the repression of the degrading vice of intemperance; of societies formed among the young men of the upper

[1] 2 Thes. iii. 1.

classes for the promotion of purity of morals and for sustaining the honor due to womanhood. For, alas, in regard to the Christian virtue of continence pernicious views are subtly creeping in, as though it were believed that a man was not so strictly bound by the precept as a woman. Moreover, reflecting men are deeply concerned at the spread of rationalism and materialism, and We Ourselves have often lifted up Our voice to denounce these evils, which weaken and paralyze not religion only, but the very springs of thought and action. The highest credit is due to those who fearlessly and unceasingly proclaim the rights of God and of Our Lord Jesus Christ, and the laws and teachings given by Him for the establishment of the divine kingdom here upon earth; in the which teachings alone strength, wisdom and safety are to be found. The various and abundant manifestations of care for the aged, for orphans, for incurables, for the destitute, the refuges, reformatories, and other forms of charity, all which the Church as a tender mother inaugurated and from the earliest times has ever inculcated as a special duty, are evidences of the spirit which animates you. Nor can We omit to mention specially the strict public observance of Sunday and the general spirit of respect for the Holy Scriptures. Every one knows the power and resources of the British nation and the civilizing influence which, with the spread of liberty, accompanies its commercial prosperity even to the most remote regions. But, worthy and noble in themselves as are all these varied manifestations of activity, Our soul is raised to the origin of all power and the perennial source of all good things, to God our Heavenly Father, most beneficent. For the labors of man, whether public or private, will not attain to their full efficacy without appeal to God in prayer and without the divine blessing. *For happy is that people whose God is the Lord.*[1] For the mind of the

---

[1] Ps. cxliii. 15.

Christian should be so turned and fixed that he places and rests the chief hope of his undertakings in the divine help obtained by prayer, whereby human effort is supernaturalized and the desire of doing good, as though quickened by a heavenly fire, manifests itself in vigorous and serviceable actions. In this power of prayer God has not merely dignified man, but with infinite mercy has given him a protector and help in the time of need, ready at hand to all, easy and void of effect to no one who has resolute recourse to it. "Prayer is our powerful weapon, our great protection, our storehouse, our port of refuge, our place of safety." [1]

But if the prayer of the righteous man rightly avail so much with God even in earthly concerns, how much more will it not avail one who is destined to an eternal existence for obtaining those spiritual blessings which Christ has procured for mankind by "the sacrament of His mercy." For He *who of God is made unto us wisdom and justice and sanctification and redemption*,[2] in addition to what He taught, instituted and effected, gave also for this purpose the salutary precept of prayer and in His great goodness confirmed it by His example.

These simple truths are indeed known to every Christian, but still by many they are neither remembered nor valued as they should be. It is for this reason that We insist the more strenuously on the confidence which should be placed in prayer, and recall the words and example of the Fatherly love of the same Christ our Lord; words of deepest import and highest encouragement; words also which show forth how in the counsels of God prayer is at the same time the expression of our helplessness and the sure hope of obtaining the strength we need. *And I say to you, Ask and it shall be given you; seek and you shall find; knock and it shall be opened to you; for every one that asketh, receiveth, and he that seeketh, findeth; and to him that knocketh it shall be opened.*[3] And

[1] Chrys. Hom. 30 in Gen.   [2] 1 Cor. i. 30.   [3] Luke xi. 9, 10.

the Son of God Himself shows us that if our prayers are to be acceptable to the divine Majesty they must be united with His name and merits. *Amen, amen, I say to you if you ask the Father anything in My name, He will give it you. Hitherto you have not asked anything in My name. Ask and you shall receive, that your joy may be full.*[1] And He enforces this by reference to the tender love of parents for their own children. *If you, then, being evil,* He says, *know how to give good gifts to your children, how much more will your Father from heaven give the good Spirit to them that ask Him.*[2]

And how abundant are not the choice gifts contained in that good Spirit. The greatest of them all is that hidden power of which Christ spoke when He said: *No man can come to Me except the Father, who hath sent Me, draw him.*[3]

It is impossible that men grounded in this teaching should not feel drawn and even impelled to the habit of faithful prayer. With what steady perseverance will they not practise it; with what fervor pursue it, having before them the very example of Christ Himself, who, having nothing to fear for Himself and needing nothing, for He was God, yet passed the whole night in prayer,[4] and with a strong cry and tears offered up prayers and supplications,[5] and doing this "He wished to stand pleading before His Father as if remembering at that time that He was our teacher,"[6] as Venerable Bede, that ornament of your nation, wisely considers. But nothing proves so clearly and forcibly both the precept and the example of our divine Lord in regard to prayer as His last discourse to the apostles during those sad moments that preceded His passion, when, raising His eyes to heaven, He again and again entreated His Holy Father, praying and beseeching Him for the most intimate union of His disciples and followers in the truth, as the most convinc-

[1] John xvi. 23, 24. [3] John vi. 44. [5] Heb. v. 7.
[2] Luke xi. 13. [4] Luke vi. 12. [6] In ev. S. Joann. xvii.

ing evidence to the world of the divine mission on which
He was about to send them.

And here no thought is more welcome to Our soul than
that happy unity of faith and wills for which our Redeemer
and divine Master prayed in that earnest supplication—a
unity which, if useful at all times even for temporal interests, both at home and abroad, is shown by the very
divisions and confusions of these days to be more than
ever needful. We on Our part, watching the signs of
the times, exhorting and taking thought for the future,
urged thereto by the example of Christ and the duty of
Our apostolic office, have not ceased to pray, and still
humbly pray, for the return of Christian nations now
divided from Us to the unity of former days. We have
more than once of late years given expression to this
object of Our desires, and have devoted sedulous care to
its realization. The time cannot be far distant when We
must appear to render an account of Our stewardship to
the Prince of pastors, and how happy, how blessed should
We be if We could bring to Him some fruit—some realization of these Our wishes which He has inspired and
sustained. In these days Our thoughts turn with love
and hope to the English people, observing as We do the
frequent and manifest works of divine grace in their
midst; how, to some, it is plain, the confusion of religious
dissensions which divide them is a cause of deep concern;
how others see clearly the need of some sure defence
against the inroad of modern errors which only too readily
humor the wishes of fallen nature and depraved reason;
how the number of those religious and discreet men,
who sincerely labor much for reunion with the Catholic
Church, is increasing. We can hardly say how strongly
these and other signs quicken the charity of Christ in Us,
and redoubling Our prayers from Our inmost soul We
call down a fuller measure of divine grace, which, poured
out on minds so well disposed, may issue in the ardently
desired fruit, the fruit, namely, that We may all meet

into the unity of faith and of the knowledge of the Son
of God [1] careful to keep the unity of the Spirit in the bond
of peace, one body and one Spirit; as you are called in
one hope of your calling—one Lord, one faith, one baptism.[2]

With loving heart, then, We turn to you all in England,
to whatever community or institution you may belong,
desiring to recall you to this holy unity. We beseech you,
as you value your eternal salvation, to offer up humble
and continuous prayer to God, our Heavenly Father, the
giver of all light, who with gentle power impels us to
the good and the right; and without ceasing to implore
light to know the truth in all its fulness, and to embrace
the designs of His mercy with single and entire faithful-
ness, calling upon the glorious name and merits of Jesus
Christ, who is *the author and finisher of our faith,*[3] who
*loved the Church and delivered Himself for it, that He might
sanctify it and might present it to Himself a glorious Church.*[4]
Difficulties there may be for us to face, but they are not
of a nature which should delay Our apostolic zeal or
stay your energy. Ah, no doubt the many changes that
have come about, and time itself, have caused the existing
divisions to take deeper root. But is that a reason to
give up all hope of remedy, reconciliation and peace?
By no means if God is with us. For we must not judge
of such great issues from a human standpoint only, but
rather must we look to the power and mercy of God.
In great and arduous enterprises, provided they are undertaken with an earnest and right intent, God stands
by man's side, and it is precisely in these difficulties that
the action of His providence shines forth with greatest
splendor. The time is not far distant when thirteen
centuries will have been completed since the English
race welcomed those apostolic men sent, as We have
said, from this very city of Rome, and, casting aside the

---

[1] Eph. iv. 13.   [2] Ib. 3–5.   [3] Heb. xii. 2.   [4] Eph. v. 25–27.

pagan deities, dedicated the first fruits of its faith to Christ our Lord and God. This encourages Our hope. It is, indeed, an event worthy to be remembered with public thanksgiving; would that this occasion might bring to all reflecting minds the memory of the faith then preached to your ancestors, the same which is now preached— *Jesus Christ yesterday, to-day, and the same forever,*[1] as the apostle says, who also most opportunely exhorts you, as He does all, to remember those first preachers *who have spoken the word of God to you, whose faith follow, considering the end of their conversation.*[2]

In such a cause We, first of all, call to Our assistance as Our allies the Catholics of England, whose faith and piety We know by experience. There can be no doubt that, weighing earnestly the value and effects of holy prayer, the virtue of which We have truly declared, they will strive by every means to succor their fellow-countrymen and brethren by invoking in their behalf the divine clemency. To pray for oneself is a need, to pray for others is a counsel of brotherly love; and it is plain that it is not prayer dictated by necessity so much as that inspired by fraternal charity which will find most favor in the sight of God. The first Christians undoubtedly adopted this practice. Especially in all that pertains to the gift of faith the early ages set us a striking example. Thus it was the custom to pray to God with ardor that relations, friends, rulers, and fellow-citizens might be blessed by a mind obedient to the Christian faith.[3]

And in regard to this there is another matter which gives Us anxiety. We have heard that in England there are some who, being Catholics in name, do not show themselves so in practice; and that in your great towns there are vast numbers of people who know not the elements of the Christian faith, who never pray to God, and live in ignorance of His justice and of His mercy. We

[1] Heb. xiii. 8. [2] Ib. 7. [3] S. Aug. de dono persev. xxiii. 63.

must pray to God, and pray yet more earnestly in this sad condition of things, since He alone can effect a remedy. May He show the measures proper to be taken; may He sustain the courage and strength of those who labor at this arduous task; may He deign to send laborers into His harvest.

Whilst We so earnestly press upon Our children the duty of prayer, We desire at the same time to warn them that they should not suffer themselves to be wanting in anything that pertains to the grace and the fruit of prayer, and that they should have ever before their minds the precept of the Apostle Paul to the Corinthians: *Be without offence to the Jews and to the Gentiles, and to the Church of God.*[1] For besides those interior dispositions of soul necessary for rightly offering prayer to God, it is also needful that they should be accompanied by actions and by words befitting the Christian profession—first of all, and chiefly, the exemplary observance of uprightness and justice, of pitifulness for the poor, of penance, of peace and concord in your own houses, of respect for the law— these are what will give force and efficacy to your prayers. Mercy favors the petition of those who in all justice study and carry out the precepts of Christ, according to His promise: *If you abide in Me, and My words abide in you, you shall ask whatever you will, and it shall be done unto you.*[2] And therefore do We exhort you that, uniting your prayer with Ours, your great desire may now be that God will grant you to welcome your fellow-citizens and brethren in the bond of perfect charity. Moreover, it is profitable to implore the help of the saints of God, the efficacy of whose prayers, specially in such a cause as this, is shown in that pregnant remark of St. Augustine as to St. Stephen: "If holy Stephen had not prayed, the Church to-day would have had no Paul."

We therefore humbly call on St. Gregory, whom the

---

[1] 1 Cor. x. 32.   [2] John xv. 7.

English have ever rejoiced to greet as the apostle of their race, on Augustine his disciple and his messenger, and on those other saints of God, through whose wonderful virtues and no less wonderful deeds England has merited the title of "Island of the Saints"; on St. Peter and St. George, those special patrons, and above all on Mary, the Holy Mother of God, whom Christ Himself from the Cross left to be the mother of mankind, to whom your kingdom was dedicated by your forefathers under that glorious title "The Dowry of Mary." All these with full confidence We call upon to be Our pleaders before the throne of God that, renewing the glory of ancient days, He may *fill you with all joy and peace in believing: that you may abound in hope and in the power of the Holy Ghost.*[1] Care should be taken that the prayers for unity already established amongst you Catholics on certain fixed days should be made more popular and recited with greater devotion. Especially that the pious practice of the Holy Rosary, which We Ourselves have so strongly recommended, should flourish, for it contains as it were a summary of the Gospel teaching, and has always been a most salutary institution for the people at large. Moreover, We are pleased of Our own will and authority to add still another to the sacred Indulgences which have been granted from time to time by Our predecessors. We grant, that is, to all those who piously recite the prayer appended to this letter, to whatever nation they may belong, an indulgence of three hundred days; moreover, a plenary indulgence once a month on the observance of the usual conditions to those who have recited it daily.

Finally, may the divine prayer of Christ Himself for unity fill up the full measure of Our desires, a prayer which on this day, through the mystery of His most holy resurrection, We repeat with the utmost confidence: *Holy Father, keep them in Thy name whom Thou hast*

---

[1] Rom. xv. 13.

given Me: that they may be one as We also are one. . . .
Sanctify them in truth. Thy word is truth. . . . *And not
for them only do I pray, but for them also who through their
word shall believe in Me: that all may be one, as Thou,
Father, in Me, and I in Thee; that they also may be one in
Us.* . . . *I in them and Thou in Me: that they may be
made perfect in one: and the world may know that Thou
hast sent Me and hast loved them, as Thou hast also loved
Me.*[1]

Finally, We desire all manner of blessings from God
for the whole of the British people, and with all Our heart
We pray that those who seek the kingdom of Christ and
salvation in the unity of faith may enter on the full realization of their desires.

––––––

To the Blessed Virgin.

Prayer for England.

O Blessed Virgin Mary, Mother of God and our most
gentle Queen and Mother, look down in mercy upon
England thy "Dowry" and upon us all who greatly hope
and trust in thee. By thee it was that Jesus our Saviour
and our hope was given unto the world; and He has given
thee to us that we might hope still more. Plead for us
thy children, whom thou didst receive and accept at the
foot of the cross. O sorrowful Mother! intercede for
our separated brethren, that with us in the one true
fold they may be united to the supreme Shepherd, the
Vicar of thy Son. Pray for us all, dear Mother, that by
faith fruitful in good works we may all deserve to see
and praise God, together with thee, in our heavenly
home. Amen.

[1] John xvii. 11, 17, 20, 21, 23.

THE UNITY OF THE CHURCH.

Encyclical Letter Satis Cognitum, June 20, 1896.

IT is sufficiently well known unto you that no small share of Our thoughts and of Our care is devoted to Our endeavor to bring back to the *fold*, placed under the guardianship of Jesus Christ, the chief Pastor of souls, sheep that have strayed. Bent upon this, We have thought it most conducive to this salutary end and purpose to describe the exemplar and, as it were, the lineaments of the Church. Amongst these the most worthy of Our chief consideration is *Unity*. This the divine Author impressed on it as a lasting sign of truth and of unconquerable strength. The essential beauty and comeliness of the Church ought greatly to influence the minds of those who consider it. Nor is it improbable that ignorance may be dispelled by the consideration; that false ideas and prejudices may be dissipated from the minds chiefly of those who find themselves in error without fault of theirs; and that even a love for the Church may be stirred up in the souls of men, like unto that charity wherewith Christ loved and united Himself to that spouse redeemed by His precious blood. *Christ loved the Church, and delivered Himself up for it.*[1]

If those about to come back to their most loving Mother (not yet fully known, or culpably abandoned) should perceive that their return involves not indeed the shedding of their blood (at which price nevertheless the Church

[1] Eph. v. 25

was bought by Jesus Christ) but some lesser trouble and labor, let them clearly understand that this burden has been laid on them not by the will of man but by the will and command of God. They may thus, by the help of heavenly grace, realize and feel the truth of the divine saying, *My yoke is sweet and My burden light.*[1]

Wherefore, having put all Our hope in the *Father of lights,* from whom *cometh every best gift and every perfect gift* [2]—from Him, namely, who alone *gives the increase* [3]— We earnestly pray that He will graciously grant Us the power of bringing conviction home to the minds of men.

Although God can do by His own power all that is effected by created natures, nevertheless in the counsels of His loving providence He has preferred to help men by the instrumentality of men. And, as in the natural order He does not usually give full perfection except by means of man's work and actions so also He makes use of human aid for that which lies beyond the limits of nature; that is to say, for the sanctification and salvation of souls. But it is obvious that nothing can be communicated amongst men save by means of external things which the senses can preceive. For this reason the Son of God assumed human nature—*who being in the form of God . . . emptied Himself, taking the form of a servant, being made in the likeness of a man* [4]—and thus living on earth He taught His doctrine and gave His laws, conversing with men.

And since it was necessary that His divine mission should be prepetuated to the end of time, He took to Himself disciples, trained by Himself, and made them partakers of His own authority. And, when He had invoked upon them from heaven the *Spirit of Truth,* He bade them go through the whole world and faithfully preach to all nations what He had taught and what He had commanded, so that by the profession of His doctrine, and the observance of His laws, the human race might

---

[1] Matt. xi. 30.　[2] James i. 17.　[3] 1 Cor. iii. 6.　[4] Philipp. ii. 6, 7.

attain to holiness on earth and never-ending happiness in heaven. In this wise, and on this principle, the Church was begotten. If we consider the chief end of this Church and the proximate efficient causes of salvation, it is undoubtedly *spiritual;* but in regard to those who constitute it, and to the things which lead to these spiritual gifts, it is *external* and necessarily visible. The apostles received a mission to teach by visible and audible signs, and they discharged their mission only by words and acts which certainly appealed to the senses. So that their voices falling upon the ears of those who heard them begot faith in souls—*Faith cometh by hearing, and hearing by the word of Christ.*[1] And faith itself—that is assent given to the first and supreme truth—though residing essentially in the intellect, must be manifested by outward profession—*For, with the heart, we believe unto justice; but with the mouth, confession is made unto salvation.*[2] In the same way, in man, nothing is more internal than heavenly grace which begets sanctity, but the ordinary and chief means of obtaining grace are external: that is to say, the sacraments which are administered by men specially chosen for that purpose, by means of certain ordinances.

Jesus Christ commanded His apostles and their successors to the end of time to teach and rule the nations. He ordered the nations to accept their teaching and obey their authority. But this correlation of rights and duties in the Christian commonwealth not only could not have been made permanent, but could not even have been initiated except through the senses, which are of all things the messengers and interpreters.

For this reason the Church is so often called in holy writ a *body,* and even *the body of Christ—Now you are the body of Christ* [3]—and precisely because it is a body is the Church visible: and because it is the body of Christ

---

[1] Rom. x. 17.　　[2] Rom. x. 10.　　[3] 1 Cor. xii. 27.

is it living and energizing, because by the infusion of His power Christ guards and sustains it, just as the vine gives nourishment and renders fruitful the branches united to it. And as in animals the vital principle is unseen and invisible, and is evidenced and manifested by the movements and action of the members, so the principle of supernatural life in the Church is clearly shown in that which is done by it.

From this it follows that those who arbitrarily conjure up and picture to themselves a hidden and invisible Church are in grievous and pernicious error, as also are those who regard the Church as a human institution which claims a certain obedience in discipline and external duties, but which is without the perennial communication of the gifts of divine grace, and without all that which testifies by constant and undoubted signs to the existence of that life which is drawn from God. It is assuredly as impossible that the Church of Jesus Christ can be the one or the other as that man should be a body alone or a soul alone. The connection and union of both elements is as absolutely necessary to the true Church as the intimate union of the soul and body is to human nature. The Church is not something dead: it is the body of Christ endowed with supernatural life. As Christ, the head and exemplar, is not wholly in His visible human nature, which Photinians and Nestorians assert, nor wholly in the invisible divine nature, as the Monophysites hold, but is one, from and in both natures, visible and invisible; so the mystical body of Christ is the true Church only because its visible parts draw life and power from the supernatural gifts and other things whence spring their very nature and essence. But since the Church is *such* by divine will and constitution, *such* it must uniformly remain to the end of time. If it did not, then it would not have been founded as perpetual and the end set before it would have been limited to some certain place and to some certain period of time; both of which are contrary to the truth. The union consequently of visible and invisible elements, because it harmonizes with the natural order and by God's will belongs to the very essence of the Church, must necessarily remain so long as the Church itself shall endure. Wherefore Chrysostom writes: "Secede not from the Church: for nothing is stronger than the Church. Thy hope is the Church; thy salvation is the Church; thy refuge is the Church. It is higher than the heavens and wider than the earth. It never grows old, but is ever full of vigor. Wherefore holy writ pointing to its strength and stability calls it a mountain." [1]

Also Augustine says: "Unbelievers think that the Christian religion will last for a certain period in the world and will then disappear. But it will remain as long as the sun—as long as the sun rises and sets; that is, as long as the ages of time shall roll, the Church of God—the true body of Christ on earth—will not disappear." [2] And in another place: "The Church will totter if its foundation shakes; but how can Christ be moved? . . . Christ remaining immovable, it (the Church) shall never be shaken. Where are they that say that the Church has disappeared from the world, when it cannot even be shaken?" [3]

He who seeks the truth must be guided by these fundamental principles. That is to say, that Christ the Lord instituted and formed the Church: wherefore when we are asked what its nature is, the main thing is to see what Christ wished, and what in fact He did. Judged by such a criterion it is the unity of the Church which must be principally considered; and of this, for the general good, it has seemed useful to speak in this Encyclical.

It is so evident from the clear and frequent testimonies of holy writ that the true Church of Jesus Christ is *one*, that no Christian can dare to deny it. But in judging and determining the nature of this unity many have erred in various ways. Not the foundation of the Church alone,

---

[1] Hom. De capto Eutropio, n. 6.   [2] In Psalm. lxx. n. 8.
[3] Enarratio in Psalm. ciii., sermo ii., n. 5.

but its whole constitution, belongs to the class of things effected by Christ's free choice. For this reason the entire case must be judged by what was actually done. We must consequently investigate not how the Church may possibly be one, but how He, who founded it, willed that it should be one.

But when we consider what was actually done we find that Jesus Christ did not, in point of fact, institute a Church to embrace several communities similar in nature, but in themselves distinct, and lacking those bonds which render the Church unique and indivisible after that manner in which in the symbol of our faith we profess: "I believe in one Church."

"The Church in respect of its unity belongs to the category of things indivisible by nature, though heretics try to divide it into many parts. . . . We say, therefore, that the Catholic Church is unique in its essence, in its doctrine, in its origin, and in its excellence. . . . Furthermore, the eminence of the Church arises from its unity, as the principle of its constitution—a unity surpassing all else, and having nothing like unto it or equal to it.[1] For this reason Christ, speaking of this mystical edifice, mentions only one Church, which He calls *His own*—"I will build My Church"; any other Church except this one, since it has not been founded by Christ, cannot be the true Church. This becomes even more evident when the purpose of the divine Founder is considered. For what did Christ the Lord ask? What did He wish in regard to the Church founded, or about to be founded? This: to transmit to it the same mission and the same mandate which He had received from the Father, that they should be perpetuated. This He clearly resolved to do: this He actually did. *As the Father hath sent Me, I also send you.[2] As thou hast sent Me into the world I also have sent them into the world.[3]*

---

[1] S. Clemens Alexandrinus, Stromatum lib. viii., c. 17
[2] John xx. 21.   [3] John xvii. 18.

But the mission of Christ is to save *that which had perished;* that is to say, not some nations or peoples, but the whole human race, without distinction of time or place. *The Son of man came that the world might be saved by Him.*[1] *For there is no other name under heaven given to men whereby we must be saved.*[2] The Church, therefore, is bound to communicate without stint to all men, and to transmit through all ages, the salvation effected by Jesus Christ, and the blessings flowing therefrom. Wherefore, by the will of its Founder, it is necessary that this Church should be one in all lands and at all times. To justify the existence of more than one Church it would be necessary to go outside this world, and to create a new and unheard-of race of men.

That the one Church should embrace all men everywhere and at all times was seen and foretold by Isaias, when looking into the future he saw the appearance of a mountain conspicuous by its all-surpassing altitude, which set forth the image of "the house of the Lord"—that is, of the Church. *And in the last days the mountain of the house of the Lord shall be prepared on the top of the mountains.*[3]

But this mountain which towers over all other mountains is *one;* and the house of the Lord to which *all nations* shall come to seek the rule of living is also *one.* "*And all nations shall flow unto it. And many peoples shall go, and say: Come, and let us go up to the mountain of the Lord, and to the house of the God of Jacob, and He will teach us His ways, and we will walk in His paths.*[4]

Explaining this passage, Optatus of Milevis says: "It is written in the prophet Isaias: 'From Sion the law shall go forth, and the word of the Lord from Jerusalem.' For it is not on Mount Sion that Isaias sees the valley, but on the holy mountain; that is, the Church, which has raised itself conspicuously throughout the entire Roman world

---

[1] John iii. 17.   [2] Acts iv. 12   [3] Isa. ii. 2.   [4] Isa. ii. 2, 3.

under the whole heavens. . . . The Church is, therefore, the spiritual Sion in which Christ has been constituted King by God the Father, and which exists throughout the entire earth, on which there is but one Catholic Church,"[1] And Augustine says: "What can be so manifest as a mountain, or so well known? There are, it is true, mountains which are unknown because they are situated in some remote part of the earth. . . . But this mountain is not unknown; for it has filled the whole face of the world, and about this it is said that it is prepared on the summit of the mountains." [2]

Furthermore, the Son of God decreed that the Church should be His mystical body, with which He should be united as the head, after the manner of the human body which He assumed, to which the natural head is physiologically united. As He took to Himself a mortal body which he gave to suffering and death in order to pay the price of man's redemption, so also He has one mystical body in which and through which He renders men partakers of holiness and of eternal salvation. God *hath made Him (Christ) head over all the Church, which is His body.*[3] Scattered and separated members cannot possibly cohere with the head so as to make one body. But St. Paul says: *All the members of the body, whereas they are many, yet are one body, so also is Christ.*[4] Wherefore this mystical body, he declares, is *compacted and fitly joined together. The head, Christ: from whom the whole body, being compacted and fitly joined together, by what every joint supplieth, according to the operation in the measure of every part.*[5] And so dispersed members, separated one from the other, cannot be united with one and the same head. "There is one God, and one Christ; and His Church is one and the faith is one; and one the people, joined together in the solid unity of the body in the bond

---

[1] De Schism. Donatist. lib. iii. n. 2.   [3] Eph. i. 22, 23.
[2] In Ep. Joan., tract i., n. 13.   [4] 1 Cor. xii. 12.
    [5] Eph. iv. 15, 16.

of concord. This unity cannot be broken, nor the one body divided by the separation of its constituent parts."[1] And to set forth more clearly the unity of the Church, he makes use of the illustration of a living body, the members of which cannot possibly live unless united to the head and drawing from it their vital force. Separated from the head they must of necessity die. "The Church," he says, "cannot be divided into parts by the separation and cutting asunder of its members. What is cut away from the mother cannot live or breathe apart."[2] What similarity is there between a dead and a living body? *For no man ever hated his own flesh, but nourisheth and cherisheth it, as also Christ doth the Church: because we are members of His body, of His flesh, and of His bones.*[3]

Another head like to Christ must be invented—that is, another Christ—if besides the one Church, which is His body, men wish to set up another. "See what you must beware of—see what you must avoid—see what you must dread. It happens that, as in the human body, some member may be cut off—a hand, a finger, a foot. Does the soul follow the amputated member? As long as it was in the body it lived; separated, it forfeits its life. So the Christian is a Catholic as long as he lives in the body: cut off from it he becomes a heretic—the life of the spirit follows not the amputated member."[4]

The Church of Christ, therefore, is one and the same forever; those who leave it depart from the will and command of Christ the Lord—leaving the path of salvation they enter on that of perdition. "Whosoever is separated from the Church is united to an adulteress. He has cut himself off from the promises of the Church, and he who leaves the Church of Christ cannot arrive at the rewards of Christ. . . . He who observes not this unity observes not

---

[1] S. Cyprianus, De Cath. Eccl. Unitate, n. 23.
[2] Ibid.
[3] Eph. v. 29, 30.
[4] S. Augustinus, Sermo cclxvii., n. 4.

the law of God, holds not the faith of the Father and the Son, clings not to life and salvation."[1]

But He, indeed, who made this one Church, also gave it *unity*, that is, He made it such that all who are to belong to it must be united by the closest bonds, so as to form one society, one kingdom, one body—*one body and one spirit, as you are called in one hope of your calling.*[2] Jesus Christ, when His death was nigh at hand, declared His will in this matter, and solemnly offered it up, thus addressing His Father: *Not for them only do I pray, but for them also who through their word shall believe in Me . . . that they also may be one in Us . . . that they may be made perfect in one.*[3] Yea, He commanded that this unity should be so closely knit and so perfect amongst His followers that it might, in some measure, shadow forth the union between Himself and His Father: *I pray that they all may be one, as Thou, Father, in Me, and I in Thee.*[4]

Agreement and union of minds is the necessary foundation of this perfect concord amongst men, from which concurrence of wills and similarity of action are the natural results. Wherefore, in His divine wisdom, He ordained in His Church *Unity* of *Faith;* a virtue which is the first of those bonds which unite man to God, and whence we receive the name of the *faithful—one Lord, one faith, one baptism.*[5] That is, as there is one Lord and one baptism, so should all Christians, without exception, have but one faith. And so the Apostle St. Paul not merely begs but entreats and implores Christians to be all of the same mind, and to avoid difference of opinions: *I beseech you, brethren, by the name of Our Lord Jesus Christ, that you all speak the same thing, and that there be no schisms amongst you, and that you be perfect in the same mind and in the same judgment.*[6] Such passages certainly need no interpreter; they speak clearly enough for themselves.

[1] S. Cyprianus, De Cath. Eccl. Unita e, n. 6.
[2] Eph. iv. 4.
[3] John xvii. 20, 21, 23.
[4] Ibid. 21.
[5] Eph. iv. 5.
[6] 1 Cor. i. 10.

Besides, all who profess Christianity allow that there can be but one faith. It is of the greatest importance, and indeed of absolute necessity, as to which many are deceived, that the nature and character of this unity should be recognized. And, as We have already stated, this is not to be ascertained by conjecture, but by the certain knowledge of what was done; that is by seeking for and ascertaining what kind of unity in faith has been commanded by Jesus Christ.

The heavenly doctrine of Christ, although for the most part committed to writing by divine inspiration, could not unite the minds of men if left to the human intellect alone. It would, for this very reason, be subject to various and contradictory interpretations. This is so not only because of the nature of the doctrine itself and of the mysteries it involves, but also because of the divergencies of the human mind and of the disturbing element of conflicting passions. From a variety of interpretations a variety of beliefs is necessarily begotten; hence come controversies, dissensions, and wranglings such as have arisen in the past, even in the first ages of the Church. Irenæus writes of heretics as follows: "Admitting the Sacred Scriptures they distort the interpretations."[1] And Augustine: "Heresies have arisen, and certain perverse views ensnaring souls and precipitating them into the abyss only when the Scriptures, good in themselves, are not properly understood."[2] Besides holy writ it was absolutely necessary to insure this union of men's minds— to effect and preserve unity of ideas—that there should be another *principle.* This the wisdom of God requires: for He could not have willed that the faith should be *one* if He did not provide means sufficient for the preservation of this unity; and this holy writ clearly sets forth as We shall presently point out. Assuredly the infinite power of God is not bound by anything; all things obey

[1] Lib. iii., cap. 12, n. 12.
[2] In Evang. Joan., tract xviii., cap. 5, n. 1

it as so many passive instruments. In regard to this external principle, therefore, we must inquire which one of all the means in His power Christ did actually adopt. For this purpose it is necessary to recall in thought the institution of Christianity.

We are mindful only of what is witnessed to by holy writ and what is otherwise well known. Christ proves His own divinity and the divine origin of His mission by miracles; He teaches the multitudes heavenly doctrine by word of mouth; and He absolutely commands that the assent of faith should be given to His teaching, promising eternal rewards to those who believe and eternal punishment to those who do not. *If I do not the works of My Father, believe Me not.*[1] *If I had not done among them the works that no other man hath done, they would not have sin.*[2] *But if I do* (the works), *though you will not believe Me, believe the works.*[3] Whatsoever He commands, He commands by the same authority. He requires the assent of the mind to all truths without exception. It was thus the duty of all who heard Jesus Christ, if they wished for eternal salvation, not merely to accept His doctrine as a whole, but to assent with their entire mind to all and every point of it, since it is unlawful to withhold faith from God even in regard to one single point.

When about to ascend into heaven He sends His apostles in virtue of the same power by which He had been sent from the Father; and He charges them to spread abroad and propagate His teaching. *All power is given to Me in heaven and in earth. Going therefore teach all nations . . . teaching them to observe all things whatsoever I have commanded you.*[4] So that those obeying the apostles might be saved, and those disobeying should perish. *He that believeth and is baptized shall be saved, but he that believeth not shall be condemned.*[5] But since it is obviously most in harmony with God's providence that no one

[1] John x. 37.   [2] John xv. 24.   [3] John x. 38.
[4] Matt. xxviii. 18, 19, 20.   [5] Mark xvi. 16.

should have confided to him a great and important mission unless he were furnished with the means of properly carrying it out, for this reason Christ promised that He would send the Spirit of Truth to His disciples to remain with them forever. *But if I go I will send Him* (the Paraclete) *to you. . . . But when He, the Spirit of Truth, is come, He will teach you all truth.*[1] *And I will ask the Father, and He shall give you another Paraclete, that He may abide with you forever, the Spirit of Truth.*[2] *He shall give testimony of Me, and you shall give testimony.*[3] Hence He commands that the teaching of the apostles should be religiously accepted and piously kept as if it were His own—*He who hears you hears Me, he who despises you despises Me.*[4] Wherefore the apostles are ambassadors of Christ as He is the ambassador of the Father. *As the Father sent Me so also I send you.*[5] Hence as the apostles and disciples were bound to obey Christ, so also those whom the apostles taught were, by God's command, bound to obey them. And, therefore, it was no more allowable to repudiate one iota of the apostles' teaching than it was to reject any point of the doctrine of Christ Himself.

Truly the voice of the apostles, when the Holy Ghost had come down upon them, resounded throughout the world. Wherever they went they proclaimed themselves the ambassadors of Christ Himself. *By whom* (Jesus Christ) *we have received grace and apostleship for obedience to the faith in all nations for His name.*[6] And God makes known their divine mission by numerous miracles. *But they going forth preached everywhere: the Lord working withal, and confirming the word with signs that followed.*[7] But what is this word? That which comprehends all things, that which they had learnt from their Master; because they openly and publicly declare that they cannot help speaking of what they had seen and heard.

[1] John xvi. 7–13.   [2] Ibid. xiv. 16, 17.   [3] Ibid. xv. 26, 27.
[4] Luke x. 16.   [5] John xx. 21.   [6] Rom. i. 5.   [7] Mark xvi. 20.

But, as We have already said, the apostolic mission was not destined to die with the apostles themselves, or to come to an end in the course of time, since it was intended for the people at large and instituted for the salvation of the human race. For Christ commanded His apostles to preach the "Gospel to every creature, to carry His name to nations and kings, and to be witnesses to Him to the ends of the earth." He further promised to assist them in the fulfilment of their high mission, and that, not for a few years or centuries only, but for all time—"even to the consummation of the world." Upon which St. Jerome says: "He who promises to remain with His disciples to the end of the world declares that they will be forever victorious, and that He will never depart from those who believe in Him." [1] But how could all this be realized in the apostles alone, placed as they were under the universal law of dissolution by death? It was consequently provided by God that the *Magisterium* instituted by Jesus Christ should not end with the life of the apostles, but that it should be perpetuated. We see it in truth propagated, and, as it were, delivered from hand to hand. For the apostles consecrated bishops, and each one appointed those who were to succeed them immediately "in the ministry of the Word."

Nay more: they likewise required their successors to choose fitting men, to endow them with like authority, and to confide to them the office and mission of teaching. *Thou, therefore, my son, be strong in the grace which is in Christ Jesus: and the things which thou hast heard of me by many witnesses, the same command to faithful men, who shall be fit to teach others also.* [2] Wherefore, as Christ was sent by God and the apostles by Christ, so the bishops and those who succeeded them were sent by the apostles. "The apostles were appointed by Christ to preach the Gospel to us. Jesus Christ was sent by God. Christ is

---

[1] In Matt., lib. iv., cap. 28, v. 20.   [2] 2 Tim. ii. 1, 2.

therefore from God, and the apostles from Christ, and both according to the will of God. . . . Preaching therefore the word through the countries and cities, when they had proved in the Spirit the first-fruits of their teaching they appointed bishops and deacons for the faithful. . . . They appointed them and then ordained them, so that when they themselves had passed away other tried men should carry on their ministry." [1] On the one hand, therefore, it is necessary that the mission of teaching whatever Christ had taught should remain perpetual and immutable, and on the other that the duty of accepting and professing all their doctrine should likewise be perpetual and immutable. "Our Lord Jesus Christ, when in His Gospel He testifies that those who are not with Him are His enemies, does not designate any special form of heresy, but declares that all heretics who are not with Him and do not gather with Him, scatter His flock and are His adversaries: He that is not with Me is against Me, and he that gathereth not with Me scattereth." [2]

The Church, founded on these principles and mindful of her office, has done nothing with greater zeal and endeavor than she has displayed in guarding the integrity of the faith. Hence she regarded as rebels and expelled from the ranks of her children all who held beliefs on any point of doctrine different from her own. The Arians, the Montanists, the Novatians, the Quartodecimans, the Eutychians, did not certainly reject all Catholic doctrine: they abandoned only a certain portion of it. Still who does not know that they were declared heretics and banished from the bosom of the Church? In like manner were condemned all authors of heretical tenets who followed them in subsequent ages. "There can be nothing more dangerous than those heretics who admit nearly the whole cycle of doctrine, and yet by one word, as with a drop of

[1] S. Clemens Rom. Epist. I. ad Corinth. capp. 42, 46.
[2] S. Cyprianus, Ep. lxix. ad Magnum, n. 1.

poison, infect the real and simple faith taught by Our Lord and handed down by apostolic tradition."[1]

The practice of the Church has always been the same, as is shown by the unanimous teaching of the Fathers, who were wont to hold as outside Catholic communion, and alien to the Church, whoever would recede in the least degree from any point of doctrine proposed by her authoritative Magisterium. Epiphanius, Augustine, Theodoret, drew up a long list of the heresies of their times. St. Augustine notes that other heresies may spring up, to a single one of which, should any one give his assent, he is by the very fact cut off from Catholic unity. "No one who merely disbelieves in all (these heresies) can for that reason regard himself as a Catholic or call himself one. For there may be or may arise some other heresies, which are not set out in this work of ours, and if any one holds to one single one of these he is not a Catholic."[2]

The need of this divinely instituted means for the preservation of unity, about which We speak, is urged by St. Paul in his epistle to the Ephesians. In this he first admonishes them to preserve with every care concord of minds: *Solicitous to keep the unity of the Spirit in the bond of peace.*[3] And as souls cannot be perfectly united in charity unless minds agree in faith, he wishes all to hold the same faith: *One Lord, one faith*, and this so perfectly *one* as to prevent all danger of error: *that henceforth we be no more children, tossed to and fro, and carried about with every wind of doctrine by the wickedness of men, by cunning craftiness, by which they lie in wait to deceive;*[4] and this he teaches is to be observed, not for a time only, but *until we all meet in the unity of faith . . . unto the measure of the age of the fulness of Christ.*[5] But, in what has Christ placed the primary principle, and the means of preserving this unity? In that—*He gave some apostles*

---

[1] Auctor Tract. de Fide Orthodoxa contra Arianos.
[2] S. Augustinus, De Haeresibus, n. 88. [4] Eph. iv. 14.
[3] Eph. iv. 3, et seq. [5] Eph. iv. 13.

. . . and other some pastors and doctors, for the perfecting of the saints, for the work of the ministry, for the edifying of the body of Christ.[1]

Wherefore, from the very earliest times the Fathers and Doctors of the Church have been accustomed to follow and with one accord to defend this rule. Origen writes: "As often as the heretics allege the possession of the canonical scriptures, to which all Christians give unanimous assent, they seem to say: 'Behold the word of truth is in the houses.' But we should believe them not and abandon not the primary and ecclesiastical tradition. We should believe not otherwise than has been handed down by the tradition of the Church of God."[2] Irenæus too says: "The doctrine of the apostles is the true faith . . . which is known to us through the episcopal succession . . . which has reached even unto our age by the very fact that the Scriptures have been zealously guarded and fully interpreted."[3] And Tertullian: "It is therefore clear that all doctrine which agrees with that of the apostolic churches —the matrices and original centres of the faith—must be looked upon as the truth, holding without hesitation that the Church received it from the apostles, the apostles from Christ, and Christ from God. . . . We are in communion with the apostolic churches, and by the very fact that they agree amongst themselves we have a testimony of the truth."[4] And so Hilary: "Christ teaching from the ship signifies that those who are outside the Church can never grasp the divine teaching; for the ship typifies the Church where the word of life is deposited and preached. Those who are outside are like sterile and worthless sand: they cannot comprehend."[5] Rufinus praises Gregory of Nazianzum and Basil because

---

[1] Eph. iv. 11, 12.
[2] Vetus Interpretatio Commentariorum in Matt. n. 46.
[3] Contra Haereses, lib. iv., cap. 33, an. 8.
[4] De Præscript., cap. xxxi.
[5] Comment. in Matt. xiii. n. 1.

" they studied the text of Holy Scripture alone, and took the interpretation of its meaning not from their own inner consciousness, but from the writings and on the authority of the ancients, who in their turn, as it is clear, took their rule for understanding the meaning from the apostolic succession." [1]

Wherefore, as appears from what has been said, Christ instituted in the Church a *living, authoritative,* and *permanent Magisterium,* which by His own power He strengthened, by the Spirit of Truth He taught, and by miracles confirmed. He willed and ordered, under the gravest penalties, that its teachings should be received as if they were His own. As often, therefore, as it is declared on the authority of this teaching that this or that is contained in the deposit of divine revelation, it must be believed by every one as true. If it could in any way be false, an evident contradiction follows; for then God Himself would be the author of error in man. "Lord, if we be in error, we are being deceived by Thee." [2] In this wise, all cause for doubting being removed, can it be lawful for any one to reject any one of those truths without by the very fact falling into heresy?—without separating himself from the Church?—without repudiating in one sweeping act the whole of Christian teaching? For such is the nature of faith that nothing can be more absurd than to accept some things and reject others. Faith, as the Church teaches, is "that supernatural virtue by which, through the help of God and through the assistance of His grace, we believe what He has revealed to be true, not on account of the intrinsic truth perceived by the natural light of reason, but because of the authority of God Himself, the Revealer, who can neither deceive nor be deceived." [3] If then it be certain that anything is revealed by God, and this is not believed,

[1] Hist. Eccl., lib. ii., c p. 9.
[2] Richardus de S. Victore, De Trin., lib. i., cap. 2.
[3] Conc. Vat., Sess. iii., cap. 3.

then nothing whatever is believed by divine faith: for what the Apostle St. James judges to be the effect of a moral delinquency, the same is to be said of an erroneous opinion in the matter of faith. *Whosoever shall offend in one point, is become guilty of all.*[1] Nay, it applies with greater force to an erroneous opinion. For it can be said with less truth that every law is violated by one who commits a single sin, since it may be that he only virtually despises the majesty of God the Legislator. But he who dissents even in one point from divinely revealed truth absolutely rejects all faith, since he thereby refuses to honor God as the supreme truth and the *formal motive of faith.* "In many things they are with me, in a few things not with me; but in those few things in which they are not with me the many things in which they are will not profit them." [2] And this indeed most deservedly; for they who take from Christian doctrine what they please lean on their own judgments, not on faith; and not *bringing into captivity every understanding unto the obedience of Christ,*[3] they more truly obey themselves than God. "You, who believe what you like of the gospels and believe not what you like, believe yourselves rather than the gospel." [4]

For this reason the Fathers of the Vatican Council laid down nothing new, but followed divine revelation and the acknowledged and invariable teaching of the Church as to the very nature of faith, when they decreed as follows: "All those things are to be believed by divine and Catholic faith which are contained in the written or unwritten word of God, and which are proposed by the Church as divinely revealed, either by a solemn definition or in the exercise of its ordinary and universal Magisterium." [5]   Hence, as it

[1] James ii. 10.
[2] S. Augustinus in Psal. liv., n. 19.
[3] 2 Cor. x. 5.
[4] S. Augustinus, lib. xvii., Contra Faustum Manichaeum, cap. 3.
[5] Sess. iii., cap. 3.

is clear that God absolutely willed that there should be unity in His Church, and as it is evident what kind of unity He willed, and by means of what principle He ordained that this unity should be maintained, We may address the following words of St. Augustine to all who have not deliberately closed their minds to the truth: "When we see the great help of God, such manifest progress and such abundant fruit, shall we hesitate to take refuge in the bosom of that Church which, as is evident to all, possesses the supreme authority of the Apostolic See through the episcopal succession? In vain do heretics rage round it; they are condemned partly by the judgment of the people themselves, partly by the weight of councils, partly by the splendid evidence of miracles. To refuse to the Church the primacy is most impious and above measure arrogant. And if all learning, no matter how easy and common it may be, in order to be fully understood requires a teacher and master, what can be greater evidence of pride and rashness than to be unwilling to learn about the books of the divine mysteries from the proper interpreter, and to wish to condemn them unknown?" [1]

It is, then, undoubtedly the office of the Church to guard Christian doctrine and to propagate it in its integrity and purity. But this is not all: the object for which the Church has been instituted is not wholly attained by the performance of this duty. For, since Jesus Christ delivered Himself up for the salvation of the human race, and to this end directed all His teaching and commands, so He ordered the Church to strive, by the truth of its doctrine, to sanctify and to save mankind. But faith alone cannot compass so great, excellent, and important an end. There must needs be also the fitting and devout worship of God, which is to be found chiefly in the divine sacrifice and in the dispensation of the sacraments, as well as salutary laws and discipline. All these must be found in the Church,

---

[1] De Unitate Credendi, cap. xvii. n. 35.

since it continues the mission of the Saviour forever. The Church alone offers to the human race that religion—that state of absolute perfection—which He wished, as it were, to be *incorporated* in it. And it alone supplies those means of salvation which accord with the ordinary counsels of Providence.

But as this heavenly doctrine was never left to the arbitrary judgment of private individuals, but in the beginning delivered by Jesus Christ, was afterwards committed by Him exclusively to the Magisterium already named, so the power of performing and administering the divine mysteries, together with the authority of ruling and governing, was not bestowed by God on all Christians indiscriminately, but on certain chosen persons. For to the apostles and their legitimate successors alone these words have reference: "Going into the whole world preach the Gospel." "Baptizing them." "Do this in commemoration of Me." "Whose sins you shall forgive they are forgiven them." And in like manner He ordered the apostles only and those who should lawfully succeed them to *feed*—that is to govern with authority—all Christian souls. Whence it also follows that it is necessarily the duty of Christians to be subject and to obey. And these duties of the apostolic office are, in general, all included in the words of St. Paul: *Let a man so account of us as of the ministers of Christ, and the dispensers of the mysteries of God.*[1]

Wherefore Jesus Christ bade all men, present and future, follow Him as their leader and Saviour; and this not merely as individuals, but as forming a society, organized and united in mind. In this way a duly constituted society should exist, formed out of the divided multitude of peoples, one in faith, one in end, one in the participation of the means adapted to the attainment of the end, and one as subject to one and the same authority.

---

[1] 1 Cor. iv. 1.

To this end He established in the Church all those principles which necessarily tend to make organized human
societies, and through which they attain the perfection
proper to each.   That is, in it (the Church) all who wished
to be the sons of God by adoption might attain to the
perfection   demanded by their high calling, and might
obtain salvation.   The Church, therefore, as we have
said, is man's guide to whatever pertains to heaven.
This is the office appointed unto it by God: that it may
watch over and may order all that concerns religion, and
may, without let or hindrance, exercise, according to its
judgment, its charge over Christianity.   Wherefore they
who pretend that the Church has any wish to interfere
in civil matters, or to infringe upon the rights of the
State, know it not, or wickedly calumniate it.

God indeed even made the Church a society far more
perfect than any other.   For the end for which the Church
exists is as much higher than the end of other societies as
divine grace is above nature, as immortal blessings are
above the transitory things on the earth.   Therefore the
Church is a society *divine* in its origin, *supernatural* in its
end and in the means proximately adapted to the attainment of that end; but it is a *human* community inasmuch
as it is composed of men.   For this reason we find it called
in holy writ by names indicating a perfect society.   It is
spoken of as *the house of God*, the *city placed upon the
mountain* to which all nations must come.   But it is also
the *fold* presided over by one Shepherd, and into which
all Christ's sheep must betake themselves.   Yea, it is called
the kingdom which God has raised up and which *will stand
forever*.   Finally it is the *body of Christ*—that is, of course,
His *mystical* body, but a body living and duly organized
and composed of many members; members indeed which
have not all the same functions, but which, united one
to the other, are kept bound together by the guidance
and authority of the head.

Indeed no true and perfect human society can be conceived which is not governed by some supreme authority. Christ therefore must have given to His Church a supreme authority to which all Christians must render obedience. For this reason, as the unity of the faith is of necessity required for the unity of the Church, inasmuch as it is the *body of the faithful,* so also for this same unity, inasmuch as the Church is a divinely constituted society, unity of government, which effects and involves *unity of communion,* is necessary *jure divino.* "The unity of the Church is manifested in the mutual connection or communication of its members, and likewise in the relation of all the members of the Church to one head." [1]

From this it is easy to see that men can fall away from the unity of the Church by schism, as well as by heresy. "We think that this difference exists between heresy and schism" (writes St. Jerome): "heresy has no perfect dogmatic teaching, whereas schism, through some episcopal dissent, also separates from the Church." [2] In which judgment St. John Chrysostom concurs: "I say and protest," he writes, "that it is as wrong to divide the Church as to fall into heresy." [3] Wherefore as no heresy can ever be justifiable, so in like manner there can be no justification for schism. "There is nothing more grievous than the sacrilege of schism . . . there can be no just necessity for destroying the unity of the Church." [4]

The nature of this supreme authority, which all Christians are bound to obey, can be ascertained only by finding out what was the evident and positive will of Christ. Certainly Christ is a King forever; and though invisible, He continues unto the end of time to govern and guard His Church from heaven. But since He willed that His kingdom should be visible He was obliged, when He

[1] St. Thomas, 2a 2æ 9, xxxix. a. 1.
[2] S. Hieronymus, Comment. in Epist. ad Titum, cap iii., v. 10, 11.
[3] Hom. xi., in Epist. ad Ephes., n. 5.
[4] S. Augustinus, Contra Epistolam Parmeniani, lib. ii., cap. ii., n. 25.

ascended into heaven, to designate a vicegerent on earth. "Should any one say that Christ is the one head and the one shepherd, the one spouse of the one Church, he does not give an adequate reply. It is clear, indeed, that Christ is the author of grace in the sacraments of the Church; it is Christ Himself who baptizes; it is He who forgives sins; it is He who is the true priest who hath offered Himself upon the altar of the cross, and it is by His power that His body is daily consecrated upon the altar; and still, because He was not to be visibly present to all the faithful, He made choice of ministers through whom the aforesaid sacraments should be dispensed to the faithful as said above."[1] "For the same reason, therefore, because He was about to withdraw His visible presence from the Church, it was necessary that He should appoint some one in His place, to have the charge of the universal Church. Hence before His ascension He said to Peter, 'Feed My sheep.'"[2]

Jesus Christ, therefore, appointed Peter to be the head of the Church; and He also determined that the authority instituted in perpetuity for the salvation of all should be inherited by His successors, in whom the same permanent authority of Peter himself should continue. And so He made that remarkable promise to Peter and to no one else: *Thou art Peter, and upon this rock I will build My Church.*[3] "To Peter the Lord spoke: to *one*, therefore, that He might establish unity upon one."[4] "Without any prelude He mentions St. Peter's name and that of his father (Blessed art thou Simon, son of John) and He does not wish Him to be called any more Simon; claiming him for Himself according to His divine authority, He aptly names him Peter, from *petra* the rock, since upon him He was about to found His Church."[5]

[1] Cap. 74.
[2] St. Thomas, Contra Gentiles, lib. iv., cap. 76.
[3] Matt. xvi. 18.
[4] S. Pacianus ad Sempronium, Ep. iii., n. 11.
[5] S. Cyrillus Alexandrinus, in Evang. Joan., lib. ii., in cap. i. v. 42.

From this text it is clear that by the will and command of God the Church rests upon St. Peter, just as a building rests on its foundation. Now the proper nature of a foundation is to be a principle of cohesion for the various parts of the building. It must be the necessary conditions of stability and strength. Remove it and the whole building falls. It is consequently the office of St. Peter to support the Church, and to guard it in all its strength and indestructible unity. How could he fulfil this office without the power of commanding, forbidding, and judging, which is properly called *jurisdiction?* It is only by this power of jurisdiction that nations and commonwealths are held together. A primacy of honor and the shadowy right of giving advice and admonition, which is called *direction,* could never secure to any society of men unity or strength. The words—*and the gates of hell shall not prevail against it*—proclaim and establish the authority of which we speak. "What is the *it?*" (writes Origen). "Is it the rock upon which Christ builds the Church, or the Church? The expression indeed is ambiguous, as if the rock and the Church were one and the same. I indeed think that this is so, and that neither against the rock upon which Christ builds His Church nor against the Church shall the gates of hell prevail."[1] The meaning of this divine utterance is, that, notwithstanding the wiles and intrigues which they bring to bear against the Church, it can never be that the Church committed to the care of Peter shall succumb or in any wise fail. "For the Church, as the edifice of Christ who has wisely built 'His house upon a rock,' cannot be conquered by the gates of hell, which may prevail over any man who shall be off the rock and outside the Church, but shall be powerless against it."[2] Therefore God confided His Church to Peter so that he might safely guard it with his unconquerable power. He invested him, there-

---

[1] Origenes, Comment. in Matt., tom. xii., n. ii.
[2] Ibid.

fore, with the needful authority; since the right to rule is absolutely required by him who has to guard human society really and effectively. This, furthermore, Christ gave: "To thee will I give the keys of the kingdom of heaven." And He is clearly still speaking of the Church, which a short time before He had called *His own,* and which He declared He wished to build on Peter as on a foundation. The Church is typified not only as an *edifice* but as a *kingdom,* and every one knows that the keys constitute the usual sign of governing authority. Wherefore when Christ promised to give to Peter the keys of the kingdom of heaven, He promised to give him power and authority over the Church. "The Son committed to Peter the office of spreading the knowledge of His Father and Himself over the whole world. He who increased the Church in all the earth, and proclaimed it to be stronger than the heavens, gave to a mortal man all power in heaven when He handed him the keys." [1] In this same sense He says: "Whatsoever thou shall bind upon earth it shall be bound also in heaven, and whatsoever thou shalt loose on earth it shall be loosed also in heaven." This metaphorical expression of binding and loosing indicates the power of making laws, of judging and of punishing; and the power is said to be of such amplitude and force that God will ratify whatever is decreed by it. Thus it is supreme and absolutely independent, so that, having no other power on earth as its superior, it embraces the whole Church and all things committed to the Church.

The promise is carried out when Christ the Lord after His Resurrection, having thrice asked Peter whether he loved Him more than the rest, lays on him the injunction: "Feed My lambs—feed My sheep." That is He confides to him, without exception, all those who were to belong to His fold. "The Lord does not hesitate. He interrogates, not to learn but to teach. When He was about to ascend

[1] S. Johannes Chrysostomus, Hom. liv., in Matt. v. 2.

into heaven He left us, as it were, a vicegerent of His love . . . and so because Peter alone of all others professes his love he is preferred to all—that being the most perfect he should govern the more perfect."[1]

These, then, are the duties of a shepherd: to place himself as leader at the head of his flock, to provide proper food for it, to ward off dangers, to guard against insidious foes, to defend it against violence: in a word, to rule and govern it. Since therefore Peter has been placed as shepherd of the Christian flock he has received the power of governing all men for whose salvation Jesus Christ shed His blood. "Why has He shed His blood? To buy the sheep which He handed over to Peter and his successors."[2]

And since all Christians must be closely united in the communion of one immutable faith, Christ the Lord, in virtue of His prayers, obtained for Peter that in the fulfilment of his office he should never fall away from the faith. *But I have asked for thee that thy faith fail not,"*[3] and He furthermore commanded him to impart light and strength to his brethren as often as the need should arise: *Confirm thy brethren.*[4] He willed then that he whom He had designated as the foundation of the Church should be the defence of its faith. "Could not Christ, who confided to him the kingdom by His own authority, have strengthened the faith of one whom He designated a rock to show the foundation of the Church?"[5] For this reason Jesus Christ willed that Peter should participate in certain names, signs of great things which properly belong to Himself alone: in order that identity of titles should show identity of power. So He who is Himself *the chief corner-stone in whom all the building being framed*

---

[1] S. Ambrosius, Exposit. in Evang. secundum Lucam, lib. x. nn. 175, 176.

[2] S. Johannes Chrysostomus, De Sacerdotio, lib. ii.

[3] Luke xxii. 32.

[4] Ibid.

[5] S. Ambrosius, De Fide, lib. iv., n. 56.

together, groweth up in a holy temple in the Lord,[1] placed
Peter as it were *a stone* to support the Church. "When
he heard *thou art a rock*, he was ennobled by the announce-
ment. Although he is a rock, not as Christ is a rock,
but as Peter is a rock. For Christ is by His very being
an immovable rock; Peter only through this rock. Christ
imparts His gifts, and is not exhausted . . . He is a
priest, and makes priests. He is a rock, and constitutes
a rock."[2] He who is the King of His Church, *who hath
the key of David, who openeth and no man shutteth, who
shutteth and no man openeth,*[3] having delivered *the keys*
to Peter declared him Prince of the Christian commonwealth. So, too, He, the Great Shepherd, who calls
Himself *the Good Shepherd,* constituted Peter the pastor
of His lambs and sheep. Feed My lambs, feed My sheep.
Wherefore Chrysostom says: "He was pre-eminent among
the apostles: He was the mouthpiece of the apostles
and the head of the apostolic college . . . at the same
time showing him that henceforth he ought to have
confidence, and as it were blotting out his denial, He
commits to him the government of his brethren . . .
He saith to him: *'If thou lovest Me, be over My brethren.'*"
Finally He who confirms in *every good work and word*[4]
commands Peter *to confirm his brethren.*

Rightly, therefore, does St. Leo the Great say: "From
the whole world Peter alone is chosen to take the lead in
calling all nations, to be the head of all the apostles and
of all the Fathers of the Church. So that, although in the
people of God there are many priests and many pastors,
Peter should by right rule all of those over whom Christ
Himself is the chief ruler."[5] And so St. Gregory the
Great, writing to the Emperor Maurice Augustus, says:

[1] Eph. ii. 21.
[2] Hom. de Poenitentia, n. 4 in Appendice opp. S. Basilii.
[3] Apoc. iii. 7.
[4] 2 Thess. ii. 16.
[5] Sermo iv., cap. 2.

"It is evident to all who know the Gospel that the charge of the whole Church was committed to St. Peter, the apostle and prince of all the apostles, by the word of the Lord. . . . Behold! he hath received the keys of the heavenly kingdom—the power of binding and loosing is conferred upon him: the care of the whole government of the Church is confided to him." [1]

It was necessary that a government of this kind, since it belongs to the constitution and formation of the Church, as its principal element—that is as the principle of unity and the foundation of lasting stability—should in no wise come to an end with St. Peter, but should pass to his successors from one to another. "There remains, therefore, the ordinance of truth, and St. Peter, persevering in the strength of the rock which he had received, hath not abandoned the government of the Church which had been confided to him." [2] For this reason the Pontiffs who succeed Peter in the Roman Episcopate receive the supreme power in the Church, *jure divino.* "We define" (declare the Fathers of the Council of Florence) "that the Holy and Apostolic See and the Roman Pontiff holds the primacy of the Church throughout the whole world: and that the same Roman Pontiff is the successor of St. Peter, the prince of the apostles, and the true Vicar of Christ, the head of the whole Church, and the father and teacher of all Christians; and that full power was given to him, in blessed Peter, by Our Lord Jesus Christ to feed, to rule, and to govern the universal Church, as is also contained in the acts of œcumenical councils and in the sacred canons." [3] Similarly the Fourth Council of Lateran declares: "The Roman Church, as the mother and mistress of all the faithful, by the will of Christ obtains primacy of jurisdiction over all other Churches." These declarations were preceded by the consent of antiquity which ever acknowledged, without the slightest

[1] Epist. lib. v. Epist. xx.   [2] S. Leo M. sermo iii., cap. 3.
[3] Conc. Florentinum.

doubt or hesitation, the Bishops of Rome, and revered them, as the legitimate successors of St. Peter.

Who is unaware of the many and evident testimonies of the holy Fathers which exist to this effect? Most remarkable is that of St. Irenæus, who, referring to the Roman Church, says: "With this Church, on account of its pre-eminent authority, it is necessary that every Church should be in concord;"[1] and St. Cyprian also says of the Roman Church, that "it is the root and mother of the Catholic Church, the chair of Peter, and the principal Church whence sacerdotal unity has its source."[2] He calls it *the chair of Peter* because it is occupied by the successor of Peter; he calls it the *principal Church,* on account of the primacy conferred on Peter himself and his legitimate successors; and *the source of unity,* because the Roman Church is the efficient cause of unity in the Christian commonwealth. For this reason Jerome addresses Damasus thus: "My words are spoken to the successor of the Fisherman, to the disciple of the cross. . . . I communicate with none save your Blessedness, that is with the chair of Peter. For this I know is the rock on which the Church is built."[3] Union with the Roman See of Peter is to him always the public criterion of a Catholic. "I acknowledge every one who is united with the See of Peter."[4] And for a like reason St. Augustine publicly attests that "the primacy of the Apostolic chair always existed in the Roman Church;"[5] and he denies that any one who dissents from the Roman faith can be a Catholic. "You are not to be looked upon as holding the true Catholic faith if you do not teach that the faith of Rome is to be held."[6] So, too, St. Cyprian:

[1] Contra Haereses, lib. iii., cap. 3, n. 2.
[2] Ep. xlviii, ad Cornelium, n. 3. and Ep. lix., ad eundem, n. 14.
[3] Ep. xv., ad Damasum, n. 2.
[4] Ep. xvi., ad Damasum, n. 2.
[5] Ep. xliii. n. 7.
[6] Sermo cxx. n. 13.

"To be in communion with Cornelius is to be in communion with the Catholic Church."[1] In the same way Maximus the Abbot teaches that obedience to the Roman Pontiff is the proof of the true faith and of legitimate communion. "Therefore if a man does not want to be, or to be called, a heretic, let him not strive to please this or that man . . . but let him hasten before all things to be in communion with the Roman See. If he be in communion with it, he should be acknowledged by all and everywhere as faithful and orthodox. He speaks in vain who tries to persuade me of the orthodoxy of those who, like himself, refuse obedience to his Holiness the Pope of the most holy Church of Rome; that is to the Apostolic See." The reason and motive of this he explains to be that "the Apostolic See has received and hath government, authority, and power of binding and loosing from the Incarnate Word Himself; and, according to all holy synods, sacred canons and decrees, in all things and through all things, in respect of all the holy churches of God throughout the whole world, since the Word in heaven who rules the heavenly powers binds and loosens there."[2]

Wherefore what was acknowledged and observed as Christian faith, not by one nation only nor in one age, but by the East and by the West, and through all ages, this Philip, the priest, the Pontifical legate at the Council of Ephesus, no voice being raised in dissent, recalls: "No one can doubt, yea, it is known unto all ages, that St. Peter, the Prince of the Apostles, the pillar of the faith and the ground of the Catholic Church, received the keys of the kingdom from Our Lord Jesus Christ. That is: the power of forgiving and retaining sins was given to him who, up to the present time, lives and exercises judgment in the persons of his successors."[3] The pronouncement

[1] Ep. lv., n. 1.
[2] Defloratio ex Epistola ad Petrum illustrem.
[3] Actio iii.

of the Council of Chalcedon on the same matter is present to the minds of all: "Peter has spoken through Leo," [1] to which the voice of the Third Council of Constantinople responds as an echo: "The chief Prince of the Apostles was fighting on our side: for we have had as our ally his follower and the successor to his see: and the paper and the ink were seen, and Peter spoke through Agatho." [2]

In the formula of Catholic faith drawn up and proposed by Hormisdas, which was subscribed at the beginning of the sixth century in the great Eighth Council by the Emperor Justinian, by Epiphanius, John and Menna, the Patriarchs, this same is declared with great weight and solemnity. "For the pronouncement of Our Lord Jesus Christ saying: *'Thou art Peter, and upon this rock I will build My Church,'* etc., cannot be passed over. What is said is proved by the result, because Catholic faith has always been preserved without stain in the Apostolic See." [3] We have no wish to quote every available declaration; but it is well to recall the formula of faith which Michael Paleologus professed in the Second Council of Lyons: "The same holy Roman Church possesses the sovereign and plenary primacy and authority over the whole Catholic Church, which, truly and humbly, it acknowledges to have received together with the plenitude of power from the Lord Himself, in the person of St. Peter, the Prince or Head of the Apostles, of whom the Roman Pontiff is the successor. And as it is bound to defend the truth of faith beyond all others, so also if any question should arise concerning the faith it must be determined by its judgment." [4]

But if the authority of Peter and his successors is plenary and supreme, it is not to be regarded as the sole authority. For He who made Peter the foundation of the Church also *chose twelve, whom He called apostles;* [5] and

[1] Actio ii.
[2] Actio xviii.
[3] Post Epistolam, xxvi., ad omnes Episc. Hispan., n. 4.
[4] Actio iv.
[5] Luke vi. 13.

just as it is necessary that the authority of Peter should be perpetuated in the Roman Pontiff, so, by the fact that the bishops succeed the apostles, they inherit their ordinary power, and thus the episcopal order necessarily belongs to the essential constitution of the Church. Although they do not receive plenary, or universal or supreme authority, they are not to be looked upon as *vicars* of the Roman Pontiffs; because they exercise a power really their own, and are most truly called the *ordinary* pastors of the peoples over whom they rule.

But since the successor of Peter is one, and those of the apostles are many, it is necessary to examine into the relations which exist between him and them according to the divine constitution of the Church. Above all things the need of union between the bishops and the successors of Peter is clear and undeniable. This bond once broken, Christians would be separated and scattered, and would in no wise form one body and one flock. "The safety of the Church depends on the dignity of the chief priest, to whom if an extraordinary and supreme power is not given, there are as many schisms to be expected in the Church as there are priests."[1] It is necessary, therefore, to bear this in mind, viz., that nothing was conferred on the apostles apart from Peter, but that several things were conferred upon Peter apart from the apostles. St. John Chrysostom in explaining the words of Christ asks: "Why, passing over the others, does He speak to Peter about these things?" And he replies unhesitatingly and at once, "Because he was pre-eminent among the apostles, the mouthpiece of the disciples, and the head of the college."[2] He alone was designated as the foundation of the Church. To him He gave the power of *binding* and *loosing;* to him alone was given the power of *feeding.* On the other hand, whatever authority and office the apostles received, they received in conjunction with

[1] S. Hieronymus, Dialog. contra Luciferianos, n. 9.
[2] Hom. lxxxviii. in Joan., n. 1.

Peter. "If the divine benignity willed anything to be in common between him and the other princes, whatever He did not deny to the others He gave only through him. So that whereas Peter alone received many things, He conferred nothing on any of the rest without Peter participating in it." [1]

From this it must be clearly understood that bishops are deprived of the right and power of ruling, if they deliberately secede from Peter and his successors; because, by this secession, they are separated from the foundation on which the whole edifice must rest. They are therefore outside the *edifice* itself; and for this very reason they are separated from the *fold*, whose leader is the Chief Pastor; they are exiled from the *Kingdom*, the keys of which were given by Christ to Peter alone.

These things enable us to see the heavenly ideal, and the divine exemplar of the constitution of the Christian commonwealth, namely: When the divine Founder decreed that the Church should be one in faith, in government, and in communion, He chose Peter and his successors as the principal and centre, as it were, of this unity. Wherefore St. Cyprian says: "The following is a short and easy proof of the faith. The Lord saith to Peter: 'I say to thee thou art Peter'; on him alone He buildeth His Church; and although after His Resurrection He gives a similar power to all the apostles and says: 'As the Father hath sent me,' etc., still in order to make the need of unity clear, by His own authority He laid down the source of that unity as beginning from one." [2] And Optatus of Milevis says: "You cannot deny that you know that in the city of Rome the Episcopal chair was first conferred on Peter. In this Peter, the head of all the apostles (hence his name Cephas), has sat; in which chair alone unity was to be preserved for all, lest any of the other apostles should claim anything as exclusively his own. So much so, that he who would place another

[1] S. Leo M. sermo iv., cap. 2.   [2] De Unit. Eccl., n. 4.

chair against that one chair, would be a schismatic and a sinner." [1] Hence the teaching of Cyprian, that heresy and schism arise and are begotten from the fact that due obedience is refused to the supreme authority. "Heresies and schisms have no other origin than that obedience is refused to the priest of God, and that men lose sight of the fact that there is one judge in the place of Christ in this world." [2] No one, therefore, unless in communion with Peter can share in his authority, since it is absurd to imagine that he who is outside can command in the Church. Wherefore Optatus of Milevis blamed the Donatists for this reason: "Against which gates (of hell) we read that Peter received the saving keys, that is to say, our prince, to whom it was said by Christ: 'To thee will I give the keys of the kingdom of heaven, and the gates of hell shall not conquer them.' Whence is it therefore that you strive to obtain for yourselves the keys of the kingdom of heaven—you who fight against the chair of Peter?" [3]

But the Episcopal order is rightly judged to be in communion with Peter, as Christ commanded, if it be subject to and obeys Peter; otherwise it necessarily becomes a lawless and disorderly crowd. It is not sufficient for the due preservation of the unity of the faith that the head should merely have been charged with the office of superintendent, or should have been invested solely with a power of direction. But it is absolutely necessary that he should have received real and sovereign authority which the whole community is bound to obey. What had the Son of God in view when He promised the keys of the kingdom of heaven to Peter *alone?* *Biblical usage* and the unanimous teaching of the Fathers clearly show that supreme authority is designated in the passage by the word *keys*. Nor is it lawful to interpret in a different sense what was given to Peter alone, and what was given to the other apostles conjointly with him. If the power of binding,

---

[1] De Schism. Donat., lib. ii.   [2] Epist. xii. ad Cornelium, n. 5.
[3] Lib. ii., n. 4, 5.

loosening, and feeding confers upon each and every one of the bishops, the successors of the apostles, a real authority to rule the people committed to him, certainly the same power must have the same effect in his case to whom the duty of feeding the lambs and sheep has been assigned by God. "Christ constituted [Peter] not only pastor, but pastor of pastors; Peter therefore feeds the lambs and feeds the sheep, feeds the children and feeds the mothers, governs the subjects and rules the prelates, because the lambs and the sheep form the whole of the Church." [1] Hence those remarkable expressions of the ancients concerning St. Peter, which most clearly set forth the fact that he was placed in the highest degree of dignity and authority. They frequently call him "the prince of the college of the disciples; the prince of the holy apostles; the leader of that choir; the mouthpiece of all the apostles; the head of that family; the ruler of the whole world; the first of the apostles; the safeguard of the Church." In this sense St. Bernard writes as follows to Pope Eugenius: "Who art thou? The great priest—the high priest. Thou art the Prince of Bishops and the heir of the apostles. . . . Thou art he to whom the keys were given. There are, it is true, other gatekeepers of heaven and other pastors of flocks, but thou art so much the more glorious as thou hast inherited a different and more glorious name than all the rest. They have flocks consigned to them, one to each; to thee all the flocks are confided as one flock to one shepherd, and not alone the sheep, but the shepherds. You ask how I prove this? From the words of the Lord. To which—I do not say— of the bishops, but even of the apostles have all the sheep been so absolutely and unreservedly committed? If thou lovest Me, Peter, feed My sheep. Which sheep? Of this or that people, of this city, or country, or kingdom? *My* sheep, He says: to whom therefore is it not evident

[1] S. Brunonis Episcopi Signiensis comment. in Joan., part iii., cap. 21, n. 55.

that He does not designate some, but all? We can make no exception where no distinction is made." [1]

But it is opposed to the truth, and in evident contradiction with the divine constitution of the Church, to hold that while each bishop is *individually* bound to obey the authority of the Roman Pontiffs, taken *collectively* the bishops are not so bound. For it is the nature and object of a foundation to support the unity of the whole edifice and to give stability to it, rather than to *each component part;* and in the present case this is much more applicable, since Christ the Lord wished that by the strength and solidity of the foundation the gates of hell should be prevented from prevailing against the Church. All are agreed that the divine promise must be understood of the Church as a whole, and not of any certain portions of it. These can indeed be overcome by the assaults of the powers of hell, as in point of fact has befallen some of them. Moreover, he who is set over the whole flock must have authority not only over the sheep dispersed throughout the Church, but also when they are assembled together. Do the sheep when they are all assembled together rule and guide the shepherd? Do the successors of the apostles assembled together constitute the foundation on which the successor of St. Peter rests in order to derive therefrom strength and stability? Surely jurisdiction and authority belong to him in whose power have been placed the keys of the kingdom of heaven, not alone in all provinces taken singly, but in all taken collectively. And as the bishops, each in his own district, command with real power not only individuals but the whole community, so the Roman Pontiffs, whose jurisdiction extends to the whole Christian commonwealth, must have all its parts even taken collectively, subject and obedient to their authority. Christ the Lord, as we have quite sufficiently shown, made Peter and his successors His *vicars,* to exercise forever in the Church the power which He

[1] De Consideratione, lib. ii., cap. 8.

exercised during His mortal life. Can the Apostolic College be said to have been above its master in authority?

This power over the Episcopal College to which we refer, and which is clearly set forth in holy writ, has ever been acknowledged and attested by the Church, as is clear from the teaching of General Councils. "We read that the Roman Pontiff has pronounced judgments on the prelates of all the churches; we do not read that anybody has pronounced sentence on him." [1] The reason for which is stated thus: "there is no authority greater than that of the Apostolic See." [2] Wherefore Gelasius on the decrees of Councils says: "That which the First See has not approved of cannot stand; but what it has thought well to decree has been received by the whole Church." [3] It has ever been unquestionably the office of the Roman Pontiffs to ratify or to reject the decrees of Councils. Leo the Great rescinded the acts of the Conciliabulum of Ephesus. Damasus rejected those of Rimini, and Hadrian I. those of Constantinople. The twenty-eighth canon of the Council of Chalcedon, by the very fact that it lacks the assent and approval of the Apostolic See, is admitted by all to be worthless. Rightly, therefore, has Leo X. laid down in the fifth Council of Lateran "that the Roman Pontiff alone, as having authority over all Councils has full jurisdiction and power to summon, to transfer, to dissolve Councils, as is clear, not only from the testimony of holy writ, from the teaching of the Fathers and of the Roman Pontiffs, and from the decrees of the sacred canons, but from the teaching of the very Councils themselves." Indeed, holy writ attests that the keys of the kingdom of heaven were given to Peter alone, and that

[1] Hadrianus ii., in Allocutione iii., ad Synodum Romanum an. 869. Cf. Actionem vii., Conc. Constantinopolitani iv.

[2] Nicolaus in Epist. lxxxvi. ad Michael. Imperat. "It is evident that the judgment of the Apostolic See, than which there is no authority greater, may be rejected by no one, nor is it lawful for any one to pass judgment on its judgment."

[3] Epist. xxvi., ad Episcopos Dardaniæ, n. 5.

the power of binding and loosening was granted to the apostles and to Peter; but there is nothing to show that the apostles received supreme power *without Peter,* and *against Peter.* Such power they certainly did not receive from Jesus Christ. Wherefore, in the decree of the Vatican Council as to the nature and authority of the primacy of the Roman Pontiff, no newly conceived opinion is set forth, but the venerable and constant belief of every age.[1]

Nor does it beget any confusion in the administration that Christians are bound to obey a twofold authority. We are prohibited in the first place by divine wisdom from entertaining any such thought, since this form of government was constituted by the counsel of God Himself. In the second place we must note that the due order of things and their mutual relations are disturbed if there be a twofold magistracy of the same rank set over a people, neither of which is amenable to the other. But the authority of the Roman Pontiff is supreme, universal, independent; that of the bishops limited, and dependent. "It is not congruous that two superiors with equal authority should be placed over the same flock; but that two one of whom is higher than the other, should be placed over the same people is not incongruous. Thus the parish priest, the bishop, and the Pope, are placed immediately over the same people."[2] So the Roman Pontiffs, mindful of their duty, wish above all things, that the divine constitution of the Church should be preserved. Therefore, as they defend with all necessary care and vigilance their own authority, so they have always labored, and will continue to labor, that the authority of the bishops may be upheld. Yea, they look upon whatever honor or obedience is given to the bishops as paid to themselves. "My honor is the honor of the universal Church. My honor is the strength and stability

[1] Sess. iv., cap. 3.
[2] St. Thomas in iv. Sent. dist. xvii. a. 4, ad q. 4, ad 3.

of my brethren. Then am I honored when due honor is given to every one." [1]

In what has been said We have faithfully described the exemplar and form of the Church as divinely constituted. We have treated at length of its unity: We have explained sufficiently its nature, and pointed out the way in which the divine Founder of the Church willed that it should be preserved. There is no reason to doubt that all those, who by divine grace and mercy have had the happiness to have been born, as it were, in the bosom of the Catholic Church, and to have lived in it, will listen to Our apostolic voice: *My sheep hear My voice,*[2] and that they will derive from Our words fuller instruction and a more perfect disposition to keep united with their respective pastors, and through them with the Supreme Pastor, so that they may remain more securely within the one fold, and may derive therefrom a greater abundance of salutary fruit. But We, who, notwithstanding Our unfitness for this great dignity and office, govern by virtue of the authority conferred on Us by Jesus Christ, as We *look on Jesus, the author and finisher of our faith,*[3] feel Our heart fired by His charity. What Christ has said of Himself We may truly repeat of Ourselves: *Other sheep I have that are not of this fold: them also I must bring and they shall hear My voice.*[4] Let all those, therefore, who detest the widespread irreligion of our times, and acknowledge and confess Jesus Christ to be the Son of God and the Saviour of the human race, but who have wandered away from the Spouse, listen to Our voice. Let them not refuse to obey Our paternal charity. Those who acknowledge Christ must acknowledge Him wholly and entirely. "The Head and the body are Christ wholly and entirely. The Head is the only-begotten Son of God, the body is His Church; the bridegroom and the

---

[1] S. Gregorius M. Epistolarum, lib viii., ep. xxx., ad Eulogium.
[2] John x. 27.
[3] Heb. xii. 2.
[4] John x. 16.

bride, two in one flesh. All who dissent from the Scriptures concerning Christ, although they may be found in all places in which the Church is found, are not in the Church; and again all those who agree with the Scriptures concerning the Head, and do not communicate in the unity of the Church, are not in the Church." [1]

And with the same yearning Our soul goes out to those whom the foul breath of irreligion has not entirely corrupted, and who at least seek to have the true God, the Creator of heaven and earth, as their Father. Let such as these take counsel with themselves, and realize that they can in no wise be counted among the children of God, unless they take Christ Jesus as their Brother, and at the same time the Church as their Mother. We lovingly address to all the words of St. Augustine: "Let us love the Lord our God; let us love His Church; the Lord as our Father, the Church as our Mother. Let no one say, I go indeed to idols, I consult fortune-tellers and soothsayers; but I leave not the Church of God: I am a Catholic. Clinging to thy Mother, thou offendest thy Father. Another, too, says: 'Far be it from me; I do not consult fortune-telling, I seek not soothsaying, I seek not profane divinations, I go not to the worship of devils, I serve not stones: but I am on the side of Donatus.' What doth it profit thee not to offend the Father, who avenges an offence against the Mother? What doth it profit to confess the Lord, to honor God, to preach Him, to acknowledge His Son, and to confess that He sits on the right hand of the Father, if you blaspheme His Church? . . . If you had a beneficent friend, whom you honored daily—and even once calumniated his spouse, would you ever enter his house? Hold fast, therefore, O dearly beloved, hold fast altogether God as your Father, and the Church as your Mother." [2]

[1] S. Augustinus, Contra Donatistas Epistola, sive De Unit. Eccl., cap. iv., n. 7.

[2] Enarratio in Psal. lxxxviii., sermo ii., n. 14.

Above all things, trusting in the mercy of God, who is able to move the hearts of men and to incline them as and when He pleases, We most earnestly commend to His loving kindness all those ot whom We have spoken. As a pledge of divine grace. and as a token of Our affection, We lovingly impart to you, in the Lord, Venerable Brethren, to your clergy and people, Our Apostolic Blessing.

ANGLICAN ORDERS.

Apostolic Letter Apostolicæ Curæ, September 13, 1896.

WE have dedicated to the welfare of the noble English nation no small portion of the apostolic care and charity by which, helped by His grace, We endeavor to fulfil the office and follow in the footsteps of *"the Great Shepherd of the sheep,"* [1] Our Lord Jesus Christ. The Letter which last year We sent to *"the English seeking the kingdom of Christ in the unity of the faith"* is a special witness of Our good-will towards England. In it We recalled the memory of the ancient union of her people with Mother Church, and We strove to hasten the day of a happy reconciliation by stirring up men's hearts to offer diligent prayer to God. And, again, more recently, when it seemed good to Us to treat more fully the unity of the Church in a general Letter, England had not the last place in Our mind, in the hope that Our teaching might both strengthen Catholics and bring the saving light to those divided from Us.

It is pleasing to acknowledge the generous way in which Our zeal and plainness of speech, inspired by no mere human motives, have met the approval of the English people; and this testifies not less to their courtesy than to the solicitude of many for their eternal salvation.

With the same mind and intention We have now determined to turn Our consideration to a matter of no less importance, which is closely connected with the same subject and with Our desires. For an opinion already

[1] Heb. xiii. 20.

prevalent, confirmed more than once by the action and constant practice of the Church, maintained that when in England, shortly after it was rent from the centre of Christian unity, a new rite for conferring Holy Orders was publicly introduced under Edward VI., the true Sacrament of Orders, as instituted by Christ, lapsed, and with it the hierarchical succession. For some time, however, and in these last years especially, a controversy has sprung up as to whether the Sacred Orders conferred according to the Edwardine Ordinal possessed the nature and effect of a sacrament: those in favor of the absolute validity, or of a doubtful validity, being not only certain Anglican writers, but some few Catholics, chiefly non-English. The consideration of the excellency of the Christian priesthood moved Anglican writers in this matter, desirous as they were that their own people should not lack the twofold power over the body of Christ. Catholic writers were impelled by a wish to smooth the way for the return of Anglicans to holy unity. Both, indeed, thought that in view of studies brought up to the level of ecent research, and of new documents rescued from oblivion, it was not inopportune to re-examine the question by Our authority. And We, not disregarding such desires and opinions, and, above all, obeying the dictates of apostolic charity, have considered that nothing should be left untried that might in any way tend to preserve souls from injury or procure their advantage.

It has, therefore, pleased Us to graciously permit the cause to be re-examined so that through the extreme care taken in the new examination all doubt, or even shadow of doubt, should be removed for the future. To this end We commissioned a certain number of men noted for their learning and ability, whose opinions in this matter were known to be divergent, to state the grounds of their judgments in writing. We then, having summoned them to Our person, directed them to interchange writings and further to investigate and discuss all that was necessary for a full knowledge of the matter. We were careful also that they should be able to re-examine all documents bearing on this question which were known to exist in the Vatican archives, to search for new ones, and even to have at their disposal all acts relating to this subject which are preserved by the Holy Office—or as it is called the *Supreme Council*—and to consider whatever had up to this time been adduced by learned men on both sides. We ordered them, when prepared in this way, to meet together in special sessions. These to the number of twelve were held under the presidency of one of the Cardinals of the Holy Roman Church, appointed by Ourselves, and all were invited to free discussion. Finally We directed that the acts of these meetings, together with all other documents, should be submitted to Our venerable brethren, the Cardinals of the same Council, so that when all had studied the whole subject, and discussed it in Our presence, each might give his opinion.

This order for discussing the matter having been determined upon, it was necessary, with a view to forming a true estimate of the real state of the question, to enter upon it, after careful inquiry as to how the matter stood in relation to the prescription and settled custom of the Apostolic See, the origin and force of which custom it was undoubtedly of great importance to determine. For this reason, in the first place, the principal documents in which Our predecessors, at the request of Queen Mary, exercised their special care for the reconciliation of the English Church, were considered. Thus Julius III. sent Cardinal Reginald Pole, an Englishman, and illustrious in many ways, to be his Legate *a latere* for the purpose, *" as his angel of peace and love,"* and gave him extraordinary and unusual mandates or faculties and direction for his guidance. These Paul IV. confirmed and explained. And here, to interpret rightly the force of these documents, it is necessary to lay it down as a fundamental principle that they were certainly not intended to deal with an abstract state of things, but with a specific and concrete issue. For since the faculties given by these Pontiffs to the Apostolic Legate had reference to England only, and to the state of religion therein, and since the rules of action were laid down by them at the request of the said Legate, they could not have been mere directions for determining the necessary conditions for the validity of ordinations in general. They must pertain directly to providing for Holy Orders in the said kingdom, as the recognized condition of the circumstances and times demanded. This, besides being clear from the nature and form of the said documents, is also obvious from the fact that it would have been altogether irrelevant to thus instruct the Legate—one whose learning had been conspicuous in the Council of Trent—as to the conditions necessary for the bestowal of the Sacrament of Orders.

To all rightly estimating these matters it will not be difficult to understand why, in the Letters of Julius III., issued to the Apostolic Legate on March 8, 1554, there is a distinct mention, first, of those who, "*rightly and lawfully promoted,*" might be maintained in their Orders; and then of others who, "*not promoted to Sacred Orders,*" might "*be promoted if they were found to be worthy and fitting subjects.*" For it is clearly and definitely noted, as indeed was the case, that there were two classes of men: the first those who had really received Sacred Orders, either before the secession of Henry VIII., or, if after it and by ministers infected by error and schism, still according to the accustomed Catholic rite; the second, those who were initiated according to the Edwardine Ordinal, who on that account could be "*promoted,*" since they had received an ordination which was null. And that the mind of the Pope was this and nothing else is clearly confirmed by the Letter of the said Legate (January 29, 1555) subdelegating his faculties to the Bishop of Norwich. Moreover, what the Letters of Julius III. themselves say about freely using the Pontifical faculties, even in behalf of those who had received their consecration *"minus rite and not according to the accustomed form of the Church,"* is to be especially noted. By this expression those only could be meant who had been consecrated according to the Edwardine rite, since besides it and the Catholic form there was then no other in England.

This becomes even still clearer when we consider the legation which, on the advice of Cardinal Pole, the Sovereign Princes, Philip and Mary, sent to the Pope in Rome in the month of February, 1555. The royal ambassadors —three men, *"most illustrious and endowed with every virtue,"* of whom one was Thomas Thirlby, Bishop of Ely—were charged to inform the Pope more fully as to the religious condition of the country, and especially to beg that he would ratify and confirm what the Legate had been at pains to effect, and had succeeded in effecting, towards the reconciliation of the kingdom with the Church. For this purpose all the necessary written evidence and the pertinent parts of the new Ordinal were submitted to the Pope. The Legation having been splendidly received, and their evidence having been *"diligently discussed"* by several of the Cardinals, *"after mature deliberation,"* Paul IV. issued his Bull *Præclara carissimi* on June 20 of the same year. In this, whilst giving full force and approbation to what Pole had done, it is ordered in the matter of the Ordinations as follows: *"Those who have been promoted to Ecclesiastical Orders . . . by any one but by a bishop validly and lawfully ordained are bound to receive those Orders again."* But who those bishops not *"validly and lawfully ordained"* were had been made sufficiently clear by the foregoing documents and the faculties used in the said matter by the Legate: those, namely, who have been promoted to the Episcopate, as others to other Orders *"not according to the accustomed form of the Church,"* or, as the Legate himself wrote to the Bishop of Norwich, *"the form and intention of the Church"* not having been observed. These were certainly those promoted according to the new form of rite, to the examination of which the Cardinals specially deputed had given their careful attention. Neither should the passage much to the point in the same Pontifical Letter be overlooked, where, together with others needing dispensation, are enumerated those "*who had obtained as well orders as benefices nulliter et de facto.*" For to obtain orders *nulliter* means the same as by an act null and void, that is *invalid*, as the very meaning of the word and as common parlance require. This is especially clear when the word is used in the same way about orders as about "*ecclesiastical benefices.*" These, by the undoubted teaching of the sacred canons, were clearly null if given with any vitiating defect. Moreover, when some doubted as to who, according to the mind of the Pontiff, could be called and considered bishops "*validly and lawfully ordained,*" the said Pope shortly after, on October 30, issued further letters in the form of a brief, and said: "*We, wishing to remove the doubt, and to opportunely provide for the peace of conscience of those who during the schism were promoted to Orders, by expressing more clearly the mind and intention which We had in the aforesaid Letters, declare that only those bishops and archbishops who were not ordained and consecrated in the form of the Church cannot be said to have been validly and lawfully ordained.*" Unless this declaration had applied to the actual case in England, that is to say to the Edwardine Ordinal, the Pope would certainly have done nothing by these last Letters for the removal of doubt and the restoration of peace of conscience. Further, it was in this sense that the Legate understood the documents and commands of the Apostolic See, and duly and conscientiously obeyed them; and the same was done by Queen Mary and the rest who helped to restore Catholicism to its former state.

The authority of Julius III. and of Paul IV., which we have quoted, clearly shows the origin of that practice which has been observed without interruption for more than three centuries, that Ordinations conferred according to the Edwardine rite should be considered null and void. This practice is fully proved by the numerous cases of absolute reordination according to the Catholic rite even in Rome. In the observance of this practice we have a proof directly affecting the matter in hand. For if by any chance doubt should remain as to the true sense in which these Pontifical documents are to be understood, the principle holds good that *"Custom is the best interpreter of law."* Since in the Church it has ever been a constant and established rule that it is sacrilegious to repeat the Sacrament of Order, it never could have come to pass that the Apostolic See should have silently acquiesced and tolerated such a custom. But not only did the Apostolic See tolerate this practice, but approved and sanctioned it as often as any particular case arose which called for its judgment in the matter. We adduce two facts of this kind out of many which have from time to time been submitted to the Supreme Council of the Holy Office. The first was (in 1684) of a certain French Calvinist, and the other (in 1704), of John Clement Gordon, both of whom had received their Orders according to the Edwardine ritual. In the first case, after a searching investigation, the consultors, not a few in number, gave in writing their answers—or, as they call it, their *vota*— and the rest unanimously agreed with their conclusion, *for "the invalidity of the Ordination,"* and only on account of reasons of opportuneness did the Cardinals deem it well to answer by a *"dilata"* [viz., not to formulate the conclusion at the moment]. The same documents were called into use and considered again in the examination of the second case, and additional written statements of opinion were also obtained from consultors, and the most eminent doctors of the Sorbonne and of Douai were likewise asked for their opinion. No safeguard which wisdom and prudence could suggest to insure the thorough sifting of the question was neglected.

And here it is important to observe that although
Gordon himself, whose case it was, and some of the consultors had adduced, amongst the reasons which went to
prove the invalidity, the Ordination of Parker, according to their own ideas about it, in the delivery of the
decision this reason was altogether set aside, as documents of incontestable authenticity prove. Nor, in
pronouncing the decision, was weight given to any other
reason than the *"defect of form and intention";* and in
order that the judgment concerning this form might be
more certain and complete, precaution was taken that a
copy of the Anglican Ordinal should be submitted to
examination, and that with it should be collated the
Ordination forms gathered together from the various
Eastern and Western rites. Then Clement XI. himself,
with the unanimous vote of the Cardinals concerned
on the *"Feria V.,"* [1] April 17, 1704, *decreed:* "John Clement
Gordon shall be ordained from *the beginning and uncon-
ditionally* to all the Orders, even Sacred Orders, and
chiefly of priesthood, and in case he has not been confirmed he shall first receive the Sacrament of Confirmation." It is important to bear in mind that this judgment was in no wise determined by the omission of the
tradition of instruments, or in such a case, according to
the established custom, the direction would have been
to repeat the ordination *conditionally;* and still more
important it is to note that the judgment of the Pontiff
applies universally to all Anglican Ordinations, because,
although it refers to a particular case, it is not based upon
any reason special to that case, but upon the defect of

---

[1] [The term *"Feria V."* here used has a technical value. Ordinary meetings of the Supreme Council for the ratification of decrees usually take place on the Wednesdays, and are marked
"Feria IV." But the special and solemn sessions which, in matters
of graver import, are held in the presence and under the presidency
of the Pope himself, who thus in a special way makes the decisions
his own, take place on Thursdays, and are marked *"Feria V."*—
Translators' Note.]

form, which defect equally affects all these Ordinations; so much so, that when similar cases subsequently came up for decision the same decree of Clement XI. was quoted as the norma.

Hence it must be clear to every one that the controversy lately revived had been already definitely settled by the Apostolic See, and that it is to the insufficient knowledge of these documents that we must, perhaps, attribute the fact that any Catholic writer should have considered it still an open question. But, as We stated at the beginning, there is nothing We so deeply and ardently desire as to be of help to men of good-will by showing them the greatest consideration and charity. Wherefore We ordered that the Anglican Ordinal, which is the essential point of the whole matter, should be once more most carefully examined.

In the examination of any rite for the effecting and administering of a sacrament, distinction is rightly made between the part which is *ceremonial* and that which is *essential*, usually called the *matter and form*. All know that the sacraments of the New Law, as sensible and efficient signs of invisible grace, ought both to signify the grace which they effect, and effect the grace which they signify. Although the signification ought to be found in the whole essential rite—that is to say, in the matter and form—it still pertains chiefly to the form; since the matter is the part which is not determined by itself, but which is determined by the form. And this appears still more clearly in the Sacrament of Orders, the matter of which, in so far as We have to consider it in this case, is the imposition of hands, which indeed by itself signifies nothing definite, and is equally used for several Orders and for Confirmation. But the words which until recently were commonly held by Anglicans to constitute the proper form of priestly Ordination—namely, "*Receive the Holy Ghost,*" certainly do not in the least definitely express the Sacred Order of Priesthood, or its grace and power, which is chiefly the power "*of consecrating and of offering the true body and blood of the Lord*" [1] in that sacrifice which is no "*nude commemoration of the sacrifice offered on the Cross.*" [2] This form had indeed afterwards added to it the words "*for the office and work of a priest,*" etc.;—but this rather shows that the Anglicans themselves perceived that the first form was defective and inadequate. But even if this addition could give to the form its due signification, it was introduced too late, as a century had already elapsed since the adoption of the Edwardine Ordinal, for, as the hierarchy had become extinct, there remained no power of ordaining. In vain has help been recently sought for the plea of the validity of Orders from the other prayers of the same Ordinal. For, to put aside other reasons which show this to be insufficient for the purpose in the Anglican rite, let this argument suffice for all: from them has been deliberately removed whatever sets forth the dignity and office of the priesthood in the Catholic rite. That form consequently cannot be considered apt or sufficient for the sacrament which omits what it ought essentially to signify.

The same holds good of Episcopal consecration. For to the formula "*Receive the Holy Ghost*" not only were the words "*for the office and work of a bishop,*" etc., added at a later period, but even these, as we shall presently state, must be understood in a sense different to that which they bear in the Catholic rite. Nor is anything gained by quoting the prayer of the preface "*Almighty God,*" since it in like manner has been stripped of the words which denote the *summum sacerdotium*. It is not here relevant to examine whether the Episcopate be a completion of the priesthood or an Order distinct from it, or whether when bestowed, as they say *per saltum*, on one who is not a priest, it has or has not its effect. But the Episcopate undoubtedly by the institution of

---

[1] Council of Trent, Sess. XXIII., de Sacr. Ord., Can. 1.

[2] Ibid., Sess. XXII., de sacrif. Missae, Can. 3.

Christ most truly belongs to the Sacrament of Orders and constitutes the sacerdotium in the highest degree, namely, that which by the teaching of the holy Fathers and our liturgical customs is called the "*summum sacerdotium, sacri ministerii summa.*" So it comes to pass that, as the Sacrament of Orders and the true sacerdotium of Christ were utterly eliminated from the Anglican rite, and hence the sacerdotium is in no wise conferred truly and validly in the Episcopal consecration of the same rite, for the like reason, therefore, the Episcopate can in no wise be truly and validly conferred by it; and this the more so because among the first duties of the Episcopate is that of ordaining ministers for the Holy Eucharist and sacrifice.

For the full and accurate understanding of the Anglican Ordinal, besides what we have noted as to some of its parts, there is nothing more pertinent than to consider carefully the circumstances under which it was composed and publicly authorized. It would be tedious to enter into details, nor is it necessary to do so, as the history of that time is sufficiently eloquent as to the animus of the authors of the Ordinal against the Catholic Church, as to the abettors whom they associated with themselves from the heterodox sects, and as to the end they had in view. Being fully cognizant of the necessary connection between faith and worship, between "*the law of believing and the law of praying,*" under a pretext of returning to the primitive form, they corrupted the liturgical order in many ways to suit the errors of the reformers. For this reason in the whole Ordinal not only is there no clear mention of the sacrifice, of consecration, of the sacerdotium, and of the power of consecrating and offering sacrifice, but, as we have just stated, every trace of these things, which had been in such prayers of the Catholic rite as they had not entirely rejected, was deliberately removed and struck out. In this way the native character—or spirit as it is called—of the Ordinal clearly manifests itself. Hence, if vitiated in its origin it was wholly insufficient to confer Orders, it was impossible that in the course of time it could become sufficient since no change had taken place. In vain those who, from the time of Charles I., have attempted to hold some kind of sacrifice or of priesthood, have made some additions to the Ordinal. In vain also has been the contention of that small section of the Anglican body formed in recent times that the said Ordinal can be understood and interpreted in a sound and orthodox sense. Such efforts, We affirm, have been and are made in vain, and for this reason, that any words in the Anglican Ordinal, as it now is, which lend themselves to ambiguity, cannot be taken in the same sense as they possess in the Catholic rite. For once a new rite has been initiated in which, as we have seen, the Sacrament of Orders is adulterated or denied, and from which all idea of consecration and sacrifice has been rejected, the formula *"Receive the Holy Ghost,"* no longer holds good; because the Spirit is infused into the soul with the grace of the sacrament, and the words *"for the office and work of a priest or bishop"* and the like no longer hold good, but remain as words without the reality which Christ instituted.

Several of the more shrewd Anglican interpreters of the Ordinal have perceived the force of this argument, and they openly urge it against those who take the Ordinal in a new sense and vainly attach to the Orders conferred thereby a value and efficacy which they do not possess. By this same argument is refuted the contention of those who think that the prayer *"Almighty God, giver of all good things,"* which is found at the beginning of the ritual action, might suffice as a legitimate form of Orders, even in the hypothesis that it might be held to be sufficient in a Catholic rite approved by the Church.

With this inherent *defect of form* is joined the *defect of intention,* which is equally essential to the sacrament. The Church does not judge about the mind and intention in so far as it is something by its nature internal; but in so far as it is manifested externally she is bound to judge concerning it. When any one has rightly and seriously made use of the due form and the matter requisite for effecting or conferring the sacrament he is considered by the very fact to do what the Church does. On this principle rests the doctrine that a sacrament is truly conferred by the ministry of one who is a heretic or unbaptized, provided the Catholic rite be employed. On the other hand, if the rite be changed, with the manifest intention of introducing another rite not approved by the Church and of rejecting what the Church does, and what by the institution of Christ belongs to the nature of the sacrament, then it is clear that not only is the necessary intention wanting to the sacrament, but that the intention is adverse to and destructive of the sacrament.

All these matters have been long and carefully considered by Ourselves and by Our Venerable Brethren, the Judges of the Supreme Council, of whom it has pleased Us to call a special meeting on the "*Feria V.*," the 16th day of July last, upon the solemnity of Our Lady of Mount Carmel. They with one accord agreed that the question laid before them had been already adjudicated upon with full knowledge of the Apostolic See, and that this renewed discussion and examination of the issues had only served to bring out more clearly the wisdom and accuracy with which that decision had been made. Nevertheless We deemed it well to postpone a decision in order to afford time, both to consider whether it would be fitting or expedient that We should make a fresh authoritative declaration upon the matter, and to humbly pray for a fuller measure of divine guidance. Then, considering that this matter of practice, although already decided, had been by certain persons, for whatever reason, recalled into discussion, and that thence it might follow that a pernicious error would be fostered in the minds of many who might suppose that they possessed the Sacrament and effects of Orders, where these are nowise to be found, it has seemed good to Us in the Lord to pronounce Our judgment.

Wherefore, strictly adhering in this matter to the decrees of the Pontiffs Our predecessors, and confirming them most fully, and, as it were, renewing them by Our authority, of Our own motion and certain knowledge We pronounce and declare that Ordinations carried out according to the Anglican rite have been and are absolutely null and utterly void.

It remains for Us to say that even as We have entered upon the elucidation of this grave question in the name and in the love of the *Great Shepherd,* in the same We appeal to those who desire and seek with a sincere heart the possession of a hierarchy and of Orders. Perhaps until now aiming at the greater perfection of Christian virtue, and searching more devoutly the divine Scriptures, and redoubling the fevor of their prayers, they have, nevertheless, hesitated in doubt and anxiety to follow the voice of Christ, which so long has interiorly admonished them. Now they see clearly whither He in His goodness invites them and wills them to come. In returning to His one only fold, they will obtain the blessings which they seek, and the consequent helps to salvation of which He has made the Church the dispenser, and, as it were, the constant guardian and promoter of His Redemption amongst the nations. Then indeed *"they shall draw waters in joy from the fountains of the Saviour,"* His wondrous sacraments, whereby His faithful souls have their sins truly remitted, and are restored to the friendship of God, are nourished and strengthened by the heavenly Bread, and abound with the most powerful aids for their eternal salvation. May the God of Peace, the God of all consolation, in His infinite tenderness enrich and fill with all these blessings those who truly yearn for them. We wish to direct Our exhortation and Our desires in a special way to those who are ministers of religion in their respective communities. They are men who from their **very** office take precedence in learning and authority, and who have at heart the glory of God and the salvation of souls. Let them be the first in joyfully submitting to the divine call, and obey it, and furnish a glorious example to others. Assuredly with an exceeding great joy their Mother, the Church, will welcome them and will cherish with all her love and care those whom the strength of their generous souls has amidst many trials and difficulties led back to her bosom. Nor could words express the recognition which this devoted courage will win for them from the assemblies of the brethren throughout the Catholic world, or what hope or confidence it will merit for them before Christ as their Judge, or what reward it will obtain from Him in the heavenly kingdom! And We Ourselves in every lawful way shall continue to promote their reconciliation with the Church in which individuals and masses, as We ardently desire, may find so much for their imitation. In the meantime, by the tender mercy of the Lord our God, We ask and beseech all to strive faithfully to follow in the open path of divine grace and truth.

We decree that these Letters and all things contained therein shall not be liable at any time to be impugned or objected to by reason of fault or any other defect whatsoever of subreption or obreption or of Our intention, but are and shall be always valid and in force, and shall be inviolably observed both juridically and otherwise, by all of whatsoever degree and pre-eminence; declaring null and void anything which in these matters may happen to be contrariwise attempted, whether wittingly or unwittingly, by any person whatsoever by whatsoever authority or pretext, all things to the contrary notwithstanding.

We will that there shall be given to copies of these Letters, even printed, provided that they be signed by a notary and sealed by a person constituted in ecclesiastical dignity, the same credence that would be given to the expression of Our will by the showing of these presents.

THE PROHIBITION AND CENSORSHIP OF BOOKS.

Apostolic Constitution Officiorum ac Munerum,
January 25, 1897.

OF all the official duties which We are bound most carefully and most diligently to fulfil in this supreme position of the apostolate, the chief and principal duty is to watch assiduously and earnestly to strive that the integrity of Christian faith and morals may suffer no diminution. And this, more than at any other time, is especially necessary in these days, when men's minds and characters are so unrestrained that almost every doctrine which Jesus Christ, the Saviour of mankind, has committed to the custody of His Church, for the welfare of the human race, is daily called into question and doubt. In this warfare, many and varied are the stratagems and hurtful devices of the enemy; but most perilous of all is the uncurbed freedom of writing and publishing noxious literature. Nothing can be conceived more pernicious, more apt to defile souls, through its contempt of religion, and its manifold allurements to sin. Wherefore the Church, who is the custodian and vindicator of the integrity of faith and morals, fearful of so great an evil, has from an early date realized that remedies must be applied against this plague; and for this reason she has ever striven, as far as lay in her power, to restrain men from the reading of bad books, as from a deadly poison. The early days of the Church were witnesses to the earnest zeal of St. Paul in this respect; and every subsequent age has witnessed the vigilance of the Fathers, the commands of the bishops, and the decrees of Councils in a similar direction.

Historical documents bear special witness to the care and diligence with which the Roman Pontiffs have vigilantly endeavored to prevent the unchecked spread of heretical writings detrimental to the public. History is full of examples. Anastasius I. solemnly condemned the more dangerous writings of Origen, Innocent I. those of Pelagius, Leo the Great all the works of the Manicheans. The *decretal* letters, opportunely issued by Gelasius, concerning books to be received and rejected, are well known. And so, in the course of centuries, the Holy See condemned the pestilent writings of the Monothelites, of Abelard, Marsilius Patavinus, Wycliff, and Huss.

In the fifteenth century, after the invention of the art of printing, not only were bad publications which had already appeared condemned, but precautions began to be taken against the publication of similar works in the future. These prudent measures were called for by no slight cause, but rather by the need of protecting the public morals and welfare at the time; for too many had rapidly perverted into a mighty engine of destruction an art excellent in itself, productive of immense advantages, and naturally destined for the advancement of Christian culture. Owing to the rapid process of publication, the great evil of bad books had been multiplied and accelerated. Wherefore Our predecessors, Alexander VI. and Leo X., most wisely promulgated certain definite laws, well suited to the character of the times, in order to restrain printers and publishers within the limits of their duty.

The tempest soon became more violent, and it was necessary to check the contagion of heresy with still more vigilance and severity. Hence Leo X., and afterwards Clement VII., severely prohibited the reading or retaining of the books of Luther. But as, owing to the unhappy circumstances of that epoch, the foul flood of pernicious books had increased beyond measure and spread in all directions, there appeared to be need of a more complete and efficacious remedy. This remedy Our predecessor, Paul IV., was the first to employ, by opportunely publishing a list of books and other writings against which the faithful should be warned. A little later the Council of Trent took steps to restrain the ever-growing license of writing and reading by a new measure. At its command and desire, certain chosen prelates and theologians not only applied themselves to increasing and perfecting the Index which Paul IV. had published, but also drew up certain rules to be observed in the publishing, reading, and use of books; to which rules Pius IV. added the sanction of his apostolic authority.

The interests of the public welfare, which had given rise to the Tridentine Rules, necessitated in the course of time certain alterations. For which reason the Roman Pontiffs, especially Clement VIII., Alexander VII., and Benedict XIV., mindful of the circumstances of the period and the dictates of prudence, issued several decrees calculated to elucidate these rules and to accommodate them to the times.

The above facts clearly prove that the chief care of the Roman Pontiffs has always been to protect civil society from erroneous beliefs and corrupt morals, the twin causes of the decline and ruin of States, which commonly owes its origin and its progress to bad books. Their labors were not unfruitful, so long as the divine law regulated the commands and prohibitions of civil government, and the rulers of States acted in unison with the ecclesiastical authority.

Every one is aware of the subsequent course of events. As circumstances and men's minds gradually altered, the Church, with her wonted prudence, observing the character of the period, took those steps which appeared most expedient and best calculated to promote the salvation of men. Several prescriptions of the rules of the Index, which appeared to have lost their original opportuneness, she either abolished by decree, or, with equal gentleness and wisdom, permitted them to grow obsolete. In recent times, Pius IX., in a letter to the archbishops and bishops of the States of the Church, considerably mitigated Rule X. Moreover, on the eve of the Vatican Council, he instructed the learned men of the preparatory commission to examine and revise all the rules of the Index, and to advise how they should be dealt with. They unanimously decided that the rules required alteration; and several of the Fathers of the Council openly professed their agreement with this opinion and desire. A letter of the French bishops exists urging the necessity of immediate action in "republishing the rules and the whole scheme of the Index in an entirely new form, better suited to our times and easier to observe." A similar opinion was expressed at the same time by the bishops of Germany, who definitely petitioned that "the rules of the Index might be submitted to a fresh revision and a rearrangement." With these bishops many bishops of Italy and other countries have agreed.

Taking into account the circumstances of our times, the conditions of society, and popular customs, all these requests are certainly justified and in accordance with the maternal affection of Holy Church. In the rapid race of intellect, there is no field of knowledge in which literature has not run riot, hence the daily inundation of most pernicious books. Worst of all, the civil laws not only connive at this serious evil but allow it the widest license. Thus, on the one hand, many minds are in a state of anxiety; whilst, on the other, there is unlimited opportunity for every kind of reading.

Believing that some remedy ought to be applied to these evils, We have thought well to take two steps which will supply a certain and clear rule of action in this matter. First, to diligently revise the Index of books forbidden to be read; and We have ordered this revised edition to be published when complete. Secondly, We have turned Our attention to the rules themselves, and have determined, without altering their nature, to make them somewhat milder, so that it cannot be difficult or irksome for any person of good-will to obey them. In this we have not only followed the example of Our predecessors, but imitated the maternal affection of the Church, who desires nothing more earnestly than to show herself indulgent, and, in the present, as in the past, ever cares for her children in such a manner as gently and lovingly to have regard to their weakness.

Wherefore, after mature deliberation, and having consulted the Cardinals of the Sacred Congregation of the Index, We have decided to issue the following General Decrees appended to this Constitution, and the aforesaid Sacred Congregation shall, in the future, follow these exclusively, and all Catholics throughout the world shall strictly obey them. We will that they alone shall have the force of law, abrogating the rules published by order of the Sacred Council of Trent, and the Observations, Instructions, Decrees, Monita, and all other statutes and commands whatsoever of Our predecessors, with the sole exception of the Constitution *Sollicita et provida* of Benedict XIV., which We will to retain in the future the full force which it has hitherto had.

GENERAL DECREES CONCERNING THE PROHIBITION AND CENSORSHIP OF BOOKS.

ARTICLE I.

Of the Prohibition of Books.

CHAPTER I.

Of the Prohibited Books of Apostates, Heretics, Schismatics, and Other Writers.

1. All books condemned before the year 1600 by the Sovereign Pontiffs, or by Œcumenical Councils, and which

are not recorded in the new Index, must be considered as condemned in the same manner as formerly, with the exception of such as are permitted by the present General Decrees.

2. The books of apostates, heretics, schismatics, and all writers whatsoever, defending heresy or schism, or in any way attacking the foundations of religion, are altogether prohibited.

3. Moreover, the books of non-Catholics, *ex professo* treating of religion, are prohibited, unless they clearly contain nothing contrary to Catholic faith.

4. The books of the above-mentioned writers, not treating *ex professo* of religion, but only touching incidentally upon the truths of faith, are not to be considered as prohibited by ecclesiastical law, unless proscribed by special decree.

CHAPTER II.

Of Editions of the Original Text of Holy Scripture and of Versions not in the Vernacular.

5. Editions of the original text and of the ancient Catholic versions of Holy Scripture, as well as those of the Eastern Church, if published by non-Catholics, even though apparently edited in a faithful and complete manner, are allowed only to those engaged in theological and biblical studies, provided also that the dogmas of Catholic faith are not impugned in the prolegomena or annotations.

6. In the same manner, and under the same conditions, other versions of the Holy Bible, whether in Latin or in any other dead language, published by non-Catholics, are permitted.

CHAPTER III.

Of Vernacular Versions of Holy Scripture.

7. As it has been clearly shown by experience that, if the Holy Bible in the vernacular is generally permitted without any distinction, more harm than utility is thereby

caused, owing to human temerity: all versions in the vernacular, even by Catholics, are altogether prohibited, unless approved by the Holy See, or published, under the vigilant care of the bishops, with annotations taken from the Fathers of the Church and learned Catholic writers.

8. All versions of the Holy Bible, in any vernacular language, made by non-Catholics are prohibited; and especially those published by the Bible societies, which have been more than once condemned by the Roman Pontiffs, because in them the wise laws of the Church concerning the publication of the sacred books are entirely disregarded.

Nevertheless, these versions are permitted to students of theological or biblical science, under the conditions laid down above (No. 5).

CHAPTER IV.

Of Obscene Books.

9. Books which professedly treat of, narrate, or teach lewd or obscene subjects are entirely prohibited, since care must be taken not only of faith but also of morals, which are easily corrupted by the reading of such books.

10. The books of classical authors, whether ancient or modern, if disfigured with the same stain of indecency, are, on account of the elegance and beauty of their diction, permitted only to those who are justified on account of their duty or the function of teaching; but on no account may they be placed in the hands of, or taught to, boys or youths, unless carefully expurgated.

CHAPTER V.

Of Certain Special Kinds of Books.

11. Those books are condemned which are derogatory to Almighty God, or to the Blessed Virgin Mary, or the

Saints, or to the Catholic Church and her worship, or to the sacraments, or to the Holy See. To the same condemnation are subject those works in which the idea of the inspiration of Holy Scripture is perverted, or its extension too narrowly limited. Those books, moreover, are prohibited which professedly revile the ecclesiastical hierarchy, or the clerical or religious state.

12. It is forbidden to publish, read, or keep books in which sorcery, divination, magic, the evocation of spirits, and other superstitions of this kind are taught or commended.

13. Books or other writings which narrate new apparitions, revelations, visions, prophecies, miracles, or which introduce new devotions, even under the pretext of being private ones, if published without the legitimate permission of ecclesiastica superiors, are prohibited.

14. Those books, moreover, are prohibited which defend as lawful, duelling, suicide, or divorce; which treat of Freemasonry, or other societies of the kind, teaching them to be useful, and not injurious to the Church and to Society; and those which defend errors proscribed by the Apostolic See.

CHAPTER VI.

Of Sacred Pictures and Indulgences.

15. Pictures, in any style of printing, of Our Lord Jesus Christ, the Blessed Virgin Mary, the angels and saints, or other servants of God, which are not conformable to the sense and decrees of the Church, are entirely forbidden. New pictures, whether produced with or without prayers annexed, may not be published without permission of ecclesiastical authority.

16. It is forbidden to all to give publicity in any way to apocryphal indulgences, and such as have been proscribed or revoked by the Apostolic See. Those which have already been published must be withdrawn from the hands of the faithful.

17. No books of indulgences, or compendiums, pamphlets, leaflets, etc., containing grants of indulgences, may be published without permission of competent authority.

CHAPTER VII.

Of Liturgical Books and Prayer Books.

18. In authentic editions of the Missal, Breviary, Ritual, Ceremonial of Bishops, Roman Pontifical, and other liturgical books approved by the holy Apostolic See, no one shall presume to make any change whatsoever; otherwise such new editions are prohibited.

19. No litanies—except the ancient and common litanies contained in the breviaries, missals, pontificals, and rituals, as well as the Litany of Loretto, and the Litany of the Most Holy Name of Jesus already approved by the Holy See—may be published without the examination and approbation of the ordinary.

20. No one, without license of legitimate authority, may publish books or pamphlets of prayers, devotions, or of religious, moral, ascetic, or mystic doctrine and instruction, or others of like nature, even though apparently conducive to the fostering of piety among Christian people; otherwise they are to be considered as prohibited.

CHAPTER VIII.

Of Newspapers and Periodicals.

21. Newspapers and periodicals which designedly attack religion or morality are to be held as prohibited not only by the natural but also by the ecclesiastical law.

Ordinaries shall take care, whenever it be necessary, that the faithful shall be warned against the danger and injury of reading of this kind.

22. No Catholics, particularly ecclesiastics, shall pub-

lish anything in newspapers or periodicals of this character, unless for some just and reasonable cause.

CHAPTER IX.

Of Permission to Read and Keep Prohibited Books.

23. Those only shall be allowed to read and keep books prohibited, either by special decrees or by these General Decrees, who shall have obtained the necessary permission, either from the Apostolic See or from its delegates.

24. The Roman Pontiffs have placed the power of granting licenses for the reading and keeping of prohibited books in the hands of the Sacred Congregation of the Index. Nevertheless the same power is enjoyed both by the Supreme Congregation of the Holy Office, and by the Sacred Congregation of Propaganda for the regions subject to its administration. For the city of Rome this power belongs also to the Master of the Sacred Apostolic Palace.

25. Bishops and other prelates with quasi-episcopal jurisdiction may grant such license for individual books, and in urgent cases only. But if they have obtained from the Apostolic See a general faculty to grant permission to the faithful to read and keep prohibited books, they must grant this only with discretion and for a just and reasonable cause.

26. Those who have obtained apostolic faculties to read and keep prohibited books may not on this account read and keep any books whatsoever or periodicals condemned by the local ordinaries, unless in the apostolic indult express permission be given to read and keep books by whomsoever prohibited. And those who have obtained permission to read prohibited books must remember that they are bound by grave precept to keep books of this kind in such a manner that they may not fall into the hands of others.

CHAPTER X.

Of the Denunciation of Bad Books.

27. Although all Catholics, especially the more learned, ought to denounce pernicious books either to the bishops or to the Holy See, this duty belongs more especially to apostolic nuncios and delegates, local ordinaries, and rectors of universities.

28. It is expedient, in denouncing bad books, that not only the title of the book be expressed, but also, as far as possible, the reasons be explained why the book is considered worthy of censure. Those to whom the denunciation is made will remember that it is their duty to keep secret the names of the denouncers.

29. Ordinaries, even as delegates of the Apostolic See, must be careful to prohibit evil books or other writings published or circulated in their dioceses, and to withdraw them from the hands of the faithful. Such works and writings should be referred by them to the judgment of the Apostolic See as appear to require a more careful examination, or concerning which a decision of the supreme authority may seem desirable in order to procure a more salutary effect.

ARTICLE II.

OF THE CENSORSHIP OF BOOKS.

CHAPTER I.

Of the Prelates entrusted with the Censorship of Books.

30. From what has been laid down above (No. 7), it is sufficiently clear what persons have authority to approve or permit editions and translations of the Holy Bible.

31. No one shall venture to republish books condemned by the Apostolic See. If, for a grave and reasonable cause, any particular exception appears desirable in this respect, this can only be allowed on obtaining beforehand a license from the Sacred Congregation of the Index and observing the conditions prescribed by it.

32. Whatsoever pertains in any way to causes of beatification and canonization of the servants of God may not be published without the approval of the Congregation of Sacred Rites.

33. The same must be said of collections of decrees of the various Roman congregations: such collections may not be published without first obtaining the license of the authorities of each congregation, and observing the conditions by them prescribed.

34. Vicars apostolic and missionaries apostolic shall faithfully observe the decrees of the Sacred Congregation of Propaganda concerning the publication of books.

35. The approbation of books of which the censorship is not reserved by the present decrees either to the Holy See or to the Roman congregations belongs to the ordinary of the place where they are published.

36. Regulars must remember that, in addition to the license of the bishop, they are bound by a decree of the Sacred Council of Trent to obtain leave for publishing any work from their own superior. Both permissions must be printed either at the beginning or at the end of the book.

37. If an author, living in Rome, desires to print a book, not in the city of Rome but elsewhere, no other approbation is required beyond that of the Cardinal Vicar and the Master of the Apostolic Palace.

CHAPTER II.

Of the Duty of Censors in the Preliminary Examination of Books.

38. Bishops whose duty it is to grant permission for the printing of books shall take care to employ in the examination of them men of acknowledged piety and learning.

concerning whose faith and honesty they may feel sure that they will show neither favor nor ill-will, but, putting aside all human affections, will look only to the glory of God and the welfare of the people.

39. Censors must understand that, in the matter of various opinions and systems, they are bound to judge with a mind free from all prejudice, according to the precept of Benedict XIV. Therefore they should put away all attachment to their particular country, family, school, or institute, and lay aside all partisan spirit. They must keep before their eyes nothing but the dogmas of Holy Church, and the common Catholic doctrine as contained in the decrees of General Councils, the Constitutions of the Roman Pontiffs, and the unanimous teaching of the Doctors of the Church.

40. If, after this examination, no objection appears to the publication of the book, the ordinary shall grant to the author, in writing and without any fee whatsoever, a license to publish, which shall be printed either at the beginning or at the end of the work.

CHAPTER III.

Of the Books to be Submitted to Censorship.

41. All the faithful are bound to submit to preliminary ecclesiastical censorship at least those books which treat of Holy Scripture, sacred theology, ecclesiastical history, canon law, natural theology, ethics, and other religious or moral subjects of this character; and in general all writings specially concerned with religion and morality.

42. The secular clergy, in order to give an example of respect towards their ordinaries, ought not to publish books, even when treating of merely natural arts and sciences, without their knowledge.

They are also prohibited from undertaking the management of newspapers or periodicals without the previous permission of their ordinaries.

CHAPTER IV.

Of Printers and Publishers of Books.

43. No book liable to ecclesiastical censorship may be printed unless it bear at the beginning the name and surname of both the author and the publisher, together with the place and year of printing and publishing. If in any particular case, owing to a just reason, it appears desirable to suppress the name of the author, this may be permitted by the ordinary.

44. Printers and publishers should remember that new editions of an approved work require a new approbation; and that an approbation granted to the original text does not suffice for a translation into another language.

45. Books condemned by the Apostolic See are to be considered as prohibited all over the world, and into whatever language they may be translated.

46. Booksellers, especially Catholics, should neither sell, lend, nor keep books professedly treating of obscene subjects. They should not keep for sale other prohibited books, unless they have obtained leave through the ordinary from the Sacred Congregation of the Index; nor sell such books to any person whom they do not prudently judge to have the right to buy them.

CHAPTER V.

Of Penalties Against Transgressors of the General Decrees.

47. All and every one knowingly reading, without authority of the Holy See, the books of apostates and heretics defending heresy; or books of any author which are by name prohibited by Apostolic Letters; also those keeping, printing, and in any way defending such works; incur *ipso facto* excommunication reserved in a special manner to the Roman Pontiff.

48. Those who, without the approbation of the ordinary, print, or cause to be printed, books of Holy Scripture, or notes or commentaries on the same, incur *ipso facto* excommunication, but not reserved.

49. Those who transgress the other prescriptions of these General Decrees shall, according to the gravity of their offence, be seriously warned by the bishop, and, if it seem expedient, may also be punished by canonical penalties.

We decree that these presents and whatsoever they contain shall at no time be questioned or impugned for any fault of subreption, or obreption, or of Our intention, or for any other defect whatsoever; but are and shall be ever valid and efficacious, and to be inviolably observed, both judicially and extra-judicially, by all of whatsoever rank and pre-eminence. And We declare to be invalid and of no avail, whatsoever may be attempted knowingly or unknowingly contrary to these, by any one, under any authority or pretext whatsoever; all to the contrary notwithstanding.

And We will that the same authority be attributed to copies of these Letters, even if printed, provided they be signed by the hand of a notary, and confirmed by the seal of some one in ecclesiastical dignity, as to the indication of Our will by the exhibition of these presents.

No man, therefore, may infringe or temerariously venture to contravene this document of Our constitution, ordination, limitation, derogation, and will. If any one shall so presume, let him know that he will incur the wrath of Almighty God, and of the blessed apostles Peter and Paul.

THE HOLY SPIRIT.

Encyclical Letter Divinum Illud, May 4, 1897.

THAT divine office which Jesus Christ received from His Father for the welfare of mankind, and most perfectly fulfilled, had for its final object to put men in possession of the eternal life of glory, and proximately during the course of ages to secure to them the life of divine grace, which is destined eventually to blossom into the life of heaven. Wherefore Our Saviour never ceases to invite, with infinite affection, all men, of every race and tongue, into the bosom of His Church: *Come ye all to Me, I am the Life, I am the Good Shepherd.* Nevertheless, according to His inscrutable counsels, He did not will to entirely complete and finish this office Himself on earth, but as He had received it from the Father, so He transmitted it for its completion to the Holy Ghost. It is consoling to recall those assurances which Christ gave to the body of His disciples a little before He left the earth: *It is expedient to you that I go: for if I go not, the Paraclete will not come to you: but if I go, I will send Him to you.*[1] In these words He gave as the chief reason of His departure and His return to the Father the advantage which would most certainly accrue to His followers from the coming of the Holy Ghost, and at the same time He made it clear that the Holy Ghost is equally sent by—and therefore proceeds from—Himself and the Father; that He would complete, in His office of Intercessor, Consoler, and Teacher, the work which Christ Himself had begun in His mortal

[1] John xvi. 7.

life. For, in the redemption of the world, the completion of the work was by divine Providence reserved to the manifold power of that Spirit who, in the creation, *adorned the heavens* [1] and *filled the whole world.*[2]

Now We have earnestly striven, by the help of His grace, to follow the example of Christ Our Saviour, the Prince of pastors, and the Bishop of our souls, by diligently carrying on His office, entrusted by Him to the apostles and chiefly to Peter, "whose dignity faileth not, even in his unworthy successor." [3] In pursuance of this object We have endeavored to direct all that we have attempted and persistently carried out during a long pontificate towards two chief ends: in the first place, towards the restoration, both in rulers and peoples, of the principles of the Christian life in civil and domestic society, since there is no true life for men except from Christ; and, secondly, to promote the reunion of those who have fallen away from the Catholic Church either by heresy or by schism, since it is most undoubtedly the will of Christ that all should be united in one flock under one Shepherd. But now that We are looking forward to the approach of the closing days of Our life, Our soul is deeply moved to dedicate to the Holy Ghost, who is the life-giving Love, all the work We have done during Our pontificate, that He may bring it to maturity and fruitfulness. In order better and more fully to carry out this Our intention, We have resolved to address you at the approaching sacred season of Pentecost concerning the indwelling and miraculous power of the Holy Ghost; and the extent and efficiency of His action, both in the whole body of the Church and in the individual souls of its members, through the glorious abundance of His divine graces. We earnestly desire that, as a result, faith may be aroused in your minds concerning the mystery of the adorable Trinity, and espe-

---

[1] Job xxvi. 13.
[2] Wisdom i. 7.
[3] St. Leo the Great, Sermon ii., on the Anniversary of his Election.

cially that piety may increase and be inflamed towards the Holy Ghost, to whom especially all of us owe the grace of following the paths of truth and virtue, for, as St. Basil said, "Who denieth that the dispensations concerning man, which have been made by the great God and our Saviour Jesus Christ, according to the goodness of God, have been fulfilled through the grace of the Spirit?" [1]

Before We enter upon this subject, it will be both desirable and useful to say a few words about the mystery of the Blessed Trinity. This dogma is called by the Doctors of the Church "the substance of the New Testament," that is to say, the greatest of all mysteries, since it is the fountain and origin of them all. In order to know and contemplate this mystery, the angels were created in heaven and men upon earth. In order to teach more fully this mystery, which was but foreshadowed in the Old Testament, God Himself came down from the angels unto men: *No man hath seen God at any time; the only begotten Son, who is in the bosom of the Father, He hath declared Him.*[2] Whosoever then writes or speaks of the Trinity must keep before His eyes the prudent warning of the Angelic Doctor: "When we speak of the Trinity, we must do so with caution and modesty, for, as St. Augustine saith, nowhere else are more dangerous errors made, or is research more difficult, or discovery more fruitful". [3] The danger that arises is lest the divine persons be confounded one with the other in faith or worship, or lest the one nature in them be separated: for "This is the Catholic faith, that we should adore one God in Trinity and Trinity in Unity." Therefore Our predecessor Innocent XII. absolutely refused the petition of those who desired a special festival in honor of God the Father. For, although the separate mysteries connected with the Incarnate Word are celebrated on certain fixed days, yet there is no special feast on which the Word is honored according to His divine nature alone.

[1] Of the Holy Ghost, c. xvi., v. 39.　　[2] John i. 18.
[3] Summ. Th. 1a., q. xxxi. De Trin. l. i., c. 3.

And even the Feast of Pentecost was instituted in the earliest times, not simply to honor the Holy Ghost in Himself, but to commemorate His coming, or His external mission. And all this has been wisely ordained, lest from distinguishing the persons men should be led to distinguish the divine essence. Moreover the Church, in order to preserve in her children the purity of faith, instituted the Feast of the Most Holy Trinity, which John XXII. afterwards extended to the Universal Church. He also permitted altars and churches to be dedicated to the Blessed Trinity, and with the divine approval, sanctioned the Order for the Ransom of Captives, which is specially devoted to the Blessed Trinity and bears its name. Many facts confirm its truths. The worship paid to the saints and angels, to the Mother of God, and to Christ Himself, finally redounds to the honor of the Blessed Trinity. In prayers addressed to one person, there is also mention of the others; in the litanies, after the individual persons have been separately invoked, a common invocation of all is added; all psalms and hymns conclude with the doxology to the Father, Son, and Holy Ghost; blessings, sacred rites, and sacraments are either accompanied or concluded by the invocation of the Blessed Trinity. This was already foreshadowed by the Apostle in those words: *For of Him, and by Him, and in Him, are all things: to Him be glory forever,*[1] thereby signifying both the trinity of persons and the unity of nature: for as this is one and the same in each of the persons, so to each is equally owing supreme glory, as to one and the same God. St. Augustine commenting upon this testimony writes: "The words of the Apostle, *of Him, and by Him, and in Him,* are not to be taken indiscriminately; *of Him* refers to the Father, *by Him* to the Son, *in Him* to the Holy Ghost."[2] The Church is accustomed most fittingly to attribute to the Father those works of the divinity in which power excels, to the Son those in which wisdom excels, and those in which love excels to the Holy Ghost.

[1] Rom. xi 36.   [2] De Trin. l. vi., c. 10; l. i., c. 6.

Not that all perfections and external operations are not common to the divine persons; for "the operations of the Trinity are indivisible, even as the essence of the Trinity is indivisible"[1] because as the three divine persons "are inseparable, so do they act inseparably."[2] But by a certain comparison, and a kind of affinity between the operations and the properties of the persons, these operations are attributed or, as it is said, "appropriated" to one person rather than to the others. "Just as we make use of the traces of similarity or likeness which we find in creatures for the manifestation of the divine persons, so do we use their essential attributes; and this manifestation of the persons by their essential attributes is called *appropriation.*"[3] In this manner the Father, who is "the principal of the whole Godhead,"[4] is also the efficient cause of all things, of the Incarnation of the Word, and the sanctification of souls; "of Him are all things," *of Him* referring to the Father. But the Son, the Word, the Image of God, is also the exemplary cause, whence all creatures borrow their form and beauty, their order and harmony. He is for us the way, the truth, and the life: the reconciler of man with God. "By Him are all things," *by Him* referring to the Son. The Holy Ghost is the ultimate cause of all things, since, as the will and all other things finally rest in their end, so He, who is the divine goodness and the mutual love of the Father and Son, completes and perfects, by His strong yet gentle power, the secret work of man's eternal salvation. "In Him are all things," *in Him* referring to the Holy Ghost.

THE HOLY GHOST AND THE INCARNATION.

Having thus paid the due tribute of faith and worship owing to the Blessed Trinity, and which ought to be more

[1] St. Aug. De Trin., l. i., cc. 4, 5
[2] St. Aug., ib.
[3] St. Th. 1a., q. xxxix., a. 7.
[4] St. Aug. De Trin. l. iv., c. 20.

and more inculcated upon the Christian people, We now turn to the exposition of the power of the Holy Ghost. And, first of all, we must look to Christ, the Founder of the Church and Redeemer of our race. Among the external operations of God, the highest of all is the mystery of the Incarnation of the Word, in which the splendor of the divine perfections shines forth so brightly that nothing more sublime can even be imagined, nothing else could have been more salutary to the human race. Now this work, although belonging to the whole Trinity, is still appropriated especially to the Holy Ghost, so that the gospels thus speak of the Blessed Virgin: *She was found with child of the Holy Ghost,*[1] and *that which is conceived in her is of the Holy Ghost.*[1] And this is rightly attributed to Him who is the Love of the Father and the Son, since this *great mystery of piety*[2] proceeds from the infinite love of God towards man, as St. John tells us: *God so loved the world as to give His only begotten Son.*[3] Moreover, human nature was thereby elevated to a *personal* union with the Word; and this dignity is given, not on account of any merits, but entirely and absolutely through grace, and therefore, as it were, through the special gift of the Holy Ghost. On this point St. Augustine writes: "The manner in which Christ was born of the Holy Ghost indicates to us the grace of God, by which humanity, with no antecedent merits, at the first moment of its existence, was united with the Word of God by so intimate a personal union that He who was the Son of man was also the Son of God, and He who was the Son of God was also the Son of man."[4] By the operation of the Holy Spirit, not only was the conception of Christ accomplished, but also the sanctification of His soul, which, in Holy Scripture is called His *anointing.*[5] Wherefore all His actions were *performed in the Holy Ghost,*[6] and especially the sac-

---

[1] Matt. i. 18, 20.
[2] 1 Tim. iii. 16.
[3] John iii. 16.
[4] Enchir., c. xl.; St. Th. 3a., q. xxxii., a. 1.
[5] Acts x. 38.
[6] St. Basil de Sp. S., c. xvi.

rifice of Himself: *Christ, through the Holy Ghost, offered Himself without spot to God.*[1] Considering this no one can be surprised that all the gifts of the Holy Ghost inundated the soul of Christ. In Him resided the absolute fulness of grace, in the greatest and most efficacious manner possible; in Him were all the treasures of wisdom and knowledge, graces *gratis datæ*, virtues, and all other gifts foretold in the prophecies of Isaias,[2] and also signified in that miraculous dove which appeared at the Jordan, when Christ, by His Baptism, consecrated its waters for a new sacrament. On this the words of St. Augustine may appropriately be quoted: "It would be absurd to say that Christ received the Holy Ghost when He was already thirty years of age, for He came to His Baptism without sin, and therefore not without the Holy Ghost. At this time, then (that is at His Baptism), He was pleased to prefigure His Church, in which those especially who are baptized receive the Holy Ghost." [3] Therefore, by the conspicuous apparition of the Holy Ghost over Christ and by His invisible power in His soul, the twofold mission of the Spirit is foreshadowed, namely, His outward and visible mission in the Church, and His secret indwelling in the souls of the just.

THE HOLY GHOST AND THE CHURCH.

The Church which, already conceived, came forth from the side of the second Adam in His sleep on the cross, first showed herself before the eyes of men on the great day of Pentecost. On that day the Holy Ghost began to manifest His gifts in the mystic body of Christ, by that miraculous outpouring already foreseen by the prophet Joel,[4] for the Paraclete "sat upon the apostles as though new spiritual crowns were placed upon their heads in tongues of fire." [5] Then the apostles "descended from

---

[1] Heb. ix. 14.
[2] Isa. iv. 1; xi. 23.
[3] De Trin. l. xv., c. 26.
[4] Joel ii. 28, 29
[5] S. Cyril Hier. Catech. 17.

the mountain," as St. John Chrysostom writes, "not bearing in their hands tables of stone like Moses, but carrying the Spirit in their mind, and pouring forth the treasure and the fountain of doctrines and graces."[1]   Thus was fully accomplished that last promise of Christ to His apostles of sending the Holy Ghost, who was to complete and, as it were, to seal the deposit of doctrine committed to them under His inspiration. *I have yet many things to say to you, but you cannot bear them now; but when He, the Spirit of Truth, shall come, He will teach you all truth.*[2] For He who is the Spirit of Truth, inasmuch as He proceedeth both from the Father, who is the eternally True, and from the Son, who is the substantial Truth, receiveth from each both His essence and the fulness of all truth. This truth He communicates to His Church, guarding her by His all-powerful help from ever falling into error, and aiding her to foster daily more and more the germs of divine doctrine and to make them fruitful for the welfare of the peoples.   And since the welfare of the peoples, for which the Church was established, absolutely requires that this office should be continued for all time, the Holy Ghost perpetually supplies life and strength to preserve and increase the Church. *I will ask the Father, and He will give you another Paraclete, that He may abide with you forever, the Spirit of Truth.*[3]

By Him the bishops are constituted, and by their ministry are multiplied not only the children, but also the fathers—that is to say, the priests—to rule and feed the Church by that blood wherewith Christ has redeemed her. *The Holy Ghost hath placed you bishops to rule the Church of God, which He hath purchased with His own blood.*[4]   And both bishops and priests, by the miraculous gift of the Spirit, have the power of absolving sins, according to those words of Christ to the apostles: *Receive ye the Holy Ghost; whose sins you shall forgive they are for-*

---

[1] In Matt. Hom. I., 2 Cor. iii. 3.   [3] John xiv. 16, 17.
[2] John xvi. 12, 13.   [4] Acts xx. 28.

given them, and whose you shall retain they are retained.[1]
That the Church is a divine institution is most clearly
proved by the splendor and glory of those gifts and graces
with which she is adorned, and whose author and giver
is the Holy Ghost. Let it suffice to state that, as Christ
is the Head of the Church, so is the Holy Ghost her soul.
"What the soul is in our body, that is the Holy Ghost in
Christ's body, the Church."[2] This being so, no further
and fuller "manifestation and revelation of the divine
Spirit" may be imagined or expected; for that which
now takes place in the Church is the most perfect possible,
and will last until that day when the Church herself,
having passed through her militant career, shall be taken
up into the joy of the saints triumphing in heaven.

THE HOLY GHOST IN THE SOULS OF THE JUST.

The manner and extent of the action of the Holy Ghost
in individual souls is no less wonderful, although somewhat
more difficult to understand, inasmuch as it is entirely
invisible. This outpouring of the Spirit is so abundant,
that Christ Himself, from whose gift it proceeds, compares
it to an overflowing river, according to those words of
St. John: "He that believeth in Me, as the Scripture
saith, out of his midst shall flow rivers of living water";
to which testimony the Evangelist adds the explanation:
*Now this He said of the Spirit which they should receive
who believed in Him.*[3] It is indeed true that in those of
the just who lived before Christ, the Holy Ghost resided
by grace, as we read in the Scriptures concerning the
prophets, Zachary, John the Baptist, Simeon, and Anna;
so that on Pentecost the Holy Ghost did not communicate
Himself in such a way "as then for the first time to begin
to dwell in the saints, but by pouring Himself forth more
abundantly: crowning, not beginning His gifts; not

---

[1] John xx, 22, 23,   [2] St. Aug. Serm, 187, de Temp.
[3] John vii. 38, 39,

commencing a new work, but giving more abundantly."[1]
But if they also were numbered among the children of
God, they were in a state like that of servants, for *as long
as the heir is a child he differeth nothing from a servant,
but is under tutors and governors.*[2] Moreover, not only
was their justice derived from the merits of Christ who
was to come, but the communication of the Holy Ghost
after Christ was much more abundant, just as the price
surpasses in value the earnest and the reality excels the
image. Wherefore St. John declares: *As yet the spirit
was not given, because Jesus was not yet glorified.*[3] So
soon, therefore, as Christ, "ascending on high," entered
into possession of the glory of His Kingdom which He
had won with so much labor, He munificently opened out
the treasures of the Holy Ghost: *He gave gifts to men.*[4]
For that giving or sending forth of the Holy Ghost after
Christ's glorification was to be such as had never been
before; not that there had been none before, but it had
not been of the same kind.[5]

Human nature is by necessity the servant of God:
"The creature is a servant, we are the servants of God
by nature."[6] On account, however, of original sin, our
whole nature had fallen into such guilt and dishonor that
we had become enemies to God. *We were by nature the
children of wrath.*[7] There was no power which could
raise us and deliver us from this ruin and eternal destruction. But God, the Creator of mankind and infinitely
merciful, did this through His only-begotten Son, by
whose benefit it was brought about that man was restored
to that rank and dignity whence he had fallen, and was
adorned with still more abundant graces. No one can

[1] St. Leo the Great, Hom. iii, de Pentec.
[2] Gal. iv. 1, 2.
[3] John vii. 39.
[4] Eph. iv. 8.
[5] St. Aug., de Trin., l. iv. c. 20.
[6] St. Cyr. Alex., Thesaur, l, v., c. 5.
[7] Eph. ii. 3.

express the greatness of this work of divine grace in the
souls of men. Wherefore, both in Holy Scripture and
in the writings of the fathers, men are styled regenerated,
new creatures, partakers of the divine nature, children
of God, god-like, and similar epithets. Now these great
blessings are justly attributed as especially belonging to
the Holy Ghost. He is "the Spirit of adoption of sons,
whereby we cry: Abba, Father." He fills our hearts
with the sweetness of paternal love: *The Spirit Himself
giveth testimony to our spirit that we are the sons of God.*[1]
This truth accords with the similitude observed by the
Angelic Doctor between both operations of the Holy
Ghost; for through Him "Christ was conceived in holiness
to be by nature the Son of God," and "others are sanctified
to be the sons of God by adoption."[2] This spiritual generation proceeds from love in a much more noble manner
than the natural: namely, from the uncreated Love.

The beginnings of this regeneration and renovation of
man are by Baptism. In the sacrament, when the unclean
spirit has been expelled from the soul, the Holy Ghost
enters in and makes it like to Himself. *That which is
born of the Spirit, is spirit.*[3] The same Spirit gives Himself
more abundantly in Confirmation, strengthening and confirming Christian life; from which proceeded the victory
of the martyrs and the triumph of the virgins over temptations and corruptions. We have said that the Holy
Ghost gives Himself: *the charity of God is poured out into
our hearts by the Holy Ghost who is given to us.*[4] For He
not only brings to us His divine gifts, but is the Author
of them and is Himself the supreme gift, who, proceeding
from the mutual love of the Father and the Son, is justly
believed to be and is called "Gift of God most high."
To show the nature and efficacy of this gift it is well to
recall the explanation given by the Doctors of the Church
of the words of Holy Scripture. They say that God is

---

[1] Rom viii. 15, 16.
[2] St. Th. 3a, q. xxxii., a. 1.
[3] John iii. 6.
[4] Rom. v. 5.

present and exists in all things, "by His power, in so far as all things are subject to His power; by His presence, inasmuch as all things are naked and open to His eyes; by His essence, inasmuch as He is present to all as the cause of their being." [1] But God is in man, not only as in inanimate things, but because He is more fully known and loved by him, since even by nature we spontaneously love, desire, and seek after the good. Moreover God by grace resides in the just soul as in a temple, in a most intimate and peculiar manner. From this proceeds that union of affection by which the soul adheres most closely to God, more so than the friend is united to his most loving and beloved friend, and enjoys God in all fulness and sweetness. Now this wonderful union, which is properly called "indwelling," differing only in degree or state from that with which God beatifies the saints in heaven, although it is most certainly produced by the presence of the whole Blessed Trinity—*We will come to Him and make our abode with Him,*[2]—nevertheless is attributed in a peculiar manner to the Holy Ghost. For, whilst traces of divine power and wisdom appear even in the wicked man, charity, which, as it were, is the special mark of the Holy Ghost, is shared in only by the just. In harmony with this, the same Spirit is called holy, for He, the first and supreme Love, moves souls and leads them to sanctity, which ultimately consists in the love of God. Wherefore the Apostle, when calling us the temple of God, does not expressly mention the Father, or the Son, or the Holy Ghost: *Know ye not that your members are the temple of the Holy Ghost, who is in you, whom you have from God?*[3] The fulness of divine gifts is in many ways a consequence of the indwelling of the Holy Ghost in the souls of the just. For, as St. Thomas teaches, "when the Holy Ghost proceedeth as love, He proceedeth in the character of the first gift; whence Augustine saith that through

---

[1] St. Th. 1a. q. viii., a. 3.   [2] John xiv. 23.
[3] 1 Cor. vi. 19.

the gift which is the Holy Ghost, many other special gifts are distributed among the members of Christ." [1] Among these gifts are those secret warnings and invitations which from time to time are excited in our minds and hearts by the inspiration of the Holy Ghost. Without these there is no beginning of a good life, no progress, no arriving at eternal salvation. And since these words and admonitions are uttered in the soul in an exceedingly secret manner, they are sometimes aptly compared in holy writ to the breathing of a coming breeze, and the Angelic Doctor likens them to the movements of the heart which are wholly hidden in the living body. "Thy heart has a certain hidden power, and therefore the Holy Ghost, who invisibly vivifies and unites the Church, is compared to the heart." [2] More than this, the just man, that is to say he who lives the life of divine grace, and acts by the fitting virtues as by means of faculties, has need of those seven *gifts* which are properly attributed to the Holy Ghost. By means of them the soul is furnished and strengthened so as to be able to obey more easily and promptly His voice and impulse. Wherefore these gifts are of such efficacy that they lead the just man to the highest degree of sanctity; and of such excellence that they continue to exist even in heaven, though in a more perfect way. By means of these gifts the soul is excited and encouraged to seek after and attain the evangelical beatitudes which, like the flowers that come forth in the spring-time, are the signs and harbingers of eternal beatitude. Lastly there are those blessed *fruits*, enumerated by the Apostle,[3] which the Spirit, even in this mortal life, produces and shows forth in the just; fruits filled with all sweetness and joy, inasmuch as they proceed from the Spirit, "who is in the Trinity the sweetness of both Father and Son, filling all creatures with infinite

---

[1] Summ. Th., 1a, q. xxxviii., a. 2. St. Aug. de Trin., l. xv., c. 19.
[2] Summ. Th., 3a, q. vii., a. 1, ad 3.
[3] Gal. v. 22.

fulness and profusion." [1]   The divine Spirit, proceeding from the Father and the Word in eternal light of sanctity, Himself both Love and Gift, after having manifested Himself through the veils of figures in the Old Testament, poured forth all His fulness upon Christ and upon His mystic Body, the Church; and called back by His presence and grace men who were going away in wickedness and corruption with such salutary effect that, being no longer of the earth earthy, they relished and desired quite other things, becoming of heaven heavenly.

These sublime truths, which so clearly show forth the infinite goodness of the Holy Ghost towards us, certainly demand that we should direct towards Him the highest homage of our love and devotion.   Christians may do this most effectually if they will daily strive to know Him, to love Him, and to implore Him more earnestly; for which reason may this Our exhortation, flowing spontaneously from a paternal heart, reach their ears.   Perchance there are still to be found among them, even nowadays, some who, if asked, as were those of old by St. Paul the Apostle, whether they have received the Holy Ghost, might answer in like manner: *We have not so much as heard whether there be a Holy Ghost*.[2]   At least there are certainly many who are very deficient in their knowledge of Him.   They frequently use His name in their religious practices, but their faith is involved in much darkness.   Wherefore all preachers and those having care of souls should remember that it is their duty to instruct their people more diligently and more fully about the Holy Ghost—avoiding, however, difficult and subtle controversies, and eschewing the dangerous folly of those who rashly endeavor to pry into divine mysteries.   What should be chiefly dwelt upon and clearly explained is the multitude and greatness of the benefits which have been bestowed, and are constantly bestowed, upon us by this divine Giver, so that errors

---

[1] St. Aug. de Trin. l. vi., c. 9.   [2] Acts xix. 2.

and ignorance concerning matters of such moment may be entirely dispelled, as unworthy of "the children of light." We urge this not only because it affects a mystery by which we are directly guided to eternal life, and which must therefore be firmly believed, but also because the more clearly and fully the good is known the more earnestly it is loved. Now we owe to the Holy Ghost, as we mentioned in the second place, love, because He is God: *Thou shalt love the Lord thy God with thy whole heart, and with thy whole soul, and with thy whole strength.*[1] He is also to be loved because He is the substantial, eternal, primal Love, and nothing is more lovable than love. And this all the more because he has overwhelmed us with the greatest benefits, which both testify to the benevolence of the Giver and claim the gratitude of the receiver. This love has a twofold and most conspicuous utility. In the first place it will excite us to acquire daily a clearer knowledge about the Holy Ghost; for, as the Angelic Doctor says, "the lover is not content with the superficial knowledge of the beloved, but striveth to inquire intimately into all that appertains to the beloved, and thus to penetrate into the interior; as is said of the Holy Ghost, who is the love of God, that He searcheth even the profound things of God."[2] In the second place it will obtain for us a still more abundant supply of heavenly gifts; for whilst a narrow heart contracteth the hand of the giver, a grateful and mindful heart causeth it to expand. Yet we must strive that this love should be of such a nature as not to consist merely in dry speculations or external observances, but rather to run forward towards action, and especially to fly from sin, which is in a more special manner offensive to the Holy Spirit. For whatever we are, that we are by the divine goodness; and this goodness is specially attributed to the Holy Ghost. The sin-

[1] Deut. vi. 5.
[2] 1 Cor. ii. 10; Summ. Theol., 1a, 2æ., q. 28, a. 2.

ner offends this his Benefactor, abusing His gifts; and taking advantage of His goodness becomes more hardened in sin day by day. Again, since He is the Spirit of Truth, whosoever faileth by weakness or ignorance may perhaps have some excuse before Almighty God; but he who resists the truth through malice and turns away from it, sins most grievously against the Holy Ghost. In our days this sin has become so frequent that those dark times seem to have come which were foretold by St. Paul, in which men, blinded by the just judgment of God, should take falsehood for truth, and should believe in "the prince of this world," who is a liar and the father thereof, as a teacher of truth: *God shall send them the operation of error, to believe lying.*[1] *In the last times some shall depart from the faith; giving heed to the spirits of error and the doctrines of devils.*[2] But since the Holy Ghost, as We have said, dwells in us as in His temple, We must repeat the warning of the Apostle: *Grieve not the Holy Spirit of God, whereby you are sealed.*[3] Nor is it enough to fly from sin; every Christian ought to shine with the splendor of virtue so as to be pleasing to so great and so beneficent a guest: and first of all with chastity and holiness, for chaste and holy things befit the temple. Hence the words of the Apostle: *Know you not that you are the temple of God, and that the Spirit of God dwelleth in you? But if any man violate the temple of God, him shall God destroy. For the temple of God is holy, which you are* [4]—a terrible, indeed, but a just warning.

Lastly, we ought to pray to and invoke the Holy Spirit, for each one of us greatly needs His protection and His help. The more a man is deficient in wisdom, weak in strength, borne down with trouble, prone to sin, so ought he the more to fly to Him who is the never-ceasing fount of light, strength, consolation, and holiness. And chiefly that first requisite of man, the forgiveness of sins, must be sought for from Him: "It is the special character

---

[1] 2 Thess. ii. 10.
[2] 1 Tim. iv. 1.
[3] Eph. iv. 30.
[4] 1 Cor. iii 16, 17.

of the Holy Ghost that He is the Gift of the Father and
the Son.   Now the remission of sins is given by the Holy
Ghost as by the Gift of God."[1]   Concerning this Spirit
the words of the liturgy are very explicit: "For He
is the remission of all sins."[2]   How He should be invoked
is clearly taught by the Church, who addresses Him in
humble supplication, calling upon Him by the sweetest of
names: "Come, Father of the poor! Come, Giver of gifts!
Come, Light of our hearts!   O best of Consolers, sweet
Guest of the soul, our refreshment!"[3]   She earnestly
implores Him to wash, heal, water our minds and hearts,
and to give us who trust in Him "the merit of virtue,
the acquirement of salvation, and joy everlasting."   Nor
can it be in any way doubted that He will listen to such
prayer, since we read the words written by His own inspiration: *The Spirit Himself asketh for us with unspeak-
able groanings.*[4]   Lastly, we ought confidently and continually to beg of Him to illuminate us daily more and more
with His light and inflame us with His charity: for, thus
inspired with faith and love, we may press onward earnestly towards our eternal reward, since He *is the pledge of
our inheritance.*[5]

Such, Venerable Brethren, are the teachings and exhortations which We have seen good to utter, in order to
stimulate devotion to the Holy Ghost. We have no
doubt that, chiefly by means of your zeal and earnestness,
they will bear abundant fruit among Christian peoples.
We Ourselves shall never in the future fail to labor towards
so important an end; and it is even Our intention, in
whatever ways may appear suitable, to further cultivate
and extend this admirable work of piety. Meanwhile,
as two years ago, in Our Letter *Provida Matris*, We recom-

---

[1] Summ. Th. 3a, q. iii. a. 8, ad 3m.
[2] Roman Missal, Tuesday after Pentecost.
[3] Hymn, Veni Sancti Spiritus.
[4] Rom. viii. 26.
[5] Eph. i. 14.

mended to Catholics special prayers at the Feast of Pentecost, for the reunion of Christendom, so now We desire to
make certain further decrees on the same subject.

Wherefore, We decree and command that throughout
the whole Catholic Church, this year and in every subsequent year, a novena shall take place before Whit-
Sunday, in all parish churches, and also, if the local ordinaries think fit, in other churches and oratories. To
all who take part in this novena and duly pray for Our
intention, We grant for each day an indulgence of seven
years and seven quarantines; moreover, a plenary indulgence on any of the days of the novena, or on Whit-
Sunday itself, or on any day during the octave; provided
they shall have received the Sacraments of Penance and
the Holy Eucharist, and devoutly prayed for Our intention. We will that those who are legitimately prevented
from attending the novena, or who are in places where
the devotions cannot, in the judgment of the ordinary,
be conveniently carried out in church, shall equally enjoy
the same benefits, provided they make the novena privately and observe the other conditions. Moreover We
are pleased to grant, in perpetuity, from the Treasury of
the Church, that whosoever, daily during the octave
of Pentecost up to Trinity Sunday inclusive, offer again
publicly or privately any prayers, according to their
devotion, to the Holy Ghost, and satisfy the above conditions, shall a second time gain each of the same indulgences. All these indulgences We also permit to be
applied as suffrages for the souls in purgatory.

And now Our mind and heart turn back to those hopes
with which We began, and for the accomplishment of
which We earnestly pray, and will continue to pray, to
the Holy Ghost. Unite, then, Venerable Brethren, your
prayers with Ours, and at your exhortation let all Christian peoples add their prayers also, invoking the powerful
and ever-acceptable intercession of the Blessed Virgin.
You know well the intimate and wonderful relations

existing between her and the Holy Ghost, so that she is justly called His spouse. The intercession of the Blessed Virgin was of great avail both in the mystery of the Incarnation and in the coming of the Holy Ghost upon the apostles. May she continue to strengthen our prayers with her suffrages, that, in the midst of all the stress and trouble of the nations, those divine prodigies may be happily revived by the Holy Ghost, which were foretold in the words of David: *Send forth Thy Spirit and they shall be created, and Thou shalt renew the face of the earth.*[1]

As a pledge of divine favor and a testimony of Our affection, Venerable Brethren, to you, to your clergy and people, We gladly impart in the Lord the Apostolic Benediction.

[1] Ps. ciii. 30.

TRUE AND FALSE AMERICANISM IN RELIGION.

Apostolical Letter Testem Benevolentiœ, January 22, 1899, addressed to His Eminence Cardinal Gibbons, Archbishop of Baltimore.

WE send you this letter as a testimony of that devoted affection in your regard, which during the long course of Our Pontificate, We have never ceased to profess for you, for your colleagues in the Episcopate, and for the whole American people, willingly availing Ourselves of every occasion to do so, whether it was the happy increase of your church, or the works which you have done so wisely and well in furthering and protecting the interests of Catholicity. The opportunity also often presented itself of regarding with admiration that exceptional disposition of your nation, so eager for what is great, and so ready to pursue whatever might be conducive to social progress and the splendor of the State. But although the object of this letter is not to repeat the praise so often accorded, but rather to point out certain things which are to be avoided and corrected, yet because it is written with that same apostolic charity which We have always shown you, and in which We have often addressed you, We trust that you will regard it likewise as a proof of Our love; and all the more so as it is conceived and intended to put an end to certain contentions which have arisen lately among you, and which disturb the minds, if not of all, at least of many, to the no slight detriment of peace.

You are aware, beloved Son, that the book entitled "The Life of Isaac Thomas Hecker," chiefly through the action of those who have undertaken to publish and

441

interpret it in a foreign language, has excited no small controversy on account of certain opinions which are introduced concerning the manner of leading a Christian life. We, therefore, on account of Our apostolic office, in order to provide for the integrity of the faith, and to guard the security of the faithful, desire to write to you more at length upon the whole matter.

The principles on which the new opinions We have mentioned are based may be reduced to this: that, in order the more easily to bring over to Catholic doctrine those who dissent from it, the Church ought to adapt herself somewhat to our advanced civilization, and, relaxing her ancient rigor, show some indulgence to modern popular theories and methods. Many think that this is to be understood not only with regard to the rule of life, but also to the doctrines in which the *deposit of faith* is contained. For they contend that it is opportune, in order to work in a more attractive way upon the wills of those who are not in accord with us, to pass over certain heads of doctrines, as if of lesser moment, or to so soften them that they may not have the same meaning which the Church has invariably held. Now, Beloved Son, few words are needed to show how reprehensible is the plan that is thus conceived, if we but consider the character and origin of the doctrine which the Church hands down to us. On that point the Vatican Council says: "The doctrine of faith which God has revealed is not proposed like a theory of philosophy which is to be elaborated by the human understanding, but as a divine deposit delivered to the Spouse of Christ to be faithfully guarded and infallibly declared. . . . That sense of the sacred dogmas is to be faithfully kept which Holy Mother Church has once declared, and is not to be departed from under the specious pretext of a more profound understanding." [1]

Nor is the suppression to be considered altogether free from blame, which designedly omits certain principles of

[1] Const. de Fid. cath. c. iv.

Catholic doctrine and buries them, as it were, in oblivion. For there is the one and the same Author and Master of all the truths that Christian teaching comprises: *the only-begotten Son who is in the bosom of the Father.*[1] That they are adapted to all ages and nations is plainly deduced from the words which Christ addressed to His apostles: *Going therefore teach ye all nations: teaching them to observe all things whatsoever I have commanded you: and behold I am with you all days even to the consummation of the world.*[2] Wherefore the same Vatican Council says: "By the divine and Catholic faith those things are to be believed which are contained in the word of God either written or handed down, and are proposed by the Church whether in solemn decision or by the ordinary universal magisterium, to be believed as having been divinely revealed."[3] Far be it, then, for any one to diminish or for any reason whatever to pass over anything of this divinely delivered doctrine; whosoever would do so, would rather wish to alienate Catholics from the Church than to bring over to the Church those who dissent from it. Let them return; indeed, nothing is nearer to Our heart; let all those who are wandering far from the sheepfold of Christ return; but let it not be by any other road than that which Christ has pointed out.

The rule of life which is laid down for Catholics is not of such a nature as not to admit modifications, according to the diversity of time and place. The Church, indeed, possesses what her Author has bestowed on her, a kind and merciful disposition; for which reason from the very beginning she willingly showed herself to be what Paul proclaimed in his own regard: *I became all things to all men, that I might save all.*[4] The history of all past ages is witness that the Apostolic See, to which not only the office of teaching but also the supreme government of the whole Church was committed, has constantly adhered

---

[1] John i. 18.
[2] Matt. xxviii. 19 s.
[3] Const. de Fid. cath. c. iii.
[4] 1 Cor. ix. 22.

to the same doctrine, in the same sense and in the same mind:[1] but it has always been accustomed to so modify the rule of life that, while keeping the divine right inviolate, it has never disregarded the manners and customs of the various nations which it embraces. If required for the salvation of souls, who will doubt that it is ready to do so at the present time? But this is not to be determined by the will of private individuals, who are mostly deceived by the appearance of right, but ought to be left to the judgment of the Church. In this all must acquiesce who wish to avoid the censure of Our predecessor Pius VI., who proclaimed the 18th proposition of the Synod of Pistoia "to be injurious to the Church and to the Spirit of God which governs her, inasmuch as it subjects to scrutiny the discipline established and approved by the Church, as if the Church could establish a useless discipline or one which would be too onerous for Christian liberty to bear."

But in the matter of which we are now speaking, Beloved Son, the project involves a greater danger and is more hostile to Catholic doctrine and discipline, inasmuch as the followers of these novelties judge that a certain liberty ought to be introduced into the Church, so that, limiting the exercise and vigilance of its powers, each one of the faithful may act more freely in pursuance of his own natural bent and capacity. They affirm, namely, that this is called for in order to imitate that liberty which, though quite recently introduced, is now the law and the foundation of almost every civil community. On that point We have spoken very much at length in the Letter written to all the bishops about the constitution of States; where We have also shown the difference between the Church, which is of divine right, and all other associations which subsist by the free will of men. It is of importance, therefore, to note particularly an opinion which is adduced as a sort of argument to urge the granting of such liberty to Catho-

[1] Conc. Vatic. Ibid. c. iv.

lics. For they say, in speaking of the infallible teaching of the Roman Pontiff, that after the solemn decision formulated in the Vatican Council, there is no more need of solicitude in that regard, and, because of its being now out of dispute, a wider field of thought and action is thrown open to individuals. A preposterous method of arguing, surely. For if anything is suggested by the infallible teaching of the Church, it is certainly that no one should wish to withdraw from it; nay, that all should strive to be thoroughly imbued with and be guided by its spirit, so as to be the more easily preserved from any private error whatsoever. To this we may add that those who argue in that wise quite set aside the wisdom and providence of God; who when He desired in that very solemn decision to affirm the authority and teaching office of the Apostolic See, desired it especially in order the more efficaciously to guard the minds of Catholics from the dangers of the present times. The license which is commonly confounded with liberty; the passion for saying and reviling everything; the habit of thinking and of expressing everything in print, have cast such deep shadows on men's minds, that there is now greater utility and necessity for this office of teaching than ever before, lest men should be drawn away from conscience and duty. It is far, indeed, from Our intention to repudiate all that the genius of the time begets; nay, rather, whatever the search for truth attains, or the effort after good achieves, will always be welcome by Us, for it increases the patrimony of doctrine and enlarges the limits of public prosperity. But all this, to possess real utility, should thrive without setting aside the authority and wisdom of the Church.

We come now in due course to what are adduced as consequences from the opinions which We have touched upon; in which if the intention seem not wrong, as We believe, the things themselves assuredly will not appear by any means free from suspicion. For, in the first place, all external guidance is rejected as superfluous, nay even as somewhat of a disadvantage, for those who desire to devote themselves to the acquisition of Christian perfection; for the Holy Ghost, they say, pours greater and richer gifts into the hearts of the faithful now than in times past; and by a certain hidden instinct teaches and moves them with no one as an intermediary. It is indeed not a little rash to wish to determine the degree in which God communicates with men; for that depends solely on His will; and He Himself is the absolutely free giver of His own gifts. *The Spirit breatheth where He will.*[1] *But to every one of us is given grace according to the measure of the giving of Christ.*[2] For who, when going over the history of the apostles, the faith of the rising Church, the struggles and slaughter of the valiant martyrs, and finally most of the ages past so abundantly rich in holy men, will presume to compare the past with the present times and to assert that they received a lesser outpouring of the Holy Ghost? But, aside from that, no one doubts that the Holy Ghost, by His secret incoming into the souls of the just, influences and arouses them by admonition and impulse. If it were otherwise, any external help and guidance would be useless. "If any one positively affirms that he can consent to the saving preaching of the Gospel without the illumination of the Holy Ghost, who imparts sweetness to all to consent to and accept the truth, he is misled by a heretical spirit."[3] But as we know by experience these promptings and impulses of the Holy Ghost for the most part are not discerned without the help, and, as it were, without the preparation of an external guidance. In this matter Augustine says: "It is he who in good trees co-operates in their fruiting, who both waters and cultivates them by any servant whatever from without, and who by himself gives increase within."[4] That is to say, the whole matter is according to the common law

---

[1] John iii. 8.
[2] Eph. iv. 7.

[3] Conc. Arausic. ii. can. vii.
[4] De Grat. Christi. c. xix.

by which God in His infinite providence has decreed that
men for the most part should be saved by men; hence He
has appointed that those whom He calls to a loftier degree
of holiness should be led thereto by men, "in order that,"
as Chrysostom says, "we should be taught by God through
men." [1] We have an illustrious example of this put
before us in the very beginning of the Church, for
although Saul, who was *breathing threatenings and slaughter,* [2]
heard the voice of Christ Himself, and asked from Him,
Lord, what wilt Thou have me to do? he was nevertheless
sent to Ananias at Damascus: *Arise and go into the city,
and there it shall be told thee what thou must do.* It must
also be kept in mind that those who follow what is more
perfect are by the very fact entering upon a way of life
which for most men is untried and more exposed to error,
and therefore they, more than others, stand in need of a
teacher and a guide. This manner of acting has invariably obtained in the Church. All, without exception,
who in the course of ages have been remarkable for science
and holiness have taught this doctrine. Those who reject
it, assuredly do so rashly and at their peril.

For one who examines the matter thoroughly, it is hard
to see, if we do away with all external guidance as these
innovators propose, what purpose the more abundant influence of the Holy Ghost, which they make so much of,
is to serve. In point of fact, it is especially in the cultivation of virtue that the assistance of the Holy Spirit is
indispensable; but those who affect these novelties extol
beyond measure the natural virtues as more in accordance
with the ways and requirements of the present day, and
consider it an advantage to be richly endowed with them,
because they make a man more ready and more strenuous
in action. It is hard to understand how those who are
imbued with Christian principles can place the natural
ahead of the supernatural virtues, and attribute to them
greater power and fecundity. Is nature, then, with grace

---

[1] Hom. i. in Inscr. altar.   [2] Act. Ap. c. ix.

added to it, weaker than when left to its own strength? and have the eminently holy men whom the Church reveres and pays homage to, shown themselves weak and incompetent in the natural order, because they have excelled in Christian virtue? Even if we admire the sometimes splendid acts of the natural virtues, how rare is the man who really possesses the habit of these natural virtues? Who is there who is not disturbed by passions, sometimes of a violent nature, for the persevering conquest of which, just as for the observance of the whole natural law, man must needs have some divine help? If we scrutinize more closely the particular acts We have above referred to, we shall discover that oftentimes they have more the appearance than the reality of virtue. But let us grant that these are real. If we do not wish *to run in vain*, if we do not wish to lose sight of the eternal blessedness to which God in His goodness has destined us, of what use are the natural virtues unless the gift and strength of divine grace be added? Aptly does St. Augustine say: "Great power, and a rapid pace, but out of the course."[1] For as the nature of man, because of our common misfortune, fell into vice and dishonor, yet by the assistance of grace is lifted up and borne onward with new honor and strength; so also the virtues which are exercised not by the unaided powers of nature, but by the help of the same grace, are made productive of a supernatural beatitude and become solid and enduring.

With this opinion about natural virtue, another is intimately connected, according to which all Christian virtues are divided as it were into two classes, *passive* as they say, and *active;* and they add the former were better suited for the past times, but the latter are more in keeping with the present. It is plain what is to be thought of such division of the virtues. There is not and cannot be a virtue which is really passive. "Virtue," says St. Thomas, "denotes a certain perfection of a power; but

[1] In Ps. xxxi. 4.

the object of a power is an act; and an act of virtue is nothing else than the good use of our free will";[1] the divine grace of course helping, if the act of virtue is supernatural. The one who would have Christian virtues to be adapted, some to one age and others to another, has forgotten the words of the Apostle: *Whom he foreknew, he also predestinated to be made conformable to the image of His Son.*[2] The Master and exemplar of all sanctity is Christ, to whose rule all must conform who wish to attain to the thrones of the blessed. Now, then, Christ does not at all change with the progress of the ages, but is *yesterday and to-day, and the same forever.*[3] To the men of all ages, the phrase is to be applied: *Learn of Me because I am meek, and humble of heart,*[4] and at all times Christ shows Himself to us as becoming *obedient unto death,*[5] and in every age also the word of the Apostle holds: *And they that are Christ's have crucified their flesh with the vices and concupiscences.*[6] Would that more would cultivate those virtues in our days, as did the holy men of bygone times! Those who by humbleness of spirit, by obedience and abstinence, were *powerful in word and work,* were of the greatest help not only to religion but to the State and society.

From this species of contempt of the evangelical virtues, which are wrongly called *passive,* it naturally follows that the mind is imbued little by little with a feeling of disdain for the religious life. And that this is common to the advocates of these new opinions we gather from certain expressions of theirs about the vows which religious orders pronounce. For, say they, such vows are altogether out of keeping with the spirit of our age, inasmuch as they narrow the limits of human liberty; are better adapted to weak minds than to strong ones; avail little for Christian perfection and the good of human society, and rather obstruct and interfere with it. But how false these

[1] I. II. a. I.
[2] Rom. viii. 29.
[3] Heb. xiii. 8.
[4] Matt. xi. 29.
[5] Philip. ii. 8.
[6] Galat. v. 24.

assertions are, is evident from the usage and doctrine of the Church, which has always given the highest approval to religious life. And surely not undeservedly. For those who, not content with the common duties of the precepts, enter of their own accord upon the evangelical counsels, in obedience to a divine vocation, present themselves to Christ as His prompt and valiant soldiers. Are we to consider this a mark of weak minds? In the more perfect manner of life is it unprofitable or hurtful? Those who bind themselves by the vows of religion are so far from throwing away their liberty that they enjoy a nobler and fuller one—that, namely, *by which Christ has set us free.*[1]

What they add to this—namely, that religious life helps the Church not at all or very little—apart from being injurious to religious orders, will be admitted by no one who has read the history of the Church. Did not your own United States receive from the members of religious orders the beginning of its faith and civilization? For one of them recently, and it redounds to your credit, you have decreed that a statue should be publicly erected. And at this very time, with what alacrity and success are these religious orders doing their work wherever we find them! How many of them hasten to impart to new lands the life of the Gospel and to extend the boundaries of civilization with the greatest earnestness of soul and amid the greatest dangers! From them no less than from the rest of the clergy the Christian people obtain preachers of the Word of God, directors of conscience, instructors of youth, and the entire Church examples of holy lives. Nor is there any distinction of praise between those who lead an active life and those who, attracted by seclusion, give themselves up to prayer and mortification of the body. How gloriously they have merited from human society, and do still merit, they should be aware who are not ignorant of how *the continual prayer of a just*

---

[1] Galat. iv. 31.

man,[1] especially when joined to affliction of the body, avails to propitiate and conciliate the majesty of God.

If there are any, therefore, who prefer to unite together in one society without the obligation of vows, let them do as they desire. That is not a new institution in the Church, nor is it to be disapproved. But let them beware of setting such association above religious orders; nay rather, since mankind is more prone now than heretofore to the enjoyment of pleasure, much greater esteem is to be accorded to those *who have left all things and have followed Christ.*

Lastly, not to delay too long, it is also maintained that the way and the method which Catholics have followed thus far for recalling those who differ from us is to be abandoned and another resorted to. In that matter, it suffices to advert that it is not prudent, Beloved Son, to neglect what antiquity, with its long experience, guided as it is by apostolic teaching, has stamped with its approval. From the word of God we have it that it is the office of all to labor in helping the salvation of our neighbor in the order and degree in which each one is. The faithful indeed will most usefully fulfil their duty by integrity of life, by the works of Christian charity, by instant and assiduous prayer to God. But the clergy should do so by a wise preaching of the Gospel, by the decorum and splendor of the sacred ceremonies, but especially by expressing in themselves the form of doctrine which the apostles delivered to Titus and Timothy. So that if among the different methods of preaching the word of God, that sometimes seems preferable by which those who dissent from us are spoken to, not in the church but in any private and proper place, not in disputation but in amicable conference, such method is indeed not to be reprehended; provided, however, that those who are devoted to that work by the authority of the bishop be men who have first given proof of science and virtue. For We think that there are

[1] James v. 16.

very many among you who differ from Catholics rather through ignorance than because of any disposition of the will, who, perchance, if the truth is put before them in a familiar and friendly manner, may more easily be led to the one sheepfold of Christ.

Hence, from all that We have hitherto said, it is clear, Beloved Son, that We cannot approve the opinions which some comprise under the head of Americanism. If, indeed, by that name be designated the characteristic qualities which reflect honor on the people of America, just as other nations have what is special to them; or if it implies the condition of your commonwealths, or the laws and customs which prevail in them, there is surely no reason why We should deem that it ought to be discarded. But if it is to be used not only to signify, but even to commend the above doctrines, there can be no doubt but that our Venerable Brethren the bishops of America would be the first to repudiate and condemn it, as being especially unjust to them and to the entire nation as well. For it raises the suspicion that there are some among you who conceive of and desire a church in America different from that which is in the rest of the world. One in the unity of doctrine as in the unity of government, such is the Catholic Church, and, since God has established its centre and foundation in the Chair of Peter, one which is rightly called Roman, for where Peter is there is the Church. Wherefore he who wishes to be called by the name of Catholic ought to employ in truth the words of Jerome to Pope Damasus, "I following none as the first except Christ am associated in communion with your Beatitude, that is, with the Chair of Peter; upon that Rock I know is built the Church; whoever gathereth not with thee scattereth." [1]

What We write, Beloved Son, to you in particular, by reason of Our office, we shall take care to have communicated to the rest of the bishops of the United States,

[1] S. Ambr. in Ps. xi. 57.

expressing again that love in which we include your whole nation, which as in times past has done much for religion and bids fair with God's good grace to do still more in the future.

To you and all the faithful of America We give most lovingly as an augury of divine assistance Our Apostolical Benediction.

ON THE CONSECRATION OF MANKIND TO THE SACRED HEART OF JESUS.

Encyclical Letter Annum Sacrum, May 25, 1899.

But a short time ago, as you well know, We, by letters apostolic, and following the custom and ordinances of Our predecessors, commanded the celebration in this city, at no distant date, of a Holy Year. And now, to-day in the hope and with the object that this religious celebration shall be more devoutly performed, We have traced and recommended a striking design from which, if all shall follow it out with hearty good-will, We not unreasonably expect extraordinary and lasting benefits for Christendom in the first place, and also for the whole human race.

Already more than once We have endeavored, after the example of Our predecessors Innocent XII., Benedict XIII., Clement XIII., Pius VI., Pius VII., and Pius IX., devoutly to foster and bring out into fuller light that most excellent form of devotion which has for its object the veneration of the Sacred Heart of Jesus: this We did especially by the decree given on June 28, 1889, by which We raised the feast under that name to the dignity of the first class. But now We have in mind a more signal form of devotion which shall be in a manner the crowning perfection of all the honors that people have been accustomed to pay to the Sacred Heart, and which We confidently trust will be most pleasing to Jesus Christ, our Redeemer. This is not the first time, however, that the design of which We speak has been mooted. Twenty-five years ago, on the approach of the solemnities of the second centenary of the blessed Margaret Mary Alacoque's reception of the divine command to propagate the worship of the Sacred Heart, many letters from all parts, not merely from private persons but from bishops also, were sent to Pius IX. begging that he would consent to consecrate the whole human race to the most Sacred Heart of Jesus. It was thought best at the time to postpone the matter in order that a well-considered decision might be arrived at: meanwhile permission was granted to individual cities which desired it thus to consecrate themselves and a form of consecration was drawn up. Now, for certain new and additional reasons, We consider that the plan is ripe for fulfilment.

This world-wide and solemn testimony of allegiance and piety is especially appropriate to Jesus Christ, who is the Head and supreme Lord of the race. His empire extends not only over Catholic nations and those who having been duly washed in the waters of holy Baptism, belong of right to the Church, although erroneous opinions keep them astray, or dissent from her teaching cuts them off from her care; it comprises also all those who are deprived of the Christian faith, so that the whole human race is most truly under the power of Jesus Christ. For He who is the only-begotten Son of God the Father, having the same substance with Him and being the brightness of His glory and the figure of His substance,[1] necessarily has everything in common with the Father, and therefore sovereign power over all things. This is why the Son of God thus speaks of Himself through the Prophet: *But I am appointed king by Him over Sion, His holy mountain. . . . The Lord said to Me, Thou art My Son, this day have I begotten Thee. Ask of Me and I will give Thee the Gentiles for Thy inheritance, and the utmost parts of the earth for Thy possession.*[2] By these words He declares that He has power from God over the whole Church, which is signified by Mount Sion, and also over the rest of the

---

[1] Hebrews i. 3.   [2] Ps. ii. 6–8.

world to its uttermost ends. On what foundation this sovereign power rests is made sufficiently plain by the words, *Thou art My Son.* For by the very fact that He is the Son of the King of all, He is also the heir of all His Father's power: hence the words—*I will give Thee the Gentiles for Thy inheritance,* which are similar to those used by Paul the Apostle, *whom He hath appointed heir of all things.*[1]

But we should now give most special consideration to the declarations made by Jesus Christ, not through the apostles or the prophets, but by His own words. To the Roman governor who asked Him, *Art Thou a king, then?* He answered unhesitatingly, *Thou sayest that I am a king.*[2] And the greatness of this power and the boundlessness of His kingdom is still more clearly declared in these words to the apostles: *All power is given to Me in heaven and on earth.*[3] If, then, all power has been given to Christ, it follows of necessity that His empire must be supreme, absolute and independent of the will of any other, so that none is either equal or like unto it: and since it has been given in heaven and on earth it ought to have heaven and earth obedient to it. And verily He has acted on this extraordinary and peculiar right when He commanded His apostles to preach His doctrine over the earth, to gather all men together into the one body of the Church by the baptism of salvation, and to bind them by laws which no one could reject without risking his eternal salvation.

But this is not all. Christ reigns not only by natural right as the Son of God but also by a right that He has acquired. For He it was who snatched us *from the powers of darkness,*[4] and *gave Himself for the redemption of all.*[5] Therefore not only Catholics, and those who have duly received Christian Baptism, but also all men, individually

---

[1] Heb. i. 2.   [3] Matt. xxviii. 18.
[2] John xviii. 37.   [4] Coloss. i. 13.
[5] 1 Tim. ii. 6.

and collectively, have become to Him *a purchased people.*[1]
St. Augustine's words are therefore to the point when he
says: "You ask what price He paid? See what He gave
and you will understand how much He paid. The price
was the blood of Christ What could cost so much but
the whole world, and all its people? The great price He
paid was paid for all." [2]

How it comes about that infidels themselves are subject to the power and dominion of Jesus Christ is clearly
shown by St. Thomas, who gives us the reason and its
explanation. For having put the question whether His
judicial power extends to all men, and having stated that
judicial authority flows naturally from royal authority, he
concludes decisively as follows: "All things are subject to
Christ as far as His power is concerned, although they are
not all subject to Him in the exercise of that power." [3] This
sovereign power of Christ over men is exercised by truth,
justice, and, above all, by charity.

To this twofold ground of His power and domination
He graciously allows us, if we think fit, to add voluntary consecration. Jesus Christ, our God and our Redeemer, is rich in the fullest and perfect possession of
all things: we, on the other hand, are so poor and needy
that we have nothing of our own to offer Him as a gift.
But yet, in His infinite goodness and love, He in no way
objects to our giving and consecrating to Him what is
already His, as if it were really our own; nay, far from
refusing such an offering, He positively desires it and asks
for it: "My son, give Me thy heart." We are, therefore,
able to be pleasing to Him by the good-will and the affection of our soul. For by consecrating ourselves to Him
we not only declare our open and free acknowledgment
and acceptance of His authority over us, but we also
testify that if what we offer as a gift were really our own,
we would still offer it with our whole heart. We also beg

[1] 1 Peter ii. 9.   [2] T. 120 Jon.
[3] 3 P., Q. 59 A.

of Him that He would vouchsafe to receive it from us, though clearly His own. Such is the efficacy of the act of which We speak, such is the meaning underlying Our words.

And since there is in the Sacred Heart a symbol and a sensible image of the infinite love of Jesus Christ which moves us to love one another, therefore is it fit and proper that we should consecrate ourselves to His most Sacred Heart—an act which is nothing else than an offering and a binding of one's self to Jesus Christ, seeing that whatever honor, veneration, and love is given to this divine Heart is really and truly given to Christ Himself.

For these reasons We urge and exhort all who know and love this divine Heart willingly to undertake this act of piety; and it is Our earnest desire that all should make it on the same day, that so the aspirations of so many thousands who are performing this act of consecration may be borne to the temple of heaven on the same day. But shall We allow to slip from Our remembrance those innumerable others upon whom the light of Christian truth has not yet shined? We hold the place of Him who came to save that which was lost, and who shed His blood for the salvation of the whole human race. And so We greatly desire to bring to the true life those who sit in the shadow of death. As We have already sent messengers of Christ over the earth to instruct them, so now, in pity for their lot, with all Our soul We commend them, and as far in Us lies We consecrate them to the Sacred Heart of Jesus. In this way this act of devotion, which We recommend, will be a blessing to all. For having performed it, those in whose hearts are the knowledge and love of Jesus Christ will feel that faith and love increased. Those who knowing Christ, yet neglect His law and its precepts, may still gain from His Sacred Heart the flame of charity. And lastly, for those still more unfortunate, who are struggling in the darkness of superstition, we shall all with one mind implore the assistance of heaven that Jesus Christ, to whose power they are subject, may also one day render them submissive to its exercise; and that not only in the life to come, when He will fulfil His will upon all men, by saving some and punishing others (St. Thomas), but also in this mortal life by giving them faith and holiness. May they by these virtues strive to honor God as they ought, and to win everlasting happiness in heaven.

Such an act of consecration, since it can establish or draw tighter the bonds which naturally connect public affairs with God, gives to States a hope for better things. In these latter times especially, a policy has been followed which has resulted in a sort of wall being raised between the Church and civil society. In the constitution and administration of States the authority of sacred and divine law is utterly disregarded, with a view to the exclusion of religion from having any constant part in public life. This policy almost tends to the removal of the Christian faith from our midst, and, if that were possible, of the banishment of God Himself from the earth. When men's minds are raised to such a height of insolent pride, what wonder is it that the greater part of the human race should have fallen into such disquiet of mind and be buffeted by waves so rough that no one is suffered to be free from anxiety and peril? When religion is once discarded it follows of necessity that the surest foundations of the public welfare must give way, whilst God, to inflict on His enemies the punishment they so richly deserve, has left them the prey of their own evil desires, so that they give themselves up to their passions and finally wear themselves out by excess of liberty.

Hence that abundance of evils which have now for a long time settled upon the world, and which pressingly call upon us to seek for help from Him by whose strength alone they can be driven away. Who can he be but Jesus Christ, the only-begotten Son of God? *For there is no other name under heaven given to men whereby we must be saved.*[1]

[1] Acts iv. 12.

We must have recourse to Him who is the Way, the Truth, and the Life. We have gone astray and we must return to the right path: darkness has overshadowed our minds, and the gloom must be dispelled by the light of truth: death has seized upon us, and we must lay hold of life. It will at length be possible that our many wounds be healed and all justice spring forth again with the hope of restored authority; that the splendors of peace be renewed, and swords and arms drop from the hand when all men shall acknowledge the empire of Christ and willingly obey His word, and *every tongue shall confess that the Lord Jesus Christ is in the glory of God the Father.*[1]

When the Church, in the days immediately succeeding her institution, was oppressed beneath the yoke of the Cæsars, a young emperor saw in the heavens a cross, which became at once the happy omen and cause of the glorious victory that soon followed. And now, to-day, behold another blessed and heavenly token is offered to our sight—the most Sacred Heart of Jesus, with a cross rising from it and shining forth with dazzling splendor amidst flames of love. In that Sacred Heart all our hopes should be placed, and from it the salvation of men is to be confidently besought.

Finally, there is one motive which We are unwilling to pass over in silence, personal to Ourselves it is true, but still good and weighty, which moves Us to undertake this celebration. God, the author of every good, not long ago preserved Our life by curing Us of a dangerous disease. We now wish, by this increase of the honor paid to the Sacred Heart, that the memory of this great mercy should be brought prominently forward, and Our gratitude be publicly acknowledged.

For these reasons, We ordain that on the ninth, tenth, and eleventh of the coming month of June, in the principal church of every town and village, certain appointed prayers be said, and on each of these days there be added

[1] Phil. ii. 11.

to the other prayers the Litany of the Sacred Heart approved by Our authority. On the last day the form of consecration shall be recited which, Venerable Brethren, We send to you with these letters.

As a pledge of divine benefits, and in token of Our paternal benevolence to you, and to the clergy and people committed to your care, We lovingly grant in the Lord the Apostolic Benediction.

CHRIST OUR REDEEMER.

Encyclical Letter Tametsi, November 1, 1900.

THE outlook, Venerable Brethren, is not without concern for us; nay, there are many grave reasons for alarm, and the causes of evil in public and private are numerous and of long standing. And yet the end of the century does seem, by the divine mercy, to bring some hope and consolation.

No one can doubt that the reawakened attention to spiritual things and the revival of piety and faith are helping to avert disaster. That there is a very general growth in these virtues at the present time we have ample assurance. In the midst of the allurements of the world, and in spite of many obstacles in the path of piety, great multitudes, at the mere suggestion of the Pontiff, flock from all sides to the threshold of the holy apostles; coming from far and near to show their devotion to their religion, and, confiding in the proffered indulgences of the Church, to seek with eagerness the means of attaining their eternal salvation. Nor could any one fail to be moved by the extraordinary outburst of piety which has been displayed towards the Saviour of mankind.

The ardor with which so many thousands from all parts of the world have united in confessing the name of Jesus Christ and celebrating His praises is not unworthy of the best ages of the Christian faith. Would that this fire of the faith of our forefathers might leap into a conflagration! Would that the excellent example of so many might arouse the rest of the world! For the age needs

more than anything else the restoration among the nations
of the Christian spirit and the virtues of former days.
It is a calamity that so many turn a deaf ear and hear
not the admonition conveyed by such a reawakening of
piety. If they "knew the gift of God," if they considered
that nothing more miserable could happen to them than
to have revolted against the Liberator of the world and
to have abandoned the law and the life of Christianity,
they would surely rouse themselves and hasten of their
own accord to turn and flee from the destruction most
certainly impending over them.

To uphold on earth and to extend the empire of the
Son of God and to promote the salvation of men by the
dissemination of divine benefits is so greatly and so
peculiarly the office of the Church that her authority and
power rests mainly on the performance of this task. To
this end We trust We have labored to the best of Our
ability in the difficult and anxious administration of
Our Pontificate; while it is your ordinary and, indeed,
daily practice, Venerable Brethren, to give especial thought
and care in the same work. But both you and We ought,
in these times, to make still greater efforts, and in particular on the occasion of the Jubilee, to endeavor to spread
more widely the knowledge and love of Jesus Christ, by
teaching, persuading, and exhorting, if perchance Our
voice may be heard, not only by those who are accustomed
to hear Christian doctrine attentively, but also by the
unhappy remainder, who, while nominally Christian, pass
their lives without either faith in Christ or love for Him.
For these especially We grieve; and these, in particular,
We would fain have consider both what they are doing and
whither they are sure to go unless they repent in time.

Never to have known Jesus Christ in any way is the
greatest of misfortunes, but it involves no perversity or
ingratitude. But, after having known, to reject or forget
Him, is such a horrible and mad crime as to be scarcely
credible. For He is the origin and source of all good,

and just as mankind could not be freed from slavery but by the sacrifice of Christ, so neither can it be preserved but by His power. *Neither is there salvation in any other. For there is no other name under heaven given to men, whereby we must be saved.*[1] What the life of men is from which Jesus has been expelled, Jesus "the Power of God and the Wisdom of God," what is its morality and its end, may be learned from the example of nations which have not the light of Christianity. Any one who recalls for a moment that mental blindness which St. Paul alludes to,[2] the depravity of their nature, the abominable character of their vices and superstitions, must feel penetrated with horror, and, at the same time, with pity for them.

What We here speak of is a matter of common knowledge, but not usually dwelt upon or thought of. There would not be so many alienated by pride or buried in sloth if they recollected what benefits they had received from God, what Christ has rescued them from and to what He has brought them. Disinherited and exiled, the human race for ages was hurrying to destruction, enthralled by those dreadful evils which the sin of our first parents had begotten and by other woes beyond the power of man to remedy, when Christ our Lord came down from heaven and appeared as our Redeemer. In the first dawn of the world's history, God Himself had promised Him to us, as the victor and conqueror of "the serpent"; succeeding ages looked forward to His advent with eager longing; holy prophets had long and plainly foretold that on Him all our hopes depended; nay, the various fortunes of the chosen people, their history, their institutions, their laws, their sacrifices and ceremonies, had clearly and distinctly prefigured that the salvation of humanity would be wrought and completed in Him, who it was declared should be at once the High Priest and propitiatory Victim, the Restorer of human liberty, the Prince of peace, the Teacher of all nations, founding a

[1] Acts iv. 12.   [2] Rom. i. 21.

kingdom which should endure forever. By these titles, and under these images and prophetic utterances, various in kind, but agreeing in sense, He was designated as the One who for the exceeding love wherewith He loved us should one day give His life for our salvation. Accordingly, when the time of the divine counsel was ripe, the only-begotten Son of God, being made man, offered an abundant and complete satisfaction for men to His offended Father, and by so great a price redeemed and made the human race His own. *You are not redeemed with corruptible things as gold and silver . . . but with the precious blood of Christ, as of a lamb unspotted and undefiled.*[1] Accordingly, although all men without exception were already subject to His power and sway, because He is the Creator and Preserver of all, He made them His a second time by redeeming them in the truest and most literal sense. *You are not your own, for you are bought with a great price.*[2] Hence all things are re-established in Christ by God. *The mystery of His will, according to His good pleasure, which He hath purposed in Him, in the dispensation of the fulness of times, to re-establish all things in Christ.*[3] So that when Jesus had blotted out the handwriting which was contrary to us, and fastened it to the cross, the wrath of heaven was immediately appeased; the disordered and erring race of man had the bonds of their ancient slavery loosed, the will of God was reconciled to them, grace restored, the way to eternal happiness opened, and the title to possess and the means of attaining it both given back. Then, as though awakened from a long-lingering and deadly lethargy, man beheld the light of truth so long desired, but for generations sought in vain; he recognized, in particular, that he was born for much higher and more splendid things than the frail and fleeting objects of sense, to which he had formerly confined his thoughts and pursuits, and that this was

[1] 1 Peter i. 18, 19.   [2] 1 Cor. vi. 19, 20.
[3] Eph. i. 9, 10.

in fine the constitution and supreme law of human life, and the end to which all must tend, that as we came from God so we should one day return to Him. From this beginning and on this foundation consciousness of human dignity was restored and lived again; the sense of a common brotherhood took possession of men's hearts; their rights and duties in consequence were perfected or established anew and virtues beyond the imagination or conception of ancient philosophy were revived. So men's purposes, tenor of life, and characters were changed, and the knowledge of the Redeemer having spread far and wide, and His power having penetrated into the very life-blood of nations, expelling their ignorance and their ancient vices, a marvellous transformation took place, which, originating in Christian civilization, utterly changed the face of the earth.

In recalling these things, Venerable Brethren, there is an infinite sweetness experienced, but at the same time, a serious warning is conveyed—namely to return thanks with our whole heart and soul and to see that others, so far as in us lies, return thanks to our divine Saviour.

We live in an age remote from the inception and beginning of our redemption; but what matters it, since the power of redemption is perpetual, and the benefits thereof are abiding and everlasting. He who once restored our fallen nature, preserves, and will continue to preserve it. *He gave Himself a redemption for all;*[1] *in Christ all shall be made alive;*[2] *and of His kingdom there shall be no end.*[3] Thus, according to the eternal counsel of God, the salvation of all and each wholly depends on Christ Jesus; those who forsake Him, in their blind fury, seek by that very act their own personal destruction, and at the same time as far as they can, make society in general fall back into the very abyss of evils and disasters from which the Redeemer out of His love had delivered mankind.

[1] Tim. ii. 6.　　[2] 1 Cor. xv. 22.
[3] Luke i. 33.

Men wander very far in aimless error from the goal once they have entered upon devious paths. Likewise, if the pure and unsullied light of truth be rejected, men's minds must needs be buried in darkness and deceived by the depraved fancies that meet them at every step. What hope can there be of health for those who forsake the fountain and source of life? Christ is alone the way, the truth, and the life,[1] and if we despise Him, we lose these three indispensable requisites of salvation.

There is no need to dilate upon what experience continually teaches, and in his heart every one feels, even when abounding in earthly goods that only in God can the heart of man find absolute and complete repose. In very truth, the end of man is God; and the time we spend on earth is more truly likened and compared to a pilgrimage. Christ, then, is for us *the way,* because from this mortal journeying of ours, which is so especially toilsome and so beset with danger, we can only attain to God, our chief and final good, with Christ to guide and direct us. *No man cometh to the Father but by Me.*[2] *But by Me—* that is to say, first and chiefly, by His grace. Yet, if His precepts and laws are despised, His grace is *void.* As it behooved him to do, when He had wrought our salvation, Jesus Christ left us His law, as the custodian and director of the human race, so that under its guidance men might turn from evil ways and safely attain to God. *Go teach ye all nations . . . teaching them to observe all things whatsoever I have commanded you;*[3] *keep My commandments.*[4] By this we ought to understand that it is the chief and absolutely essential thing for those who confess Christ to be docile to the precepts of Jesus Christ, and to hold our will submissive and devoted to Him as Our Lord and supreme Ruler. A great undertaking and frequently entailing a hard struggle and demanding much labor and steadiness of purpose. For, albeit human

---

[1] John xiv. 6.
[2] Ibid.
[3] Matt. xxviii. 19, 20.
[4] John xiv. 15.

nature has been restored by the sacrifice of Our Redeemer, yet there remains in every one a certain debility, weakness and corruption.

Various appetites drag a man hither and thither, and the allurements of external things impel the soul to follow its own pleasure in place of Christ's command. But yet we must struggle and fight against our desires "unto the obedience of Christ"; and, unless they are subservient to reason, they become our masters, and separating us from Christ make us body and soul their slaves. "Men corrupt in mind, reprobate concerning the Faith, do not deliver themselves from slavery . . . for they are slaves to three sorts of desire, that of pleasure, or pride of place, or display of worldly pomp." [1] In this contest every one ought to be so disposed as to feel bound to take upon himself trouble and inconvenience for the sake of Christ. It is difficult to refuse things which so strongly attract and charm; it is hard to despise qualities of body and earthly possessions, in submission to the will and command of Christ our Lord, but a Christian must be always brave and strong to endure, if he would pass his time of life like a Christian. Have we forgotten what is the body of which we are members, and who is our Head? He having joy set before Him endured the cross, and He has given us His precept to deny ourselves. The very dignity of human nature depends on this disposition of mind of which we speak. For, as even the ancient philosophy often perceived, it is not at all meanness of spirit to rule oneself and to make the lower part of nature obey the higher, but it is rather a noble kind of virtue and is marvellously consistent with reason and human dignity.

Besides, to suffer and to bear is the lot of humanity. Man can no more construct for himself a life free from pain and replete with every happiness than he can annul the counsels of his divine Creator, who has willed that the consequences of our fault should remain in perpetuity.

[1] St. Aug. De Vera nl. 37.

It is proper, therefore, not to look for an end of pain upon the earth, but to strengthen our mind to bear pain, which, in fact, educates us to the attainment of the greatest of all good things for which we hope. For it is not to wealth and luxury, nor to worldly honors and powers that Christ has promised eternal happiness in heaven, but to patient suffering and tears, to the desire of justice and to cleanness of heart.

Hence it is easy to see what ought ultimately to be expected from the error and pride of those who, despising the supremacy of the Redeemer, give man the highest place, and hold that human nature should bear rule everywhere and in every case; although they can neither attain such control, nor even define its nature The kingdom of Jesus Christ obtains its form and virtue from divine charity; holy and pure affection is its foundation and completion. The punctual observance of our duties necessarily follows, viz., not to wrong our neighbor, to esteem the earthly less than the heavenly, to set the love of God before all else. But the reign of man, either openly rejecting Christ or neglecting Him, consists entirely in the love of self; charity there is none, and self-immolation is ignored. Rule, indeed, man may but in Jesus Christ, and only on the condition that first of all he serves God, and religiously finds in His law the rule and discipline of life.

By the law of Christ we mean not merely the natural precepts of morality, or what supernatural knowledge the ancient world acquired, all which Jesus Christ perfected and raised to the highest plane by His explanation, interpretation, and ratification; but we mean, besides, all the doctrine and in particular the institutions He has left us. Of these the Church is the chief. Indeed, what institution of Christ is there that she does not fully embrace and include? By the ministry of the Church, so gloriously founded by Him, He willed to perpetuate the office assigned to Him by His Father, and having on the one hand conferred upon her all effectual aids for human salvation, He ordained with the utmost emphasis on the other that men should be subject to her as to Himself, and zealously follow her guidance in every department of life: *He that heareth you, heareth Me; and he that despiseth you, despiseth Me.*[1] So the law of Christ is always to be sought from the Church, and therefore as Christ is for man the way, so likewise the Church is the way. He in Himself and by His proper nature, she by His commission and by a share in His power. On this account those who would strive for salvation apart from the Church, wander from the way and are struggling in vain.

The case of governments is much the same as that of the individual; they also must run into fatal issues, if they depart from *the way.* The Creator and Redeemer of human nature, the Son of God, is King and Lord of the world, and holds absolute sovereignty over men, both as individuals and as members of society. *He hath given to Him power and honor and dominion, and all peoples, tribes, and languages shall serve Him.*[2] *Yet am I established King by Him. . . . I will give Thee the nations for Thine inheritance, and the ends of the earth for Thy possession.*[3] Therefore, the law of Christ ought to hold sway in human society, and in communities so far as to be the teacher and guide of public no less than private life. This being divinely appointed and provided, no one may resist with impunity, and it fares ill with any commonwealth in which Christian institutions are not allowed their proper place. Let Jesus be excluded, and human reason is left without its greatest protection and illumination; the very notion is easily lost of the end for which God created human society, to wit: that by help of their civil union the citizens should attain their natural good, but nevertheless in a way not to conflict with that highest and most perfect and enduring good which is above nature. Their

[1] Luke x. 16. [2] Dan. vii. 14.
[3] Ps. ii. 6, 8.

minds busy with a hundred confused projects, rulers and
subjects alike travel a devious road; bereft, as they are,
of safe guidance and fixed principle.

Just as it is pitiable and calamitous to wander out of
the way, so it is to desert the truth. But the first absolute and essential truth is Christ, the Word of God, con-
substantial and co-eternal with the Father, who with
the Father is one. *I am the Way and the Truth.* Accordingly, if truth is sought, let human reason first of all obey
Jesus Christ and rest secure in His authoritative teaching,
because by Christ's voice the truth itself speaks.

Human intelligence has a wide field of its own in which
to employ itself freely with investigation and experiment.
Nature not only allows this, but evidently requires it.
But it is a wicked thing and against nature for the mind
to refuse to be confined within its own limitations, to
have no proper modesty, and to scorn the authority of
Christ's teaching. The doctrine, on which our salvation
altogether depends, regards God and divine things. That
was not created by any man's wisdom, but the Son of
God received it in its entirety from His Father. *The
words which Thou gavest Me, I have given them.*[1] Accordingly, it necessarily includes much that, without being
contrary to reason, for that cannot possibly be, is still
beyond the reach of our mind as much as is the compre-
hension of God in His essential being. But if there are
so many things in nature itself which are mysterious and
obscure, and which no human intelligence can explain,
and yet which no one in his senses would presume to doubt,
it will be a perverse freedom of thought not to allow for
things existing outside the domain of nature altogether,
which are above nature, and beyond our minds to fathom.
To refuse to accept dogmas evidently means to do away
with the whole Christian religion. The mind must be
subjected humbly and submissively *to the obedience of*

[1] John xvii. 8.

Christ, so as to be held, as it were, captive to His will and sovereignty. *Bringing into captivity every understanding unto the obedience of Christ.*[1] Such is the obedience which Christ wills, and rightfully, to have offered to Him, inasmuch as He is God, and has therefore supreme sovereignty over the understanding as well as over the will of man. There is nothing servile in serving Christ our Lord with the understanding, but it is especially consonant to reason and to our personal dignity.

For a man does not thus submit his will to the sovereignty of any fellow man, but to that of God the Creator and First Cause of all, to whom he is made subject by the law of nature; nor does a man allow himself to be coerced by the imagination of any human teacher, but by the eternal and immutable truth. He attains at once the natural good of the mind and mental freedom. For truth as proceeding from the authoritative teaching of Christ, sets in a clear light the intrinsic character and relative importance of things, whatever they may be, and thus instructed and obedient to the truth which he sees, he will not subject himself to creatures, but creatures to himself, he will not let passion rule reason, but will make reason rule passion; casting off the pernicious slavery of sin and error, he will be made free with the best kind of freedom—*You shall know the truth, and the truth shall make you free.*[2] It is plain, therefore, that those whose minds refuse to acknowledge Christ, are obstinately striving against God. Having escaped from the divine subjection, they will not thereby gain greater freedom; but will come under some human authority; they will choose, indeed, as men do, some one to listen to, to obey, and to follow as their master. Besides this, debarring themselves from theological studies and confining the exercise of their minds within a more circumscribed sphere, they will come less efficiently trained to the consideration

[1] 2 Cor. x. 5.   [2] John viii. 33.

of subjects with which reason properly deals. There are many things in nature on the investigation or explanation of which theology sheds considerable light. And often, to punish men's pride, God suffers them to miss the truth, so as to chastise them in the very thing in which they have sinned. For one or other of these reasons very many men who seem endowed with great intellectual capacity, and of profound erudition, have nevertheless in their investigations of nature fallen into the most absurd and egregious mistakes.

It is certain, therefore, that in Christianity the understanding should be wholly and unreservedly resigned to the divine authority. If when reason thus submits, our spiritual pride, which is so strong in us, suffers repression, and feels pain, that proves all the more that in a Christian there ought to be patient endurance not merely of the will, but of the mind as well. And this we wish especially to note for those who dream of, and openly prefer, some discipline of thought and action in Christianity, with precepts less rigorous and more indulgent to human nature, that would demand of us to put up with little or nothing. They have no notion of the spirit of faith and of Christian institutions, they do not see that *the cross* meets us everywhere as the standard of life and the banner under which we must always fight if we would follow Christ, not in name only, but in deed and in truth.

God alone is Life. All other beings partake of, but are not, life. Moreover from all eternity, and by His proper nature Christ is *the Life* equally as He is the Truth, being God of God. From Him, as from its ultimate and most august beginning, all life has flowed down upon the world and will forever flow; all that is, has its being from Him; all that lives, lives by Him, for by the Word "all things were made, and without Him was nothing made that was made."

So much for the natural life. But above we alluded to a much better and much more desirable life, won for us by the sacrifice of Christ, viz., the life *of grace*, the most blessed end of which is the life *of glory*, to which all our thoughts and actions should be referred. The whole meaning of Christian doctrine and precepts is that *we being dead to sin, should live to justice* [1] that is to say, to virtue and holiness, in which the moral life of the soul consists with the well-founded hope of everlasting happiness.

But justice in its true and proper sense, the justice which attains to salvation, is fed by Christian faith, and by that alone. *The just man liveth by faith,* [2] *without faith it is impossible to please God.* [3] It follows that Jesus Christ, who is the author and parent and upholder of faith, maintains and supports our moral life chiefly by the ministry of the Church. To her administration, in keeping with His benign and most provident purpose, He has committed the appropriate means of generating and preserving the virtue of which We speak, and of reviving it when dead. The force, then, which generates and conserves the virtues *necessary to salvation* disappears when morality is divorced from divine faith; and, truly, those who would have morals directed in the path of virtue by the sole authority of reason, rob man of his highest dignity, and most perniciously deprive him of his supernatural life and throw him back on the merely natural. Not that man is unable to recognize and observe many natural precepts by the light of reason, but even if he recognize and observe them all without stumbling for the whole of his life, which without the grace of Our Redeemer helping him, he could not do, yet vain would be his confidence of obtaining eternal salvation if destitute of faith. *If any one abide not in Me, he shall be cast forth as a branch and shall wither, and they shall gather him up, and cast him into the fire, and he burneth.* [4] *He that believeth*

---

[1] 1 Peter ii. 24.　　[3] Heb. xi. 6.
[2] Gal. iii. 11.　　[4] John xv. 6.

not shall be condemned.[1] How little that kind of virtue which despises faith avails in the end, and what sort of fruit it brings forth, we see only too plainly.

Why is it that with so much zeal displayed for establishing and augmenting the commonwealth, nations still have to labor and yet in so many and such important matters fare worse and worse every day? They say indeed that civil society is self-dependent, that it can go on happily without the protection of Christian institutions, that by its own unaided energies it can reach its goal. Hence they prefer to have public affairs conducted on a secular basis, so that in civil discipline and public life there are always fewer and fewer traces discernible of the old religious spirit. They do not see what they are doing. Take away the supremacy of God, who judges right and wrong; and law necessarily loses its paramount authority, while at the same time justice is undermined, these two being the strongest and most essential bonds of social union. In the same way, when the hope and expectation of immortality are gone, it is only human to seek greedily after perishable things, and every one will try, in proportion to his power, to clutch a larger share of them. Hence spring, jealousies, envies, hatreds; the most iniquitous plots to overthrow all power and mad schemes of universal ruin are formed. There is no peace abroad, nor security at home, and social life is made hideous by crime.

In such strife of passions, in such impending perils, we must either look for utter ruin, or some effective remedy must be found without delay. To restrain evil-doers, to soften the manners of our populations, to deter them from committing crimes by legislative intervention, is right and necessary; but that is by no means all. The healing of the nations goes deeper; a mightier influence must be invoked than human endeavor, one that may touch the conscience and reawaken the sense of duty,

[1] Mark xvi. 16.

the same influence that has once already delivered from destruction a world overwhelmed with far greater evils.

Do away with the obstacles to the spirit of Christianity; revive and make it strong in the State, and the State will be recreated. The strife between high and low will at once be appeased, and each will observe with mutual respect the rights of the other. If they listen to Christ, the prosperous and the unfortunate will both alike remember their duty; the one will feel that they must keep justice and charity, if they would be saved, the other that they must show temperance and moderation. Domestic society will have been solidly established under a salutary fear of the divine commands and prohibitions; and so likewise in society at large, the precepts of the natural law will prevail, which tells us that it is right to respect lawful authority, and to obey the laws, to do no seditious act, nor contrive anything by unlawful association. Thus when Christian law exerts its power without being thwarted in any way, naturally and without effort the order of society is maintained as constituted by divine Providence, and prosperity and public safety are secured. The security of the State demands that we should be brought back to Him from whom we ought never to have departed to Him who is the way, the truth, and the life, not as individuals merely, but as human society through all its extent. Christ our Lord must be reinstated as the Ruler of human society. It belongs to Him, as do all its members. All the elements of the commonwealth; legal commands and prohibitions, popular institutions, schools, marriage, home-life, the workshop, and the palace, all must be made to come to that fountain and imbibe the life that comes from Him. No one should fail to see that on this largely depends the civilization of nations, which is so eagerly sought, but which is nourished and augmented not so much by bodily comforts and conveniences, as by what belongs to the soul, viz., commendable lives and the cultivation of virtue.

Many are estranged from Jesus Chrst rather through ignorance than perversity; many study man and the universe around him with all earnestness, but very few study the Son of God. Let it be the first endeavor, then, to dispel ignorance by knowledge, so that He may not be despised or rejected as unknown. We call upon Christians everywhere to labor diligently to the utmost of their power to know their Redeemer. Any one who regards Him with a sincere and candid mind, will clearly perceive that nothing can be more salutary than His law, or more divine than His doctrine. In this, your authority and co-operation, Venerable Brethren, will marvellously assist, as will also the zeal and assiduity of the clergy at large. Think it the chief part of your duty to engrave in the hearts of your people the true knowledge, and, We might almost say the image, of Jesus Christ, and to illustrate in your letters, your discourses, your schools and colleges, your public assemblies, whenever occasion serves, His charity, His benefits and institutions. About the "rights of man," as they are called, the multitude has heard enough; it is time they should hear of the rights of God. That the present is a suitable time, is shown by the good impulses of many which have already, as We have said, been awakened, and in particular by the many evidences which have been given of piety towards the Redeemer, a piety which, if it please God, we shall hand down to the next century with the promise of a better age. But as the matter in hand is one in which success can only be looked for through divine grace, let us with a common impulse and with earnest prayers invoke the mercy of Almighty God, that He would not suffer those to perish whom He has freed by shedding His blood that He would graciously regard this age, which has, indeed, been grievously remiss, but has suffered much and bitterly, too, in expiation of its sins; and that He would, benignantly embracing all peoples and classes of men, remember the word which He spoke:

If I be lifted up from the earth, I will draw all things to Myself.[1]

In promise of divine gifts, and in witness of Our paternal benevolence, Venerable Brethren, We impart to your clergy and people most lovingly in the Lord Our Apostolic Benediction.

[1] John xii. 32.

CHRISTIAN DEMOCRACY.

Apostolic Letter Graves de Communi, January 18, 1901.

THE grave discussions on economical questions which for some time past have disturbed the peace of several countries of the world are growing in frequency and intensity to such a degree that the minds of thoughtful men are filled, and rightly so, with worry and alarm. These discussions take their rise in the bad philosophical and ethical teaching which is now widespread among the people. The changes also which the mechanical inventions of the age have introduced, the rapidity of communication between places and the devices of every kind for diminishing labor and increasing gain all add bitterness to the strife; and lastly matter have been brought to such a pass by the struggle between capital and labor, fomented as it is by professional agitators, that the countries where these disturbances most frequently occur, find themselves confronted with ruin and disaster.

At the very beginning of Our Pontificate We clearly pointed out what the peril was which confronted society on this head, and We deemed it Our duty to warn Catholics, in unmistakable language, how great the error was which was lurking in the utterances of socialism, and how great the danger was that threatened not only their temporal possessions, but also their morality and religion. That was the purpose of Our Encyclical Letter *Quod Apostolici Muneris* which We published on the 28th of December in the year 1878; but as these dangers day by day threat-

479

ened still greater disaster, both to individuals and the commonwealth, We strove with all the more energy to avert them. This was the object of Our Encyclical *Rerum Novarum* of the 15th May, 1891, in which We dwelt at length on the rights and duties which both classes of society—those namely, who control capital, and those who contribute labor—are bound in relation to each other; and at the same time, We made it evident that the remedies which are most useful to protect the cause of religion, and to terminate the contest between the different classes of society, were to be found in the precepts of the Gospel.

Nor, with God's grace, were Our hopes entirely frustrated. Even those who are not Catholics, moved by the power of truth, avowed that the Church must be credited with a watchful care over all classes of society, and especially those whom fortune had least favored. Catholics of course profited abundantly by these Letters, for they not only received encouragement and strength for the admirable enterprises in which they were engaged but also obtained the light which they desired, by the help of which they were able with greater safety and with more plentiful blessings to continue the efforts which they had been making in the matter of which We are now speaking. Hence it happened that the differences of opinion which prevailed among them were either removed or their acrimony diminished and the discussion laid aside. In the work which they had undertaken this was effected, viz.: that in their efforts for the elevation of the poorer classes, especially in those places where the trouble is greatest, many new enterprises were set on foot; those which were already established were increased and all reaped the blessing of a greater stability imparted to them. Some of these works were called *Bureaus of the People*, their object being to supply information. Rural savings banks had been established, and various associations, some for mutual aid, others, of relief were organized.

There were working men's societies and other enterprises for work or beneficence. Thus under the auspices of the Church, united action of Catholics was secured as well as wise discrimination exercised in the distribution of help for the poor who are often as badly dealt with by chicanery and exploitation of their necessities, as they are oppressed by indigence and toil. These schemes of popular benevolence were, at first, distinguished by no particular appellation. The name of *Christian Socialism* with its derivatives which was adopted by some was very properly allowed to fall into disuse. Afterwards some asked to have it called *The Popular Christian Movement*. In the countries most concerned with this matter, there are some who are known as *Christian Socialists*. Elsewhere the movement is described as *Christian Democracy*, and its partisans *Christian Democrats*, in contradistinction to those who are designated as *Socialists*, and whose system is known as *Social Democracy*. Not much exception is taken to the former, *i.e.*, *Christian Socialism*, but many excellent men find the term *Christian Democracy* objectionable. They hold it to be very ambiguous and for this reason open to two objections. It seems by implication to covertly favor popular government, and to disparage other methods of political administration. Secondly, it appears to belittle religion by restricting its scope to the care of the poor, as if the other sections of society were not of its concern. More than that, under the shadow of its name, there might easily lurk a design to attack all legitimate power either civil or sacred. Wherefore, since this discussion is now so widespread, so exaggerated and so bitter, the consciousness of duty warns Us to put a check on this controversy and to define what Catholics are to think on this matter. We also propose to describe how the movement may extend its scope and be made more useful to the commonwealth.

What *Social Democracy* is and what *Christian Democracy* ought to be, assuredly no one can doubt. The first, with due consideration to the greater or less intemperance of its utterance, is carried to such an excess by many as to maintain that there is really nothing existing above the natural order of things, and that the acquirement and enjoyment of corporal and external goods constitute man's happiness. It aims at putting all government in the hands of the people, reducing all ranks to the same level, abolishing all distinction of class, and finally introducing community of goods. Hence, the right of ownership is to be abrogated, and whatever property a man possesses, or whatever means of livelihood he has, is to be common to all.

As against this, *Christian Democracy,* by the fact that it is Christian, is built, and necessarily so, on the basic principles of divine faith, and provides for the betterment of the masses, with the ulterior object of availing itself of the occasion to fashion their minds for things which are everlasting. Hence, for *Christian Democracy* justice is sacred; it must maintain that the right of acquiring and possessing property cannot be impugned, and it must safeguard the various distinctions and degrees which are indispensable in every well-ordered commonwealth. Finally it must endeavor to preserve in every human society the form and the character which God ever impresses on it. It is clear, therefore, that there is nothing in common between *Social* and *Christian Democracy.* They differ from each other as much as the sect of Socialism differs from the profession of Christianity.

Moreover it would be a crime to distort this name of *Christian Democracy* to politics, for although democracy, both in its philological and philosophical significations, implies popular government, yet in its present application it is so to be employed that, removing from it all political significance, it is to mean nothing else than a benevolent and Christian movement in behalf of the people. For the laws of nature and of the Gospel, which by right are superior to all human contingencies, are necessarily independent of all modifications of civil government, while at the same time they are in concord with everything that is not repugnant to morality and justice. They are, therefore, and they must remain absolutely free from political parties, and have nothing to do with the various changes of administration which may occur in a nation; so that Catholics may and ought to be citizens according to the constitution of any State, guided as they are by those laws which command them to love God above all things, and their neighbors as themselves. This has always been the discipline of the Church. The Roman Pontiffs acted upon this principle, whenever they dealt with different countries, no matter what might be the character of their governments. Hence, the mind and the action of Catholics who are devoted to the amelioration of the working classes, can never be actuated with the purpose of favoring and introducing one government in place of another.

In the same manner, from *Christian Democracy*, We must remove another possible subject of reproach, namely: that while looking after the advantage of the working people they should act in such a manner as to forget the upper classes of society; for they also are of the greatest use in preserving and perfecting the commonwealth. As We have explained, the Christian law of charity will prevent Us from so doing. For it extends to all classes of society, and all should be treated as members of the same family, as children of the same heavenly Father, as redeemed by the same Saviour, and called to the same eternal heritage. Hence the doctrine of the Apostle who warns us that : "We are one body and one spirit called to the one hope in our vocation; one Lord, one Faith and one Baptism; one God and the Father of all who is above all, and through all, and in us all." Wherefore on account of the nature of the union which exists between the different classes of society and which Christian brotherhood makes still closer, it follows that no matter how great Our devotion may be in helping the people, We should all the more keep Our hold upon the upper classes, because association with them is proper and necessary, as We shall explain later on, for the happy issue of the work in which We are engaged.

Let there be no question of fostering under this name of *Christian Democracy* any intention of diminishing the spirit of obedience, or of withdrawing people from their lawful rulers. Both the natural and the Christian law command us to revere those who, in their various grades are above us in the State, and to submit ourselves to their just commands. It is quite in keeping with our dignity as men and Christians to obey, not only exteriorly but from the heart, as the Apostle expresses it, *for conscience, sake,* when he commands us to keep our soul subject to the higher powers. It is abhorrent to the profession of a Christian for any one to be unwilling to be subject and obedient to those who rule in the Church, and first of all to the bishops whom (without prejudice to the universal power of the Roman Pontiff) *the Holy Ghost has placed to rule the Church of God which Christ has purchased by His blood.*[1] He who thinks or acts otherwise is guilty of ignoring the grave precept of the Apostle who bids us to obey our rulers and to be subject to them, for they watch, having to give an account of our souls. Let the faithful everywhere implant these principles deep in their souls, and put them in practice in their daily life, and let the ministers of the Gospel meditate them profoundly, and incessantly labor not merely by exhortation but especially by example to make them enter into the souls of others.

We have recalled these matters which on other occasions We have made the subject of Our instructions, in the hope that all dissension about the name of *Christian Democracy* will cease and that all suspicion of any danger coming from what the name signifies will be put at rest. And with reason do We hope so; for neglecting the opinions

[1] Acts xx. 28.

of certain men, with regard to the power and the efficacy of this kind of *Christian Democracy,* which at times are exaggerated and are not free from error, let no one, however, condemn that zeal which, according to the natural and divine law, has this for its object, viz.: to make the condition of those who toil more tolerable; to enable them to obtain, little by little, those means by which they may provide for the future; to help them to practise in public and in private the duties which morality and religion inculcate; to aid them to feel that they are not animals but men, not heathens but Christians, and so to enable them to strive more zealously and more eagerly for the one thing which is necessary, viz.: that ultimate good for which we are all born into this world. This is the intention; this is the work of those who wish that the people should be animated by Christian sentiments and should be protected from the contamination of socialism which threatens them.

We have designedly made mention here of virtue and religion. For, it is the opinion of some, and the error is already very common, that the social question is merely an economic one, whereas in point of fact, it is above all a moral and religious matter, and for that reason must be settled by the principles of morality and according to the dictates of religion. For even though wages are doubled and the hours of labor are shortened and food is cheapened, yet if the working man hearkens to the doctrines that are taught on this subject, as he is prone to do, and is prompted by the examples set before him to throw off respect for God and to enter upon a life of immorality, his labors and his gain will avail him naught.

Trial and experience have made it abundantly clear that many a workman lives in cramped and miserable quarters, in spite of his shorter hours and larger wages, simply because he has cast aside the restraints of morality and religion. Take away the instinct which Christian virtue has planted and nurtured in men's hearts, take away prudence, temperance, frugality, patience, and other correct, natural habits, no matter how much he may strive, he will never achieve prosperity. That is the reason why We have incessantly exhorted Catholics to enter these associations for bettering the condition of the laboring classes, and to organize other undertakings with the same object in view; but We have likewise warned them that all this should be done under the auspices of religion, with its help and under its guidance.

The zeal of Catholics on behalf of the masses is especially noteworthy by the fact that it is engaged in the very field in which, under the benign inspiration of the Church, the active industry of charity has always labored, adapting itself in all cases to the varying exigencies of the times. For the law of mutual charity perfects, as it were, the law of justice, not merely by giving each man his due and in not impeding him in the exercise of his rights, but also by befriending him in case of need, "not with the word alone, or the lips, but in deed and in truth"; being mindful of what Christ so lovingly said to His own: "A new commandment I give unto you, that you love one another as I have loved you, that you love also one another. By this shall all men know that you are My disciples, if you have love one for the other." This zeal in coming to the rescue of Our fellow men should, of course, be solicitous, first for the imperishable good of the soul, but it must not neglect what is necessary and helpful for the body.

We should remember what Christ said to the disciples of the Baptist who asked him: "Art Thou He that art to come or look we for another?" He invoked, as the proof of the mission given to Him among men, His exercise of charity, quoting for them the text of Isaias: *The blind see, the lame walk, the lepers are cleansed, the deaf hear, the dead rise again, the poor have the Gospel preached to them.*[1] And speaking also of the Last Judgment and of the rewards and punishments He will assign, He de-

---

[1] Matt. xi. 5.

clared that He would take special account of the charity men exercised towards each other. And in that discourse there is one thing that especially excites our surprise, viz.: that Christ omits those works of mercy which comfort the soul and refers only to external works which, although done in behalf of men, He regards as being done to Himself. *For I was hungry and you gave Me to eat; I was thirsty and you gave Me to drink; I was a stranger and you took Me in; naked and you covered Me; sick and you visited Me; I was in prison and you came to Me.*[1]

To the teachings which enjoin the twofold charity of spiritual and corporal works, Christ adds His own example so that no one may fail to recognize the importance which He attaches to it. In the present instance we recall the sweet words that came from His paternal heart: *I have pity on the multitude,*[2] as well as the desire He had to assist them even if it were necessary to invoke His miraculous power. Of His tender compassion we have the proclamation made in Holy Writ, viz.: that *He went about doing good and healing all that were oppressed by the devil.*[3] This law of charity which He imposed upon His apostles, they in the most holy and zealous way put into practice; and after them those who embraced Christianity originated that wonderful variety of institutions for alleviating all the miseries by which mankind is afflicted. And these institutions carried on and continually increased their powers of relief and were the especial glories of Christianity and of the civilization of which it was the source, so that right-minded men never fail to admire those foundations, aware as they are of the proneness of men to concern themselves about their own and neglect the needs of others.

Nor are we to eliminate from the list of good works the giving of money for charity, in pursuance of what Christ has said: *But yet that which remaineth, give alms.*[4]

[1] Matt. xxv. 35.
[2] Mark vii. 2.
[3] Acts x. 38.
[4] Luke xi. 41.

Against this, the Socialist cries out and demands its abolition as injurious to the native dignity of man. But if it is done in the manner which the Scripture enjoins,[1] and in conformity with the true Christian spirit, it neither connotes pride in the giver nor inflicts shame upon the one who receives. Far from being dishonorable for man it draws closer the bonds of human society by augmenting the force of the obligation of the duties which men are under with regard to each other. No one is so rich that he does not need another's help; no one so poor as not to be useful in some way to his fellow man; and the disposition to ask assistance from others with confidence, and to grant it with kindness is part of our very nature. Thus justice and charity are so linked with each other, under the equable and sweet law of Christ, as to form an admirable cohesive power in human society and to lead all of its members to exercise a sort of providence in looking after their own and in seeking the common good as well.

As regards not merely the temporary aid given to the laboring classes, but the establishment of permanent institutions in their behalf, it is most commendable for charity to undertake them. It will thus see that more certain and more reliable means of assistance will be afforded to the necessitous. That kind of help is especially worthy of recognition which forms the minds of mechanics and laborers to thrift and foresight so that in course of time they may be able, in part at least to look out for themselves. To aim at that is not only to dignify the duty of the rich towards the poor, but to elevate the poor themselves; for while it urges them to work for a better degree of comfort in their manner of living, it preserves them meantime from danger by checking extravagance in their desires, and acts as a spur in the practise of the virtues proper to their state. Since, therefore, this is of such great avail and so much in keeping with the spirit

[1] Matt. vi. 2.

of the times, it is a worthy object for charity to undertake with all prudence and zeal.

Let it be understood, therefore, that this devotion of Catholics to comfort and elevate the mass of the people is in keeping with the spirit of the Church and is most conformable to the examples which the Church has always held up for imitation. It matters very little whether it goes under the name of *"The Popular Christian Movement,"* or *"Christian Democracy,"* if the instructions that have been given by Us be fully carried out with the submission that is due. But it is of the greatest importance that Catholics should be one in mind, will, and action in a matter of such great moment. And it is also of importance that the influence of these undertakings should be extended by the multiplication of men and means devoted to the same object.

Especially must there be appeals to the kindly assistance of those whose rank, worldly wealth, and culture give them importance in the community. If their help is excluded, scarcely anything can be done which will be of any assistance for the wants which now clamor for satisfaction in this matter of the well-being of the people. Assuredly the more earnestly many of those who are prominent in the State conspire effectively to attain that object the quicker and surer will the end be reached. We wish them to understand that they are not at all free to look after or neglect those who happen to be beneath them, but that it is a strict duty which binds them. For no one lives only for his personal advantage in a community; he lives for the common good as well, so that when others cannot contribute their share for the general object, those who can do so are obliged to make up the deficiency. The very extent of the benefits they have received increases the burden of their responsibility, and a stricter account will have to be rendered to God who bestowed those blessings upon them. What should also urge all to the fulfilment of their duty in this regard is the widespread disaster which will eventually fall upon all classes of society if this assistance does not arrive in time; and therefore is it that he who neglects the cause of the distressed poor is not doing his duty to himself or to the State.

If this social movement extends its scope far and wide in a true Christian fashion, and grows in its proper and genuine spirit, there will be no danger, as is feared, that those other institutions, which the piety of our ancestors have established and which are now flourishing, will decline or be absorbed by new foundations. Both of them spring from the same root of charity and religion, and not only do not conflict with each other, but can be made to coalesce and combine so perfectly as to provide by a union of their benevolent resources in a more efficacious manner against the graver perils and necessities of the people which confront us to-day.

The condition of things at present proclaims, and proclaims vehemently, that there is need for a union of brave minds with all the resources they can command. The harvest of misery is before Our eyes, and the dreadful projects of the most disastrous national upheavals are threatening Us from the growing power of the socialistic movement. They have insidiously worked their way into the very heart of the State, and in the darkness of their secret gatherings, and in the open light of day, in their writings and their harangues, they are urging the masses onward to sedition; they fling aside religious discipline, they scorn duties and clamor only for rights; they are working incessantly on the multitudes of the needy which daily grow greater, and which, because of their poverty, are easily deluded and hurried off into ways that are evil. It is equally the concern of the State and of religion, and all good men should deem it a sacred duty to preserve and guard both in the honor which is their due.

That this most desirable agreement of wills should be

maintained, it is essential that all refrain from giving any causes of dissension in hurting and alienating the minds of others. Hence in newspapers and in speeches to the people, let them avoid subtle and useless questions which are neither easy to solve nor to understand except by minds of unusual ability and only after the most serious study. It is quite natural for people to think differently in doubtful questions, but those who address themselves to these subjects in a proper spirit will preserve their mental calm and not forget the respect which is due to those who differ from them. If minds see things in another light it is not necessary to become alienated forthwith. To whatever opinion a man's judgment may incline, if the matter is yet open to discussion let him keep it, provided his mental attitude is such that he is ready to yield if the Holy See should otherwise decide.

This Catholic action, of whatever description it may be, will work with greater effect if all of the various associations, while preserving their individual rights, move together under one primary and directive force.

In Italy We desire that this directive force should emanate from the Catholic Congresses and Reunions so often praised by Us, to further which Our predecessor and We Ourselves have ordered that these meetings should be controlled and guided by the bishops of the country. So let it be for other nations, in case there be any leading organization of this description to which this matter has been legitimately entrusted.

Now in all questions of this sort where the interests of the Church and the Christian people are so closely allied, it is evident what they who are in the sacred ministry should do, and it is clear how industrious they should be in inculcating right doctrine and in teaching the duties of prudence and charity. To go out and move among the people, to exert a healthy influence on them by adapting themselves to the present condition of things is what more than once in addressing the clergy We have advised. More frequently also in writing to the bishops and other dignitaries of the Church, and especially of late (to the Minister General of the Minorites, November 25, 1898) We have lauded this affectionate solicitude for the people and declared it to be the especial duty of both the secular and regular clergy. But in the fulfilment of this obligation let there be the greatest caution and prudence exerted, and let it be done after the fashion of the saints. Francis, who was poor and humble, Vincent of Paul, the Father of the afflicted classes, and very many others whom the Church keeps ever in her memory, were wont to lavish their care upon the people, but in such wise as not to be engrossed overmuch or to be unmindful of themselves or to let it prevent them from laboring with the same assiduity in the perfection of their own soul and the cultivation of virtue.

There remains one thing upon which We desire to insist very strongly, in which not only the ministers of the Gospel, but also all those who are devoting themselves to the cause of the people, can with very little difficulty bring about a most commendable result. That is to inculcate in the minds of the people, in a brotherly way and whenever the opportunity presents itself, the following principles, viz.: to keep aloof on all occasions from seditious acts and seditious men; to guard inviolate the rights of others; to show a proper respect to superiors; to willingly perform the work in which they are employed; not to grow weary of the restraint of family life which in many ways is so advantageous; to keep to their religious practices above all, and in their hardships and trials to have recourse to the Church for consolation. In the furtherance of all this, it is very efficacious to propose the splendid example of the Holy Family of Nazareth, and to advise the invocation of its protection, and it also helps to remind the people of the examples of sanctity which have shone in the midst of poverty, and to hold up before them the reward that awaits them in the better life to come.

Finally, We recur again to what We have already declared and We insist upon it most solemnly, viz.: that whatever projects individuals or associations form in this matter should be done with due regard to Episcopal authority and absolutely under Episcopal guidance. Let them not be led astray by an excessive zeal in the cause of charity. If it leads them to be wanting in proper submission it is not a sincere zeal; it will not have any useful result and cannot be acceptable to God. God delights in the souls of those who put aside their own designs and obey the rulers of His Church as if they were obeying Him; He assists them even when they attempt difficult things and benignly leads them to their desired end. Let them show also examples of virtue, so as to prove that a Christian is a hater of idleness and indulgence, that he gives willingly from his goods for the help of others, and that he stands firm and unconquered in the midst of adversity. Examples of that kind have a power of moving people to dispositions of soul that make for salvation, and have all the greater force as the condition of those who give them is higher in the social scale.

We exhort you, Venerable Brethren, to provide for all this, as the necessities of men and of places may require, according to your prudence and your zeal, meeting as usual in council to combine with each other in your plans for the furtherance of these projects. Let your solicitude watch and let your authority be effective in controlling, compelling, and also in preventing, lest any one under the pretext of good should cause the vigor of sacred discipline to be relaxed or the order which Christ has established in His Church to be disturbed. Thus by the correct, concurrent, and ever-increasing labor of all Catholics, the truth will flash out more brilliantly than ever, viz.: that truth and true prosperity flourish especially among those peoples whom the Church controls and influences: and that she holds it as her sacred duty to admonish every one of what the law of God enjoins to unite the rich and the poor in the bonds of fraternal charity, and to lift up and strengthen men's souls in the times when adversity presses heavily upon them.

Let Our commands and Our wishes be confirmed by the words which are so full of apostolic charity which the blessed Paul addressed to the Romans: "I beseech you therefore brethren, be reformed in the newness of your mind; he that giveth, with simplicity; he that ruleth, with carefulness; he that showeth mercy with cheerfulness. Let love be without dissimulation—hating that which is evil; clinging to that which is good; loving one another with the charity of brotherhood; with honor preventing one another; in carefulness, not slothful; rejoicing in hope; patient in tribulation; instant in prayer. Communicating to the necessities of the saints. Pursuing hospitality. Rejoice with them that rejoice; weep with them that weep; being of one mind to one another; to no man rendering evil for evil; providing good things not only in the sight of God but also in the sight of men."

As a pledge of these benefits receive the Apostolic Benediction which, Venerable Brethren, We grant most lovingly in the Lord to you and your clergy and people.

THE RELIGIOUS CONGREGATIONS IN FRANCE.

I. *Letter from the Pope to the Archbishop of Paris, December 23, 1900.*

AMID the consolations afforded Us during the Holy Year by the pious eagerness of the pilgrims who have flocked to Rome from all parts of the world, We have been struck with sadness at the news of the dangers which threaten the religious congregations in France. By dint of misunderstanding and prejudice it has come to be thought that it will be necessary for the good of the State to put restraints upon their liberty, and perhaps to proceed against them with even greater rigor. The duty of Our supreme ministry, and the deep affection which We bear for France, lead Us to address you on this grave and important subject in the hope that, on being better enlightened, upright and fair-minded men will hark back to more equitable counsels. And in addressing you We address also Our Venerable Brethren—your colleagues in the French episcopate.

In the name of the heavy cares which you share with Us it is for you to dissipate the prejudice which exists among your countrymen, and to prevent, as far as possible, any irreparable misfortunes befalling the Church and France.

ORIGIN AND OBJECT.

The religious orders, as every one knows, have their origin and the reason of their existence in those sublime evangelical counsels which Our divine Redeemer gave to those who, in every succeeding age, would attain to

Christian perfection—to those brave and generous souls who by prayer and contemplation, by pious austerities and the observance of certain rules, endeavor to climb to the highest summits of the spiritual life. Born and cradled under the action of the Church, whose authority gives sanction to their government and administration, the religious orders form a chosen portion of the flock of Jesus Christ. They are, according to the expression of St. Chrysostom, "the honor and ornament of spiritual grace," whilst, at the same time, they are witnesses to the sacred fecundity of the Church.

Their vows, made freely and spontaneously, after ripening in the meditations of the novitiate, have ever been regarded and respected by people in every age as sacred things and the sources of the rarest virtue. Their object is twofold: first, the raising of those who take them to a higher degree of perfection; and secondly, by purifying and strengthening their souls, to prepare them for a ministry which is exercised for the everlasting salvation of their neighbor and for the alleviation of the numberless miseries of humanity. Thus, working under the supreme direction of the Apostolic See for the realization of the ideal of perfection traced by Our Lord, and living under rules which have nothing in contradiction of any form of civil government, the religious congregations co-operate on a large scale in the mission of the Church, which consists essentially in the sanctification of souls and in doing good to men.

This is why wherever the Church is in possession of her liberty, wherever the natural right of a citizen to choose the sort of life he considers best suited to his taste and his moral advancement is respected, there, too, the religious orders have arisen as a spontaneous product of Catholic soil, and the bishops have rightly regarded them as valuable auxiliaries in the sacred ministry and in works of Christian charity.

SERVICES TO CIVIL SOCIETY.

But it is not to the Church alone that the religious orders have from their first appearance rendered immense services: they have benefited also civil society itself. They have had the merit of preaching virtue to the multitude by the apostolate of good example, as well as by that of word of mouth, of forming and adorning men's minds by the teaching of sacred and profane knowledge, and of enlarging the heritage of the fine arts by splendid works that will live.

Whilst their doctors shed renown on the universities by the depth and breadth of their learning, and their houses became the refuge of divine and human knowledge, and in the shipwreck of civilization saved from certain destruction the masterpieces of ancient wisdom, other religious have penetrated inhospitable regions, swamps or tangled forests, and there, braving every danger in draining and clearing and cultivating the land by the sweat of their brow, they founded round their monasteries and beneath the shadow of the cross centres of population which grew into villages and flourishing towns, whence, under a kindly rule, agriculture and industry began to spread abroad.

When the small number of priests or the needs of the day demanded it, legions of apostles, eminent for their piety and learning, were seen issuing forth from the cloisters, who, by their valiant co-operation with the bishops, exerted the happiest influence on society, by putting an end to feuds, stifling enmity, bringing people back to the thought of duty, and by setting up again in honor the principles of religion and Christian civilization.

Such, briefly indicated, are the merits of the religious orders in the past. They have been registered by the hand of impartial history, and it is superfluous to dwell on them at any greater length. Nor is their activity, their zeal, or their love of their fellow men diminished in our own day. The good that they do strikes every eye, and their virtues shine with a brilliance which no accusation, no attack, can tarnish.

In this noble arena in which the religious congregations vie with each other in beneficent activity, those of France, We say it again with joy, occupy a foremost and honorable place. Some devoted to teaching instruct the young in secular knowledge and the principles of religious virtue and duty, upon which public peace and the welfare of States absolutely depend. Others, consecrated to various works of charity, afford effective aid to every physical and moral misery in the numberless houses wherein they tend the sick, the infirm and the aged, the orphan, the deranged, and the incurable, without allowing the danger or unpleasantness of their work or the ingratitude they may meet with to dampen their courage or check their ardor. These meritorious services, recognized again and again by men above any suspicion of favoritism, and time after time, rewarded by public honors, make these congregations the glory of the Church at large, and the particular and shining glory of France, which they have ever nobly served, and which they love, as We have many times seen, with a patriotism that feared not to face death itself with joy.

The disappearance of these champions of Christian charity would, it is evident, bring on the country an irreparable loss. By the drying up of such an abundant source of voluntary aid, public misery would be notably increased and, at the same time, an eloquent preaching of brotherhood and concord would be silenced. A society in which so many elements of trouble and enmity are fermenting needs assuredly great examples of self-sacrifice, love, and disinterestedness. And what is better fitted to raise and pacify men's minds than the sight of these men and woman, who, giving up a happy, distinguished and, oftentimes, an illustrious position, voluntarily make themselves the brothers and sisters of the children of the people, practising in their regard true equality by utterly devoting themselves to the disinherited, the abandoned, and the suffering?

So admirable is the activity of the French congregations that it could not be kept within the frontiers of the country, but has gone forth to carry the Gospel to the ends of the earth, and with the Gospel the name, the language, and the prestige of France. Exiles of their own free will, the French missionaries go out across stormy sea and sandy desert seeking to gain souls for Christ in the most distant and often unexplored regions. They are seen settling amongst savage tribes in order to civilize them by teaching the elements of Christianity, the love of God and their neighbors, work, regard for the weak, and cleanly living; and they devote themselves to this without looking for any earthly reward even till death, which is often hastened by fatigue, the difficulties of the Church, or the sword of the executioner. Respecting the laws and submissive to the civil authorities, they bring with them, wherever they come, civilization and peace; their only ambition is to enlighten the less fortunate people to whom they devote themselves, and to lead them to Christian morality, and to a knowledge of their dignity as men. Nor is it an uncommon thing for them to make important contribution to science by the help they give to the researches which are being made in such different domains as the study of the differences of race and tongue, of history, the nature and products of the soil, and other questions.

It is, moreover, precisely upon the laborious, patient, and tireless action of these admirable missionaries that the Protectorate of France is founded, which government after government has always been jealous to preserve, and which We Ourselves have publicly acknowledged. The inviolable attachment of the French missionaries to their country, the eminent services which they render her, the great influence which they secure for her especially in the East, all these are facts recognized by men of the most varied opinions, and only lately solemnly proclaimed by the voice of the highest authority.

Under these circumstances, to deprive the religious congregations at home of the freedom and peace which alone can ensure the recruiting of their members and the long and laborious task of their training would not only be to requite so many great services with inexplicable ingratitude, but would also, at the same time, be a clear renunciation of the benefits that flow from them. Other nations have already had sorry experience of such a policy. After having checked the expansion of the religious congregations at home, and so gradually dried up their seed they have seen their own influence and prestige abroad proportionally decline; for it is useless to seek fruit of a tree from which you lop the branches.

It is easy to see that all the great interests at stake in this question would be seriously compromised, even if the missionary orders were spared that the others might be struck, for careful consideration shows that the existence and action of the one are bound up with the existence and action of the others. As a matter of fact the vocation of the missionary religious germinates and develops under the word of the preacher religious, under the pious direction of the teaching religious and even under the supernatural influence of the contemplative religious. One can imagine, too, the difficult situation in which the missionaries would be placed, and the decline of their authority and prestige which would follow on the people whom they are seeking to evangelize, learning that the religious congregations, far from meeting with protection and respect in their own country, were there treated with hostility and harshness.

But, looking at the question from a higher standpoint, we may point out that the religious congregations, as We have already said, represent the public practice of Christian perfection; and, if it be certain that there are in the Church, and always will be, elect souls aspiring to it under the influence of grace, it would be unjust to hinder their designs. It would, moreover, be an assault on the liberty of the Church which is in France guaranteed by a solemn treaty, for everything that hinders her from leading souls to perfection injures the free exercise of her divine mission.

To strike at the religious orders would be to deprive the Church of devoted co-operators: at home where they are the necessary auxiliaries of the bishops and clergy in the exercise of the sacred ministry and the function of Catholic teaching and preaching which the Church has the right and the duty of dispensing, and which is demanded by the conscience of the faithful; and abroad where the general interests of the apostolate and its chief power in all parts of the world are for the greater part represented by the French congregations. The blow which struck them would be felt everywhere, and the Holy See, bound by a divine command to provide for the spread of the Gospel, would find itself under the necessity of offering no opposition to the occupation of the vacancies left by French missionaries by the missionaries of other nations.

Lastly, We should point out that to strike the religious congregations would be to forsake to one's own undoing those democratic principles of liberty and equality which form the very foundation of constitutional right in France and guarantee the individual and collective liberty of every citizen so long as his actions and manner of living have an honest aim which in no way injures the rights and legitimate interests of any one.

Now, in a State of such advanced civilization as that of France, We refuse to think that there is neither protection nor respect for a class of citizens who are honest, peaceable, and devoted to their country, who, possessing all the rights and fulfilling all the duties of their fellow countrymen, have, either in the vows they make or the life they lead, no other end in view but to work for the perfection of their own souls and the good of their neighbor. They only ask for liberty, and the measures taken against them would appear to be all the more unjust and odious since societies of quite another sort receive at the same time a treatment altogether different.

Of course We are not unaware that as a justification for these rigors there are people who go about declaring that the religious congregations encroach upon the jurisdiction of the bishops and interfere with the rights of the secular clergy. This assertion cannot be sustained if one cares to consult the wise laws published on this point by the Church, and which We have recently reenacted. In perfect harmony with the decrees and spirit of the Council of Trent they regulate on the one hand the conditions of existence of persons vowed to the practise of the evangelical counsels and to the apostolate, and on the other they respect as far as is necessary the authority of the bishops in their respective dioceses. Whilst they safeguard the dependence due to the head of the Church, they also in a majority of cases give to the bishop supreme authority over the congregations by way of delegation apostolic. As for the attempt to make out that the episcopate and clergy of France are disposed to give a favorable welcome to the ostracism with which it is desired to strike the religious orders, it is an insult which the bishops and priests can only repel with all the energy of their priestly soul.

There is no need to give any more importance to the other reproach that is made against the congregations, of being too rich. Even if we admit that the value set upon their property is not exaggerated there is no contesting that they are in honorable and legal possession, and consequently to despoil them would be an attack upon the rights of property. It is, moreover, necessary to remark that they possess nothing for their personal

interest or for the good of their individual members, but
for works of religion, charity, and beneficence, which
turn to the profit of the French nation at home and abroad,
whither they go to increase its prestige by contributing
to the mission of civilization which Providence has entrusted to it.

Passing over in silence other considerations which
are made on the subject of the religious congregations,
We confine Ourselves to this important remark: France
maintains amicable relations with the Holy See founded
upon a solemn treaty. If then, the inconveniences indicated have upon given points any reality the way is
open to bring them to the notice of the Holy See, which
is ready to make them the subject of a serious investigation, and if need be to apply suitable remedies. We
desire, however, to reckon upon the equitable impartiality
of the men who guide the destinies of France and upon
the fairmindedness and good sense which distinguish the
French people. We feel confident that they will not wish
to lose the precious moral and social heritage of which
the religious congregations are the representatives; that
they have no desire, in seeking to secure general liberty
by laws of exception, to wound the feelings of Catholics,
and to aggravate to its own great detriment their country's
internal discords. A nation is truly great and strong,
and can regard the future with any assurance of security,
only if its people are closely united in working for the
common good in full regard for the rights of all, and with
consciences free and undisturbed. From the beginning
of Our Pontificate We have never omitted to make any
effort to further this work of pacification in France which
would have brought her incalculable benefits, not only in
the religious, but also in the civil and political order.
Undeterred by any difficulties, We have not ceased to
give France particular proofs of Our respect, solicitude,
and affection, always feeling sure that she would respond
to them as a great and generous nation should.

We should be overwhelmed with the deepest sorrow if, in the evening of Our days, We should discover that We had been deceived in these hopes, deprived of the price of Our fatherly solicitude, and condemned to watch in the country which We love a rancorous struggle between party passions, with no power to know how far their excesses would extend or to ward off the misfortunes which We have done all We could to prevent, and for which We decline, in advance, to be held in any way responsible.

In any case the duty which is at present incumbent on the French bishops is to labor in perfect harmony of thought and action to prevail upon the people to save the rights and interests of the religious congregations, which We love with all Our fatherly heart, and whose existence, liberty, and prosperity concern the Catholic Church, France, and humanity.

May the Lord vouchsafe to hear Our ardent prayers and to grant success to the efforts which We have now for so long made in this noble cause. And as a token of Our benevolence and of divine favors We grant you, dear Son, and to the whole episcopate, clergy, and people of France, the Apostolic Benediction.

II. *Letter of His Holiness Leo XIII., June* 29, 1901, *to the Superiors of the Religious Orders and Institutes in France.*

At all times the religious families have received from the Apostolic See particular assurance of loving and considerate solicitude, whether they were in the enjoyment of the benefits of peace, or, as in our days, undergoing such trials as those which now assail them. The onslaught which, in certain countries, has been recently made against the orders and the institutes subject to your authority, cause Us the profoundest grief, and holy Church is bowed down in sorrow because of it, for it feels itself cut to the quick in its own inherent rights, and seriously impeded in the fulfilment of its work which, for its proper exercise, requires the concurrence of both clergies, secular and religious. In truth, who touches its priests touches the apple of its eye. For Our part, you know that We have endeavored, by all the means in Our power, to prevent this unworthy persecution, and have striven to avert from those countries the consequent disasters which will be as great as they are undeserved. Hence it is that on many occasions, in the name of religion, of justice, and of civilization, We have pleaded your cause with all the power at Our command; but We have hoped in vain that Our remonstrances would be listened to; for, lo! a nation which was singularly fruitful in religious vocations, a nation on which We have always bestowed the greatest consideration, has, by the authority of its government, approved and promulgated these unjust and discriminating laws, against which, a few months ago, We had lifted Our voice in the hope of preventing their being put upon the statutes.

Remembering Our sacred duties, and following the example of Our illustrious predecessors, We have put the seal of condemnation on these laws as being contrary to that natural and evangelical right which is conferred by constant tradition; the right, namely, to form associations for the purpose of leading lives which are not only honest in themselves but marked by exalted sanctity: We have condemned them because they are contrary to that unquestionable right which the Church possesses of founding religious institutions exclusively subject to its authority to aid it in the accomplishment of its divine mission; especially when, in this instance, the exercise of that right has resulted in the greatest benefits in the religious and civil order and redounded to the advantage of that noble nation itself.

And now We feel moved to open to you Our paternal heart in the desire to give you, and to receive from you some holy consolation and, at the same time, to address to you the advice which the occasion calls for, in order that remaining still more firm in the time of trial you will gain greater merit in the sight of God and men.

Among the many motives of courage which spring from our faith, recall, dear Sons, that solemn word of Jesus Christ: *Blessed are ye when they shall revile and persecute you, and speak all that is evil against you untruly for My sake.*[1] Reproaches, calumnies, vexations of all kinds will be poured out upon you for My sake, but then shall you be blessed. It is in vain to multiply against you those calumnious accusations which seek to dishonor you. The sad reality is flashed only the more vividly on men's eyes, that the true reason for which you are persecuted is that deep-seated hatred which the world cherishes against the Catholic Church, the City of God; that the real intention is, if possible, to nullify in society the reparative action of Jesus Christ from which such beneficent and salutary results universally flow. No one is ignorant of the fact that the religious of both sexes form a chosen body in the City of God; that they represent particularly the spirit and the mortifications of Jesus Christ; that by the practice of the Evangelical Counsels they tend to carry Christian virtue to the summit of perfection and that, in a multitude of ways, they powerfully second the action of the Church. Hence it is not astonishing that to-day, as in other times, under other iniquitous forms, the City of the World rises against them, and chiefly those men who, by a sacrilegious compact, are most intimately united and most servilely bound to him who is Prince of this world.

It is clear that they consider the dissolution and extinction of religious orders as a successful manœuvre in the furthering of their deep-laid designs of driving the Catholic nations into the ways of apostasy and alienation from Jesus Christ, and because of that, We may say

[1] Matt. v. 11.

in all truth: *Blessed are you because you are hated and persecuted.* It is only because you have chosen your kind of life out of love for Jesus Christ.

If you followed the maxims and the ways of the world, the world would not trouble you, but would shower its favors upon you. *"If you had been of the world, the world would love its own";* but because you are walking in opposite ways you are assailed and warred against. It is because the world hates you. Christ Himself foretold it. Hence He regards you with all the more love and predilection as He sees you more like Himself in your suffering for justice' sake. But if you partake of the suffering of Christ, rejoice. Aspire to the courage of those heroes *who went from the presence of the Council rejoicing that they were accounted worthy to suffer reproach for the name of Jesus.*[1] To this glory which comes from the testimony of your conscience, there is added, though you do not seek it, the blessing of all honest men. All those who have at heart the peace and prosperity of their country are aware that there are no more honorable citizens, no more useful men, no more devoted patriots than the members of religious congregations, and they tremble at the thought of losing in you so many precious advantages which depend upon your existence. There are the throngs of the poor, the abandoned and the unfortunate for whose sake you have founded and sustained every variety of establishment with supreme intelligence and admirable charity. There are the fathers of families who have entrusted their sons to you, and who, until the present moment, relied upon you to impart that moral and religious education which is strong, vigorous, and fruitful in solid virtue, and which was never more needed than in our time. There are the priests who find in you valuable auxiliaries in their important and laborious ministry. There are the men of all ranks who, in these times of apostasy, find useful direction and encouragement in

[1] Acts v. 41.

your advice, backed as it is by the integrity of your lives. There are, above all, the bishops who honor you with their confidence, and who consider you as tried teachers of their younger clergy, and who recognize in you the true friends of their brothers and their people, offering as you do for them to the divine mercy your incessant prayers and expiatory sacrifices.

But no one appreciates the exceptional merits of religious orders with greater justice than We Ourselves who, from this Apostolic See, are watching over the needs of the universal Church.

Already, in other acts, We have made particular mention of all this. Let it suffice now, to call attention to that splendid ardor with which these religious bodies follow, not only the directions, but the least expression of wish of the Vicar of Jesus Christ; undertaking every work which may contribute to the advantage of the Church and society whenever He indicates it; hurrying to the most inhospitable shores; braving every suffering and accepting death itself, as many have done in the most glorious manner in the recent upheavals of the empire of China.

If, among the dearest remembrances of Our long Pontificate, We count the fact that by Our authority We have raised a great number of the servants of God to the honors of the altar, those remembrances are all the more dear to Us because the majority of those saints belong to religious orders, either as founders or as simple religious.

We, moreover, wish to recall for your consolation, that among people of the world, distinguished by their position, and by their knowledge of what society needs there have not been lacking many honorable and upright men who have come forward to praise your works, to defend your inviolable right as citizens, and your still more inviolable liberty as Catholics. Surely, one must be blinded by passion not to see that it is unwise and dishonorable to crush those who, hoping for nothing and asking for nothing, give themselves up entirely to the service of their fellow men. Let it be considered with what zeal these religious apply themselves to develop among the children of the people those germs of natural goodness which, without them, would perish and leave these little ones to grow up a danger to themselves and to others. These religious have, with the help of grace, cultivated patiently and assiduously these precious seeds, have preserved them from destruction and have succeeded in bringing them to maturity. Under their influence they developed a splendid fruitage of intelligent love for truth, of honesty, a sense of duty, of strength, of character, and of generosity in sacrifice. And what is there better calculated than all this for the order and prosperity of the State? Nevertheless, dear Sons, since the hatred of the world pursues you so far as to pretend that it is a useful and praiseworthy work to trample under foot in your persons the most sacred rights and that in so doing, a service is done to God, adore with a trusting humility the designs of the Almighty in permitting this. If, at times, He suffers right to succumb to violence He does so only for the purpose of some greater good; but remember that He often comes to Our rescue in unforseen ways when We suffer for Him and trust in Him.

If He places obstacles and obstructions in the path of those whose state is that of Christian perfection, it is in order to test and fortify their virtue, and it is, more particularly, to strengthen and reinvigorate their souls which might else have grown feeble in protracted peace.

Endeavor, therefore, to correspond to those paternal designs of Almighty God. Give yourselves up with redoubled ardor to a life of prayer and faith and holy works; make regular discipline reign among you; let a brotherly union of hearts prevail among you, with humble and eager obedience, austerity and detachment and a pious ardor for the glory of God. Let your thoughts be always high, your resolutions generous and your zeal indefatigable for the glory of God and the extension of His kingdom. Since by the misfortune of the times, you find yourselves either already struck or threatened by the fatal laws of dispersion you must recognize that these very circumstances impose upon you the duty of defending with more zeal than ever the integrity of your religious spirit against the contamination of the world and of holding yourselves ever ready and ever armed against all attacks.

On this point you will recall the different instructions which have been addressed to Regulars by the Apostolic See, and these other prescriptions which have emanated from your own superiors. Let both one and the other keep their full vigor and be most conscientiously observed. And now, religious of every age, young and old, lift your eyes to your illustrious founders. Their maxims speak to you, their statutes guide you; their examples are before your eyes. Let your sweetest and holiest desires be to hear them, to follow them, to imitate them. It is thus that multitudes of your ancestors have acted in times of trial; it is thus they have transmitted to you a rich heritage of sublime courage and virtue. Long to make yourselves worthy of your sires and of your brethren in order that you may be able, all of you, to say, while justly glorifying yourselves, *We are the sons and brothers of the saints.* It is thus that you will obtain the greatest advantage for yourselves, for the Church, and for society. By spurring yourselves onward to reach that degree of sanctity to which God has called you, you will fulfil the designs of Providence in your regard and you will merit the abundant recompense which He has promised you. The Church—your tender mother—who has heaped favors upon you, will obtain, in return for it all, a more faithful and more efficacious coöperation than ever in its mission of peace and salvation. Peace and salvation; they are the two urgent needs of society at the present time, which so many causes tend to corrupt and degrade.

To arouse it and to bring it repentant to the feet of the merciful Saviour we must have men of superior virtue, of living eloquence, of apostolic hearts and men who possess, at the same time, the power of drawing abundant graces from heaven. You will be such men, We doubt not, and you will thus become the most opportune and the most glorious benefactors of society.

Dear sons, the charity of the Lord inspires a last word to strengthen in you the sentiments with which you are animated towards those who attack your institutes and who wish to destroy your liberty. Just as your conscience prompts you to keep a firm and dignified attitude, so by your profession, you must always show yourselves sweet and indulgent; because it is especially in the religious that the perfection of that true charity should be resplendent, revealing itself, as always open to pity, and ever incapable of harboring hate. Without doubt, to see yourselves rewarded with ingratitude and thrust aside by those you have benefited would naturally cause bitterness of heart; but, dear Sons, let your faith, and what it tells you give you comfort. Bear in mind the sublime exhortation, *Overcome evil by good.* That faith places before your eyes the incomparable magnanimity of the Apostle. *We are reviled and we bless; we are persecuted and we suffer it; we are blasphemed and we entreat.*[1] Above all, it invites you to repeat the supplication of the supreme benefactor of the human race, Jesus Christ, suspended on His cross: *Father, forgive them.* Therefore, dear Sons, strengthen yourselves in the Lord. You have with you the Vicar of Jesus Christ; you have with you the whole Catholic world, which regards you with affection, respect, and gratitude. Your glorious founders and your glorious brothers encourage you. Your Sovereign Chief, Jesus Christ, girds you with His strength and covers you with the mantle of His virtue.

Well-beloved Sons, turn to the divine Heart with a

[1] 1 Cor. iv. 12, 13.

fervent confidence, and fervent prayers. You will find there all the strength necessary to conquer the fear of the world. There is one word which rings through the centuries, always living and always full of consolation. *Have confidence, I have conquered the world.*

May you find, besides, some consolation in Our blessing which on this day, consecrated to the triumphant memory of the apostles, We are happy to accord you in all its plenitude; to each one of you, to all of you, and to each one of your families who are most true to Us in the Lord.

CONGRATULATIONS TO THE AMERICAN HIERARCHY.

Pope Leo's Letter Addressed to Cardinal Gibbons and the American Bishops, April 15, 1902.

CERTAINLY We have reason to rejoice, and the Catholic world, on account of its reverence for the Apostolic See, has reason to rejoice at the extraordinary fact that We are to be reckoned as the third in the long line of Roman Pontiffs to whom it has been happily given to enter upon the twenty-fifth year of the Supreme Priesthood. But in this circle of congratulations, while the voices of all are welcome to Us, that of the Bishops and faithful of the United States of North America brings Us special joy, both on account of the conditions which give your country prominence over many others, and of the special love we entertain for you.

You have been pleased, beloved Son and Venerable Brothers, in your joint letter to Us to mention in detail what, prompted by love for you, We have done for your churches during the course of Our Pontificate. We, on the other hand, are glad to call to mind the many different ways in which you have ministered to Our consolation throughout this period. If We found pleasure in the state of things which prevailed among you when We first entered upon the charge of the Supreme Apostolate, now that We have advanced beyond twenty-four years in the same charge, We are constrained to confess that Our first pleasure has never been diminished, but, on the contrary, has increased from day to day by reason of the increase of Catholicity among you. The cause of this increase, although first of all to be attributed to the providence of God, must also be ascribed to your energy and activity. You have, in your prudent policy, promoted every kind of Catholic organization with such wisdom as to provide for all necessities and all contingencies, in harmony with the remarkable character of the people of your country.

Your chief praise is that you have promoted and sedulously continue to foster the union of your churches with this chief of churches and with the Vicar of Christ on earth. Herein, as you rightly confess, is the apex and centre of government, of teaching and of the priesthood; the source of that unity which Christ destined for His Church, and which is one of the most striking notes distinguishing it from all human sects. As We have never failed to exercise with advantage this most salutary office of teaching and government in every nation, so We have never permitted that you or your people should suffer the lack of it. For We have gladly availed Ourselves of every opportunity to testify the constancy of Our solicitude for you and for the interests of religion among you. And Our daily experience obliges Us to confess that We have found your people, through your influence, endowed with perfect docility of mind and alacrity of disposition. Therefore, while the changes and tendencies of nearly all the nations which were Catholic for many centuries give cause for sorrow, the state of your churches, in their flourishing youthfulness, cheers Our heart and fills it with delight. True, you are shown no special favor by the law of the land, but on the other hand your lawgivers are certainly entitled to praise for the fact that they do nothing to restrain you in your just liberty. You must, therefore, and with you the Catholic host behind, make strenuous use of the favorable time for action which is now at your disposal by spreading abroad as far as possible the light of truth against the errors and absurd imaginings of the sects that are springing up.

We are not unaware, Venerable Brothers, of all that has been done by every one of you for the establishment and the success of schools and academies for the proper education of children. By your zeal in this respect you have clearly acted in conformity with the exhortations of the Apostolic See and the prescriptions of the Council of Baltimore. Your magnificent work on behalf of the ecclesiastical seminaries has assuredly been calculated to increase the prospects of good to be done by the clergy and to add to their dignity. Nor is this all. You have wisely taken measures to enlighten dissidents and to draw them to the truth by appointing learned and worthy members of the clergy to go about from district to district to address them in public in familiar style in churches and other buildings, and to solve the difficulties that may be advanced. An excellent plan, and one which We know has already borne abundant fruit. Nor has your charity been unmindful of the sad lot of the negro and the Indian— you have sent them teachers, helped them liberally, and you are most zealously providing for their eternal salvation. We are glad to add a stimulus, if such be necessary, to enable you to continue these undertakings with full confidence that your work is worthy of commendation.

Finally, not to omit the expression of Our gratitude, We would have you know what satisfaction you have caused Us by the liberality with which your people are endeavoring to contribute by their offerings to relieve the penury of the Holy See. Many indeed and great are the necessities for which the Vicar of Christ as supreme Pastor and Father of the Church is bound to provide in order to avert evil and to promote the faith. Hence your generosity becomes an exercise and a testimony of your faith.

For all these reasons We wish to declare to you again

and again Our affection for you.   Let the Apostolic blessing, which We bestow most lovingly in the Lord upon you
all and upon the flocks entrusted to each one of you, be
taken as a token of this affection and an augury of divine
gifts.

THE MOST HOLY EUCHARIST.

Encyclical Letter Miræ Caritatis, May 28, 1902.

To examine into the nature and to promote the effects of those manifestations of His wondrous love which, like rays of light, stream forth from Jesus Christ—this, as befits Our sacred office, has ever been, and this, with His help to the last breath of Our life, will ever be Our earnest aim and endeavor. For, whereas Our lot has been cast in an age that is bitterly hostile to justice and truth, We have not failed, as you have been reminded by the apostolic letter which We recently addressed to you, to do what in Us lay, by Our instructions and admonitions, and by such practical measures as seemed best suited for their purpose, to dissipate the contagion of error in its many shapes, and to strengthen the sinews of the Christian life. Among these efforts of Ours there are two in particular, of recent memory, closely related to each other, from the recollection whereof We gather some fruit of comfort, the more seasonable by reason of the many causes of sorrow that weigh Us down. One of these is the occasion on which We directed, as a thing most desirable, that the entire human race should be consecrated by a special act to the Sacred Heart of Christ our Redeemer; the other that on which We so urgently exhorted all those who bear the name Christian to cling loyally to Him who, by divine ordinance, is "the Way, the Truth, and the Life," not for individuals alone but for every rightly constituted society. And now that same apostolic charity, ever watchful over the vicissitudes of the Church, moves and in a manner compels Us to add one thing more, in order to fill up the measure of what We have already conceived and carried out. This is, to commend to all Christians, more earnestly than heretofore, the all-holy Eucharist, forasmuch as it is a divine gift proceeding from the very Heart of the Redeemer, who "with desire desireth" this singular mode of union with men, a gift most admirably adapted to be the means whereby the salutary fruits of His redemption may be distributed. Indeed We have not failed in the past, more than once, to use Our authority and to exercise Our zeal in this behalf. It gives Us much pleasure to recall to mind that We have officially approved and enriched with canonical privileges not a few institutions and confraternities having for their object the perpetual adoration of the Sacred Host; that We have encouraged the holding of Eucharistic Congresses, the results of which have been as profitable as the attendance at them has been numerous and distinguished; that We have designated as the heavenly patron of these and similar undertakings St. Paschal Baylon, whose devotion to the mystery of the Eucharist was so extraordinary.

Accordingly, Venerable Brethren, it has seemed good to Us to address you on certain points connected with this same mystery, for the defence and honor of which the solicitude of the Church has been so constantly engaged, for which martyrs have given their lives, which has afforded to men of the highest genius a theme to be illustrated by their learning, their eloquence, their skill in all the arts; and this We will do in order to render more clearly evident and more widely known those special characteristics by virtue of which it is so singularly adapted to the needs of these our times. It was towards the close of His mortal life that Christ our Lord left this memorial of His measureless love for men, this powerful means of support *for the life of the world*.[1] And precisely for this reason, We, being so soon to depart from this

[1] John vi. 52.

life, can wish for nothing better than that it may be granted to Us to stir up and foster in the hearts of all men the dispositions of mindful gratitude and due devotion towards this wonderful Sacrament, wherein most especially lie, as We hold, the hope and the efficient cause of salvation and of that peace which all men so anxiously seek.

Some there are, no doubt, who will express their surprise that for the manifold troubles and grievous afflictions by which our age is harassed We should have determined to seek for remedies and redress in this quarter rather than elsewhere, and in some, perchance, Our words will excite a certain peevish disgust. But this is only the natural result of pride; for when this vice has taken possession of the heart, it is inevitable that Christian faith, which demands a most willing docility, should languish, and that a murky darkness in regard of divine truths should close in upon the mind; so that in the case of many these words should be made good: *whatever things they know not, they blaspheme.*[1] We, however, so far from being hereby turned aside from the design which We have taken in hand, are on the contrary determined all the more zealously and diligently to hold up the light for the guidance of the well-disposed, and, with the help of the united prayers of the faithful, earnestly to implore forgiveness for those who speak evil of holy things.

To know with an entire faith what is the excellence of the Most Holy Eucharist is in truth to know what that work is which, in the might of His mercy, God, made man, carried out on behalf of the human race. For as a right faith teaches us to acknowledge and to worship Christ as the sovereign cause of our salvation, since He by His wisdom, His laws, His ordinances, His example, and by the shedding of His blood, made all things new; so the same faith likewise teaches us to acknowledge Him and to worship Him as really present in the Eucharist, as verily abiding through all time in the midst of men, in

[1] Jude 10.

order that their Master, their Good Shepherd, their most acceptable Advocate with the Father, He may impart to them of His own inexhaustible abundance the benefits of that redemption which He has accomplished. Now if any one will seriously consider the benefits which flow from the Eucharist he will understand that conspicuous and chief among them all is that in which the rest, without exception, are included; in a word, it is for men the source of life, of that life which best deserves the name. *The bread which I will give is My flesh, for the life of the world.*[1] In more than one way, as We have elsewhere declared, is Christ *the life.* He Himself declared that the reason of His advent among men was this, that He might bring them the assured fulness of a more than merely human life. *I am come that they may have life, and may have it more abundantly.*[2] Every one is aware that no sooner had *the goodness and kindness of God our Saviour appeared*[3] than there at once burst forth a certain creative force which issued in a new order of things and pulsed through all the veins of society, civil and domestic. Hence arose new relations between man and man; new rights and new duties, public and private; henceforth a new direction was given to government, to education, to the arts; and most important of all, man's thoughts and energies were turned towards religious truth and the pursuit of holiness. Thus was life communicated to man, a life truly heavenly and divine. And thus we are to account for those expressions which so often occur in Holy Writ: *The tree of life, the word of life, the book of life, the crown of life,* and particularly *the bread of life.*

But now, since this life of which We are speaking bears a definite resemblance to the natural life of man, as the one draws its nourishment and strength from food, so also the other must have its own food whereby it may be

---

[1] John vi. 52.   [2] John x. 10.
[3] Tit. iii. 4.

sustained and augmented. And here it will be opportune
to recall to mind on what occasion and in what manner
Christ moved and prepared the hearts of men for the
worthy and due reception of the living bread which He
was about to give them. No sooner had the rumor spread
of the miracle which He had wrought on the shores of
the lake of Tiberias, when with the multiplied loaves He
fed the multitude, than many forthwith flocked to Him in
the hope that they, too, perchance, might be the recipients
of a like favor. And, just as He had taken occasion from
the water which she had drawn from the well to stir up in
the Samaritan woman a thirst for that *water which spring-
eth up unto life everlasting,*[1] so now Jesus availed Himself
of this opportunity to excite in the minds of the multitude a keen hunger for the bread *which endureth unto
life everlasting.*[2] Nor, as He was careful to explain to
them, was the bread which He promised the same as
that heavenly manna which had been given to their fathers
during their wanderings in the desert, or again the same
as that which, to their amazement, they had recently
received from Him; but He was Himself that bread: *I*, said
He, *am the bread of life.*[3] And He urges this still further
upon them all both by invitation and by precept: *If any
man shall eat of this bread, he shall live forever; and the
bread which I will give is My flesh, for the life of the world.*[4]
And in these other words He brings home to them the
gravity of the precept: *Amen, amen, I say to you, unless
you shall eat the flesh of the Son of man and drink His
blood, you shall not have life in you.*[5] Away then with
the widespread but most mischievous error of those who
give it as their opinion that the reception of the Eucharist
is in a manner reserved for those narrow-minded persons
(as they are deemed) who rid themselves of the cares of
the world in order to find rest in some kind of professedly

[1] John iv. 14.
[2] John vi. 27.
[3] John vi. 48.
[4] John vi. 52.
[5] John vi. 54.

religious life. For this gift, than which nothing can be more excellent or more conductive to salvation, is offered to all those, whatever their office or dignity may be, who wish—as every one ought to wish—to foster in themselves that life of divine grace whose goal is the attainment of the life of blessedness with God.

Indeed it is greatly to be desired that those men would rightly esteem and would make due provision for life everlasting whose industry or talents or rank have put it in their power to shape the course of human events. But, alas! we see with sorrow that such men too often proudly flatter themselves that they have conferred upon this world, as it were, a fresh lease of life and prosperity, inasmuch as by their own energetic action they are urging it on to the race for wealth, to a struggle for the possession of commodities which minister to the love of comfort and display. And yet, whithersoever we turn, we see that human society, if it be estranged from God, instead of enjoying that peace in its possessions for which it had sought, is shaken and tossed like one who is in the agony and heat of fever; for while it anxiously strives for prosperity, and trusts to it alone, it is pursuing an object that ever escapes it, clinging to one that ever eludes the grasp. For as men and states alike necessarily have their being from God, so they can do nothing good except in God through Jesus Christ, through whom every best and choicest gift has ever proceeded and proceeds. But the source and chief of all these gifts is the venerable Eucharist, which not only nourishes and sustains that life the desire whereof demands our most strenuous efforts, but also enhances beyond measure that dignity of man of which in these days we hear so much. For what can be more honorable or a more worthy object of desire than to be made, as far as possible, sharers and partakers in the divine nature? Now this is precisely what Christ does for us in the Eucharist, wherein, after having raised man by the operation of His grace to a supernatural state,

He yet more closely associates and unites him with Himself. For there is this difference between the food of the body and that of the soul, that whereas the former is changed into our substance, the latter changes us into its own; so that St. Augustine makes Christ Himself say: "You shall not change Me into yourself as you do the food of your body, but you shall be changed into Me." [1]

Moreover, in the most admirable Sacrament, which is the chief means whereby men are engrafted on the divine nature, men also find the most efficacious help towards progress in every kind of virtue. And first of all in faith. In all ages faith has been attacked; for although it elevates the human mind by bestowing on it the knowledge of the highest truths, yet because, while it makes known the existence of divine mysteries, it yet leaves in obscurity the mode of their being, it is therefore thought to degrade the intellect. But whereas in past times particular articles of faith have been made by turns the object of attack, the seat of war has since been enlarged and extended, until it has come to this, that men deny altogether that there is anything above and beyond nature. Now nothing can be better adapted to promote a renewal of the strength and fervor of faith in the human mind than the mystery of the Eucharist, the "mystery of faith,". as it has been most appropriately called. For in this one mystery the entire supernatural order, with all its wealth and variety of wonders, is in a manner summed up and contained: *He hath made a remembrance of His wonderful works, a merciful and gracious Lord; He hath given food to them that fear Him.* [2] For whereas God has subordinated the whole supernatural order to the Incarnation of His Word, in virtue whereof salvation has been restored to the human race, according to those words of the Apostle: *He hath purposed . . . to re-establish all things in Christ, that are in heaven and on earth, in Him.* [3]

[1] Confessions l. vii., c. x.   [2] Psalm cx. 4, 5.
[3] Eph. i. 9, 10.

The Eucharist, according to the testimony of the holy Fathers, should be regarded as in a manner a continuation and extension of the Incarnation. For in and by it the substance of the Incarnate Word is united with individual men, and the supreme Sacrifice offered on Calvary is in a wondrous manner renewed, as was signified beforehand by Malachy in the words: *In every place there is sacrifice, and there is offered to My name a pure oblation.*[1] And this miracle, itself the very greatest of its kind, is accompanied by innumerable other miracles; for here all the laws of nature are suspended; the whole substance of the bread and wine are changed into the body and the blood; the species of bread and wine are sustained by the divine power without the support of any underlying substance; the body of Christ is present in many places at the same time, that is to say, wherever the Sacrament is consecrated. And in order that human reason may the more willingly pay its homage to this great mystery, there have not been wanting, as an aid to faith, certain prodigies wrought in His honor, both in ancient times and in our own, of which in more than one place there exist public and notable records and memorials. It is plain that by this Sacrament faith is fed, in it the mind finds its nourishment, the objections of rationalists are brought to naught, and abundant light is thrown on the supernatural order.

But that decay of faith in divine things of which We have spoken is the effect not only of pride, but also of moral corruption. For if it is true that a strict morality improves the quickness of man's intellectual powers, and if on the other hand, as the maxims of pagan philosophy and the admonitions of divine wisdom combine to teach us, the keenness of the mind is blunted by bodily pleasures, how much more, in the region of revealed truths, do these same pleasures obscure the light of faith, or even, by the just judgment of God, entirely extinguish

[1] Mal. i. 11.

it. For these pleasures, at the present day, an insatiable appetite rages, infecting all classes as with an infectious disease, even from tender years. Yet even for so terrible an evil there is a remedy close at hand in the divine Eucharist. For in the first place it puts a check on lust by increasing charity, according to the words of St. Augustine, who says, speaking of charity: "As it grows, lust diminishes; when it reaches perfection, lust is no more." [1] Moreover the most chaste flesh of Jesus keeps down the rebellion of our flesh, as St. Cyril of Alexandria taught, "For Christ abiding in us lulls to sleep the law of the flesh which rages in our members." [2] Then, too, the special and most pleasant fruit of the Eucharist is that which is signified in the words of the prophet: *What is the good thing of Him,* that is, of Christ, *and what is His beautiful thing, but the corn of the elect and the wine that engendereth virgins,*[3] producing, in other words, that flower and fruitage of a strong and constant purpose of virginity which, even in an age enervated by luxury, is daily multiplied and spread abroad in the Catholic Church, with those advantages to religion and to human society, wherever it is found, which are plain to see.

To this it must be added that by this same Sacrament our hope of everlasting blessedness, based on our trust in the divine assistance, is wonderfully strengthened. For the edge of that longing for happiness which is so deeply rooted in the hearts of all men from their birth is whetted even more and more by the experience of the deceitfulness of earthly goods, by the unjust violence of wicked men, and by all those other afflictions to which mind and body are subject. Now the venerable Sacrament of the Eucharist is both the source and the pledge of blessedness and of glory, and this, not for the soul alone, but for the body also. For it enriches the soul

---

[1] De diversis quæstionibus, lxxxiii. q. 36.
[2] Lib. iv., c. ii., in Joan. vi. 57.
[3] Zach. ix. 17.

with an abundance of heavenly blessings, and fills it with a sweet joy which far surpasses man's hope and expectations; it sustains him in adversity, strengthens him in the spiritual combat, preserves him for life everlasting, and as a special provision for the journey accompanies him thither. And in the frail and perishable body that divine Host, which is the immortal body of Christ, implants a principle of resurrection, a seed of immortality, which one day must germinate. That to this source man's soul and body will be indebted for both these boons has been the constant teaching of the Church, which has dutifully reaffirmed the affirmation of Christ: *He that eateth My flesh and drinketh My blood hath everlasting life; and I will raise him up at the last day.*[1]

In connection with this matter it is of importance to consider that in the Eucharist, seeing that it is instituted by Christ as "a perpetual memorial of His passion,"[2] is proclaimed to the Christian the necessity of a salutary self-chastisement. For Jesus said to those first priests of His: *Do this in memory of Me;*[3] that is to say, do this for the commemoration of My pains, My sorrows, My grievous afflictions, My death upon the cross. Wherefore this Sacrament is at the same time a sacrifice, seasonable throughout the entire period of our penance; and it is likewise a standing exhortation to all manner of toil, and a solemn and severe rebuke to those carnal pleasures which some are not ashamed so highly to praise and extol: *As often as ye shall eat this bread, and drink this chalice, ye shall announce the death of the Lord, until He come.*[4]

Furthermore, if any one will diligently examine into the causes of the evils of our day, he will find that they arise from this, that as charity towards God has grown cold, the mutual charity of men among themselves has likewise

---

[1] John vi. 55.
[2] Opusc. lvii. Offic. de festo Corporis Christi.
[3] Luke xxii. 18.
[4] 1 Cor. xi. 26.

cooled. Men have forgotten that they are children of God and brethren in Jesus Christ; they care for nothing except their own individual interests; the interests and the rights of others they not only make light of, but often attack and invade.

Hence frequent disturbances and strifes between class and class: arrogance, oppression, fraud on the part of the more powerful: misery, envy, and turbulence among the poor. These are evils for which it is in vain to seek a remedy in legislation, in threats of penalties to be incurred, or in any other device of merely human prudence. Our chief care and endeavor ought to be, according to the admonitions which We have more than once given at considerable length, to secure the union of classes in a mutual interchange of dutiful services, a union which, having its origin in God, shall issue in deeds that reflect the true spirit of Jesus Christ and a genuine charity. This charity Christ brought into the world, with it He would have all hearts on fire. For it alone is capable of affording to soul and body alike, even in this life, a foretaste of blessedness; since it restrains man's inordinate self-love, and puts a check on avarice, which *is the root of all evil.*[1] And whereas it is right to uphold all the claims of justice as between the various classes of society, nevertheless it is only with the efficacious aid of charity, which tempers justice, that the *equality* which St. Paul commended,[2] and which is so salutary for human society, can be established and maintained. This then is what Christ intended when He instituted this venerable Sacrament, namely, by awakening charity towards God to promote mutual charity among men. For the latter, as is plain, is by its very nature rooted in the former, and springs from it by a kind of spontaneous growth. Nor is it possible that there should be any lack of charity among men, or rather it must needs be enkindled and

---

[1] 1 Tim. vi. 10.   [2] 2 Cor. viii. 14.

flourish, if men would but ponder well the charity which Christ has shown in this Sacrament. For in it He has not only given a splendid manifestation of His power and wisdom, but "has in a manner poured out the riches of His divine love towards men."[1] Having before our eyes this noble example set us by Christ, who bestows on us all that He has, assuredly we ought to love and help one another to the utmost, being daily more closely united by the strong bond of brotherhood. Add to this that the outward and visible elements of this Sacrament supply a singularly appropriate stimulus to union. On this topic St. Cyprian writes: "In a word the Lord's sacrifice symbolizes the oneness of heart, guaranteed by a persevering and inviolable charity, which should prevail among Christians. For when Our Lord calls His body bread, a substance which is kneaded together out of many grains, He indicates that we His people, whom He sustains, are bound together in close union; and when He speaks of His blood as wine, in which the juice pressed from many clusters of grapes is mingled in one fluid, He likewise indicates that we His flock are by the commingling of a multitude of persons made one."[2] In like manner the Angelic Doctor, adopting the sentiments of St. Augustine,[3] writes: "Our Lord has bequeathed to us His body and blood under the form of substances in which a multitude of things have been reduced to unity, for one of them, namely bread, consisting as it does of many grains is yet one, and the other, that is to say wine, has its unity of being from the confluent juice of many grapes; and therefore St. Augustine elsewhere says: 'O Sacrament of mercy, O sign of unity, O bond of charity!'"[4] All of which is confirmed by the declaration of the Council of Trent that Christ left the

---

[1] Conc. Trid., Sess. XIII. De Euch. c. ii.
[2] Ep. 96 ad Magnum n. 5 (al. 6).
[3] Tract. xxvi. in Joan. nn. 13, 17.
[4] Summ. Theol. P. III., q. lxxix., a. 1.

Eucharist in His Church "as a symbol of that unity and charity whereby He would have all Christians mutually joined and united . . . a symbol of that one body of which He is Himself the head, and to which He would have us, as members, attached by the closest bonds of faith, hope, and charity."[1] The same idea had been expressed by St. Paul when he wrote: *For we, being many, are one bread, one body, all we who partake of the one bread.*[2] Very beautiful and joyful too is the spectacle of Christian brotherhood and social equality which is afforded when men of all conditions, gentle and simple, rich and poor, learned and unlearned, gather round the holy altar, all sharing alike in this heavenly banquet. And if in the records of the Church it is deservedly reckoned to the special credit of its first ages that *the multitude of the believers had but one heart and one soul,*[3] there can be no shadow of doubt that this immense blessing was due to their frequent meetings at the divine table; for we find it recorded of them: *They were persevering in the doctrine of the apostles and in the communion of the breaking of bread.*[4]

Besides all this, the grace of mutual charity among the living, which derives from the Sacrament of the Eucharist so great an increase of strength, is further extended by virtue of the sacrifice to all those who are numbered in the communion of saints. For the communion of saints, as every one knows, is nothing but the mutual communication of help, expiation, prayers, blessings, among all the faithful, who, whether they have already attained to the heavenly country, or are detained in the purgatorial fire, or are yet exiles here on earth, all enjoy the common franchise of that city whereof Christ is the head, and the consti-

[1] Conc. Trid., Sess. XIII., De Euchar., c. ii.
[2] 1 Cor. x. 17.
[3] Acts iv. 32.
[4] Acts ii. 42.

tution is charity.   For faith teaches us, that although the
venerable Sacrifice may be lawfully offered to God alone,
yet it may be celebrated in honor of the saints reigning
in heaven with God who has crowned them, in order
that we may gain for ourselves their patronage.   And it
may also be offered—in accordance with an apostolic
tradition—for the purpose of expiating the sins of those
of the brethren who, having died in the Lord, have not
yet fully paid the penalty of their transgressions.

That genuine charity, therefore, which knows how to do
and to suffer all things for the salvation and the benefit
of all, leaps forth with all the heat and energy of a flame
from that Most Holy Eucharist in which Christ Himself
is present and lives, in which He indulges to the utmost
His love towards us, and under the impulse of that divine
love ceaselessly renews His Sacrifice.   And thus it is
not difficult to see whence the arduous labors of apostolic
men, and whence those innumerable designs of every kind
for the welfare of the human race which have been set
on foot among Catholics, derive their origin, their strength,
their permanence, their success.

These few words on a subject so vast will, We doubt
not, prove most helpful to the Christian flock, if you in
your zeal, Venerable Brethren, will cause them to be expounded and enforced as time and occasion may serve.
But indeed a Sacrament so great and so rich in all manner
of blessings can never be extolled as it deserves by human
eloquence, nor adequately venerated by the worship of
man.   This Sacrament, whether as the theme of devout
meditation, or as the object of public adoration, or best
of all as a food to be received in the utmost purity of
conscience, is to be regarded as the centre towards which
the spiritual life of a Christian in all its ambit gravitates;
for all other forms of devotion, whatsoever they may be,
lead up to it, and in it find their point of rest.   In this
mystery more than in any other that gracious invitation
and still more gracious promise of Christ is realized and

finds its daily fulfilment: *Come to Me, all ye that labor and are heavily burdened, and I will refresh you.*[1]

In a word this Sacrament is, as it were, the very soul of the Church; and to it the grace of the priesthood is ordered and directed in all its fulness and in each of its successive grades. From the same source the Church draws and has all her strength, all her glory, her every supernatural endowment and adornment, every good thing that is hers; wherefore she makes it the chiefest of all her cares to prepare the hearts of the faithful for an intimate union with Christ through the Sacrament of His body and blood, and to draw them thereto. And to this end she strives to promote the veneration of this august mystery by surrounding it with holy ceremonies. To this ceaseless and ever watchful care of the Church our mother, our attention is drawn by that exhortation which was uttered by the holy Council of Trent, and which is so much to the purpose that for the benefit of the Christian people We here reproduce it in its entirety. "The Holy Synod admonishes, exhorts, asks and implores by the tender mercy of Our God, that all and each of those who bear the name of Christian should at last unite and find peace in this sign of unity, in this bond of charity, in this symbol of concord; and that, mindful of the great majesty and singular love of Jesus Christ our Lord, who gave His precious life as the price of our salvation, and His flesh for our food, they should believe and revere these sacred mysteries of His body and blood with such constancy of unwavering faith, with such interior devotion and worshipful piety, that they may be in condition to receive frequently that supersubstantial bread, and that it may be to them the life of their souls and keep their mind in soundness of faith; so that strengthened with its strength they may be enabled after the journey of this sorrowful pilgrimage to reach the heavenly country, there to see

[1] Matt. xi. 28.

and feed upon that bread of angels which here they eat under the sacramental veils." [1]

History bears witness that the virtues of the Christian life have flourished best wherever and whenever the frequent reception of the Eucharist has most prevailed. And on the other hand it is no less certain that in days when men have ceased to care for this heavenly bread, and have lost their appetite for it, the practice of Christian religion has gradually lost its force and vigor. And indeed it was as a needful measure of precaution against a complete falling away that Innocent III., in the Council of the Lateran, most strictly enjoined that no Christian should abstain from receiving the communion of the Lord's body at least in the solemn paschal season. But it is clear that this precept was imposed with regret, and only as a last resource; for it has always been the desire of the Church that at every Mass some of the faithful should be present and should communicate. "The Holy Synod would wish that in every celebration of the Mass some of the faithful should take part, not only by devoutly assisting thereat, but also by the sacramental reception of the Eucharist, in order that they might more abundantly partake of the fruits of this holy Sacrifice." [2]

Most abundant, assuredly, are the salutary benefits which are stored up in this most venerable mystery, regarded as a Sacrifice; a Sacrifice which the Church is accordingly wont to offer daily "for the salvation of the whole world." And it is fitting, indeed in this age it is specially important, that by means of the united efforts of the devout, the outward honor and the inward reverence paid to this Sacrifice should be alike increased. Accordingly it is Our wish that its manifold excellence may be both more widely known and more attentively considered.

There are certain general principles the truth of which

[1] Conc. Trid., Sess. XXII , c. vi.
[2] Conc. Trid., Sess. XIII. de Euchar. c. viii.

can be plainly perceived by the light of reason; for instance, that the dominion of God our Creator and Preserver over all men, whether in their private or in their public life, is supreme and absolute; that our whole being and all that we possess, whether individually or as members of society, comes from the divine bounty; that we on our part are bound to show to God, as Our Lord, the highest reverence, and, as He is our greatest benefactor, the deepest gratitude. But how many are there who at the present day acknowledge and discharge these duties with full and exact observance? In no age has the spirit of contumacy and an attitude of defiance towards God been more prevalent than in our own; an age in which that unholy cry of the enemies of Christ: *We will not have this man to rule over us,*[1] makes itself more and more loudly heard, together with the utterance of that wicked purpose: *Let us make away with Him;*[2] nor is there any motive by which many are hurried on with more passionate fury, than the desire utterly to banish God not only from the civil government, but from every form of human society. And although men do not everywhere proceed to this extremity of criminal madness, it is a lamentable thing that so many are sunk in oblivion of the divine Majesty and of His favors, and in particular of the salvation wrought for us by Christ. Now a remedy must be found for this wickedness on the one hand, and this sloth on the other, in a general increase among the faithful of fervent devotion towards the Eucharistic Sacrifice, than which nothing can give greater honor, nothing be more pleasing, to God. For it is a divine Victim which is here immolated; and accordingly through this Victim we offer to the Most Blessed Trinity all that honor which the infinite dignity of the Godhead demands; infinite in value and infinitely acceptable is the gift which we present to the Father in His only-begotten Son; so that for His benefits to us we

[1] Luke xix. 14. [2] Jer. xi. 11.

not only signify our gratitude, but actually make an adequate return.

Moreover there is another twofold fruit which we may and must derive from this great sacrifice. The heart is saddened when it considers what a flood of wickedness, the result—as We have said—of forgetfulness and contempt of the divine Majesty, has inundated the world. It is not too much to say that a great part of the human race seems to be calling down upon itself the anger of heaven; though indeed the crop of evils which has grown up here on earth is already ripening to a just judgment. Here then is a motive whereby the faithful may be stirred to a devout and earnest endeavor to appease God the avenger of sin, and to win from Him the help which is so needful in these calamitous times. And they should see that such blessings are to be sought principally by means of this Sacrifice. For it is only in virtue of the death which Christ suffered that man can satisfy, and that most abundantly, the demands of God's justice, and can obtain the plenteous gifts of His clemency. And Christ has willed that the whole virtue of His death, alike for expiation and impetration, should abide in the Eucharist, which is no mere empty commemoration thereof, but a true and wonderful, though bloodless and mystical, renewal of it.

To conclude, We gladly acknowledge that it has been a cause of no small joy to Us that during these last years a renewal of love and devotion towards the Sacrament of the Eucharist has, as it seems, begun to show itself in the hearts of the faithful; a fact which encourages Us to hope for better times and a more favorable state of affairs. Many and varied, as We said at the commencement, are the expedients which an inventive piety has devised; and worthy of special mention are the Confraternities instituted either with the object of carrying out the Eucharistic ritual with greater splendor, or for the perpetual adoration of the venerable Sacrament by day and night, or for the purpose of making reparation for the blasphemies and insults of which it is the object. But neither We nor you, Venerable Brethren, can allow ourselves to rest satisfied with what has hitherto been done; for there remain many things which must be further developed or begun anew, to the end that this most divine of gifts, this greatest of mysteries, may be better understood and more worthily honored and revered, even by those who already take their part in the religious services of the Church. Wherefore, works of this kind which have been already set on foot must be ever more zealously promoted; old undertakings must be revived wherever perchance they may have fallen into decay; for instance, Confraternities of the Holy Eucharist, intercessory prayers before the Blessed Sacrament exposed for the veneration of the faithful, solemn processions, devout visits to God's tabernacle, and other holy and salutary practices of the same kind; nothing must be omitted which a prudent piety may suggest as suitable. But the chief aim of Our efforts must be that the frequent reception of the Eucharist may be everywhere revived among Catholic peoples. For this is the lesson which is taught us by the example, already referred to, of the primitive Church, by the decrees of Councils, by the authority of the Fathers and of holy men in all ages. For the soul, like the body, needs frequent nourishment; and the Holy Eucharist provides that food which is best adapted to the support of its life. Accordingly all hostile prejudices, those vain fears to which so many yield, and their specious excuses from abstaining from the Eucharist, must be resolutely put aside; for there is question here of a gift than which none other can be more serviceable to the faithful people, either for the redeeming of them from the tyranny of anxious cares concerning perishable things, or for the renewal of the Christian spirit and perseverance therein. To this end the exhortations and example of all those who occupy a prominent position will powerfully contribute, but most especially the resourceful and diligent zeal of the clergy. For priests, to whom Christ our Redeemer entrusted the office of consecrating and dispensing the mystery of His body and blood, can assuredly make no better return for the honor which has been conferred upon them, than by promoting with all their might the glory of His Eucharist, and by inviting and drawing the hearts of men to the health-giving springs of this great Sacrament and Sacrifice, seconding hereby the longings of His Most Sacred Heart.

May God grant that thus, in accordance with Our earnest desire, the excellent fruits of the Eucharist may daily manifest themselves in greater abundance, to the happy increase of faith, hope, and charity, and of all Christian virtues; and may this turn to the recovery and advantage of the whole body politic; and may the wisdom of God's most provident charity, who instituted this mystery for all time "for the life of the world," shine forth with an ever brighter light.

Encouraged by such hopes as these, Venerable Brethren, We, as a presage of the divine liberality and as a pledge of Our own charity, most lovingly bestow on each of you, and on the clergy and flock committed to the care of each, Our Apostolic Benediction.

THE HOLY SCRIPTURES; THE BIBLICAL COMMISSION.

Apostolical Letter Vigilantiœ, October 30, 1902.

FAITHFUL to the tradition of watchfulness and zeal by which We, first of all, because of Our office, are bound to preserve the deposit of faith safe and inviolate, We gave to the world in the year 1893 the Encyclical *Providentissimus.* In it We included, after due examination, a number of questions concerning the study of Holy Scripture. The grandeur and extreme utility of the subject impelled Us, in effect, to determine, as far as in Us lay, the directive principle of those studies so necessary now that the increase of erudition confronts us every day with the consideration of novel questions which are sometimes in danger of being treated in a manner fraught with rashness.

Wherefore, We have warned all Catholics, and especially those in Holy Orders, of the work which each one should undertake in this matter in accordance with the abilities with which he is endowed, and We applied Ourselves with the greatest care to show how and in what manner these studies should be developed in conformity with the needs of our epoch. This document has not been without result, and it is with joy that We recall the testimonies of submission which the bishops and a great number of men eminent in science hastened to give Us while proclaiming at the same time the opportuneness and the importance of what We had written; and promising to conform with the greatest diligence to Our instructions. Another remembrance no less agreeable comes to Us in the fact that excellent beginnings were immediately made by some in the direction indicated, and an enthusiasm awakened in various places in the prosecution of such studies.   Nevertheless, We remark that the causes which prompted Us to publish the previous Letter are still persistent and more serious.   It is therefore necessary to insist more emphatically on what has already been enjoined and more than ever to express Our desire that Our Venerable Brethren of the episcopate should watch with the greatest vigilance over these studies.   To ensure greater facility as well as fruitfulness, We have resolved to add new strength to Our authority in this matter.   As the task now before Us of explaining these divine books and maintaining them intact is too difficult for Our Catholic interpreters to acquit themselves well of, if left to their individual efforts, and because the work is nevertheless so necessary on account of the manifold developments of science and the appearance of such multitudinous error, it is deemed proper that a federation of energies should be made, and that assistance should be afforded under the auspices and direction of the Apostolic See.   This result, it appears to Us, can be easily attained if we make use in the present instance of the means which We have already employed for advancing other studies.

Wherefore, it has seemed good to Us to institute a council or, as it is termed, a commission of men of learning whose duty shall be to effect that in every possible manner the divine text will find here and from every quarter the most thorough interpretation which is demanded by our times, and be shielded not only from every breath of error, but also from every temerarious opinion. It is proper that the principal seat of this commission should be in Rome, under the very eyes of the Sovereign Pontiff.   As it is the seat of the mistress and guardian of Christian knowledge, it should also be the centre from which there should flow through the whole body of the

Christian commonwealth the pure and incorruptible teaching of this science which is now so indispensable. The men of whom this commission shall be composed, in order to satisfy fully the serious obligation which is laid upon them and which confers on them such distinction, should regard as peculiarly and especially their own the tasks which are here proposed to their zeal.

In the first place, having established exactly what is the actual intellectual trend of the present day with regard to this science, they should bear in mind that none of the recent discoveries which the human mind has made is foreign to the purpose of their work. On the contrary, let them make haste in any case where our times have discovered something useful in the matter of biblical exegesis to avail themselves of it forthwith and by their writings to put it at the service of all.

Wherefore they should devote themselves with the greatest care to the study of philology and kindred sciences and keep themselves abreast of the progress of the day. As it is generally on this point that the attacks on Holy Scripture are made, it is there that we should likewise gather our arms of defence; so that there may be no inequality in the struggle between truth and error. Likewise they shall take measures that the knowledge of the ancient and oriental languages, and above all the art of deciphering the ancient texts, should be assiduously cultivated. Both of these branches are, as a matter of fact, a precious help in biblical studies.

In what concerns the integral safeguarding of the authority of the Scriptures, the members of the commission will employ an active vigilance and unremitting assiduity. The main point to be attained is that Catholics should not admit the malignant principle of granting more than is due to the opinion of heterodox writers, and of thinking that the true understanding of the Scriptures should be sought first of all in the researches which the erudition of unbelievers has arrived at. Indeed, no Catholic can consider as subject to doubt these truths which We have elsewhere referred to at greater length, and they must know that God has not delivered the Scriptures to the private judgment of the learned, but has confided the interpretation of them to the teaching of the Church. "In the matter of faith and morals which pertain to the teaching of Christian doctrine, the sense of Holy Scripture, which must be considered as the true sense, is that which has been adopted and is adopted by our holy mother, the Church, whose office it is to judge of the real meaning and interpretation of Holy Scriptures. It is therefore not permitted to any one to interpret the Holy Scripture in any way contrary to this sense, or even in any way contrary to the universal opinion of the Fathers."[1] As We were saying, the nature of the divine books is such that in order to dissipate the religious obscurity with which they are shrouded we must never count on the laws of hermeneutics, but must address ourselves to the Church which has been given by God to mankind as a guide and mistress. In brief, the legitimate sense of the divine Scriptures is not to be found outside the Church, nor can it be pronounced by those who have repudiated her teaching and authority. The men who are to compose this commission should therefore watch with great care to safeguard these principles and to keep them, as time goes on, with still greater strictness. And if certain minds profess an exaggerated admiration for heterodox writers, they must be led by persuasion to follow and to obey more faithfully the direction of the Church.

Doubtless there may arise an occasion when the Catholic interpreter may find some assistance in authors outside of the Church, especially in matters of criticism, but here there is need of prudence and discernment. Let our doctors cultivate with care the science of criticism, for it is of great utility in order to grasp in its complete sense the

[1] Conc. Vatic. sess. iii., cap. ii.

opinion of hagiographers; and in that they will receive Our warmest approbation. Let them draw from this science new resources by availing themselves even of the assistance of non-Catholic scholars. In doing so they need not fear Our disapprobation. They should, however, be careful not to draw from habitual association with such writers independence of judgment, for in point of fact the system which is known in our days as higher criticism frequently leads to such results. Its dangerous rashness We have more than once already condemned.

In the third place, it is of importance that this commission should consecrate its most special attention to that part of these studies which properly concerns the explanation of the Scriptures and which opens to the faithful a great source of spiritual profit. In whatever touches the texts whose sense has been fixed in an authentic manner, either by the sacred writers or by the Church, the commission, it is needless to say, should be convinced that only that interpretation can be adopted. Such is the rule of sound hermeneutics. But there exist numerous passages upon which the Church has not yet given any fixed or precise definition, with regard to which it is permitted to each doctor in his individual capacity to profess and to sustain the opinion which seems to him to be correct. They must know, however, that on these points they should keep as the rules of interpretation the analogy of faith and of Catholic doctrine. Moreover, we must be on our guard in this matter against transgressing, in the excessive ardor of debate, the limits of mutual charity. It is also of importance not to seem to discuss revealed truths and divine traditions. If they make light of intellectual concord, and if these principles are not safeguarded, we cannot have any right to expect that the divergent labors of such a great number of scholars will accomplish any notable progress in this science.

Hence this commission will have as its task to regulate in a legitimate and suitable manner the principal questions which are pending between Catholic doctors in order to arrive at a conclusion. To settle them the assembly will lend sometimes the light of its judgment, sometimes the weight of its authority. Their investigations will also have a result of the greatest advantage, namely, that of furnishing to the Holy See an opportune occasion to declare what ought to be inviolably maintained by Catholics, what ought to be reserved for more profound research, and what ought to be left to the free judgment of each.

Having, therefore, in view to ensure the maintenance of Catholic authority in its integrity, and to promote the studies which relate to Holy Scripture in conformity with the rules which have been herein laid down, We, by these present Letters, establish in this illustrious city a council or a special commission. We wish it to be composed of some cardinals of the Holy Roman Church who shall be chosen in virtue of Our authority. It is Our intention to add to them with the functions and titles of consultors taking part in the same studies and the same labors, as it is customary in the sacred Roman commissions, certain eminent men who belong to different nationalities, who are recommended by their knowledge in sacred studies, and above all, in whatever appertains to biblical science.

The commission will hold its fixed reunions and publish its writings, which will appear periodically or as need may require. If advice is asked of it, it will reply to those who consult it. In a word, it will labor by all means in its power to maintain and to develop the studies of which We speak. We desire that a report concerning all the questions which may be treated in common should be addressed to the Sovereign Pontiff by the consultor, to whom the commission will have confided the office of secretary.

In order to furnish members of the commission with available help, which will be of service to them in any of these studies, We herewith assign to them for this purpose a certain portion of Our Vatican Library. We shall take care that a numerous collection of manuscripts and volumes of every epoch which treat of biblical questions shall without delay be classified and placed at the disposition of the commissioners. It is very desirable that well-to-do Catholics should come to Our assistance to establish and enlarge this library in sending to Us resources to be employed for this end, or useful books, and in so doing they will render a service in a most fitting manner to Almighty God, who is the Author of Scriptures and of the Church.

Moreover, We have confidence that divine Providence will amply bless this undertaking, which has for its direct object the safeguarding of Christian faith and the eternal salvation of souls, and that Catholics who are devoted to the Holy Books will respond with an absolute and complete submission to the declarations of the Holy See on this point. We wish and We ordain that all and every one of these prescriptions and decisions which it has seemed good to Us to make and to formulate on this point shall be and shall remain ratified and confirmed in the manner which We have adopted and formulated, any clause to the contrary notwithstanding.

THE CHURCH IN THE PHILIPPINES.

THE broad stretch of islands bounded by the China Sea and the Pacific Ocean which Philip II., King of Spain, called the Philippines, were scarcely opened up by Ferdinand Magellan at the beginning of the sixteenth century when, with the image of the holy cross planted on their shores, they were consecrated to God and offered as a first-fruit offering of the Catholic religion.

From that time the Roman Pontiffs, with the aid of Charles V. and Philip his son, both remarkable for their zeal for spreading the faith, have thought nothing more urgent than to convert the islanders, who were idol-worshippers, to the faith of Christ. With God's help, by the strenuous efforts of the members of different religious orders, this came about very favorably and in such a short time that Gregory XIII. decided to appoint a bishop for the growing Church there, and constituted Manila an Episcopal See. With this happy beginning the growth which followed in after years corresponded in every way. Owing to the united measures of Our predecessors and of the Spanish kings, slavery was abolished, the inhabitants were trained in the ways of civilization by the study of arts and letters, so that the people and Church in the Philippines were deservedly distinguished by the renown of their nation and their meritorious zeal for religion. In this way, under the direction of the kings of Spain and the patronage of the Roman Pontiffs, Catholicity was maintained with due order in the Philippine Islands. But the change which the fortunes of war have wrought in civil matters there has affected religion also; for when the Spanish yoke was removed the patronage of the Spanish kings ceased, and as a result the Church attained to a larger share of liberty, ensuring for every one rights which are safe and unassailable.

To provide against the relaxation of ecclesiastical discipline in this new state of affairs, a plan of action and of organization had to be sought promptly and with great care. For this purpose We sent Our Venerable Brother Placide Louis Chapelle, Archbishop of New Orleans, as Our Delegate Extraordinary to the Philippine Islands, who, after examining in person and putting to rights whatever would not admit of delay or postponement, was then to report to Us. The duties thus imposed he has discharged faithfully in Our behalf, and deserves for this reason that We should bestow on him well-merited praise. Later it happened auspiciously that the Government of the United States of America undertook, by means of a special legation, to consider plans for a way of adjusting certain questions regarding Catholic interests in the Philippines. This enterprise We gladly encouraged, and by the skill and moderation of the negotiators a way has been opened for a settlement, which is to be effected on the ground itself. After hearing the opinions of some of the Holy Roman and Eminent Cardinals of the Sacred Congregation presiding over Extraordinary Affairs, We decree and declare in this Apostolical Constitution what has seemed, after long deliberation, to be most conducive for the interests of the Church in the Philippine Islands, trusting that what We, by Our supreme authority ordain, may, with the civil government righteously and favorably disposed, be zealously and piously observed.

First of all, therefore, it is Our intention and purpose to increase the sacred hierarchy. When the diocese of Manila had been created by Gregory XIII., as We have said, as the faithful rapidly increased in numbers, both by reason of the natives who embraced the Catholic religion and of the arrivals from Europe, Clement VIII.

decided to increase the number of bishops. He therefore elevated the Church in Manila to the dignity of an Archiepiscopate, making the Bishops of the three new dioceses he created, Cebu, Caceres, and Nueva Segovia, suffragans to it. To these was added later, in the year 1865, the Episcopal See of Jaro.

Now these dioceses are so vast that, owing to the distance by which the settlements are separated and the difficulties of travel, the bishops can scarcely visit them thoroughly without extreme labor. Wherefore it is necessary to avail Ourselves of the present opportunity to reduce the dioceses already established to narrower limits, and to form new ones. Hence, keeping the Archiepiscopal See of Manila, and the dioceses of Cebu, Caceres, Nueva Segovia, and Jaro, We add to them and create four new dioceses: Lipa, Tuguegarao, Capiz, and Zamboanga, all, like the others, suffragan to the Manilan Metropolis. Moreover, in the Marian Islands, We create a Prefecture Apostolic subject, without any intermediate authority, to Ourselves and to Our successors.

The Archbishop of Manila is the one who will bear the title of "Metropolitan" in the Philippine Islands; and all the other bishops, those who fill the old as well as those who are to occupy the newly created sees, will be subject to him, as suffragans both in rank and in name. The rights and the functions of the Metropolitan are laid down by the ecclesiastical laws already extant. As We wish that these laws be inviolably observed, so also do We wish that the bonds of holy friendship and charity between the Metropolitan and his suffragans be ever unimpaired, and grow always closer and more binding by mutual services, exchange of counsel, and especially by frequent episcopal conventions, so far as distance may permit. Concord is the mother and guardian of the greatest benefits.

The dignity and precedence of the Metropolitan Church require that it should be honored by a College of Canons.

The Delegate Apostolic will see and determine how to obtain in future the stipend for each of the canons, which hitherto was paid by the Spanish government. If, owing to the shrinkage of revenue, the number of canons cannot be maintained as heretofore, let it be reduced so as to consist of ten at least, and retain those who are canons by right of their office. The archbishop may by his own unrestricted right confer the aforementioned dignities, the canonry, and all the benefices which belong to the Metropolitan Church; except, indeed, those which either by common law are reserved to the Apostolic See, or are the gift of some other person, or are controlled by the conditions of the concursus. We earnestly desire to have colleges of canons formed in the other cathedral churches also. Until such time as this can be done, the bishops are to choose for consultors some priests, secular and religious, distinguished by their piety, learning, and experience in administration, as is done in other dioceses in which there is no canonical chapter. To provide for the proper dignity of the sacred ceremonies, the consultors, just mentioned, should attend the bishop when officiating. If for any reason they be prevented from so doing, the bishop will substitute others, worthy members of the clergy, both secular and religious.

Should it happen that any suffragan diocese, in which there is no canonical chapter, should lose its bishop, the Metropolitan will assume its administration; should there be none, the charge will fall to the nearest bishop, with the condition, however, that a vicar be chosen as soon as possible. Meanwhile the vicar-general of the deceased bishop will manage the diocese.

Since it is proved by experience that a native clergy is most useful everywhere, the bishops must make it their care to increase the number of native priests, in such a manner, however, as to form them thoroughly in piety and character, and to make sure that they are worthy to be entrusted with ecclesiastical charges.

Let them gradually appoint to the more responsible positions those whom practical experience will prove to be more efficient.   Above all things, the clergy should hold to the rule that they are not to allow themselves to be mixed up in party strifes.   Although it is a maxim of common law that he who fights for God should not be involved in worldly pursuits, We deem it necessary that men in Holy Orders in the present condition of affairs in the Philippine Islands should avoid this in a special manner.   Moreover, since there is great power in harmony of sentiment for accomplishing every great useful work for the sake of religion, let all the priests, whether secular or religious, cultivate it most zealously.   It is certainly proper that they who are one body of the one head Christ should not envy one another, but be of one will, loving one another with brotherly charity.   To foster this charity and maintain a vigorous discipline the bishops are reminded how very useful it is to convene a synod occasionally as time and place may require.   In this way there will easily be unity in thought and action.   To keep the first fervor of the priests from cooling and to preserve and increase the virtues which are worthy of the priesthood, the practice of the spiritual exercises is most helpful.   The bishops must therefore see that all who have been called to the vineyard of the Lord should at least every third year go into retreat in some suitable place to meditate on the eternal truths, to remove the stains contracted by worldly contamination and renew their ecclesiastical spirit.   Effort must be made to have the study of the sacred sciences kept alive among the clergy by frequent exercise.   *For the lips of the priest shall keep knowledge,* which he can teach the faithful, *who shall seek the law at his mouth.*[1] For this purpose there is nothing better than to have conferences frequently, both on moral and on liturgical questions.   If the difficulties of travelling, or the small number of priests, or any other similar cause prevents

[1] Malachy ii. 7.

them from meeting for such discussions, it will be well
to have those who cannot attend the conferences treat
in writing the questions proposed and submit them to
the bishop at the appointed time.

How much the Church thinks of seminaries for the
young men who are educated with a view to the priesthood, is clear from the decree of the Council of Trent, by
which they were first instituted. The bishops should
therefore make the most diligent effort to have one in
each diocese, in which young candidates for the sacred
warfare may be received and trained for a holy living
and in the lower and higher sciences. It is advisable that
the boys who are studying literature should occupy their
own building, and the young men who, after finishing the
humanities, are devoted to philosophy and theology should
dwell in another. In both departments the students
should remain until, if deserving, they shall have been
ordained priests, and never be permitted, except for grave
reasons, to return to their homes. The bishop will en-
trust the administration of the seminary to one of the
clergy, whether secular or religious, who is distinguished
for his prudence and experience in governing and for
holiness of life. The rules laid down by Us and Our
predecessors show very clearly in what way the studies
are to be regulated in seminaries. Where there is no
seminary the bishop will have candidates educated in one
of the seminaries of the neighboring diocese. On no
account should the bishops admit to these seminaries any
but the young men who are likely to give themselves to
God in Holy Orders. Those who wish to study for the
civil professions should have other schools, if it be possible, known as episcopal institutions or colleges. Above
all things the bishop, following the precept of the Apostle,
is not lightly to lay hands on any one; but to raise to Orders and to employ in sacred things only those who when
well tried and duly advanced in science and virtue can be
of credit and of service to a diocese. They are not to

leave those who go out from the seminary entirely to themselves; but to keep them from idleness and from abandoning the study of the sacred sciences, it is an excellent thing to have them every year for at least five years after ordination submit to an examination in dogmatic and moral theology before men of learning and authority. Since the halls of Rome also are open to young students from the Philippines who may wish to pursue the higher studies, it will afford Us much pleasure if the bishops send hither from time to time young men who may one day communicate to their fellow citizens the knowledge of religion acquired in this very centre of truth. This Holy See will do its share in the most effective way to advance the secular clergy in higher learning and better ecclesiastical training, so that in good time it may be worthy to assume the pastoral charges now administered by the regular priests.

It is not to the ecclesiastical seminaries only that the bishops are to devote their attention; the young laymen who go to other schools are also committed to their care and providence. It is therefore the duty of the consecrated bishops to make every effort that the minds of the young who are instructed in the public schools should not lack knowledge of their religion. To have it taught properly, the bishops must see and insist that the teachers are fitted for this task and that the books in use contain no errors. Since there is question of public schools, We do not wish to proceed without a word of praise well deserved for the great Lyceum of Manila, founded by the Dominicans, and authorized by Innocent X. Since it has always been distinguished for sound doctrine and excellent teachers, for the great good it has accomplished, not only do We wish that it be treated with favor by all the bishops, but besides We take it under Our own care and that of Our successors. Wherefore confirming absolutely the privileges and honors granted to it by the Roman Pontiffs Innocent X. and Clement XII., We bestow upon it the title of Pontifical University, and wish that the academic degrees conferred by it may have the same value as the degrees given by other Pontifical Universities.

Yielding to the opportunities of the new order of things in that region, the Holy Apostolic See has decided to make suitable provision for the religious men who look to a manner of life proper to their Institute, devoted entirely to the duties of the sacred ministry, for the advancement of public morality, the increase of Christianity and peaceful social intercourse. We recommend earnestly, therefore, to the members of the religious orders to discharge holily the duties which they have assumed when pronouncing their vows, "giving no offense to any man." We command them to keep their rule of cloister inviolably; and wish therefore that all should be bound by the decree issued by the Congregation of Bishops and Regulars, July 20, 1731, which Clement XIII., Our predecessor, confirmed by Apostolic Letters *Nuper pro parte*, August 26, the same year. The rule and boundary of the cloister are those which are laid down in another decree issued with the approbation of Pius VI. by the Sacred Congregation for the Propagation of the Faith, August 24, 1780. For the rest, the religious who labor in the Philippines must remember to treat with great reverence and honor those whom the Holy Ghost hath placed to rule the Church of God: and bound together with the secular clergy by the closest ties of concord and charity, let them hold nothing more pressing than to work hand in hand, throwing all their energy into the work of the ministry and the building up of the body of Christ. Furthermore, to remove every element of dissension, We wish that in future in the Philippine Islands the constitution *Formandis* of Benedict XII., dated November 6, 1744, and the other *Romanos Pontifices*, May 8, 1881, in which We decided certain points in dispute between the bishops and missionary regulars in England and Scotland, be observed.

The bishops will determine what parishes are to be en-

trusted to pastors from the religious orders after conferring with the superiors of these orders. Should any
question arise in this matter which cannot be settled privately, the case is to be referred to the Delegate Apostolic.

To the other means, by which the Church as teacher
provides that faith and good morals and all that makes
for the salvation of souls should suffer no harm, must be
added one of the very greatest utility, the spiritual exercises commonly known as missions. It is altogether desirable, therefore, that in each province at least one house
be founded, as a dwelling for about eight religious men,
whose one duty it will be to visit occasionally the towns
and villages and better the people by pious exhortations.
If this is so useful for the faithful, it is surely necessary
for those who have not yet received the light of the Gospel. Wherever, therefore, uncivilized peoples are still
buried in monstrous idolatry, the bishops and priests must
know that they are bound to try to convert them. Let
them, therefore, establish stations among them for priests
who will act as their apostles, and not only lead the idolaters to Christian practices, but also devote themselves to
the instruction of the children. These stations are to be
so located that in due time they may be made Prefectures
or Vicariates Apostolic. To provide those who labor in
them with means for support and for the propagation of
the faith, We recommend that in each diocese, without
interfering with the Lyons Society for the Propagation
of the Faith, special congregations of men and women be
formed to manage the collection of the alms of the faithful
and hand over the contributions to the bishops, to be
distributed entirely and equally to the missions.

To win the esteem of the faithful there is no better way
than for the clergy to do in effect what as priests they
preach. For, since, as the Council of Trent says, they are
regarded as removed above worldly things to a higher
plane, others lift their eyes to them for a model and imitate what they get from them. Wherefore it is highly

proper that priests should so regulate all their manners that in their dress, carriage, walk, conversation, and in all things they may appear grave, moderate and altogether religious; they should avoid even lighter faults, which in them are serious, so that all their actions may inspire veneration. It is for this restoration of ecclesiastical discipline and for the full execution of this Constitution We have sent our Venerable Brother John Baptist Guidi, Archbishop of Stauropolis, as Extraordinary Delegate Apostolic to the Philippine Islands, carrying thither Our person. On him We have conferred all necessary faculties; and We have given him besides Our mandate to convene and hold a provincial Synod, as soon as circumstances permit.

It remains for Us now only to address Ourselves with paternal charity to all the inhabitants of the Philippine Islands, and to exhort them with all the persuasion in Our power to maintain union in the bonds of peace. This the duty of our Christian profession requires: "For greater is the brotherhood in Christ, than of blood: for the brotherhood of blood means only a likeness of body, but brotherhood in Christ is unanimity in heart and in soul, as it is written in Acts iv. 32, 'and the multitude of believers had but one heart and one soul.'" This, too, is required for the good of religion, which is the chief source and ground of the praiseworthy things which have distinguished the Philippine peoples in the past. This, finally, is required by a sincere love of country, which will derive nothing but loss and destruction from public disturbances. Let them reverence those who exercise authority, according to the Apostle, "for all power is from God." And although separated from Us by the broad expanse of ocean, let them know that they are one in faith with the Apostolic See, which embraces them with special affection and will never abandon its charge of protecting their interests.

[Here follow the usual affirmation of the validity of this Constitution, and the penalties for disobeying and opposing it.]

REVIEW OF HIS PONTIFICATE.

Apostolical Letter, March 19, 1902.

HAVING come to the twenty-fifth year of Our Apostolic Ministry, and being astonished Ourselves at the length of the way which We have travelled amidst painful and continual cares, We are naturally inspired to lift Our thoughts to the ever-blessed God, who, with so many other favors, has deigned to accord Us a Pontificate the length of which has scarcely been surpassed in history. To the Father of all mankind, therefore; to Him who holds in His hands the mysterious secret of life, ascends, as an imperious need of the heart, the canticle of Our thanksgiving. Assuredly the eye of man cannot pierce all the depths of the designs of God in thus prolonging Our old age beyond the limits of hope: here We can only be silent and adore. But there is one thing which We do well understand; namely, that as it has pleased Him, and still pleases Him, to preserve Our existence, a great duty is incumbent on Us—to live for the good and the development of His immaculate spouse, the holy Church; and far from losing courage in the midst of cares and pains, to consecrate to Him the remainder of Our strength unto Our last sigh.

After paying a just tribute of gratitude to Our heavenly Father, to whom be honor and glory for all eternity, it is most agreeable to Us to turn Our thoughts and address Our words to you, Venerable Brothers, who, called by the Holy Ghost to govern the appointed portions of the flock of Jesus Christ, share thereby with Us in the struggle and triumph, the sorrows and joys, of the ministry of pastors. No, they shall never fade from Our memory, those frequent and striking testimonials of religious veneration which you have lavished upon Us during the course of Our Pontificate, and which you still multiply with emulation full of tenderness in the present circumstances. Intimately united with you already by Our duty and Our paternal love, We are more closely drawn by those proofs of your devotedness, so dear to Our hearts, less for what was personal in them in Our regard than for the inviolable attachment which they denote to this Apostolic See, centre and mainstay of all the Sees of Catholicity. If it has always been necessary that, according to the different grades of the ecclesiastical hierarchy, all the children of the Church should be sedulously united by the bonds of mutual charity and by the pursuit of the same objects, so as to form but one heart and one soul, this union is become in our day more indispensable than ever. For who can ignore the vast conspiracy of hostile forces which aims to-day at destroying and making disappear the great work of Jesus Christ, by endeavoring, with a fury which knows no limits, to rob man, in the intellectual order, of the treasure of heavenly truths, and, in the social order, to obliterate the most holy, the most salutary Christian institutions. But by all this you yourselves are impressed every day. You who, more than once, have poured out to Us your anxieties and anguish, deploring the multitude of prejudices, the false systems and errors which are disseminated with impunity amongst the masses of the people. What snares are set on every side for the souls of those who believe! What obstacles are multiplied to weaken, and if possible to destroy the beneficent action of the Church! And, meanwhile, as if to add derision to injustice, the Church herself is charged with having lost her pristine vigor, and with being powerless to stem the tide of overflowing passions which threaten to carry everything away.

We would wish, Venerable Brothers, to entertain you with subjects less sad and more in harmony with the great and auspicious occasion which induces Us to address you. But nothing suggests such tenor of discourse— neither the grievous trials of the Church which call with instance for prompt remedies; nor the conditions of contemporary society which, already undermined from a moral and material point of view, tend toward a yet more gloomy future by the abandonment of the great Christian traditions; a law of Providence, confirmed by history, proving that the great religious principles cannot be renounced without shaking at the same time the foundations of order and social prosperity. In those circumstances, in order to allow souls to recover, to furnish them with a new provision of faith and courage, it appears to Us opportune and useful to weigh attentively, in its origin, causes, and various forms, the implacable war that is waged against the Church; and in denouncing its pernicious consequences to indicate a remedy. May Our words, therefore, resound loudly, though they but recall truths already asserted; may they be hearkened to, not only by the children of Catholic unity, but also by those who differ from Us, and even by the unhappy souls who have no longer any faith; for they are all children of one Father, all destined for the same supreme good: may Our words, finally, be received as the testament which, at the short distance that separates Us from eternity, We would wish to leave to the people as a presage of the salvation which We desire for all.

During the whole course of her history the Church of Christ has had to combat and suffer for truth and justice. Instituted by the divine Redeemer Himself to establish throughout the world the kingdom of God, she must, by the light of the Gospel law, lead fallen humanity to its immortal destinies; that is, to make it enter upon the possession of the blessings without end which God has promised us, and to which our unaided natural power could never rise—a heavenly mission in the pursuit of which the Church could not fail to be opposed by the countless passions begotten of man's primal fall and consequent corruption—pride, cupidity, unbridled desire of material pleasures; against all the vices and disorders springing from those poisonous roots the Church has ever been the most potent means of restraint. Nor should we be astonished at the persecutions which have arisen, in consequence, since the divine Master foretold them, and they must continue as long as this world endures. What words did He address to His disciples when sending them to carry the treasure of His doctrines to all nations? They are familiar to us all: "You will be persecuted from city to city: you will be hated and despised for My Name's sake: you will be dragged before the tribunals, and condemned to extreme punishment." And wishing to encourage them for the hour of trial, He proposed Himself as their example: *If the world hate you, know ye that it hath hated Me before you.*[1]

Certainly, no one who takes a just and unbiassed view of things can explain the motive of this hatred. What offence was ever committed, what hostility deserved by the divine Redeemer? Having come down amongst men through an impulse of divine charity, He had taught a doctrine that was blameless, consoling, most efficacious to unite mankind in a brotherhood of peace and love; He had coveted neither earthly greatness nor honor; He had usurped no one's right; on the contrary, He was full of pity for the weak, the sick, the poor, the sinner, and the oppressed: hence His life was but a passage to distribute with munificent hand His benefits amongst men. We must acknowledge, in consequence, that it was simply by an excess of human malice, so much the more deplorable because unjust, that, nevertheless, He became, in truth, according to the prophecy of Simeon, "a sign to be contradicted."

What wonder, then, if the Catholic Church, which

---

[1] St. John xv. 18.

continues His divine mission, and is the incorruptible depositary of His truths, has inherited the same lot. The world is always consistent in its way. Near the sons of God are constantly present the satellites of that great adversary of the human race, who, a rebel from the beginning against the Most High, is named in the Gospel the prince of this world. It is on this account that the spirit of the world, in the presence of the law and of him who announces it in the name of God, swells with the measureless pride of an independence that ill befits it. Alas, how often, in more stormy epochs, with unheard-of cruelty and shameless injustice, and to the evident undoing of the whole social body, have the adversaries banded themselves together for the foolhardy enterprise of dissolving the work of God! And not succeeding with one manner of persecution, they adopted others. For three long centuries, the Roman Empire, abusing its brute force, scattered the bodies of martyrs through all its provinces, and bathed with their blood every foot of ground in this sacred city of Rome; while heresy, acting in concert, whether hidden beneath a mask or with open effrontery, with sophistry and snare, endeavored to destroy at least the harmony and unity of faith. Then were set loose, like a devastating tempest, the hordes of barbarians from the north, and the Moslems from the south, leaving in their wake only ruins in a desert. So has been transmitted from age to age the melancholy heritage of hatred by which the Spouse of Christ has been overwhelmed. There followed a Cæsarism as suspicious as powerful, jealous of all other power, no matter what development it might itself have thence acquired, which incessantly attacked the Church, to usurp her rights and tread her liberties under foot. The heart bleeds to see this mother so often oppressed with anguish and woes unutterable. However, triumphing over every obstacle, over all violence and all tyrannies, she pitched her peaceful tents more and more widely; she saved from disaster the glorious patrimony of arts, history, science, and letters; and imbuing deeply the whole body of society with the spirit of the Gospel, she created Christian civilization—that civilization to which the nations, subjected to its beneficent influence, owe the equity of their laws, the mildness of their manners, the protection of the weak, pity for the afflicted and the poor, respect for the rights and dignity of all men and thereby, as far as it is possible amidst the fluctuations of human affairs, that calm of social life which springs from the just and prudent alliance between justice and liberty.

Those proofs of the intrinsic excellence of the Church are as striking and sublime as they have been enduring. Nevertheless, as in the Middle Ages and during the first centuries, so in those nearer our own, we see the Church assailed more harshly, in a certain sense at least, and more distressingly than ever. Through a series of well-known historical causes, the pretended Reformation of the sixteenth century raised the standard of revolt; and, determining to strike out straight into the heart of the Church, audaciously attacked the Papacy. It broke the precious link of the ancient unity of faith and authority, which, multiplying a hundredfold power, prestige, and glory, thanks to the harmonious pursuit of the same objects, united all nations under one staff and one shepherd. This unity being broken, a pernicious principle of disintegration was introduced amongst all ranks of Christians.

We do not, indeed, hereby pretend to affirm that from the beginning there was a set purpose of destroying the principle of Christianity in the heart of society; but by refusing, on the one hand, to acknowledge the supremacy of the Holy See, the effective cause and bond of unity, and by proclaiming, on the other, the principle of private judgment, the divine structure of faith was shaken to its deepest foundations and the way was opened to infinite variations, to doubts and denials of the most important things, to an extent which the innovators themselves had not foreseen. The way was opened. Then came the contemptuous and mocking philosophism of the eighteenth century, which advanced farther. It turned to ridicule the sacred canon of the Scriptures and rejected the entire system of revealed truths, with the purpose of being able ultimately to root out from the conscience of the people all religious belief and stifling within it the last breath of the spirit of Christianity. It is from this source that have flowed rationalism, pantheism, naturalism, and materialism—poisonous and destructive systems which, under different appearances, renew the ancient errors triumphantly refuted by the Fathers and Doctors of the Church; so that the pride of modern times, by excessive confidence in its own lights, was stricken with blindness; and, like paganism, subsisted thenceforth on fancies, even concerning the attributes of the human soul and the immortal destinies which constitute our glorious heritage.

The struggle against the Church thus took on a more serious character than in the past, no less because of the vehemence of the assault than because of its universality. Contemporary unbelief does not confine itself to denying or doubting articles of faith. What it combats is the whole body of principles which sacred revelation and sound philosophy maintain; those fundamental and holy principles which teach man the supreme object of his earthly life, which keep him in the performance of his duty, which inspire his heart with courage and resignation, and which, in promising him incorruptible justice and perfect happiness beyond the tomb, enable him to subject time to eternity, earth to heaven. But what takes the place of these principles which form the incomparable strength bestowed by faith? A frightful scepticism, which chills the heart and stifles in the conscience every magnanimous aspiration.

This system of practical atheism must necessarily cause, as in point of fact it does, a profound disorder in the domain of morals; for, as the greatest philosophers of antiquity have declared, religion is the chief foundation of justice and virtue. When the bonds are broken which unite man to God, who is the Sovereign Legislator and Universal Judge, a mere phantom of morality remains; a morality which is purely civic and, as it is termed, independent, which, abstracting from the Eternal Mind and the laws of God, descends inevitably till it reaches the ultimate conclusion of making man a law unto himself. Incapable, in consequence, of rising on the wings of Christian hope to the goods of the world beyond, man will seek a material satisfaction in the comforts and enjoyments of life. There will be excited in him a thirst for pleasure, a desire of riches, and an eager quest of rapid and unlimited wealth, even at the cost of justice. There will be enkindled in him every ambition and a feverish and frenzied desire to gratify them even in defiance of law, and he will be swayed by a contempt for right and for public authority, as well as by licentiousness of life which, when the condition becomes general, will mark the real decay of society.

Perhaps We may be accused of exaggerating the sad consequences of the disorders of which We speak. No; for the reality is before our eyes and warrants but too truly Our forebodings. It is manifest that if there is not some betterment soon, the bases of society will crumble and drag down with them the great and eternal principles of law and morality.

It is in consequence of this condition of things that the social body, beginning with the family, is suffering such serious evils. For the lay State, forgetting its limitations and the essential object of the authority which it wields, has laid its hands on the marriage bond to profane it and has stripped it of its religious character; it has dared as much as it could in the matter of that natural right which parents possess to educate their children, and in many countries it has destroyed the stability of marriage by giving a legal sanction to the licentious institution of divorce. All know the result of these attacks. More than words can tell they have multiplied marriages which are prompted only by shameful passions, which are speedily dissolved, and which, at times, bring about bloody tragedies, at others the most shocking infidelities. We say nothing of the innocent offspring of these unions, the children who are abandoned or whose morals are corrupted on one side by the bad example of the parents, on the other by the poison which the officially lay State constantly pours into their hearts.

Along with the family, the political and social order is also endangered by doctrines which ascribe a false origin to authority, and which have corrupted the genuine conception of government. For if sovereign authority is derived formally from the consent of the people and not from God, who is the supreme and Eternal Principle of all power, it loses in the eyes of the governed its most august characteristic and degenerates into an artificial sovereignty which rests on unstable and shifting bases, namely, the will of those from whom it is said to be derived. Do we not see the consequences of this error in the carrying out of our laws? Too often these laws instead of being sound reason formulated in writing are but the expression of the power of the greater number and the will of the predominant political party. It is thus that the mob is cajoled in seeking to satisfy its desires; that a loose rein is given to popular passion, even when it disturbs the laboriously acquired tranquillity of the State, when the disorder in the last extremity can only be quelled by violent measures and the shedding of blood.

Consequent upon the repudiation of those Christian principles which had contributed so efficaciously to unite the nations in the bonds of brotherhood, and to bring all humanity into one great family, there has arisen little by little, in the international order, a system of jealous egoism, in consequence of which the nations now watch each other, if not with hate, at least with the suspicion of rivals. Hence, in their great undertakings they lose sight of the lofty principles of morality and justice and forget the protection which the feeble and the oppressed have a right to demand. In the desire by which they are actuated to increase their national riches, they regard only the opportunity which circumstances afford, the advantages of successful enterprises, and the tempting bait of an accomplished fact, sure that no one will trouble them in the name of right or the respect which right can claim. Such are the fatal principles which have consecrated material power as the supreme law of the world, and to them is to be imputed the limitless increase of military establishments and that armed peace which in many respects is equivalent to a disastrous war.

This lamentable confusion in the realm of ideas has produced restlessness among the people, outbreaks, and the general spirit of rebellion. From these have sprung the frequent popular agitations and disorders of our times which are only the preludes of much more terrible disorders in the future. The miserable condition, also, of a large part of the poorer classes, who assuredly merit our assistance, furnishes an admirable opportunity for the designs of scheming agitators, and especially of socialist factions, which hold out to the humbler classes the most extravagant promises and use them to carry out the most dreadful projects.

Those who start on a dangerous descent are soon hurled down in spite of themselves into the abyss. Prompted by an inexorable logic, a society of veritable criminals has been organized, which, at its very first appearance, has, by its savage character, startled the world. Thanks to the solidarity of its construction and its international ramifications, it has already attempted its wicked work, for it stands in fear of nothing and recoils before no danger. Repudiating all union with society, and cynically scoffing at law, religion, and morality, its adepts have adopted the name of Anarchists, and propose to utterly subvert the actual conditions of society by making use of every means that a blind and savage passion can suggest. And as society draws its unity and its life from the authority which governs it, so it is against authority that anarchy directs its efforts. Who does not feel a thrill of horror, indignation, and pity at the remembrance of the many victims that of late have fallen beneath its blows, emperors, empresses, kings, presidents of powerful republics, whose only crime was the sovereign power with which they were invested?

In presence of the immensity of the evils which overwhelm society and the perils which menace it, Our duty compels Us to again warn all men of good will, especially those who occupy exalted positions, and to conjure them as We now do, to devise what remedies the situation calls for and with prudent energy to apply them without delay.

First of all, it behooves them to inquire what remedies are needed, and to examine well their potency in the present needs. We have extolled liberty and its advantages to the skies, and have proclaimed it as a sovereign remedy and an incomparable instrument of peace and prosperity which will be most fruitful in good results. But facts have clearly shown us that it does not possess the power which is attributed to it. Economic conflicts, struggles of the classes are surging around us like a conflagration on all sides, and there is no promise of the dawn of the day of public tranquillity. In point of fact, and there is no one who does not see it, liberty as it is now understood, that is to say, a liberty granted indiscriminately to truth and to error, to good and to evil, ends only in destroying all that is noble, generous, and holy, and in opening the gates still wider to crime, to suicide, and to a multitude of the most degrading passions.

The doctrine is also taught that the development of public instruction, by making the people more polished and more enlightened, would suffice as a check to unhealthy tendencies and to keep man in the ways of uprightness and probity. But a hard reality has made us feel every day more and more of how little avail is instruction without religion and morality. As a necessary consequence of inexperience, and of the promptings of bad passions, the mind of youth is enthralled by the perverse teachings of the day. It absorbs all the errors which an unbridled press does not hesitate to sow broadcast and which depraves the mind and the will of youth and foments in them that spirit of pride and insubordination which so often trouble the peace of families and cities.

So also was confidence reposed in the progress of science. Indeed the century which has just closed, has witnessed progress that was great, unexpected, stupendous. But is it true that it has given us all the fulness and healthfulness of fruitage that so many expected from it? Doubtless the discoveries of science have opened new horizons to the mind; it has widened the empire of man over the forces of matter, and human life has been ameliorated in many ways through its instrumentality. Nevertheless, every one feels and many admit that the results have not corresponded to the hopes that were cherished. It cannot be denied, especially when we cast our eyes on the intellectual and moral status of the world as well as on the records of criminality, when we hear the dull murmurs which arise from the depths, or when we witness the predominance which might has won over right. Not to speak of the throngs who are a prey to every misery, a superficial glance at the condition of the world will suffice to convince us of the indefinable sorrow which weighs upon souls and the immense void which is in human hearts. Man may subject nature to his sway, but matter cannot give him what it has not, and to the questions which most deeply affect our gravest interests human science gives no reply. The thirst for truth, for good, for the infinite, which devours us, has not been slaked, nor have the joys and riches of earth, nor the increase of the comforts of life ever soothed the anguish which tortures the heart.

Are we then to despise and fling aside the advantages which accrue from the study of science, from civilization and the wise and sweet use of our liberty? Assuredly not. On the contrary, we must hold them in the highest esteem, guard them and make them grow as a treasure of great price, for they are means which of their nature are good, designed by God Himself, and ordained by the Infinite Goodness and Wisdom for the use and advantage of the human race. But we must subordinate the use of them to the intentions of the Creator, and so employ them as never to eliminate the religious element in which their real advantage resides, for it is that which bestows on them a special value and renders them really fruitful. Such is the secret of the problem When an organism perishes and corrupts, it is because it had ceased to be under the action of the causes which had given it its form and constitution. To make it healthy and flourishing again it is necessary to restore it to the vivifying action of those same causes. So society in its foolhardy effort to escape from God has rejected the divine order and revelation; and it is thus withdrawn from the salutary efficacy of Christianity which is manifestly the most solid guarantee of order, the strongest bond of fraternity, and the inexhaustible source of all public and private virtue. This sacrilegious divorce has resulted in bringing about the trouble which now disturbs the world. Hence it is the pale of the Church which this lost society must re-enter, if it wishes to recover its well-being, its repose, and its salvation.

Just as Christianity cannot penetrate in the soul without making it better, so it cannot enter into public life without establishing order. With the idea of a God who governs all, who is infinitely wise, good, and just, the idea of duty seizes upon the consciences of men. It assuages sorrow, it calms hatred, it engenders heroes. If it has transformed pagan society—and that transformation was a veritable resurrection—for barbarism disappeared in proportion as Christianity extended its sway, so, after the terrible shocks which unbelief has given to the world in our days, it will be able to put that world again on the true road, and bring back to order the states and peoples of modern times. But the return of Christianity will not be efficacious and complete if it does not restore the world to a sincere love of the one Holy Catholic and Apostolic Church. In the Catholic Church Christianity is incarnate. It identifies itself with that perfect, spiritual, and, in its own order, sovereign society, which is the mystical body of Jesus Christ and which has for its visible head the Roman Pontiff, successor of the Prince of the apostles. It is the continuation of the mission of the Saviour, the daughter and the heiress of His redemption. It has preached the Gospel, and has defended it at the price of its blood, and strong in the divine assistance and of that immortality which have been promised it, it makes no terms with error, but remains faithful to the commands which it has received to carry the doctrine of Jesus Christ to the uttermost limits of the world and to the end of time, and to protect it in its inviolable integrity. Legitimate dispenser of the teachings of the Gospel it does not reveal itself only as the consoler and redeemer of souls, but it is still more the internal source of justice and charity, and the propagator as well as the guardian of true liberty, and of that equality which alone is possible here below. In applying the doctrine of its divine Founder, it maintains a wise equilibrium and marks the true limits between the rights and privileges of society. The equality which it proclaims does not destroy the distinction between the different social classes. It keeps them intact, as nature itself demands, in order to oppose the anarchy of reason emancipated from faith, and abandoned to its own devices. The liberty which it gives in no wise conflicts with the rights of truth, because those rights are superior to the demands of liberty. Nor does it infringe upon the rights of justice, because those rights are superior to the claims of mere numbers or power. Nor does it assail the rights of God because they are superior to the rights of humanity.

In the domestic circle, the Church is no less fruitful in good results. For not only does it oppose the nefarious machinations which incredulity resorts to in order to attack the life of the family, but it prepares and protects the union and stability of marriage, whose honor, fidelity, and holiness it guards and develops. At the same time it sustains and cements the civil and political order by giving on one side most efficacious aid to authority, and on the other by showing itself favorable to the wise reforms and the just aspirations of the classes that are governed; by imposing respect for rulers and enjoining whatever obedience is due to them, and by defending unwaveringly the imprescriptible rights of the human conscience. And thus it is that the people who are subject to her influence have no fear of oppression because she checks in their efforts the rulers who seek to govern as tyrants.

Fully aware of this divine power, We, from the very beginning of Our Pontificate, have endeavored to place in the clearest light the benevolent designs of the Church and to increase as far as possible, along with the treasures of her doctrine the field of her salutary action. Such has been the object of the principal acts of Our Pontificate, notably in the Encyclicals on *Christian Philosophy*, on *Human Liberty*, on *Christian Marriage*, on *Freemasonry*, on *The Powers of Government*, on *The Christian Constitution of States*, on *Socialism*, on the *Labor Question*, and the *Duties of Christian Citizens* and other analogous subjects. But the ardent desire of Our souls has not been merely to illumine the mind. We have endeavored to move and to purify hearts by making use of all Our powers to cause Christian virtue to flourish among the peoples. For that reason We have never ceased to bestow encouragement and counsel in order to elevate the minds of men to the goods of the world beyond; to enable them to subject the body to the soul; their earthly life to the heavenly one;

man to God. Blessed by the Lord, Our word has been able to increase and to strengthen the convictions of a great number of men; to throw light on their minds in the difficult questions of the day; to stimulate their zeal and to advance the various works which have been undertaken.

It is especially for the disinherited classes that these works have been inaugurated, and have continued to grow in every country, as is evident from the increase of Christian charity which has always found in the midst of the people its favorite field of action. If the harvest has not been more abundant, Venerable Brothers, let us adore God who is mysteriously just and beg Him, at the same time, to have pity on the blindness of so many souls, to whom unhappily the terrifying word of the Apostle may be addressed: *The god of this world has blinded the minds of unbelievers, that the light of the Gospel of the glory of Christ, who is the image of God, should not shine to them.*[1]

The more the Catholic Church devotes itself to extend its zeal for the moral and material advancement of the peoples, the more the children of darkness arise in hatred against it and have recourse to every means in their power to tarnish its divine beauty and paralyze its action of life-giving reparation. How many false reasonings have they not made and how many calumnies have they not spread against it! Among their most perfidious devices is that which consists in repeating to the ignorant masses and to suspicious governments that the Church is opposed to the progress of science, that it is hostile to liberty, that the rights of the State are usurped by it and that politics is a field which it is constantly invading. Such are the mad accusations that have been a thousand times repudiated and a thousand times refuted by sound reason and by history and, in fact, by every man who has a heart for honesty and a mind for truth.

[1] 2 Cor. iv. 4.

The Church the enemy of knowledge and instruction! Without doubt she is the vigilant guardian of revealed dogma, but it is this very vigilance which prompts her to protect science and to favor the wise cultivation of the mind.   No! in submitting his mind to the revelation of the Word, who is the supreme truth from whom all truths must flow, man will in no wise contradict what reason discovers.   On the contrary, the light which will come to him from the divine Word will give more power and more clearness to the human intellect, because it will preserve it from a thousand uncertainties and errors. Besides, nineteen centuries of a glory achieved by Catholicism in all the branches of learning amply suffice to refute this calumny.   It is to the Catholic Church that we must ascribe the merit of having propagated and defended Christian philosophy, without which the world would still be buried in the darkness of pagan superstitions and in the most abject barbarism.   It has preserved and transmitted to all generations the precious treasure of literature and of the ancient sciences.   It has opened the first schools for the people and crowded the universities which still exist, or whose glory is perpetuated even to our own days.   It has inspired the loftiest, the purest, and the most glorious literature, while it has gathered under its protection men whose genius in the arts has never been eclipsed.

The Church the enemy of liberty!   Ah, how they travesty the idea of liberty which has for its object one of the most precious of God's gifts when they make use of its name to justify its abuse and excess!   What do we mean by liberty?   Does it mean the exemption from all laws; the deliverance from all restraint, and as a corollary, the right to take man's caprice as a guide in all our actions?   Such liberty the Church certainly reproves, and good and honest men reprove it likewise.   But do they mean by liberty the rational faculty to do good, magnanimously, without check or hindrance and according to the rules which eternal justice has established? That liberty which is the only liberty worthy of man, the only one useful to society, none favors or encourages or protects more than the Church. By the force of its doctrine and the efficaciousness of its action the Church has freed humanity from the yoke of slavery in preaching to the world the great law of equality and human fraternity. In every age it has defended the feeble and the oppressed against the arrogant domination of the strong. It has demanded liberty of Christian conscience while pouring out in torrents the blood of its martyrs; it has restored to the child and to the woman the dignity and the noble prerogatives of their nature in making them share by virtue of the same right that reverence and justice which is their due, and it has largely contributed, both to introduce and maintain civil and political liberty in the heart of the nations.

The Church the usurper of the rights of the State! The Church invading the political domain! Why, the Church knows and teaches that her divine Founder has commanded us to give to Cæsar what is Cæsar's and to God what is God's, and that He has thus sanctioned the immutable principle of an enduring distinction between those two powers which are both sovereign in their respective spheres, a distinction which is most pregnant in its consequences and eminently conducive to the development of Christian civilization. In its spirit of charity it is a stranger to every hostile design against the State. It aims only at making these two powers go side by side for the advancement of the same object, namely, for man and for human society, but by different ways and in conformity with the noble plan which has been assigned for its divine mission. Would to God that its action were received without mistrust and without suspicion. It could not fail to multiply the numberless benefits of which We have already spoken. To accuse the Church of ambitious views is only to repeat the ancient calumny, a calumny which its powerful enemies have more than once employed as a pretext to conceal their own purposes of oppression.

Far from oppressing the State, history clearly shows when it is read without prejudice, that the Church like its divine Founder has been, on the contrary, most commonly the victim of oppression and injustice. The reason is that its power rests not on the force of arms but on the strength of thought and of truth.

It is therefore assuredly with malignant purpose that they hurl against the Church accusations like these. It is a pernicious and disloyal work, in the pursuit of which above all others a certain sect of darkness is engaged, a sect which human society these many years carries within itself and which like a deadly poison destroys its happiness, its fecundity, and its life. Abiding personification of the revolution, it constitutes a sort of retrogressive society whose object is to exercise an occult suzerainty over the established order and whose whole purpose is to make war against God and against His Church. There is no need of naming it, for all will recognize in these traits the society of Freemasons, of which We have already spoken, expressly in Our Encyclical *Humanum Genus* of the twentieth of April, 1884. While denouncing its destructive tendency, its erroneous teachings, and its wicked purpose of embracing in its far-reaching grasp almost all nations, and uniting itself to other sects which its secret influence puts in motion, directing first and afterwards retaining its members by the advantages which it procures for them, bending governments to its will, sometimes by promises and sometimes by threats, it has succeeded in entering all classes of society, and forms an invisible and irresponsible state existing within the legitimate State. Full of the spirit of Satan who, according to the words of the Apostle, knows how to transform himself at need into an angel of light, it gives prominence to its humanitarian object, but it sacrifices everything to its sectarian purpose and protests that it has no political aim, while in reality it exercises the most profound action on the legislative and administrative life of the nations, and while loudly professing its respect for authority and even for religion, has for its ultimate purpose, as its own statutes declare, the destruction of all authority as well as of the priesthood, both of which it holds up as the enemies of liberty.

It becomes more evident day by day that it is to the inspiration and the assistance of this sect that we must attribute in great measure the continual troubles with which the Church is harassed, as well as the recrudescence of the attacks to which it has recently been subjected. For the simultaneousness of the assaults in the persecutions which have so suddenly burst upon us in these later times, like a storm from a clear sky, that is to say without any cause proportionate to the effect; the uniformity of means employed to inaugurate this persecution, namely, the press, public assemblies, theatrical productions; the employment in every country of the same arms, to wit, calumny and public uprisings, all this betrays clearly the identity of purpose and a program drawn up by one and the same central direction. All this is only a simple episode of a prearranged plan carried out on a constantly widening field to multiply the ruins of which We speak. Thus they are endeavoring by every means in their power first to restrict and then to completely exclude religious instruction from the schools so as to make the rising generation unbelievers or indifferent to all religion; as they are endeavoring by the daily press to combat the morality of the Church, to ridicule its practices and its solemnities. It is only natural, consequently, that the Catholic priesthood, whose mission is to preach religion and to administer the sacraments, should be assailed with a special fierceness. In taking it as the object of their attacks this sect aims at diminishing in the eyes of the people its prestige and its authority. Already their audacity grows hour by hour in proportion as it flatters itself that it can do so with impunity. It puts a malignant interpretation on all the acts of the clergy, bases suspicion upon the slenderest proofs and overwhelms it with the vilest accusations. Thus new prejudices are added to those with which the clergy are already overwhelmed, such for example as their subjection to military service, which is such a great obstacle for the preparation for the priesthood, and the confiscation of the ecclesiastical patrimony which the pious generosity of the faithful had founded.

As regards the religious orders and religious congregations, the practice of the evangelical counsels made them the glory of society and the glory of religion. These very things rendered them more culpable in the eyes of the enemies of the Church and were the reasons why they were fiercely denounced and held up to contempt and hatred. It is a great grief for Us to recall here the odious measures which were so undeserved and so strongly condemned by all honest men by which the members of religious orders were lately overwhelmed. Nothing was of avail to save them, neither the integrity of their life which their enemies were unable to assail, nor the right which authorizes all natural associations entered into for an honorable purpose, nor the right of the constitutions which loudly proclaimed their freedom to enter into those organizations, nor the favor of the people who were so grateful for the precious services rendered in the arts, in the sciences, and in agriculture, and for the charity which poured itself out upon the most numerous and poorest classes of society. And hence it is that these men and women who themselves had sprung from the people and who had spontaneously renounced all the joys of family to consecrate to the good of their fellow men, in those peaceful associations, their youth, their talent, their strength, and their lives, were treated as malefactors as if they had formed criminal associations, and have been excluded from the common and prescriptive rights at the very time when men are speaking loudest of liberty. We must not be astonished that the most beloved children are struck when the father himself, that is to say the head of Catholicity, the Roman Pontiff, is no better treated. The facts are known to all. Stripped of the temporal sovereignty and consequently of that independence which is necessary to accomplish his universal and divine mission; forced in Rome itself to shut himself up in his own dwelling because the enemy has laid siege to him on every side, he has been compelled in spite of the derisive assurances of respect and of the precarious promises of liberty to an abnormal condition of existence which is unjust and unworthy of his exalted ministry. We know only too well the difficulties that are each instant created to thwart his intentions and to outrage his dignity. It only goes to prove what is every day more and more evident that it is the spiritual power of the head of the Church which little by little they aim at destroying when they attack the temporal power of the papacy. Those who are the real authors of this spoliation have not hesitated to confess it.

Judging by the consequences which have followed, this action was not only impolitic, but was an attack on society itself; for the assaults that are made upon religion are so many blows struck at the very heart of society.

In making man a being destined to live in society, God in His providence has also founded the Church, which as the holy text expresses it, He has established on Mount Zion in order that it might be a light which, with its life-giving rays, would cause the principle of life to penetrate into the various degrees of human society by giving it divinely inspired laws, by means of which society might establish itself in that order which would be most conducive to its welfare. Hence in proportion as society separates itself from the Church, which is an important element in its strength, by so much does it decline, or its woes are multiplied for the reason that they are separated whom God wished to bind together.

As for Us, We never weary as often as the occasion presents itself to inculcate these great truths, and We desire to do so once again and in a very explicit manner on this extraordinary occasion. May God grant that the faithful will take courage from what We say and be guided to unite their efforts more efficaciously for the common good; that they may be more enlightened and that Our adversaries may understand the injustice which they commit in persecuting the most loving mother and the most faithful benefactress of humanity.

We would not wish that the remembrance of these afflictions should diminish in the souls of the faithful that full and entire confidence which they ought to have in the divine assistance. For God, in His own hour and in His mysterious ways, will bring about a certain victory. As for Us, no matter .how great the sadness which fills Our heart, We do not fear for the immortal destiny of the Church. As We have said in the beginning, persecution is its heritage, because in trying and in purifying its children, God thereby obtains for them greater and more precious advantages. And in permitting the Church to undergo these trials He manifests the divine assistance which He bestows upon it, for He provides new and un-looked-for means of assuring the support and the development of His work, while revealing the futility of the powers which are leagued against it. Nineteen centuries of a life passed in the midst of the ebb and flow of all human vicissitudes teach us that the storms pass by without ever affecting the foundations of the Church. We are able all the more to remain unshaken in this confidence, as the present time affords indications which forbid depression. We cannot deny that the difficulties that confront us are extraordinary and formidable, but there are also facts before our eyes which give evidence, at the same time, that God is fulfilling His promises with admirable wisdom and goodness.

While so many powers conspire against the Church and

while she is progressing on her way deprived of all human help and assistance, is she not in effect carrying on her gigantic work in the world and is she not extending her action in every clime and every nation? Expelled by Jesus Christ, the prince of this world can no longer exercise his proud dominion as heretofore; and although doubtless the efforts of Satan may cause us many a woe they will not achieve the object at which they aim. Already a supernatural tranquillity due to the Holy Ghost, who provides for the Church and who abides in it, reigns not only in the souls of the faithful but also throughout Christianity; a tranquillity whose serene development we witness everywhere, thanks to the union ever more and more close and affectionate with the Apostolic See; a union which is in marvellous contrast with the agitation, the dissension, and the continual unrest of the various sects which disturb the peace of society. There exists also between bishops and clergy a union which is fruitful in numberless works of zeal and charity. It exists likewise between the clergy and laity who, more closely knit together and more completely freed from human respect than ever before, are awakening to a new life and organizing with a generous emulation in defence of the sacred cause of religion. It is this union which We have so often recommended and which We recommend again, which We bless that it may develop still more and may rise like an impregnable wall against the fierce violence of the enemies of God.

There is nothing more natural than that, like the branches which spring from the roots of the tree, these numberless associations which we see with joy flourish in our days in the bosom of the Church should arise, grow strong and multiply. There is no form of Christian piety which has been omitted whether there is question of Jesus Christ Himself, or His adorable mysteries, or His divine Mother, or the saints whose wonderful virtues have illumined the world. Nor has any kind of charitable work been forgotten.

On all sides there is a zealous endeavor to procure Christian instruction for youth; help for the sick; moral teaching for the people and assistance for the classes least favored in the goods of this world. With what remarkable rapidity this movement would propagate itself and what precious fruits it would bear if it were not opposed by the unjust and unfriendly efforts with which it finds itself so often in conflict.

God, who gives to the Church such great vitality in civilized countries where it has been established for so many centuries, consoles us besides with other hopes. These hopes we owe to the zeal of Catholic missionaries. Not permitting themselves to be discouraged by the perils which they face; by the privations which they endure; by the sacrifices of every kind which they accept, their numbers are increasing and they are gaining whole countries to the Gospel and to civilization. Nothing can diminish their courage, although after the manner of their divine Master they receive only accusations and calumnies as the reward of their untiring labors.

Thus our sorrows are tempered by the sweetest consolations, and in the midst of the struggles and the difficulties which are our portion we have wherewith to refresh our souls and to inspire us with hope. This ought to suggest useful and wise reflections to those who view the world with intelligence, and who do not permit passions to blind them; for it proves that God has not made man independent in what regards the last end of life, and just as He has spoken to him in the past so He speaks again in our day by His Church, which is visibly sustained by the divine assistance and which shows clearly where salvation and truth can be found. Come what may, this eternal assistance will inspire our hearts with an incredible hope and persuade us that at the hour marked by Providence and in a future which is not remote, truth will scatter the mists in which men endeavor to shroud it and will shine forth more brilliantly than ever.

The spirit of the Gospel will spread life anew in the heart of our corrupted society and in its perishing members.

In what concerns Us, Venerable Brethren, in order to hasten the day of divine mercy, We shall not fail in Our duty to do everything to defend and develop the kingdom of God upon earth. As for you, your pastoral solicitude is too well known to Us to exhort you to do the same. May the ardent flame which burns in your hearts be transmitted more and more to the hearts of all your priests. They are in immediate contact with the people. If, full of the spirit of Jesus Christ and keeping themselves above political passion, they unite their action with yours they will succeed with the blessing of God in accomplishing marvels. By their word they will enlighten the multitude; by their sweetness of manners they will gain all hearts, and in succoring with charity their suffering brethren, they will help them little by little to better the condition in which they are placed.

The clergy will be firmly sustained by the active and intelligent coöperation of all men of good will. Thus the children who have tasted the sweetness of the Church will thank her for it in a worthy way, viz., by gathering around her to defend her honor and her glory. All can contribute to this work which will be so splendidly meritorious for them; literary and learned men, by defending her in books or in the daily press, which is such a powerful instrument now made use of by her enemies; fathers of families and teachers, by giving a Christian education to children; magistrates and representatives of the people, by showing themselves firm in the principles which they defend as well as by the integrity of their lives and in the profession of their faith without any vestige of human respect. Our age exacts lofty ideals, generous designs, and the exact observance of the laws. It is by a perfect submission to the directions of the Holy See that this discipline will be strengthened, for it is the best means of causing to disappear or at least of diminishing the evil which party opinions produce in fomenting divisions; and it will assist us in uniting all our efforts for attaining that higher end, namely, the triumph of Jesus Christ and His Church. Such is the duty of Catholics. As for her final triumph she depends upon Him who watches with wisdom and love over His immaculate spouse, and of whom it is written, *Jesus Christ, yesterday, to-day and the same forever.*[1]

It is therefore to Him, that at this moment we should lift our hearts in humble and ardent prayer, to Him who, loving with an infinite love our erring humanity, has wished to make Himself an expiatory victim by the sublimity of His martyrdom; to Him who, seated although unseen in the mystical bark of His Church, can alone still the tempest and command the waves to be calm and the furious winds to cease. Without doubt, Venerable Brethren, you with Us will ask this divine Master for the cessation of the evils which are overwhelming society, for the repeal of all hostile law, for the illumination of those who more perhaps through ignorance than through malice, hate and persecute the religion of Jesus Christ; and also for the drawing together of all men of good will in close and holy union.

May the triumph of truth and of justice be thus hastened in the world, and for the great family of men may better days dawn; days of tranquillity and of peace.

Meanwhile as a pledge of the most precious and divine favor may the benediction which We give you with all Our heart, descend upon you and all the faithful committed to your care.

[1] Heb. xiii. 8.

If you have enjoyed this book, consider making your next selection from among the following . . .

At your Bookdealer or direct from the Publisher.

Prices guaranteed through June 30, 1997.

"When Christian law exerts its power without being thwarted in any way, naturally and without effort the order of society is maintained as constituted by divine Providence, and prosperity and public safety are secured. The security of the State demands that we should be brought back to Him from whom we ought never to have departed, to Him who is the way, the truth, and the life, not as individuals merely, but as human society through all its extent. Christ our Lord must be reinstated as the Ruler of human society. It belongs to Him, as do all its members. All the elements of the commonwealth; legal commands and prohibitions, popular institutions, schools, marriage, home-life, the workshop, and the palace, all must be made to come to that fountain and imbibe the life that comes from Him. No one should fail to see that on this largely depends the civilization of nations, which is so eagerly sought, but which is nourished and augmented not so much by bodily comforts and conveniences, as by what belongs to the soul, viz., commendable lives and the cultivation of virtue."

—Pope Leo XIII
Christ Our Redeemer
Page 476